Paul Schrodt

The Problem of the Beginning of Dogma in Recent Theology

PETER LANG

Frankfurt am Main · Bern · Las Vegas

CIP-Kurztitelaufnahme der Deutschen Bibliothek

Schrodt, Paul

The problem of the beginning of dogma in recent
theology. – Frankfurt am Main, Bern, Las Vegas:
Lang, 1978.
   (Europäische Hochschulschriften: Reihe 23,
   Theologie; Bd. 103)
   ISBN 3-261-02464-X

ISBN 3-261-02464-X

Auflage 300 Ex.

© Verlag Peter Lang GmbH, Frankfurt am Main 1978

Druck: Fotokop Wilhelm Weihert KG, Darmstadt
Titelsatz: Fotosatz Aragall, Wolfsgangstraße 92, Frankfurt am Main.

TABLE OF CONTENTS

LIST OF ABBREVIATIONS

Cath	*Catholica*
DThC	*Dictionnaire de Théologie Catholique*
DS	Denzinger-Schönmetzer, *Enchiridion Symbolorum*
EThL	*Ephemerides Theologicae Lovanienses*
EvTheol	*Evangelische Theologie*
FZThPh	*Freiburger Zeitschrift für Theologie und Philosophie*
HThG	*Handbuch Theologischer Grundbegriffe*
JBL	*Journal of Biblical Literature*
JThS	*Journal of Theological Studies*
KuD	*Kerygma und Dogma*
LThK	*Lexicon für Theologie und Kirche*
MG	Migne, *Patrologia Graeca*
ML	Migne, *Patrologia Latina*
MThZ	*Münchener Theologische Zeitschrift*
RAC	*Reallexikon für Antike und Christentum*
RGG	*Die Religion in Geschichte und Gegenwart*
RSPhTh	*Revue des Sciences Philosophiques et Théologiques*
StdZ	*Stimmen der Zeit*
ThZ	*Theologische Quartalschrift*
ThSt	*Theological Studies*
ThWb	*Theologisches Wörterbuch zum Neuen Testament*
ThZ	*Theologische Zeitschrift*
TThZ	*Trierer Theologische Zeitschrift*
ZKG	*Zeitschrift für Kirchengeschichte*
ZKTh	*Zeitschrift für Katholische Theologie*
ZThK	*Zeitschrift für Theologie und Kirche*

ACKNOWLEDGMENTS

The following study is a somewhat abbreviated version of my dissertation which was accepted by the Faculty of Catholic Theology at the Ludwig-Maximilian University at Munich in 1975 for the degree of doctorate in theology. It was inspired and guided by Professor Doctor Leo Scheffczyk, whose personal interest in students rivals his dedication to theology. Special thanks are also due to Professor Doctor Josef Finkenzeller who, as second reader, studied the manuscript and offered perceptive criticisms.

To list all the other members of the teaching faculty at Munich whose seminars, lectures, and spirit of critical inquiry have made an indelible impression on me would be too long. Yet mention must be made of Professor Doctor Hans Schilling, then Rector of the Faculty and moderator of my rigorosum, as well as of Professor Doctor Walter Dürig, who as Rector of the Herzögliches Georgianum kindly made available to me a comfortable place to live and work in the shadow of the University.

Finally, my gratitude must be registered to the Holy Cross Province of the Passionists in North America for its support through years of study and, most especially to Reverend Paul I. Bechtold, C.P., provincial moderator of studies, without whose direction my graduate work would not have been possible.

Paul R. Schrodt, C.P.
Denver, Colorado

x

PREFACE

The problem to which this work addresses itself is that of the beginning of dogma. It is, strangely enough, a topic which has hardly been considered in Catholic theology, although there are in Protestant theology well-known and influential theories which propose to explain the origin of that dogmatic teaching which is so much a part of historical Christianity. We are referring, of course, to the Hellenization theory of Adolf von Harnack and to the 'consequent eschatological' theory of Martin Werner. These two schemes are explanations of extreme detail and even today not without influence in the world of theology. The publications of Leslie Dewart within the past several years testify to the fact that the influence of Harnack is still very much with us.[1]

If one were to summarize in a few words the import of the work of Harnack and Werner on the problem of the origin of dogma one would have to point to the rather generally accepted position that there is a great cleft between the structure of Christian dogma and the gospel, that is to say, that the relationship between Church dogma and the essentials of Christianity is at best tenuous.

In the area of Catholic dogmatic studies there are many works on the development of dogma. It seems, however, that no one has taken up at length that other but related concern -- the problem of dogma's origin within the self-understanding of Catholic dogma. We call this the problem of the beginning of dogma. It is the exegete, Heinrich Schlier, who

---

1. *The Future of Belief*, (New York, 1966), and *The Foundations of Belief*, (New York, 1969).

comes closest to doing this in his essay of 1951, "Kerygma und Sophia: Zur neutestamentlichen Grundlegung des Dogmas."[2] We believe that Schlier's ideas are of fundamental importance to an understanding of the origins of dogma in the way it is understood in Catholic theology. The tendency of Schlier's work is to elucidate the presuppositional relationship between dogma and scripture. It is unfortunate that, although his essay has often been cited in bibliographies, no one has attempted to draw out the full implications of his ideas for the foundation of a Catholic theory of dogmatic origins.

In this age of ecumenical theological effort it may sound anachronistic to speak of a "Catholic theory of dogmatic origins." We believe, however, that even today the understanding of dogma in Catholic theology distinguishes it enough from the understanding of dogma in the systematic theology of most of our brethren in the ecumenical world to justify the effort in elucidating this theory of its origins. The explication of these various approaches and of their presuppositions can ultimately only be of service to the serious work of ecumenism.

In the course of such a study it will be understood as completely necessary to investigate the notion of dogma itself. Terms have sometimes the unfortunate fate of meaning different things to different people. The investigation of the history of the notion of dogma is in this regard particularly fruitful.

Since the first years of the nineteenth century the problem of the development of dogma has occupied a significant position in the study of Catholic theology. It is the problem which occupied to the greatest degree the theologians of Tübingen and John Henry Newman. Their concern

2. In *Die Zeit der Kirche*, (Freiburg, 1966), pp. 206-232.

was in the first instance the development of dogma from the deposit of faith; our problem is the development of dogma in the sense of its origin.

We have chosen to consider the theologians of Tübingen and John Henry Newman within the general chapter on the history of the notion of dogma, although their own perspectives focus more clearly on the psychological origins of dogma. The same is true of the work of the founder of process philosophy, Alfred North Whitehead, who also has addressed himself to the origin of dogma, as has the "Bultmannschuler," Hans Jonas. Their reflections, coming as they do from very different areas, certainly add something to the understanding of the origin of dogma, even if not all their conclusions are found to be acceptable.

To study the origin of every dogma would be an endless task. History reveals that in the process of dogma's development there have been various forces at work such as analytic deduction, the sensus fidelium, the official magisterium, the dialectic caused by heresy, the incentive of genuine piety. Our purpose is rather to study the appearance of dogma as an historical datum. Following H. Schlier's suggestions, we believe that it is precisely here that the self-understanding of dogma in Catholic thought comes most clearly into focus.

BIBLIOGRAPHY

A. Histories of Dogma and of the Creeds

Adam, Alfred. *Lehrbuch der Dogmengeschichte*. 2 vols. Gütersloh, 1965-1968.

Alberigo, J., Joannon, P. P., etc. *Conciliorum Oecumenicorum Decreta*. Freiburg, 1962.

Aulén, Gustav. *Die Dogmengeschichte in Licht der Lutherforschung*. Gütersloh, 1962.

Baur, Ferdinand Christian. *Lehrbuch der christlichen Dogmengeschichte*.
_____. *Vorlesungen über die Christliche Dogmengeschichte*. 3 vols. Leipzig, 1865-1867.

Bethune-Baker, J. F. *An Introduction to the Early History of Christian Doctrine*. London, 1903; 1949[8].

Caspari, P. *Ungedruckte, unbeachtete und wenig beachtete Quellen zur Geschichte des Taufsymbols und der Glaubensregel*. 4 vols. Christiana, 1866-1869.
_____. *Alte und neue Quellen zur Geschichte des Taufsymbols und der Glaubensregel*. Christiana, 1879.

Cullmann, Oscar. *The Earliest Christian Confessions*. London, 1949.

Daniélou, Jean. *The Theology of Jewish Christianity, The Development of Christian Doctrine before the Council of Nicea*. Trans. and ed. by John A. Baker. London, 1964--.

Denzinger, H. and Schönmetzer, A. *Enchiridion Symbolorum*. Freiburg, 1965[34].

Eynde, Damien van den. *Les Normes de l'Enseignement Chrétien dans la Littérature Patristique des Trois Premiers Siècles*. Gemblous, 1933.

Grabmann, Martin. *Die Geschichte der Scholastischen Methode nach Gedruckten und Ungedruckten Quellen*. 2 vols. 1909-1911. Reprint: Graz, 1957.

Hahn, A. *Bibliothek der Symbole und Glaubensregeln der Alten Kirche*. Ed. by G. L. Hahn. Breslaus, 1897.

Harnack, Adolf von. *Lehrbuch der Dogmengeschichte*. 3 vols. 1886ff. Revised edition. Tübingen, 1909-1910[4].
_____. *Das Apostolische Glaubensbekenntnis*.
_____. *Die Entstehung der Christlichen Theologie und des Kirchlichen Dogmas*. 1926. Revised edition: Tübingen, 1909-1910[4].
_____. *Grundriss der Dogmengeschichte*. 1889-1891. Revised edition: Freiburg, 1931[7].

Kattenbusch, Ferdinand. *Das Apostolische Symbol, seine Entstehung, sein geschichtlicher Sinn, seine ursprüngliche Stellung im Kultus und in der Theologie der Kirche*. 2 vols. Leipzig, 1894-1900.

Kelly, J. N. D. *Early Christian Creeds*. London, 1960[2].

_____. *Early Christian Doctrines*. London, 1968[4].

Kleutgen, Joseph. *Die Theologie der Vorzeit*. 3 vols. 1853-1870. 5 vols. Münster, 1867-1874[2].

Köhler, Walter. *Dogmengeschichte als Geschichte des Christlichen Selbstbewusstseins*. 2 vols. Zürich, 1938-1951.

Lietzmann, Hans. "Symbolstudien I-XIV, 1922-1927. *Kleine Schriften*. Vol. 3. Berlin, 1962.

Lohse, Bernhard. *Epochen der Dogmengeschichte*. Stuttgart, 1963.

Loofs, Friedrich. *Leitfaden zum Studium der Dogmengeschichte*. 1889. Fourth, fully revised edition: 1906. Reprinted and edited by K. Aland: Halle-Saale, 1950-1953.

McGiffert, A. C. *The Apostles' Creed, its Origin, its Purpose and its Historical Interpretation*. New York, 1902.

Neufeld, Vernon H. *The Earliest Christian Confessions*. Leiden, 1963.

Pelikan, Jaroslav. *The Christian Tradition*. Vol. 1, *The Emergence of the Catholic Tradition (100-600)*. Chicago, 1971--.

Schaff, Philip. *Bibliotheca Symbolica Ecclesiae Universalis, The Creeds of Christendom, with a History and Critical Notes*. 3 vols. 1877. Sixth edition edited by David Schaff: New York, 1931.

Schultes, Reginaldo-Maria. *Introductio in Historiam Dogmatum*. Paris, 1922.

Seeberg, Reinhold. *Lehrbuch der Dogmengeschichte*. 3 vols. 1908-1913[2]. Fourth revised edition. 4 vols. Basel, 1953-1954.

_____. *Grundriss der Dogmengeschichte*. Leipzig, 1901.

Schwane, Joseph. *Dogmengeschichte*. 4 vols. 1862-1890. Second printing: Freiburg, 1892-1905.

Thomasius, D. *Die Dogmengeschichte der Alten Kirche als Entwicklungs-Geschichte des kirchlichen Lehrbegriffs*. 2 vols. Erlangen, 1874-1876.

Tixeront, Joseph. *Histoire des Dogmes dans l'Antiquité Chrétienne*. 3 vols. Eleventh revised edition: Paris, 1930.

Vorgrimler, Herbert, ed. *Das Zweite Vatikanische Konzil, Documente und Kommentare*. Freiburg, 1966-1968.

Werner, Martin. *Die Entstehung des christlichen Dogmas*. 1941. Bern, 1954[2].

B. Monographs and Articles

Althaus, Paul. *Das Sogenannte Kerygma und der Historische Jesus.*
    Gütersloh, 1958.
Anspach, Lucien. "La Formation des Dogmes." *Conférences Faites à*
    l'Université de Bruxelles. Brussels, 1907.
Aquilina, Annunt. S. *De Progressu Dogmatis secundam Melchioris Cani*
    Doctrinam. Naples, 1963.
Aquinas, Thomas. *Commentaria in Octo Libros Physicorum Aristotelis,* in
    Opera Omnia, iussu impensaque Leonis XIII edita, vol. 2. Rome,
    1884.
_____. *Summa Theologica,* in *Opera Omnia,* vols. 4-12. Rome, 1888-1906.
Baird, William. "What is the Kerygma?" *JBL* 76 (1957), pp. 181-191.
Barbel, Joseph. *Christos Angelos, die Anschauung von Christus als Bote*
    und Engel in den gelehrten und volkstümlichen Literatur des
    christlichen Altertums. Bottrop in W., 1941.
_____. "Christos Angelos, die frühchristliche und patristische Engel-
    christologie im Lichte der neuen Forschung." *Liturgie und*
    Monchtum 21 (1957), pp. 71-90.
Barth, Karl. *Römerbrief.* München, 1922[2].
_____. *Kirchliche Dogmatik,* I. Zürich, 1947.
Bauer, Walter. *Rechtglaubigkeit und Ketzerei im Ältesten Christentum.*
    Tübingen, 1963[2].
Baum, Gregory. *Faith and Doctrine, A Contemporary View.* New York, 1969.
Benoit, Pierre. "Les Origines du Symbole des Apôtres dans le Nouveau
    Testament." *Exégèse et Théologie.* Vol. 2. Paris, 1961.
Bicknell, E. J. "Dogma in the New Testament." *Dogma in History and*
    Thought. Preface signed by W. R. Matthews. London, 1929.
    Pp. 29-49.
Biemer, Günter. *Überlieferung und Offenbarung, die Lehre von der Tradi-*
    tion nach John Henry Newman. Freiburg, 1961.
Blair, H. A. *A Creed Before The Creeds.* London, 1955.
Boman, Thorlief. *Das Hebräische Denken im Vergleich mit dem Griechi-*
    schen. Gottingen, 1954.
_____. "Hebraic and Greek Thought Forms in the New Testament." *Current*
    Essays in New Testament Interpretation, Essays in Honor of Otto
    A. Piper. Edited by W. Klassen and G. F. Snyder. New York,
    1962. Pp. 1-22.
Bornkamm, Gunther. "Homologia." *Hermas* 71 (1936), pp. 377-393.
_____. "Das Bekenntnis im Hebräerbrief." *Studien zu Antike und Ur-*
    christentum, Gesamelte Aufsätze. Vol. 2. München, 1959.
Brox, N. "Bekenntnis." *HThG* München, 1962. Vol. 1, pp. 151-160.
Brunner, Emil. *Wahrheit als Begegnung.* Zurich, 1938.
Brunner, Peter. "Wesen und Funktion von Glaubensbekenntnissen."
    Veraltetes Glaubensbekenntnis? Edited by P. Brunner, G. Fried-
    rich, etc. Regensburg, 1968.
Byrne, J. J. "Newman's Anglican Notion of Doctrinal Development." *EThL*
    14 (1937), pp. 230-286.
Buuck, Friedrich. "Zum Rechtfertigungsdekret. Die Unterscheidung
    zwischen fehlbarem und unfehlbarem Glauben in den vorbereitenden
    Verhandlungen." *Das Weltkonzil von Trient.* Vol. 1. Freiburg,
    1951. Pp. 117-143.
Cano, Melchior. *De Locis Theologicis Libri Duodecim.* Salamanca, 1563.

Chadwick, Owen. *From Bossuet to Newman, the Idea of Doctrinal Development.* Cambridge, 1957.

Charpenter, H. J. "Symbolum as a Title of the Creed." *JThS* 43 (1942), pp. 1-11.

_____. "Creeds and Baptismal Rites in the First Four Centuries." *JThS* 44 (1943), pp. 1-11.

Chrismann, Philip Neri. *Regula Fidei Catholicae et Collectio Dogmatum Credendorum.* Kempten, 1792.

Conzelmann, Hans. "Was glaubte die frühe Christenheit?" *Schweizerische Theologische Umschau* 25 (1955), pp. 61-74.

_____. *Grundriss der Theologie des Neuen Testaments.* München, 1967.

Crehan, Joseph. *Early Christian Baptism and the Creed, a Study in Ante-Nicene Theology.* London, 1950.

Dalham, Florian. *De Canone Dogmatum Christianorum.* Vienna, 1784.

Davies, W. D. "Torah and Dogma: A Comment." *The Harvard Theological Review* 61 (1968), pp. 87-106.

Deferrari, R. J. and Barry, M. I. "Dogma." *A Lexicon of St. Thomas Aquinas.* Washington, 1948. Pp. 337-338.

Deichgräber, Reinhard. *Gotteshymnus und Christushymnus in der frühen Christenheit.* Göttingen, 1967.

Delling, Gerhard. *Der Gottesdienst im Neuen Testament.* Göttingen, 1952.

_____. "Geprägte partizipiale Gottesaussagen in der urchristlichen Verkündigung." *Studien zum Neuen Testament und zum hellenistischen Judentum.* Gottingen, 1970. Pp. 401-416.

Deneffe, August. "Dogma. Wort und Begriff." *Scholastik* 6 (1931), pp. 381-400, 505-538.

Dewart, Leslie. *The Future of Belief.* New York, 1966.

_____. *The Foundations of Belief.* New York, 1969.

Diem, Hermann. *Dogmatik.* Vol. 2. München, 1955.

Dobschütz, Ernst von. *Das Apostolicum in biblisch-theologischer Beleuctung.* Giessen, 1932.

Dodd, Charles H. *The Apostolic Preaching and Its Developments.* London, 1936.

_____. *History and the Gospel.* Welwyn, Herts, 1938.

_____. *The Parables of the Kingdom.* Revised edition: New York, 1961.

Dorner, August. *Die Entstehung der christlichen Glaubenslehren.* München, 1906.

Dörries, Hermann. *Das Bekenntnis in der Geschichte der Kirche.* Göttingen, 1947.

Drey, Johann Sebastian. *Kurze Einleitung in das Studium der Theologie, mit Rücksicht auf den wissenschaftlichen Standpunkt und das katholische System.* Tübingen, 1819.

_____. "Vom Geist und Wesen des Katholizismus." *Geist des Christentums und des Katholizismus, ausgewählte Schriften Katholischer Theologie im Zeitalter des Deutschen Idealismus und der Romantik.* Pp. 193-234. Edited by J. R. Geiselmann. Mainz, 1940.

Driedo, Johann. *De Ecclesiasticis Scripturis et Dogmatibus.* Louvain, 1533.

Dulles, Avery. *Apologetics and the Biblical Christ.* Westminster, Md., 1964.

_____. *The Survival of Dogma.* New York, 1971.

Ebeling, Gerhard. *Theologie und Verkündigung.* Tübingen, 1962.

Eichenseer, C. *Das Symbolum Apostolicum beim heiligen Augustinus.* St. Ottilien, 1960.

Elert, Werner. *Der christliche Glaube.* Hamburg, 1956[3].

_____. *Der Ausgang der altkirchlichen Christologie, eine Untersuchung über Theodor von Pharan und seine Zeit als Einführung in die alte Dogmengeschichte.* Berlin, 1957.

Elze, Martin. "Der Begriff des Dogmas in der alten Kirche." *ZThK* 61 (1964), pp. 421-438.

Evans, C. F. "The Kerygma." *JThS* New Series. 7 (1956), pp. 25-41.

Feine, Paul. *Die Gestalt des apostolischen Glaubensbekenntnisses in der Zeit des Neuen Testaments.* Leipzig, 1925.

Flückiger, Felix. *Der Ursprung des christlichen Dogmas.* Zürich, 1955.

Foakes-Jackson, F. J., and Lake, Kirsopp, editors. *The Beginnings of Christianity.* Part 1, *The Acts of the Apostles.* London, 1920.

Fries, Heinrich. "Tübinger Schule." *LThK* 10, 390-392.

Fritzsche, Hans-Georg. *Lehrbuch der Dogmatik.* Vol. 1. Göttingen, 1964.

Fuller, Reginald H. *The Foundations of New Testament Christology.* New York, 1965.

Fürst, Dieter. *Kirche oder Gnosis, Heinrich Schliers Absage an den Protestantismus.* München, 1961.

_____. "Bekennen." *Theologisches Begriffslexikon zum Neuen Testament.* Vol. 1. Wuppertal, 1967.

Gardeil, A. *Le Donné Révélé et la Théologie.* Liége, 1932.

Geiselmann, J. R. *Jesus der Christus, die Urform des apostolischen Kerygmas als Norm unserer Verkündigung und Theologie von Jesus Christus.* Stuttgart, 1951.

_____. *Die lebendige Überlieferung als Norm des christlichen Glaubens, dargestellt im Geiste der Traditionslehre Johannes Ev. Kuhns.* Freiburg, 1959.

_____. "Dogma." *HThG*, vol. 1, pp. 225-241.

_____. *Die katholische Tübinger Schule, ihre theologische Eigenart.* Freiburg, 1964.

_____. *Lebendiger Glaube aus geheiligter Überlieferung, der Grundgedanke der Theologie Johann Adam Möhlers und der katholischen Tübinger Schule.* Freiburg, 1966[2].

Gennadius de Marseilles. *De Ecclesiasticis Dogmatibus.* In: *Corpus Haereseologici*, vol. 1. Edited by Franciscus Oehler. Berlin, 1856.

Ghellinck, J. De. "Dialectique et dogme aux Xe -- XIIe siecles." *Festgabe für Clemens Baeumker.* Münster, 1913. Pp. 79-99.

_____. *Patristique et Moyen Age*, vol. 1, *Les Recherches sur les Origines du Symbole des Apôtres.* Brussels, 1949[2].

Glick, G. Wayne. *The Reality of Christianity, A Study of Adolf von Harnack as Historian and Theologian.* New York, 1967.

Gloege, G. "Dogma." *RGG*, vol. 2, pp. 222-225.

Gollwitzer, Franciscus W. *Bibliographia Dogmatica: Compendii dogmatices usui pernecessaria, collecta et edita.* Sulzbach, 1831.

Gore, Charles. "Dogma in the Early Church." *Dogma in History and Thought.* Preface signed by W. R. Matthews. London, 1929. Pp. 53-81.

Grabmann, Martin. "Das Konzil von Trient als Fortschrittsprinzip der katholischen Dogmatik." *Das Weltkonzil von Trient.* Vol. 1, pp. 33-53. Edited by Georg Schreiber. Freiburg, 1951.

Grandmaison, Léonce de. "Le développement du dogme chrétien." *Revue Pratique d'Apologétique* 5 (1907-1908), pp. 521-542, 6 (1908), pp. 5-33, 81-104, 401-436, 881-905.

Grillmeier, Aloys. "Hellenisierung -- Judaisierung des Christentums." *Scholastik* 33 (1958), pp. 321-355, 528-558.

_____, and Bacht, Heinrich, editors. *Das Konzil von Chalkedon, Geschichte und Gegenwart.* 3 vols. Würzburg, 1962³.

_____. *Christ and Christian Tradition.* New York, 1965. (This work is a complete revision of "Die theologische und sprachliche Vorbereitung der christologischen Formel von Chalkedon," which appeared in *Das Konzil von Chalkedon,* vol. 1.

Guitton, Jean. *La Philosophie de Newman: Essai sur l'idée de Développement.* Paris, 1933.

Hägglund, B. "Die Bedeutung der 'regula fidei' als Grundlage theologischer Aussagen." *Studia Theologica* 12 (1958), pp. 1-44.

Hahn, Ferdinand. *Christological Hoheitstitel, ihre Geschichte im frühen Christentum.* Göttingen, 1963.

Hammans. Herbert. *Die Neueren Katholischen Erklärungen der Dogmenentwicklung.* Essen, 1965.

Harnack, Adolf von. *Das Wesen des Christentums.* 1900. Reprinted: München, 1964.

Hatch, Edwin. *The Influence of Greek Ideas and Usages upon the Christian Church.* London, 1891.

Haussleiter, J. *Trinitarischer Glaube und Christusbekenntnis in der alten Kirche, neue Untersuchung zur Geschichte des Apostolischen Glaubensbekenntnisses.* Gütersloh, 1920.

Heidegger, Marin. *Unterwegs zur Sprache.* Pullingen, 1959.

_____. *Was heisst Denken?* Tübingen, 1954.

Hödl, Ludwig. "Articulus fidei. Eine begriffsgeschichtliche Arbeit." *Einsicht und Glaube, Gottlieb Söhngen zum 70. Geburtstag.* Pp. 358-376. Edited by Joseph Ratzinger and Heinrich Fries. Freiburg, 1962.

Horst, Ulrich. "Das Verhaltnis von Schrift und Tradition nach Melchior Cano." *TThZ* 69 (1960), pp. 207-223.

Hunter, A. M. *Paul and his Predecessors.* Philadelphia, 1961².

Joest, W., Mussner, F., Scheffczyk, L., etc., *Was heisst Auslegung der Heiligen Schrift.* Regensburg, 1966.

Jonas, Hans. *Augustin und das paulinische Freiheitsproblem.* Anhang I: *Über die hermeneutische Struktur des Dogmas.* Göttingen, 1965.

Journet, Charles. "Scripture and the Immaculate Conception: A Problem in the Evolution of Dogma." *The Dogma of the Immaculate Conception, History and Significance.* Edited by Edward D. O'Connor. Notre Dame, Ind., 1958.

Justin Martyr. *Apologia. Opera.* Edited by J. C. T. Otto. Jena, 1842.

Kantzenbach, Friedrich Wilhelm. *Evangelium und Dogma, die Bewältigung des theologischen Problems der Dogmengeschichte im Protestantismus.* Stuttgart, 1959.

Käsemann, Ernst. "Begründet der n.t. Kanon die Einheit der Kirche?" *Ev Theol* 11 (1951-52), pp. 13-21.

Kasper, Walter. *Dogma unter dem Wort Gottes.* Mainz, 1965.

_____. "Evangelium und Dogma." *Cath* 19 (1965), pp. 199-209.

_____. *Die Methoden der Dogmatik, Einheit und Vielheit.* München, 1967.

_____. "Geschichtlichkeit der Dogmen?" *StdZ* 179 (1967), pp. 401-416.

_____. "Das Verhältnis von Evangelium und Dogma." *Concilium* 3 (1967), pp. 69-75.

Kelly, J. N. D. *Rufinus, A Commentary on the Apostles' Creed. Ancient Christian Writers.* Westminster, Md., 1955.

Kittel, Gerhard. "ˮΑγγελος. *ThWb,* vol. 1, pp. 79-87.

_____. "Δόγμα, Δογματίζω." *ThWb,* vol. 2, pp. 233-235.

_____. *Biblioa Hebraica.* Stuttgart, 1949.

Kleist, James A., and Lilly, Joseph L. *The New Testament, Rendered from the Greek with Explanatory Notes.* Milwaukee, 1956.

Koopmans, Jan. *Das altkirchliche Dogma in der Reformation.* München, 1955.

Kramer, Werner. *Christos Kyrios Gottessohn.* Zürich, 1963.

Kretschmar, Georg. *Studien zur frühchristlichen Trinitatstheologie.* Tübingen, 1956.

_____. "Wahrheit als Dogma -- die alte Kirche." *Was ist Wahrheit?* Edited by H. R. Müller-Schefe. Göttingen, 1965. Pp. 94-120.

Kroll, Josef. "Die Hymnendichtung des fruhen Christentums." *Antike* 2 (1926), pp. 258-281.

Küng, Hans. *Strukturen der Kirche.* Freiburg, 1961.

_____. *Die Kirche.* Freiburg, 1967.

_____. *Unfehlbar? Eine Anfrage.* Zürich, 1970.

Kunze, Johannes. *Das apostolische Glaubensbekenntnis und das Neue Testament.* Berlin, 1911.

Ladd, G. E. "Revelation and Tradition in Paul." *Apostolic History and the Gospel, Essays Presented to F. F. Bruce.* Edited by W. Ward Gasque and Ralph P. Martin. Pp. 223-230.

Lang, Albert. *Die Loci Theologici des Melchior Cano und die Methode des Dogmatischen Beweises, ein Beitrag zur theologischen Methodologie und ihrer Geschichte.* München, 1925.

_____. "Die Gliederung und Reichweite des Glaubens nach Thomas von Aquin und den Thomisten." *Divus Thomas* (Fribourg) 20 (1942), pp. 207-236, 335-346; 21 (1943), pp. 79-97.

_____. "Der Bedeutungswandel der Begriffe 'fides' und 'haeresis' und die dogmatische Wertung der Konzilsentscheidungen von Vienne und Trient." *Studien zur Historischen Theologie, Festgabe für Franz Xavier Seppelt.* Edited by Walter Dürig and Bernhard Panzram. München, 1953. Pp. 133-146.

Lehmann, Karl, and Rahner, Karl. "Kerygma und Dogma." *Mysterium Salutis.* Vol. 1. Köln, 1965. Pp. 622-707.

_____, and Rahner, Karl. "Geschichtlichkeit der Vermittlung." *Mysterium Salutis.* Vol. 1, pp. 727-787.

_____. *Auferweckt am dritten Tag nach der Schrift, Früheste Christologie, Bekenntnisbildung und Schriftauslegung im Lichte von 1. Kor 15, 3-5.* Freiburg, 1968.

_____. "Bedarf das Glaubensbekenntnis einer Neufassung?" *Veraltetes Glaubensbekenntnis?"* Edited by Peter Brunner, Gerhard Friedrich, etc. Regensburg, 1968. Pp. 125-186.

Lengsfeld, Peter. *Überlieferung, Tradition und Schrift in der evangelischen und katholischen Theologie der Gegenwart.* Paderborn, 1960.

Lichtenstein, Ernst. "Die älteste christliche Glaubensformel." *ZKG* 63 (1950), pp. 1-74.

Locher, Gottfried W. *Glaube und Dogma.* Zollikon, 1959.

Lodrioor, J. "La Notion de Tradition chez Driedo." *EThL* 26 (1950) Pp. 37-53.

Lohmeyer, Ernst. *Kyrios Jesus, eine Untersuchung zu Phil 2, 5-11.* Heidelberg, 1928.

Macarius a Sancto Elia. *Introductio ad Historicam Litterariam Theologiae.* Grezium, 1785³.

Malmberg, Felix. "Die mittelbar-unmittelbare Verbindung mit Godd im Dogmenglauben." *Gott in Welt, Festgabe für Karl Rahner.* Vol. 2. Edited by Herbert Vorgrimler. Freiburg, 1964. Pp. 92-102.

Mangenot, E. "Chrismann." *DThC* , vol. 2b, 2415.

Marin-Sola, Fr. F. *La Evolución Homogenia del Dogma Católico.* Madrid, 1923.

Matthews, W. R., editor. *Dogma in History and Thought, Studies by Various Writers.* London, 1929.

_____. "The Nature and Basis of Dogma." *Dogma in History and Thought.* Pp. 1-26.

Maurer, W. *Bekenntnis und Sakrament.* Berlin, 1939.

Meinhold, Peter. "Geschichtskritik und Kirchenerneuerung." *Saeculum* 9 (1958), pp. 1-21.

_____. "Zur Grundlegung der Dogmengeschichte." *Saeculum* 10 (1960), pp. 1-20.

_____. "Der Ursprung des Dogmas in der Verkündigung Jesu." *ZKTh* 89 (1967), pp. 121-138.

_____. "Die Bemühungen um die Grundlegung der Dogmengeschichte." *Geschichte der Kirchlichen Historiographie.* Vol. 2. München, 1967. Pp. 515-544.

Mercier, J. "Tapper." *DThC,* vol. 15, 52-59.

Meunier, A. "Le Dogme Catholique." *Revue Écclesiastique de Liége* 38 (1951), pp. 3-15, 77-98.

Michel, Otto. "Biblisches Bekennen und Bezeugen." *EvTheol* 2 (1935), pp. 231-235.

_____. "Ὁμολογία." *ThWb,* vol. 5, pp. 199-220.

_____. *Der Brief an die Römer.* Göttingen, 1966¹².

Minon, A. "L'attitude de Jean-Adam Moehler (1796-1838) dans la question du développement du dogme." *EThL* 16 (1939), pp. 248-291.

Möhler, Johann Adam. *Die Einheit der Kirche, oder das Prinzip des Katholicismus, dargestellt im Geiste der Kirchenväter der drei ersten Jahrhunderte.* Tübingen, 1825.

_____. *Athanasius der Grosse und die Kirche seiner Zeit, besonders im Kampfe mit dem Arianismus.* 1827. Mainz, 1844².

_____. *Symbolik oder Darstellungen der dogmatischen Gegensätze der Katholiken und Protestanten nach ihren öffentlichen Bekenntnisschriften.* 1832. Mainz, 1838².

Murphy, J. L. *The Notion of Tradition in Driedo.* Milwaukee, 1959.

Nestle, Eberhard, and Aland, Kurt. *Novum Testamentum, Graece et Latine.* Stuttgart, 1963²⁵.

Newman, John Henry. *The Arians of the Fourth Century.* 1833. Westminster, Md., 1968.

_____. "The Nature of Faith in Relation to Reason." *Fifteen Sermons Preached before the University of Oxford.* 1843. Westminster, Md., 1966. Pp. 202-221.

_____. "Implicit and Explicit Reason." *Fifteen Sermons,* pp. 312-351.

xxi

_____. "The Theory of Developments in Religious Doctrine." *Fifteen Sermons,* pp. 312-351.

_____. *On Consulting the Faithful in Matters of Doctrine.* 1859. Edited by John Coulson. London, 1961.

_____. *An Essay on the Development of Christian Doctrine.* 1878. Westminster, Md., 1968.

_____. "Causes of the Rise and Successes of Arianism." *Tracts Theological and Ecclesiastical.* London, 1895. Pp. 137-299.

_____. "On St. Cyril's Formula ΜΙΑ ΦΥΣΙΣ ΣΕΣΑΡΚΩΜΕΝΗ." *Tracts Theological and Ecclesiastical.* Pp. 329-382.

_____. *De Catholici Dogmatis Evolutione.* Edited by Rev. T. Lynch. *Gregorianum* 16 (1935), pp. 403-444.

Nienaltowski, H. R. *Johann Adam Möhler's Theory of Doctrinal Development, its Genesis and Formulation.* Washington, 1959.

Nolte, Josef. *Dogma in Geschichte.* Freiburg, 1971.

Norden, Eduard. *Agnostos Theos, Untersuchungen zur Formgeschichte religiöser Rede.* 1913. Stuttgart, 1956[4].

Ott, Ludwig. *Grundriss der Dogmatik.* Freiburg, 1963.

Pannenberg, Wolfhart, editor together with Rolf Rendtorff, Trutz Rendtorff, and Ulrich Wilkens. *Offenbarung als Geschichte.* Göttingen, 1961.

_____. "Was ist eine dogmatische Aussage?" *Grundfragen systematischer Theologie, Gesammelte Aufsätze.* Göttingen, 1967. Pp. 159-180.

Parent, J. M. "La notion de dogme au XIIIe siècle." *Études d'Histoire Littéraire et Doctrinale du XIIIe siècle.* Ottawa, 1932. Pp. 141-163.

Pelikan, Jaroslav. *Development of Christian Doctrine, Some Historical Prolegomena.* New Haven, Conn., 1969.

_____. *Historical Theology, Continuity and Change in Christian Doctrine.* New York, 1971.

Peresius d'Ayala, Martinus. *De Divinis Apostolicis atque Ecclesiasticis Traditionibus, deque auctoritate ac vi earum sacrosancta adsertiones.* Coloniae, 1549.

Persson, Per Erik. *Sacra Doctrina, Reason and Revelation in Aquinas.* Philadelphia, 1970.

Petri, Heinrich. *Exegese und Dogmatik in der Sicht der Katholischen Theologie.* München, 1966.

Pissarek-Hudelist, Herlinde. "Das ordentliche Lehramt als kollegialer Akt des Bischofskollegiums." *Gott in Welt, Festgabe für Karl Rahner.* Vol. 2. Freiburg, 1964. Pp. 166-185.

Petavius. *De Dogmatibus Theologicis.* Paris, 1644-1650.

Plato. ῞ΟΡΟΙ. Edited by C. F. Hermannus. Leipzig, 1894.

Poulpiquet, E. A. de. *Le Dogme, Source d'Unité et de Sainteté dans l'Église.* Paris, 1912.

Procksch, Otto. *Das Bekenntnis im Alten Testament.* Leipzig, 1936.

Rad, Gerhard von. *Theologie des Alten Testamentes.* Vol. 1. München, 1958.

Rahlfs, Alfred, ed. *Septuaginta, id est Vetus Testamentum Graece iuxta LXX Interpretes.* Stuttgart, 1949[3].

Rahner, Karl. "Chalkedon -- Ende oder Anfang?" *Das Konzil von Chalkedon.* Edited by Aloys Grillmeier and Heinrich Bacht. Vol. 3, pp. 3-49. Würzburg, 1962[3].

_____. "Zur Frage der Dogmenentwicklung." *Schriften zur Theologie.* Vol. 1. Einsiedeln, 1964[7]. Pp. 49-90.

_____. "Überlegungen zur Dogmenentwicklung." *Schriften.* Vol. 4. Einsiedeln, 1964[4]. Pp. 11-50.

_____. "Theologie im Neuen Testament." *Schriften.* Vol. 5. Einsiedeln, 1964[2]. Pp. 33-53.

_____. "Was ist eine dogmatische Aussage?" *Schriften.* Vol. 5, pp. 54-81.

_____. "Exegese und Dogmatik." *Schriften.* Vol. 5, pp. 82-111.

_____. "Kleines Fragment 'über die kollektive Findung der Wahrheit'." *Schriften.* Vol. 6. Einsiedeln, 1965. Pp. 104-110.

_____. "Heilige Schrift und Theologie." *Schriften.* Vol. 6, pp. 111-120.

_____. "Die Forderung nach einer 'Kurzformel' des christlichen Glaubens." *Schriften.* Vol. 8. Einsiedeln, 1967. Pp. 153-164.

_____. "Der Pluralismus in der Theologie und die Einheit des Bekenntnisses in der Kirche." *Schriften.* Vol. 10. Zürich, 1972. Pp. 11-33.

_____. "Kirchliche Christologie zwischen Exegese und Dogmatik." *Schriften.* Vol. 10, pp. 197-226.

_____. "Reflexionen zur Problematik einer Kurzformel des Glaubens." *Schriften.* Vol. 10, pp. 242-256.

_____. "Bemerkungen zur Bedeutung der Geschichte Jesu für die katholische Dogmatik." *Die Zeit Jesu, Festschrift für Heinrich Schlier.* Edited by G. Bornkamm and K. Rahner. Freiburg, 1970. Pp. 273-283.

_____. "Dogma." *LThK,* vol. 3, 438-441.

_____. "Dogma." *Sacramentum Mundi,* vol. 2, pp. 102-107.

_____. "History of Dogma." *Sacramentum Mundi,* vol. 2, pp. 102-107.

_____, and Lehmann, Karl. "Kerygma und Dogma." *Mysterium Salutis.* Vol. 1. Köln, 1965. Pp. 622-707.

Ranft, J. "Dogma." *RAC,* vol. 3, 1257-1260.

Ratschow, C. H. *Der angefochtene Glaube, Anfangs- und Grundprobleme der Dogmatik.* Gütersloh, 1957.

Ratzinger, Joseph. *Das Problem der Dogmengeschichte in der Sicht der katholischen Theologie.* Köln, 1966.

Reinhardt, Klaus. *Der dogmatische Schriftgebrauch in der katholischen und protestantischer Christologie von der Aufklarung bis zur Gegenwart.* München, 1970.

Ritschl, Otto. "Literarhistorische Beobachtungen über die Nomenklatur der theologischen Disziplinen im 17. Jahrhundert." *Festgabe für Theodor von Haering.* Tübingen, 1918.

_____. "Das Wort dogmaticus in der Geschichte des Sprauchs bis zum Aufkommen des Ausdrucks theologia dogmatica." *Festgabe für Julius Kaftan.* Tübingen, 1920. Pp. 260-272.

Robinson, John A. T. "The Most Primitive Christology of All?" *JThL,* new series, 7 (1956), pp. 177-189.

Robinson, James M. "A Formel Analysis of Colosians 1:15-20." *JBL* 76 (1957), pp. 270-287.

Sanday, W., and Williams, N. P. *Form and Content in the Christian Tradition, a friendly Discussion between W. Wanday and N. P. Williams.* London, 1916.

Sanders, Jack T. *The New Testament Christological Hymns, their Histori-cal Religious Background.* Cambridge, 1971
Scheffczyk, Leo. "Biblische und dogmatische Theologie." *TThZ* 67 (1958), pp. 193-209.
_____. "Die Einheit des Dogmas und die Vielheit der Denkformen." *MThZ* 17 (1966), pp. 228-242.
_____. "Die Auslegung der Heiligen Schrift als dogmatische Aufgabe." *Was heisst Auslegung der Heiligen Schrift?* Edited by W. Joest, F. Mussner, L. Scheffczyk, etc. Regensburg, 1966. Pp. 135-171.
_____. "Dogmatik." *Was ist Theologie?* Edited by Engelbert Neuhäusler and Elisabeth Gössmann. München, 1966.
_____. *Von der Heilsmacht des Wortes.* München, 1966.
_____. "Lehramtliche Formulierungen und Dogmengeschichte der Trinität." *Mysterium Salutis.* Vol. 2. Einsiedeln, 1967. Pp. 146-220.
Schille, Gottfried. *Frühchristliche Hymnen.* Berlin, 1965.
Schillebeeckx, Edward. "Exegese, Dogmatik und Dogmenentwicklung." *Exegese und Dogmatik.* Edited by Herbert Vorgrimler. Mainz, 1962. Pp. 91-114.
_____. "The Development of the Apostolic Faith into the Dogma of the Church." *Revelation and Theology.* Vol. 1. New York, 1967. Pp. 57-83.
_____. "The Bible and Theology." *Revelation and Theology.* Vol. 1. Pp. 167-195.
_____. "The Concept of 'Truth'." *Revelation and Theology.* Vol. 2. New York, 1968. Pp. 5-29.
_____. "The New Appeal to Human Existential Experience." *Revelation and Theology.* Vol. 2. Pp. 113-121.
_____, ed. *Dogma and Pluralism, Concilium.* New York, 1970.
Schlette, Heinz Robert. "Dogmengeschichte und Geschichtlichkeit des Dogmas." *Geschichtlichkeit und Offenbarungswahrheit.* München, 1964. Pp. 67-90.
Schlier, Heinrich. *Wort Gottes.* Würzburg, 1962.
_____. "Über Sinn und Aufgabe einer Theologie des Neuen Testaments." *Besinnung auf das Neue Testament.* Freiburg, 1964. Pp. 7-24.
_____. "Biblische und dogmatische Theologie." *Besinnung,* pp. 25-41.
_____. "Was heisst Auslegung der Heiligen Schrift?" *Besinnung,* pp. 35-62.
_____. "Die Ordnung der Kirche nach den Pastoralbriefen." *Die Zeit der Kirche.* Freiburg, 1966. Pp. 129-147.
_____. "Über das Hauptanliegen des 1. Briefes an die Korinther." *Die Zeit der Kirche,* pp. 147-159.
_____. "Kerygma und Sophia, Zur neutestamentlichen Grundlegung des Dogmas." *Die Zeit der Kirche.* Pp. 206-232.
Schlink, Edmund. "Die Struktur der dogmatischen Aussage als oekumenis-ches Problem." *KuD* 3 (1957), pp. 251-306.
Schmaus, Michael. *Katholische Dogmatik.* Vol. 1. München, 1960[6].
_____. *Der Glaube der Kirche, Handbuch katholischer Dogmatik.* Vol. 1. München, 1969.
Schnackenburg, Rudolf. "Zur dogmatischen Auswertung des Neuen Testa-ments." *Exegese und Dogmatik.* Edited by Herbert Vorgrimler. Mainz, 1962.
Schneemelcher, W. "Das Problem der Dogmengeschichte." *ZThK* 48 (1951), pp. 63-89.

Schoof, T. M. *A Survey of Catholic Theology 1800-1970.* Paramus, N. J., 1970.

Schoonenberg, Piet, ed. *Die Interpretation des Dogmas.* Düsseldorf, 1969.
_____. "Geschichtlichkeit und Interpretation des Dogmas." *Die Interpretation des Dogmas,* pp. 58-110.

Schweitzer, A. *Das Messiasgeheimnis in den Evangelien.* Göttingen, 1901.
_____. *Das Messianitäts- und Leidensgeheimnis, eine Skizze des Lebens Jesu.* 1901. Tübingen, 1956[3].
_____. *Vom Reimarus zu Wrede.* 1906.
_____. *Geschichte der Leben-Jesu-Forschung.* 1913. München, 1966.
_____. *Geschichte der paulinischen Forschung.* Tübingen, 1911.

Schweitzer, Eduard. "Πνεῦμα, Πνευματικός." *ThWb,* vol. 6, p. 44f.
_____. *Erniedrigung und Erhöhung bei Jesus und seinen Nachfolgern.* Zürich, 1962[2].
_____. "Two New Testament Interpretation Creeds Compared." *Current Issues in New Testament Interpretation, Essays in honor of Otto A. Piper.* Edited by W. Klassen and G. F. Snyder. New York, 1962. Pp. 166-177.

Seeberg, Alfred. *Der Katechismus der Urchristenheit.* Leipzig, 1903.

Seeberg, Reinhold. "Zur Geschichte der Entstehung des apostolischen Symbols." *ZKG* 40 (1922), pp. 1-41

Semmelroth, Otto. "Wesen und Werden der Dogmen." *Bindung und Freiheit des katholischen Denkens.* Edited by A. Hartmann. Frankfurt am Main, 1952. Pp. 216-233.

Söll, Georg. "Das Problem der Dogmenentwicklung im Licht des Neuen Testaments." *Salesianum* 25 (1963), pp. 319-340.
_____. "Dogmenfortschritt durch neue Offenbarung? Ein Beitrag zur Geschichte der Theorie der Dogmenentwicklung." *FZThPh* 18 (1971), pp. 72-87.
_____. *Dogma und Dogmenentwicklung, Handbuch der Dogmengeschichte.* Freiburg, 1971.

Spaemann, Robert. "Das neue Dogma und die Dogmengeschichte." *MThZ* 3 (1952), pp. 151-160.

Stange, Carl. *Das Dogma und seine Beurteilung in der neueren Dogmengeschichte.* Berlin, 1898.

Staudenmaier, F. A. *Die Christliche Dogmatik.* 4 vols. Freiburg, 1844-1852. Photomechanical reproduction: Frankfurt/Main, 1967.

Stauffer, Ethelbert. *Die Theologie des Neuen Testaments.* 1941. Stuttgart, 1948[4].

Stern, Jan. *Bible et Tradition chez Newman, aux origines de la théorie du développement.* Paris, 1967.

Stöhr, Johannes. "Modellvorstellungen im Verstandnis der Dogmenentwicklung." *Reformata Reformanda, Festgabe für Hubert Jedin.* Vol. 2. Münster, 1965. Pp. 595-630.

Stuhlmueller, Carroll. "The Prophet and the Word of God." *Thomist* 28 (1964), pp. 133-173.

Tapper, Ruard. *Explicationis Articulorum, venerandae Facultatis Sacrae Theologiae generalis studii Lovaniensis circa dogmata ecclesiastica ab annis triginta quattuor controversa, una cum responsione ad argumenta adversariorum.* Louvain, 1555-1557.

Thompson, Claude H. *Theology of the Kerygma, A Study in Primitive Preaching.* Englewood Cliffs, N. J., 1962.

Tresmontant, Claude. *A Study of Hebrew Thought.* New York, 1960.

Tristram, H. "A. Moehler et J. H. Newman." *RSPhTh* 27 (1938), pp. 184-204.

Turner, H. E. W. *The Pattern of Christian Truth, A Study in the Relations between Orthodoxy and Heresy in the Early Church.* London, 1954.

Tyrrell, George. *Through Scylla and Charybdis.* London, 1907.

Vasquez, Gabriel. *Commentariorum ac Disputationum in Sanctam Thomam.* London, 1631.

Veron, Francis. *De Regula Fidei Catholicae seu de Fide Catholica.* Louvain, 1702².

Vincent of Lérin. *Commonitorium ML* 50, 637-686.

Vogl, Bertholdo. *Prolegomenon Sacrae Theologiae seu Introductio in Theologiam Scholastico-Dogmaticam.* Salzburg, 1743.

Völker, Walter. "Adolf von Harnack als Kirchenhistoriker." *ThZ* 7 (1951), pp. 209-227.

Vorgrimler, Herbert, ed. *Exegese und Dogmatik.* Mainz, 1962.

Voss, Gustav. "Johann Adam Möhler and the Development of Dogma." *ThSt* 4 (1943), pp. 420-444.

Wainwright, Arthur W. *The Trinity in the New Testament.* London, 1962.

Walgrave, Jan H. *Newman the Theologian, the Nature of Belief and Doctrine as Exemplified in his Life and Works.* London, 1960.

_____. *Unfolding Revelation.* Philadelphia, 1972.

Walther, Christian. *Typen des Reich-Gottes Verständnisses.* München, 1961.

Wegenast, Klaus. *Das Verständnis der Tradition bei Paulus und in den Deuteropaulinen.* Neukirchen, 1962.

Weiss, Johannes. *Die Predigt Jesu vom Reiche Gottes.* 1892. 1900². Göttingen, 1964.

_____. *Christus. Die Anfänge des Dogmas.* Tübingen, 1909.

Wehrlé, J. "De la nature du dogme." *Revue Biblique*, new series, 2 (1905), pp. 323-349.

Werner, Marin. *Der protestantische Weg des Glaubens.* Bern, 1955.

Whitehead, Alfred North. *Religion in the Making.* Cambridge, 1926.

Wiles, Maurice. *The Making of Christian Doctrine, a Study of Early Doctrinal Development.* Cambridge, 1967.

Wilkens, Ulrich. "Kreuz und Weisheit." *KuD* 3 (1957), pp. 77-108.

_____. *Die Missionsreden der Apostelgeschichte.* Neukirchen, 1961.

Wrede, Williams. *Das Messiasgeheimnis in den Evangelien.* 1901. Göttingen, 1969.

Zahn-Harnack, Agnes von. *Adolf von Harnack.* Berlin-Tempelhof, 1936.

Zahrnt, Heinz. *Die Sache mit Gott.* München, 1967.

Zeller, Hermann. "Bekenntnis." *LThK*, vol. 2, 142-143.

PART ONE

THE DEVELOPMENT OF THE PROBLEM

CHAPTER ONE

THE FORMATION OF CHRISTIAN DOGMA ACCORDING TO ADOLF VON HARNACK

1. INTRODUCTION

The great historian of Christian dogma and scholar in matters of early Church history, Adolf von Harnack, represents a view of dogma understood as a creation of the Greek spirit added to the apostolic faith. At least, this is the sense in which the gist of his work in the history of dogma, particularly in his *Lehrbuch der Dogmengeschichte*,[1] is commonly understood. His own later opinion seems not to have been quite so sanguine. "Man hört seit langer Zeit und auch heute noch die Antwort der spekulative Trieb der Griechen habe das [d.h., die Entstehung des Dogmas] verursacht und der Kampf gegen die Irrlehren habe dazu geführt, und unstreitig liegt Wahrheit in dieser Antwort; allein sie reicht nicht aus."[2] Be that as it may for the moment -- we shall return to the consideration of the more precise relationship of the Greek speculative

---

1. Berlin, 1885-1889. Darmstadt, 1931-1932[5]. All references here are made to the fourth edition: Tübingen, 1909-1910.
2. *Die Entstehung der christlichen Theologie und des kirchlichen Dogmas,* (Darmstadt, 1967), p. 75.

drive to dogma later -- one can hardly forget Harnack's rhetorically
excellent and oft quoted statement, "Das Dogma ist in seiner Conception
und in seinem Ausbau ein Werk des griechischen Geistes auf dem Boden
des Evangeliums."[3] It is necessary, however, to seek in detail just how
Harnack conceived of the relationship existing between dogma and the
gospel.[4]

   With this in mind, let us proceed to the consideration of what
Harnack understands under the concept "gospel." As will be seen, he
speaks of a twofold gospel, one "of Jesus" and one "about Jesus."[5] There
follows then naturally a study of the relationship existing between the
two gospels. And thereafter we propose to precise his notion of dogma.
It will be seen that Harnack gives scant place to the confessional
formulae in the development of doctrine.

2. THE GOSPEL OF JESUS

   Almost from the very beginning the word, "gospel," εὐαγγέλιον,
has been used in a double sense. On the one hand it means the preaching
of the apostles and the Christian community about Jesus. The first is
his good news of the coming of the kingdom of God, the beatitudes, and
the evangelical counsels (in the wide sense). The second, the apostolic
preaching of the crucified and risen Christ, who died for the sins of men

---

3. *Dogmengeschichte*, I, p. 20.
4. *Cf. Das Wesen des Christentums*, (München, 1964), p. 94: "Das Evangel-
    ium ist keine theoretische Lehre ....Wie weit entfernt man sich also
    von seinen (d.h., von Christi) Gedanken und von seiner Anweisung,
    wenn man ein 'christologisches' Bekenntnis dem Evangelium voranstellt
    und lehrt, erst müsse man über Christus richtig denken, dann erst
    könne man an das Evangelium herantreten! Das ist eine Verkehrung."
5. One could rightly speak here of a "subjective genitive" and of an
    "objective genitive."

and who has brought them a new life. Harnack sees a particularly intimate relationship existing between the two preachings: "Diese beiden
Bedeutungen sind ganz verschieden, und doch liegen eben in ihrem Neben-
und Ineinander die Eigenart, die inneren Spannungen und der Reichtum der
christlichen Religion beschlossen."[6] Their relationship to each other we
shall examine shortly; first let us see how Harnack sees each in its
individuality.

Jesus' preaching is in its essence the message of the even now
breaking-into-this-world rule of the almighty God, who is at once father
and judge.[7] Jesus, as many another preacher in those inter-testamental
times, was deeply impressed by the great differences existing between the
kingdom of God and the kingdom of men.[8] Because of the dramatic oppo-
sites existing in the two kingdoms, the one must be destroyed and pass.
This will take place in a great battle, but only the kingdom of God will
remain, can remain. The apocalyptic and eschatological elements of his
message belong not just to its form, but also to its content. For even
now through his person the lame walk, the blind see, the poor have the
gospel preached to them.

Those who heed his message and allow themselves to be converted
from their sinful ways are assured of a place in the coming kingdom of
his Father. But Jesus spoke also of the preservation of the individual
person's soul, that is, of a man's keeping himself free of the service of
gold and pleasure, and of living in humility before his god, and in this

6. *Dogmengeschichte*, I, p. 67.
7. *Cf. ibidem*, #4, "Das Evangelium Jesu Christi nach seinem Selbstzeug-
   nisse," pp. 65-85; and, *Wesen*, 3,2, "Die Verkündigung von Gott, dem
   einzigen und allmächtigen Vater," pp. 42-55.
8. *Cf. Wesen*, p. 43.

way he effected a movement of religion away from the political to the individual, and also to the holy, "...denn das 'Leben' wird durch das Wort Gottes ernährt, Gott aber ist der Heilige."[9]

Initial conversion is, however, only the beginning of a man's allowing the kingdom of God to take form in his life. Admission to the kingdom requires in one's personal ethical life the realization of a new law and of a newer justice (in place of the law and justification in Judaism), which is that of individed love for God and for one's fellow man. This "bessere Gerechtigkeit" corresponds to the holiness of God. And it is even available to sinners, who are included in the call to conversion and to the practice of the beatitudes.

Harnack several times summarizes the preaching of Jesus. It is: "Erstlich, das Reich Gottes und sein Kommen, Zweitens, Gott der Vater und der unendliche Wert der Menschenseele, Drittens, die bessere Gerechtig-keit und das Gebot der Liebe."[10] Or, more shortly: "Gottesherrschaft, Sündenvergebung und bessere Gerechtigkeit (Gebot der Liebe)."[11]

3. THE GOSPEL ABOUT JESUS

Although Jesus himself founded no community, the circle of his disciples who had gathered around him during his lifetime (most impor-tantly, of course, "the twelve"), were quick to form themselves into a community after his death. He had been simply their teacher; they made of themselves a cult community.[12] As a community they were characterized

---

9. *Dogmengeschichte*, I, pp. 67-68.
10. *Wesen*, p. 42.
11. *Dogmengeschichte*, I, p. 69.
12. This understanding of the community's preaching about Jesus depends on #5, "Die gemeinsame Verkündigung von Jesus Christus in der ersten Generation seiner Gläubigen," of the *Dogmengeschichte*, I, pp. 85-111.

by the fact that they, each and every one, had experienced in the man, Jesus, the Messiah of promise. They were grasped and united by his spirit and word. They were convinced that God had made of him justice and holiness, wisdom and redemption. Of him could be pronounced every honor that could be imagined. This acknowledgment of the worth of his person is traced back not just to the overpowering influence on them of his personality, but also to the two facts that his life had been given as a sacrifice for sin, and that through his resurrection he now sits at the right hand of God.[13] As the risen one, Jesus was alive and Messiah. "Weil man ihn als den Lebendigen wusste, pries man ihn als den zur Rechten Gottes Erhöhten, als den Überwinder des Todes, als den Fürsten des Lebens, als die Kraft eines neuen Daseins, als den Weg, die Wahrheit und das Leben."[14] And, "Die messianischen Vorstellungen gestatteten es, ihn an den Thron Gottes zu stellen, ohne den Monotheismus zu gefährden.[15] This developing faith and confession would end in the two- and three-member formulae,[16] but as yet everything was still in the embryonic stage.

---

and on the 9th Vorlesung in *Das Wesen des Christentums*, pp. 97-106.
13. *Cf. Wesen*, p. 98: "Paulus hat allerdings den Tod und die Auferstehung Christi zum Gegenstand einer besonderen Spekulation gemacht und das ganze Evangelium in diese Ereignisse sozusagen eingeschmolzen; aber bereits fur den persönlichen Jüngerkreis Jesu und die Urgemeinde galten sie als grundlegend."
14. *Ibidem.*
15. *Ibidem.*
16. *Cf. Dogmengeschichte*, I, p. 90: "Das Bekenntniss zu dem Vater, dem Sohn und dem Geist ist somit die Entfaltung des Glaubens, dass Jesus der Christ sei; aber es war nicht beabsichtigt, in diesem Bekenntnis die wesenhafte Gleichheit der drei Grössen oder auch nur die Gleichartigkeit der Beziehungen des Christen zu ihnen auszudrücken; vielmehr kommt in ihm der Vater als der Gott und Vater über Alles, der Sohn als der Offenbarer, Erlöser und Herr, der Geist als Besitz (Prinzip des neuen überirdischen Lebens und der Heiligkeit) in Betracht."

Inasmuch as the community felt itself the natural heir to all the promises made to Israel -- it was the "true Israel" living in the end-time, it was able to maintain all the apocalyptic features of the Jewish hopes as it awaited the return of Jesus. Indeed, the community already possessed guarantees for the fulfillment of his return not only in the resurrection of its Lord, but also in the manifold manifestations of the Spirit in its members.

Harnack summarizes the content of the disciples' faith and the preaching which bound them together in the following few sentences:

> Jesus von Nazareth ist der von den Propheten verheissene Messias. -- Jesus, nach dem Tode durch göttliche Auferweckung zur Rechten Gottes erhöht, wird demnächst wiederkommen und das Reich sichtbar aufrichten. -- Wer an Jesum als den Christ glaubt, in der Taufe die Sündenvergebung empfangen hat und in die Gemeinde aufgenommen ist, Gott als den Vater anruft und in Kraft des Geistes Gottes nach den Geboten Jesu lebt, ist ein Heiliger Gottes und darf als solcher des ewigen Lebens und des Antheils an dem himmlischen Reich gewiss sein.[17]

In his *Wesen des Christentums*, Harnack summarizes somewhat differently, and states that the new community was characterized through the following features:

> 1. durch die Anerkennung Jesu als des lebendigen Herrn, 2. dadurch, dass jeder einzelne in der neuen Gemeinde -- auch die Knechte und Mägde -- die Religion wirklich erlebte und sich in eine lebendige Verbindung mit Gott gesetzt wusste, 3. durch ein heiliges Leben in Reinheit und Brüderlichkeit und in der Erwartung der nahe bevorstehenden Wiederkunft Christi.[18]

This summary is not so complete as the foregoing one and, while omitting the notion of Jesus as the Jewish Messiah, does acknowledge him as the Lord, which is, of course, that most important part of the Pauline kerygma declaring Jesus worthy of divine honors because of his being

---

17. *Dogmengeschichte*, I, pp. 87-88. Harnack introduces this summary with the words: "Der Inhalt des Glaubens der Jünger Jesu und die gemeinsame Verkündigung, welche sie unter einander verband...."
18. *Wesen*, p. 97.

8

raised to God's right hand. It seems that Harnack does not distinguish carefully enough between the very different significances of the two titles, "Lord" and "Messiah." So, for example: "Als dem Messias -- dem 'Herrn' gilt Jesus anbetende Verehrung, d.h. sie gilt dem Namen, den ihm sein Vater gegeben hat."[19]

4. THE RELATIONSHIP BETWEEN THE TWO GOSPELS

"Nicht der Sohn, sondern allein der Vater gehört in das Evangelium, wie es Jesus verkündigt hat, hinein."[20] This sentence, which appeared first in *Das Wesen des Christentums*, was repeated in later editions of the *Dogmengeschichte* with emphasis.[21] With its first appearance it had been attacked on many sides from his critics, but unjustly so, as Rudolf Bultmann points out.[22] For Harnack's critics had overlooked the importance of "...wie Jesus es verkündigt hat," as well as the following sentence: "Nicht wie ein Bestandteil gehört er in das Evangelium hinein, sondern er ist die persönliche Verwirklichung und die Kraft des Evangeliums gewesen und wird noch immer als solche empfunden."[23]

"Soll das Evangelium Christi gelten oder das von Christus?"[24] In considering this question, Harnack sees it as incorrect to draw a sharp dividing line between the two. The gospel, either gospel -- that from Jesus or, that about Jesus -- is the gospel of Jesus, and achieves its meaning only where the Father becomes known as Jesus knows him. And

---

19. *Dogmengeschichte*
20. *Wesen*, p. 92.
21. *Dogmengeschichte*, (4th edition), I, p. 81. *Cf.* also p. 82.
22. Preface to *Das Wesen des Christentums* in the Siebenstern edition, (München, 1964), p. 13
23. *Wesen*, p. 93.
24. *Dogmengeschichte*, I, p. 81.

Jesus is experienced and recognized as the way to the Father.[25]

> ....denn in dem Jesus Christus dieses Evangelium verkündigt,
> ruft er überall die Menschen zu sich selber. In ihm ist das Evan-
> gelium Wort und That; es ist seine Speise und darum sein persön-
> liches Leben geworden, und in dieses sein Leben zieht er alle
> Anderen hinein. An ihm sollen sie wahrnehmen, welch' ein Vater der
> heilige Gott ist; an ihm sollen sie die Macht und Herrschaft Gottes
> über die Welt empfinden und dieses Trostes gewiss werden; ihm, dem
> Demüthigen und Sanftmüthigen, sollen sie nachfolgen, und indem er,
> der Heilige und Reine, die Sunder zu sich ruft, sollen sie die
> Gewissheit erhalten, dass Gott durch ihn Sünde vergiebt.[26]

Moreover, Jesus did not press the connection between his gospel and
his own person. However, he lived, worked, and spoke from the richness
of his personal life with the Father, and in this way he became for his
followers the revelation of the Father. But at bottom this connection
between him and the Father was assured through "der überwältigende
Eindruck seiner Person."[27]

What Jesus did, however, press, at least from a determined point in
his life, was himself as the "Son of God" and the "Messiah." This was a
consciousness which grew with him throughout his life and which expressed
in a meaningful way his significance for his disciples. And in the
appearance of the Messiah God himself would be visible. For, "In der
Anerkennung Jesus als des Messias war für jeden gläubigen Juden die
innigste Verbindung der Botschaft Jesu mit seiner Person gegeben: in dem
Wirken des Messias kommt Gott selbst zu seinem Volke; dem Messias, der
Gottes Werk treibt und der zur Rechten Gottes auf den Wolken des Himmels
sitzt, gebührt Anbetung."[28] In foretelling his death, he explained it as
a victory and redemption and the passing over to his glory. He had even

---

25. *Ibidem.*
26. *Ibidem*, p. 69.
27. *Ibidem.*
28. *Wesen*, p. 91.

influenced his followers so deeply that after his death they were convinced that he was not dead but even now the living Lord and Judge.[29]

Thus, the connection between the gospel (preaching) of Jesus with
the gospel (preaching) about Jesus was assured not through his revealing
mysteries about his own person, but through the overwhelming impression
of his person.

5. THE BEGINNINGS OF DOGMA

Where comes then the great change from a "kerygmatic" to a
"dogmatic" Christianity? It almost goes without saying that "Jesus war
kein Schullehrer, sondern ein Menschenfischer."[30] Moreover, his preaching was so simple and at the same time so rich that it was best simply
repeated, and only with great difficulty and lack of fidelity to its
original character can it be systematized. According to Harnack's view,
dogma (or dogmas) is not coexistent with the beginning of Christianity.
It (dogma) is the conceptual formulation of what is presumed to exist in
the "depositum" (the teachings of faith) in statements of determined
expression for scientific-apologetic discussion. His own classic
definition must be quoted:

> Die kirchlichen Dogmen sind die begrifflich formulirten und
> für eine wissenschaftlich-apologetische Behandlung ausgeprägten
> christlichen Glaubenslehren, welche die Erkenntniss Gottes, der
> Welt und der durch Christus geschehenen Erlösung umfassen und den
> objektiven Inhalt der Religion darstellen. Sie gelten in der
> christlichen Kirchen als die in den heiligen Schriften (bez. auch
> in der Tradition) enthaltenen, das Depositum fidei umschreibenden
> Wahrheiten, deren Anerkennung die Vorbedingung der von der Religion
> in Aussicht gestellten Seligkeit ist.[31]

---

29. *Cf. Dogmengeschichte*, I, p. 70.
30. *Ibidem.*
31. *Ibidem, p. 3.*

The religion of Jesus in Harnack's conception was, as we have seen, an enthusiastic movement of piety. Although it made mention of several facts, such as the fatherhood of God, the coming judgment and kingdom of God, and the nearness of Jesus to God, dogma was something entirely foreign to the movement. Instead of a teaching, it was simply a message: "....ursprünglich keine Lehre, sondern eine Botschaft."[32] Harnack believes that originally the attempt at summarizing this message of faith beyond a "couple of confessional phrases" was hardly undertaken.

> In Bezug auf den "Glauben" und die "Hoffnung" aber ist ursprünglich nicht einmal der Versuch einer Zusammenfassung gemacht, bzw. nicht über ein paar Bekenntnisssätze hinaus geführt worden; denn noch war das, um was es sich hier handelte, viel zu lebendig und mächtig, um sich schulmässig formulieren zu lassen. Es lebte in der Predigt, in liturgischen Anrufungen, vor allem in den Lob- und Dankgebeten, in Hymnen und Liedern und fand in ihnen den entsprechenden Ausdruck.[33]

In that springtime of Christianity there were only the most simple expressions of the faith which, while witnessing to the Father and a few other facts, had no determined form, because in this earliest of Christian times there was still much room for the free expression of Christian excitement and enthusiasm.[34] That is to say, Catholicism, as the political union of various local churches through a legal system of laws and dogmas, had not yet come to be.[35]

It is now obvious that Harnack's notion of dogma must be examined in somewhat more detail. Two characteristics of his concept deserve special notice: first, that the logical or conceptual expression of dogma

---

32. *Entstehung*, p. 37.
33. *Ibidem*, p. 38. Harnack does, however, admit the existence of a type of summary of moral teaching, probably used as preparation for baptism and dependent on a Jewish pattern.
34. *Cf. Dogmengeschichte*, I, p. 354.
35. *Cf. ibidem*, p. 52

belongs to its nature ("...begrifflich formulirten und für eine wissen-schaftlich-apologetische Behandlung...."); and secondly, dogmas find their expression in a determined form ("...ausgeprägte christlichen Glaubenslehren...", "...in einer festen Form ausgeprägt....").[36] Harnack discusses the second of these two points in relation to historical facts which, if they are expressed scientifically and in a determined formula, he considers to be capable of becoming dogmas as much as any other truth which should be believed toward salvation.

The most characteristic feature of Harnack's understanding of the formation of Christian dogma is the interpolation and absorption of the Greek spirit: "...ein Werk des griechischen Geistes auf dem Boden des Evangeliums."

At one point in history we see the gospel in all its purity, and at another, later point, the systematic structure of Catholic dogmatic teaching. It is the task of the historian of dogma to determine both what has caused this transformation and when. The second question Harnack answers, in so far as such a question can be given a dated answer, with the point when the teaching that Jesus Christ is the pre-existent Logos was made official Church doctrine. "Das ist aber zuerst damals geschehen, als die Lehre, Christus sei der praexistente und persönliche Logos Gottes, in den Kirchen als die fundamentale Glaubens-lehre zum Siege kam, d.h. um die Wende des dritten Jahrhunderts zum vierten."[37]

What is the "Greek spirit" that has become a constitutive part of Christian dogma? Christian dogma developed in the Roman world and in

---

36. *Ibidem*, p. 1, footnote 2.
37. *Ibidem*, p. 4.

Hellenic culture, and it almost goes without saying that with the breaking of the apostolic Church from Judaism and the subsequent destruction
of Jerusalem in 70 A.D., Christianity, if it was to survive, found it
more necessary than ever to "quarry its stones" for the building of the
great Church from the Graeco-Roman world around it. The Jewish-Christian
tradition was conscious of the nearness of the living God and this was
its treasure, but that did not prevent it from exploiting the "riches,
power, delicacy and freedom of the Greek."[38]

Is the "Greek spirit" then to be limited to the speculative drive
of the Greek way of looking at reality and the world applied to the
Christian deposit of faith? It is in Harnack's estimation certainly that
but includes also more, namely, definite areas of philosophic inquiry and
specific interpretations.

In the second century there was a resurgence of interest in
religious feeling and in religious philosophy. Under the influence of
the Platonic and Stoic schools and of thinkers such as Plutarch and
Marcus Aurelius a climate was generated in which, "Die Gedanken der
göttlichen gnädigen Vorsehung, der Zusammengehörigkeit aller Menschen,
der allgemeinen Bruderliebe, der breitwilligen Vergebung des Unrechts,
der nachsichtigen Geduld, der Einsicht in die eigenen Schwächen --
freilich noch mit manchen Schatten behaftet -- sind nicht minder ein
Erwerb der praktischen Philosophie der Griechen für weite Kreise
geworden, wie die Ueberzeugung von der inhärenten Sündhaftigkeit, von
der Erlösungsbedürftigkeit und von dem ewigen Werth und der Würde einer
menschlichen Seele, die nur in Gott ihre Ruhe findet."[39] Specifically,

38. *Ibidem*, p. 54.
39. *Ibidem*, p. 144.

14

the "Greek spirit" means the acknowledgment of a natural theology which saw in Christian revelation elements which confirmed its own dim but certain conclusions about God and the soul and expanded them. Christianity dignified in a fresh and overpowering way the Greeks' basic faith in the infinite worth of the individual human soul.[40]

Finally, the thirst of an intellectually mature searcher could find in the mysteries celebrating the death and resurrection of a Christ, with their clear reference to historical happenings, a depth of satisfaction which no serious searcher would ever find in the polytheistic official cults, and which was tantalizingly aimed at in the mystery cults from the East.[41]

What was of (infinitely) more importance to the Greek conquest of the Christian religion was the assimilation of the philosophical, Greek Logos notion to the person of Jesus. As we have said, this moment is for Harnack "articulus constitutivus ecclesiae." "Die Folgen dieses Unternehmens können gar nicht hoch genug geschätzt werden; denn die Logoslehre, mögen in sie auch nachträglich ursprüngliche Interessen eingefügt sein, ist doch die griechische Philosophie in nuce."[42]

Although gnostics had made the first attempts (in the first century) to intellectualize Christianity by appealing to its revelation to confirm their religious philosophy, credit must be given to the apologists for introducing the Logos notion to the general stream of Christian thought.[43] The aims which motivated the gnostics were

---

40. *Cf. ibidem*, p. 80ff.
41. *Cf. ibidem*, p. 346.
42. *Ibidem*.
43. St. John's Gospel did, of course, do this too, but at this time the New Testament canon did not exist, and this particular Gospel was very likely just taking its final shape.

different than those which the apologists sought to achieve. The
gnostics wanted to use Christianity only is so far as it helped in
setting forth their doctrines of eons, "light," "mystery," "truth,"
"wisdom," etc. Men such as Tatian and Justin set out to demonstrate
rationally that Christianity was the true philosophy and worthy of consideration among other schools of philosophy as scientific knowledge
about God and the world. Justin can on the same page proclaim that
Christ is a new Socrates and that this teacher is the incarnate reason
of God. "Aber dieser Lehrer war die Vernunft selber; sie war in ihm
sichtbar, ja sie ist in ihm leibhaftig erschienen."[44] The transcendent
and immutable God had manifested himself in the cosmos through his Logos,
and this Logos was his Son, Jesus.

> Da aber nach der Fundamentalanschauung der Apologeten das
> Princip der Religion, d.h. der Wahrheitserkenntniss, auch das
> Princip der Welt ist, so muss jenes göttliche Wort, welches die
> richtige Erkenntniss der Welt bringt, identisch sein mit der
> göttlichen Vernunft, welche die Welt selbst hervorgebracht hat,
> d.h. der Logos ist nicht nur die schaffende Vernunft Gottes,
> sondern auch das Offenbarungswort Gottes.[45]

Surely the time when Paul could write, "Let no man lead you astray
through philosophy and vain decits" (Col 2:8), was now long gone.[46]
The apologist, Marcianus Aristides, even introduces himself as a
"philosopher of the Athenians." The Christian religion was becoming an
exercise of reason. Wherever God revealed himself, whether in the philosophers or through the prophets of the Old Testament, there was the
Logos. For the apologists the Christian "dogmas" are, as Harnack
interprets, "...die durch die Propheten in den h. Schriften geoffenbarten

---

44. *Apol.* I,5; quoted from the *Dogmengeschichte*, I, p. 508.
45. *Dogmengeschichte*, I, p. 531.
46. Harnack mentions that this warning had been constantly repeated by
    Christians, as Celsus witnesses. *Cf. ibidem*, p. 505.

16

Vernunftwahrheiten, die in der Erkenntniss des Christus zusammen-
geschlossen sind (Χριστὸς λόγος καὶ νόμος) und in ihrer Einheit die
göttliche Weisheit darstellen, deren Anerkennung die Tugend und das
ewige Leben zur Folge hat."[47] The theology of the apologists was based
on the monotheism of God, a truth of reason and of the Old Testament,
and on the manifestation of the Logos in the world and in the Son, to
whom the Old Testament prophets give detailed witness.

Harnack believes that the reason for the apologists adopting the
concept of the Logos for the Son is to be seen in the fact that the Logos
concept hypostasized the reason in God without prejudicing his unity,
because he (the Logos) was derived from God without being created. And,
through the Logos concept God could be active in the world while preserving his transcendence.[48] Thus, the monotheism of the Old Testament is
preserved and even attested to by many of the philosophers when they
viewed the Logos as the unifying principle of reason behind the world of
phenomena. Indeed, if one searches in the scriptures (i.e., the Old
Testament), he finds that all the prophets attested to the appearance of
the Logos. Since according to his essence the Logos is the unfolding of
God (οἰκονομία), he is God and worthy of divine honors.

The Logos theology is, however, not always completely clear, for
sometimes the Logos is identified with the Spirit, and with some (e.g.,
Tertullian) there was a time before creation when the Logos did not
exist.[49] Although he is the mediator between God and creation, the
Logos is spoken of as proceeding from God in the manner of being

47. *Ibidem*, p. 526.
48. *Cf. ibidem*, p. 530f.
49. *Cf. ibidem*, p. 533ff.

egendered.[50] God "begot" (γεννᾶν) the Logos. But Justin and Tatian also use the same word (γεννᾶν) for the creation of the world. The confusion then is evident. For the apologists Christ the redeemer is principally Christ the "divine teacher," who leads men away from the bad influence of the demons.[51]

As the central part of early Christian theology the Logos doctrine would be developed further, as for example, in the thought of Origen. It is noteworthy, however, that in the thought of Athanasius, which played such an important role at Nicea and in the following controversies, the theology of the Logos is set somewhat to the side. For him Christ is no longer the reason behind the world, but the "image," the "reflection," and the "Son."[52] Jesus is, instead of the Logos, separate form God, the Son who is consubstantial (ὁμοούσιος) with the Father.

"Alle Apologeten sind aber davon durchdrungen, dass diese Erkenntniss Gottes und der Welt, der Logo- und Kosmogonie, der wesentlichste Theil des Christenthums selbst ist."[53] And inasmuch as Christ was looked upon as a great "teacher," and that the apologists made such splended use of current philosophy by adopting the Logos teaching to their own purposes, it certainly is no wonder that the intellectualization of Christianity received its appropriate expression when they also spoke of the "dogmas" of Christianity, a term which at that time was almost thoroughly a philosophical one.

---

50. *Cf. ibidem*, footnote 1.
51. This is, of course, a generality and it is certainly not to be denied that the theology of redemption was never developed further by the apologists than seeing Christ as a teacher. Justin, in particular, also saw him as the bringer of immortality.
52. *Cf. Dogmengeschichte*, II, p. 207ff.
53. *Cf. ibidem*, I, p. 536.

6. THE QUESTION OF DOGMA AND CREEDS IN HARNACK'S THOUGHT

The question of "Christological utterances" in the New Testament
is treated by Harnack in approximately three footnotes appended to a
subsection within the chapter, "Die Voraussetzungen der Dogmengeschichte," in the first volume of the *Dogmengeschichte*.[54] In other
words, whatever Christological utterances there may be in the New
Testament, they do not have more than a presuppositional function to the
formation and beginning of dogma.

The chapter in question treats of what the first disciples thought
of Jesus. He was primarily looked upon as Messiah inasmuch as God had
chosen him, according to the prophecies of the Old Testament, to restore
the kingdom. Through him God had also chosen the new Israel. Jesus was
also referred to as "Lord" inasmuch as through his suffering and death he
was raised to a position of sovereignty and glory at God's right hand.
Because his work would only reach its conclusion through his return, his
imminent coming was the most important part of the early Christian
belief.

The confession of the Father, Son, and Holy Spirit is part of the
development of the belief that Jesus is the Christ. However, it was not
meant that this confession express the equality of the three persons or
the similarity of the Christian's relationship to them: "...vielmehr
kommt in ihm [d.h. in dem Bekenntnis] der Vater als der Gott und Vater

---

54. *Cf.* the footnotes: 3, **pp.** 89-90; 1, p. 90; 1, p. 92. In the
appendix to Hahn's *Bibliothek der Symbole und Glaubensregeln der
Alten Kirche*, (Breslau, 1897), Harnack collected a large amount of
material towards the history and explanation of the old Roman creed.
Although he refers to this material in such terms as "Glaube,"
"Glaubensregel," "κήρυγμα," "Wahrheit," "παράδοσις," *etc.*, (p. 365)
he fails to discuss the dogmatic significance of these notions.

über Alles, der Sohn als der Offenbarer, Erlöser und Herr, der Geist, als Besitz (Prinzip des neuen überirdischen Lebens und Besitz der Heiligkeit) in Betracht."[55]

Basing himself on the work of Caspari,[56] Zahn,[57] and Hahn,[58] Harnack believes that the earliest date at which one can posit the existence of "ein festes Bekenntnis" to be about 150 and certainly not before 135, which form was the ancient Roman creed. Before this time it can only be said: "Direct lässt sich mit unseren heutigen Mitteln nicht zu Erkenntnissen über die Symbolbildung vor dem römischen Symbol gelangen."[59]

He allows, however, that at the same time there existed the baptismal formula, or formulae, and other short kerygmatic utterances. Beyond the confession of the Father, Son, and Holy Spirit, a rather free proclamation of the history of Jesus was common.[60] The _regulae_ _fidei_ to be found in Irenaeus and Tertullian seem not so much to depend on the ancient Roman creed as on the earlier kerygmatic formulae.[61] The peculiar contribution of the Roman community seems to have been the uniting of the proclamation about the one God with those about Jesus, and inserting both into the Roman creed proper. In the meantime, though, the baptismal formula itself was set up as the rule of faith.

In the face of Gnosticism and Marcionism and their variant teachings, Irenaeus, Tertullian, and Hippolytus placed the baptismal

---

55. _Dogmengeschichte_, I, p. 90, footnote 1.
56. _Quellen a. Gesch. des Taufsymbols_, III, p. 3ff., & Patr. App. Opp. 1.2., pp. 115-142.
57. _Das Apostol. Symbolum_, 1893.
58. _Bibliothek d. Symbole u. Glaubensregeln der alten Kirche_, 1877[2].
59. Harnack, _op. cit._, p. 177 (footnote).
60. _Cf. ibidem_, p. 175.
61. _Cf. ibidem_, pp. 354-372.

confession, which they interpreted as containing individual doctrines and thus, in a limited sense, one may say that the apologists were the first to set up dogmas. That is, if we were to accept as a definition of ecclesiastical dogma: "...Sätze, die, in dem Bekenntniss der Kirche überliefert, in der h. Schrift beider Testamente nachgewiesen und verstandesmässig reproducirt und formulirt werden, so sind die gennanten Männer die ersten, welche Dogmen aufgestellt haben...."[62] Such a definition is, however, not the definition favored by Harnack since it is not scientific enough for his purposes.

The result of the apologists setting up the baptismal formula for the rule of faith was the continuing displacement of the real rule of faith -- the gospel as Jesus had preached it. Because the Roman Church was eventually able to set the Roman creed through as the touchstone of orthodox faith, faith itself became ever less the pure enthusiastic experience of the first disciples, and ever more a submission to a judicial decree. "In der modernen römischen Kirche ist das Dogma vor allem eine Rechtsordnung, der man sich zu unterwerfen hat, und unter Umständen reicht die Unterwürfigkeit allein aus (fides implicita).[63]

Before the violent conflicts with gnosticism and therefore before the need to set up an "apostolic" rule of faith there were only short, formulated summaries which grew up out of the missionary activity of the Church. In addition to belief in monotheism, as found in the formulary in Hermas (Mand. I), πιστέυω εἰς ἕνα θεὸν παντάκρατορα, other such formulae expressed belief in the Father, Son, and Spirit. They appear to have been used on such occasions as baptism and the Lord's supper,

---

62. *Ibidem*, p. 345.
63. *Ibidem*, p. 10, footnote 1.

as well as in exorcisms.[64]

Gnosticism subjected Christianity to the testing of its own foundations. In answer to it splendid theories for Christianity's apostolic
origins were developed by Irenaeus (*Adversus Haereses*) and Tertullian
(*De Praescriptione Haereticorum*). In addition, the Roman creed which
eventually became normative in the West was looked upon as deriving from
the preaching of the apostles and eventually became known in its
developed form as the "Apostles' Creed." But in judging the ancient
Roman creed Harnack insists: "...es ist keine Lehr-, sondern eine
Bekenntnissformel, ...es hat, von allem Polemischen frei..., eine
hymnisch-cultische Form, die sich in der asyndetischen Aufeinanderfolge
der einzelnen Glieder und in dem Rhythmus zeigt...."[65] What Irenaeus and
Tertullian had accomplished theoretically the Roman Church did practically -- it used the baptismal formula, interpreted in a definite way, i.e.,
in an antignostic way, as a means of measuring adherence to the Church.[66]

7. DEVELOPMENT OF THE TRINITARIAN DOGMA

The confession of Father, Son, and Holy Spirit in the baptismal
formula is a part of the development of faith in Jesus as the Christ.
Nevertheless, Harnack did not believe that this confession expressed an
assumed equality between the various persons. His statement in the above
quote that the three members of the baptismal formula are only asyndeti-
cally related to one another represents his true view of the Trinitarian
dogma. Although the baptismal formula ranked the persons next to one

---

64. *Cf. ibidem*, pp. 355-356.
65. *Ibidem*, p. 176, footnote 4.
66. *Cf. ibidem*, p. 359ff.

22

another, he sees no unanimity in early Christianity on the function,

form of existence, or dignity of the Spirit. Part of the difficulty

Harnack attributes to the concept of spirit itself: "1) ...sofern πνεῦμα,

...auch das Wesen Gottes und des Logos bezeichnete, 2) in dem Unvermögen,

eine specifische Wirkung des Geistes in der Gegenwart anzuerkennen, 3) in

dem Interesse, vielmehr dem Logos die Wirksamkeit in dem Kosmos und in

der Offenbarungsgeschichte zuzuschreiben."[67] And so the presence of the

three persons in the tripartite formula for baptism confirms in no way

for Harnack a dogma of the Trinity. The most that can be said is that

all three somehow belonged to the "Oekonomie Gottes."

Although the references in Justin and Irenaeus about the Spirit

are not without importance, it is Tertullian who first names the Spirit

"God." It was, however, Origen who, after acknowledging the uncertainity

of the tradition, treated the doctrine of the Holy Spirit entirely

according to the analogy of the doctrine of the Logos. Nevertheless, he

called the Spirit, which exists within God one step lower than the Son, a

creature. It was again Athanasius who in the fifties came to the

conclusion that if the Spirit is a part of the Godhead, it must also be

worshiped, for what is true of the Son is true also of the Spirit.[68]

Otherwise the Trinity would be broken (ὅλη τριὰς εἰς θεός ἐστιν).

Moreover, the principle of salvation cannot be the same according to

nature as that which is saved. He, who for us is the source of life,

cannot himself then be a creature; that which communicates the divine

nature must itself possess that nature. This position, which became the

orthodox one, was first confirmed by the Synod of Alexandria (362). It

---

67. *Ibidem*, II, p. 285.
68. *Cf. ibidem*, II, pp. 288-289.

was then the Cappadocians who are most responsible that the argumentation of Athanasius was carried on.

> In der Verlegenheit, dem Geist eine eigenthümliche Seins-
> weise im Verhältniss zum Vater zu geben, verfiel man darauf, nach
> johanneischen Stellen ihm die ewige ἔκπεμψις und ἐκπόρευσις beizu-
> legen. Wie also schon im 2. Jahrhundert aus der Zeugung Christi
> ins irdische Dasein eine überirdische, dann eine ewige Zeugung
> geworden ist und man dann das 'Gezeugtsein' zum Characteristicum
> der 2. Hypostase innerhalb der h. Trias in ihr gesehen. Deutlicher
> kann man die Arbeit der Begriffsphantasie nirgends erkennen als
> hier. Hinter eine an sich schon wunderbare Geschichte, die
> zwischen der Gottheit und Menschheit spielt, wird durch Abstraction
> und Verdoppelung eine zweite Geschichte gesetzt, die ganz in die
> Gottheit selbst fallen soll.[69]

Thus Harnack sees the formation of the dogma of the Trinity as "Begriffsphantasie." It is the product of pure and even, at least to some extent, of wild speculation. He lacks the understanding that although there is in scripture no completed dogma of the Trinity, there was nevertheless a certain truth content behind the early Church's experiences of the three persons, indeed a content which could and would be developed in a more scientific way. Harnack lacked the insight that already in the time of Ignatius of Antioch, in whose work are to be found a number of Trinitarian formulas,[70] the belief of the Church about the three persons was also already a firm part of the teaching on faith.

69. *Ibidem*, II, pp. 292-293.
70. *Ad Eph.*, 18,2; *Ad Magn.*, 13,1.

8. BELIEF WITHOUT DOGMA?

Harnack's antipathy to a dogmatic Christianity, together with his stature as a scholar of early Christianity, have contributed greatly during the last several generations to the reinforcement in the public mind of the not uncommon view of an unbridgeable cleft between the gospel and dogma. Because for him 'dogmatic Christianity' corresponded to the ancient manner of thinking, it had to remain a very limited and conditioned expression of Christianity.[71] He thought that the end of this "zeitbedingte Ausdrucksform" was heralded in particular by Luther who sought a purer form of Christianity by returning to its origins in faith and personal experience. Luther, he thought, "rediscovered" the gospel.

The implicit antipathy between faith and thinking in Harnack's thought raises many serious questions. Is it at all possible to have faith without formulatable propositions standing behind the personal experience? Can the enthusiastic experience of religion at any level of historic cultural development, let alone the Greek, be realizable without at the same time being expressable, albeit imperfectly, in concepts? Finally, is faith even possible without dogmatic presuppositions? In other words, is it possible for faith to "happen" without the hearer being confronted through preaching with the word of God, expressed in some way through the preaching of the Church drawing from its dogmatic foundations and expressing the truth of Christ in some one or other

---

71. Peter Meinhold believes that the source of Harnack's valuing of "individuelle Frömigkeit" as the absolute form of piety, together with his narrow conception of dogma are drawn from "der idealisthischen Identitätsphilosophie, nach der das Ich der Punkt ist, in dem Subjekt und Objekt zusammenfallen." He does not, however, develop this thought. *Cf.* "Geschichte und Kirchenerneuerung," in *Saeculum* 9 (1958), p. 9.

'dogmatic' way?[72]

A second criticism of Harnack's work must come from his failure to see the relationship between creeds and dogma. His treatment of the development leading to the Roman creed runs parallel to, but hardly touches his development of the history of dogma. His admission that there were perhaps "ein paar Bekenntnissätze" in earliest Christianity bypasses completely the wealth of dogmatic content those sentences must have held.[73] Since the advent of form criticism it is apparent that any study of dogma on its earliest level must begin with the confessional formulae in the New Testament. It is true that Harnack's work was done before the real advent of form criticism.[74] Nevertheless, his anti-dogmatic bias prevented him from recognizing the dogmatic significance of the developing creeds in the early post-apostolic Church. Perhaps the deeper reason for Harnack's failing to see the early creeds of the Church as the dogma of that time was his rigid adherence to his own restrictive definition of dogma. Hence, Loof's criticism of his work, "a monograph of the fourth century," seems to be justified.

In our exploration, "The Question of Dogma and Creeds in Harnack's Thought," it became abundantly clear that the relationship between doctrinal norms and liturgical celebration was neither fully explored

---

72. *Cf.* Felix Malmberg, "Die mittelbar-unmittelbare Verbindung mit Gott im Dogmenglauben," in *Gott in Welt, Festgabe für Karl Rahner*, vol. II, edit. by H. Vorgrimler, (Freiburg, 1964), pp. 92-102; and Emil Brunner, *Wahrheit als Begegnung*, (Zürich, 1938).
73. *Cf.* Harnack, *Entstehung*, p. 38.
74. The form criticism of the New Testament really began only around the end of World War I with the publication of the following works: M. Dibelius, *Formgeschichte des Evangeliums*, (Tübingen, 1919); K. L. Schmidt, *Der Rahmen der Geschichte Jesu*, (Berlin, 1919); R. Bultmann, *Die Geschichte der synoptischen Tradition*, (Göttingen, 1921). The first publication of Harnack's *Dogmengeschichte* (first volume) was in 1886.

nor appreciated in Harnack's thought. He seemed somehow to suppose that the original rule of faith was the gospel as Jesus preached it and that all kerygmatic formulae which antedate the formation of the Roman creed (c. 150 A.D.), the first "festes Bekenntnis" in his terminology, were confessional and not teaching formulae. Such a position ignores the ancient axiom, "Legem credendi lex statuit supplicandi." There simply is no better way of ascertaining the belief of the Church than the study of its liturgical practice, for liturgy is the living tradition of the Church in its most dynamic form.

That which can be prayed and which is expressed in the manifold faith-forms of the liturgy, its acclamations, hymns, creeds, prayers, etc., is eminently rule for the Church's belief. For such public affirmations are at once declarations of the belief that is in the whole social body, as they are also forms the validity of which is assured by the continual presence of the Church's magisterium and tradition. Thus the liturgy has elements of both confession and catechesis. In its preaching as in its action it constantly employs formulae which proclaim and teach the mystery of Christ and the Church's beliefs about him.

No movement can survive without some type of principles governing its origin and continuance. Yet Harnack's admiration for enthusiastic Christianity blinded him even to the point of writing: "Es hat eine Zeit lang überhaupt kein festes und einheitliches Ritual besessen, und als sich ein solches ausbildete oder ausgebildet hatte, dauerte es noch ziemlich lange, bis das Ritual eine Quelle und Unterlage für die Dogmatik wurde."[75] Indeed, neither enthusiastic Christianity nor

---

75. *Dogmengeschichte*, I, p. 806.

liturgical practice preclude dogmatic Christianity; both are rather based on it. Yet how this movement known as Christianity could express the principles of its origin and continuance now in determined concepts and sentences, now in more free forms, is a question which will receive consideration in a later chapter.

From the time of Thomasius to J. Pelikan historians of dogma have avoided a definition of dogma so narrow as that of Harnack. So Thomasius saw the Church's task in forming dogma grounded in the duty of giving witness and clear expression to the faith that is in her in some type of "lehrhaften Ausdruck." "Die Kirche muss sagen, nicht nur dass, d.h., was in der Schrift geschrieben ist, sondern was sie glaubt, was der ihr anvertrauten Offenbarungswahrheit Sinn und Inhalt ist, und muss es so sagen, dass es verständlich, fassbar, greifbar wird sowohl für die an sie Herantretenden als für ihre eigenen Glieder. ...Wo sie als sichtbares, verfasstes Gemeinwesen in der Welt sich darstellt, versteht es sich ohnehin von selbst, dass sie ihrem Glauben irgend einen erkennbaren Ausdruck gibt."[76] Thus, although the Church has need of some type of articulated and formulated confession, its dogma is not in the first instance the ratiocinations of its theologians or the determined sentences and concepts of its leaders. The Church's dogma is the belief that is in her, as she sees herself entrusted and instructed with the word of God, and as she faces the world in which she finds herself with its various philosophies, thought forms, yearnings. From the central point of her belief, "Jesus is Lord" (Rom 10:2), she develops her dogma "aus ihrem Gemeinglauben zum Lehrbegriff. ...Dogma ist nicht subjective

76.   D. Thomasius, *Die Dogmengeschichte als Entwicklungs-Geschichte des kirchlichen Lehrbegriffs*, (Erlangen, 1874), I, pp. 6-7.

Meinung, die individuelle, etwa theologische Ansicht der einzelnen
Kirchenlehrer, sondern die kirchliche Glaubensbestimmung, näher die Form,
in der sich der christliche Gemeinglaube nach seinen wesentlichen
Momenten einen bestimmten und gemeingiltigen Ausdruck gibt."[77]

The expressive and rhetorically excellent definition of dogma of
Harnack's *Dogmengeschichte* is then simply too narrow and scientifically
oriented ("Dogmen sind die begrifflich formulirten und für eine wissen-
schaftlich-apologetische Behandlung ausgeprägten christlichen Glaubenslehren...") to encompass the breadth of belief that is always in
Christianity.

For that reason Pelikan's substitute definition of doctrine rather
than dogma, which will be discussed later, more closely approximates the
actual state of belief in the Church.

> To find a substitute for Harnack's definition of the history
> of doctrine as history of dogma, it is necessary to define doctrine
> in a manner that is simultaneously more comprehensive and more
> restrictive: more comprehensive in that the polemical and juridical
> expressions of doctrine in the form of dogmatic decrees and promul-
> gations are not isolated from other expressions of doctrine, such
> as preaching, instruction, exegesis, liturgy, and spirituality;
> more restrictive in that the range and content of the doctrines
> considered are not determined in the first place by the quarrels
> among theologians but by the development of those doctrines them-
> selves. Christian doctrine, then, may be defined as what the
> Church believes, teaches, and confesses on the basis of the word
> of God.[78]

Today we know that the history of doctrine and dogma does not begin
in the fourth century. It was already in full swing when the words of
the New Testament first came to be written down. Harnack's supposed
cleft between the divinized Christ as Logos and the simple figure of the

---

77. *Ibidem*, p. 7.
78. Jaroslav Pelikan, *Historical Theology:* Continuity and Change in
    Christian Doctrine, (New York, 1971), p. 95.

Jesus of the scriptures is false.[79] For already in the scriptures he is looked upon as "functionally" divine, as in the Philippians Hymn (2:6-11). This means that the history of dogma, above all of that teaching which is dogma in the fullest sense, the divinity of Jesus, begins below the level of the New Testament and not in the subsequent history of Christianity. The unfolding of dogma in the New Testament is what this book is about.

---

79. *Cf. ibidem*, pp. 71-72.

CHAPTER TWO

THE 'CONSISTENT ESCHATOLOGICAL' SCHOOL AND

THE FORMATION OF CHRISTIAN DOGMA

1. INTRODUCTION

The 'consistent eschatological' viewpoint agrees with Harnack that
the beginning of Christian dogma is not coexistent with the beginnings of
Christianity itself, and that its "birth" represents an assimilation of
Hellenistic elements. Nevertheless, the 'consistent eschatological'
viewpoint has become an independent theory of dogmatic origins. Martin
Werner cites approvingly the thesis of Ferdinand Christian Baur, "Der
Anfang der Dogmengeschichte kann nur der Anfang der Bewegung des Dogmas
selbst sein,"[1] and begins therewith his own development and view of
those origins.[2] It is then a separate theory providing its own explan-
ation of why dogma has become a part of the history of Christianity.
Even though our own interest is in that theory, it seems necessary to

---

1. *Vorlesungen über die christliche Dogmengeschichte*, (1865), I, p. 15;
    quoted by Werner in *Die Entstehung des christlichen Dogmas*, (Bern,
    1954[2]), p. 24.
2. In addition to Werner's *Entstehung* compare also his *Der protestan-
    tische Weg des Glaubens*, (Bern, 1955).

introduce it by way of the eschatological interpretation of the life and ministry of Jesus, since this is the context in which its proponents first expounded it.

Although Martin Werner has been the most articulate spokesman of the 'consistent eschatological' viewpoint, Albert Schweitzer was its originator.[3] Accordingly we shall examine the 'consistent eschatological' viewpoint as represented in the thought of these two men, but in the context of the theological debate around the turn of the nineteenth century in which it was born, which is that of the place and meaning of eschatology in the preaching of Jesus and to Christianity.

In his monumental study of the history of research on the life of Jesus, *Geschichte der Leben-Jesu-Forschung*, Albert Schweitzer comes to the conclusion that the various attempts to present Jesus objectively, that is, according to the nineteenth century's view of history, had failed. Avery Dulles summarizes this search:

> In the late eighteenth century, he shows, Jesus was portrayed as an enlightened teacher of God, virtue, and immortality. In the early nineteenth century the romantic imagination saw in Him a religious genius, exuding the poetry of God. The Hegelian idealists then tried to show that Christ had ushered in a new stage in the evolution of man's religious consciousness. The moralizing writers of the late nineteenth century, influenced by Albert Ritschl, depicted Jesus as a teacher of Kantian ethics. Toward the end of the century social revolutionaries found in Jesus a protagonist of the poor and oppressed.[4]

"Die geschichtliche Erforschung des Lebens Jesu ging nicht von dem rein geschichtlichen Interesse aus, sondern suchte den Jesus der Geschichte

---

3. Cf. Schweitzer, *Das Messianitäts- und Leidensgeheimnis, eine Skizze des Lebens Jesu*, (Tübingen, 1956[3]), and *Vom Reimarus zu Wrede*, (1906), which since 1913 has appeared in expanded form as *Geschichte der Leben-Jesu-Forschung*. All references here are made to the Siebenstern Taschenbuch edition, (München, 1966).
4. *Apologetics and the Biblical Christ*, (Westminster, Md., 1964), pp. 5-6.

als Helfer im Befreiungskampf vom Dogma. Dann, als sie vom πάθος

befreit war, suchte sie den historischen Jesus, wie er ihrer Zeit ver-

ständlich war. ...So fand jede folgende Epoche der Theologie ihre

Gedanken in Jesus, und anders konnte sie ihn nicht beleben."[5]

Only Hermann Samuel Reimarus and Bruno Bauer saw through the

variety of problems besetting any study of the life of Jesus and, in the

midst of their own "Phantasterien," touched on essentials to its logical

reconstruction. Reimarus, the first to write a "Life of Jesus," which

was only published by Lessing ten years after Reimarus' death in 1778,[6]

grasped what is entirely necessary for an _historical_ representation of

the life of Jesus: that his thought-world (Vorstellungswelt) is that of

the late Jewish apocalyptic eschatology. From this insight of Reimarus

until Johannes Weiss who takes it up again all of theology is, Schweitzer

judges, a "Rückschritt." Bruno Bauer, going from the study of the Fourth

Gospel as a literary construction (schriftstellerisches Produkt) to the

Gospel of Mark, enunciates the hypothesis that it too has the same type

of origin: it is more a product of the evangelist or of the community

than a reflection of history (Kunst, nicht Geschichte). Mark's presen-

tation of Jesus as the Messiah is an eminent part of this process.[7]

---

5. Schweitzer, _Geschichte_, I, pp. 47-48.
6. It is not strictly true that Reimarus was the first to write a biog-
    raphy of Jesus since the Jesuit, Hieronymus Xavier, had written such
    a life in the Persian language in the sixteenth century, and Johann
    Jacob Hess published one in 1768. Despite a Latin translation of the
    first it remained of little value because of its highly selective
    character intended to glorify Christ. The second was little more
    than a paraphrase of the gospels. Cf. Schweitzer, _ibidem_, I, pp. 56-
    57.
7. _Cf_. Schweitzer's quoting of Bruno Bauer, _op. cit._, p. 181: "Gibt es
    eine abgeschmacktere Unmöglichkeit? 'Jesus,' sagt Bauer, 'muss diese
    zahllosen, diese himmelschreienden Wunder verrichten, weil er der
    evangelischen Anschauung als der Messias gilt; er muss sie ver-
    richten, um sich als den Messias zu beweisen -- und niemand erkennt

Although in the beginning Bauer wanted to "save face" for Jesus and restore his relationship to history, he came to the position that the historical existence of Jesus was at least problematic, perhaps even unnecessary. At a later period Bauer did factually reach the conclusion that Jesus had not existed. For this reason what was worthwhile in his work was neglected until William Wrede was able to rehabilitate it in another form.[8]

William Wrede called into question the very possibility of an "historical" as opposed to a "dogmatic" representation of the life of Jesus.[9] His work showed that even the Gospel of Mark, obviously the most uningenious and naive among the synoptics, was governed by a theological presupposition. Mark was not motivated so much by the ideals of a nineteenth century historical science as by his purpose of marshaling the facts in the life of Jesus to illustrate the "Messiasgeheimnis." Jesus

---

ihm den Messias! Es ist selbst das allergrösste Wunder, dass das Volk in diesem Wundertäter nicht schon längst den Messias erkannt hatte. Jesus konnte erst als der Messias gelten, als er Wunder tat: Wunder tat er aber erst, als er im Glauben der Gemeinde als der Messias auferstand, und das war ein und dasselbe Faktum, dass er als Messias auferstand und Wunder tat.'"

8. Cf. Schweitzer, op. cit., p. 189: "Man kann Bauer nur mit Reimarus vergleichen. Beide habe erschrekend und lähmend auf ihre Zeit gewirkt. Niemand hatte wie sie die gewaltige Komplexität des Problems des Lebens Jesu empfunden. Darum sahen sie sich gezwungen, die Lösung ausserhalb des Gebietes der kontrollierbaren Geschichte zu verlegen, Reimarus, indem er sein Leben-Jesu auf dem Trug der Jünger erbaute, Bauer, indem er einen Geschichte produzierenden Urevangelisten statuierte. Dadurch fielen sie unter das Gericht. Mit der Lösung verurteilten die Zeitgenossen die Probleme, welche zu jener Lösung gedrängt hatten; sie verurteilten sie, weil sie diese Schwierigkeiten weder zu begreifen noch zu heben vermochten."

9. Cf. Wrede, Das Messiasgeheimnis in den Evangelien, (Göttingen, 1901), p. 131: "...als Gesamtdarstellung bietet das Evangelium keine historische Anschauung mehr vom wirklichen Leben Jesu. Nur blasse Reste einer solchen sind in eine übergeschichtliche Glaubensauffassung übergegangen. Das Markusevangelium gehört in diesem Sinne in die Dogmengeschichte."

had never considered himself as the Messiah. This view of him is the construction of the community and of Mark trying to give meaning to Jesus' person after they witnessed the appearances of the risen one. Schweitzer calls this view "literarisch-kritisch," and his own "eschatologisch-historisch."[10] His principle criticism of Wrede is that the elimination of messianism from Jesus' life makes his execution and passion unintelligible.

Despite the failure of his predecessors, Schweitzer himself set about describing what he thought was the ultimately historical about Jesus -- his eschatological and messianic consciousness. The two factors are intimately related.[11] For Schweitzer Jesus is an apocalyptic figure whose ideas derive from the late Jewish eschatology as found, for example, in the Fourth Book of Enoch and in Daniel. Whereas Wrede had denied that Jesus had considered himself as the Messiah, Schweitzer thought that despite the dogmatic redactional character of Mark's gospel, it was impossible not to attribute messianic consciousness to Jesus himself.

In pointing to the eschatological undercurrent which forms the basis of Jesus' expectation Schweitzer was doing nothing stupendous. Johannes Weiss published in 1892 the first edition of his work, *Die Predigt Jesu vom Reiche Gottes*, which turned theology once again to the centrality of eschatology in the message of Jesus, and which even to the present day exerts a wide influence. Harnack almost failed to notice and completely failed to appreciate the eschatological in the teaching of Jesus. For in the theology of Ritschl, which was so important in the

10. Schweitzer, *op. cit.*, II, p. 382.
11. *Ibidem*, I, pp. 53-54.

latter part of the nineteenth century and which definitely influenced Harnack, the view prevailed that Jesus preached a kingdom-of-God teaching which found its realization almost entirely in this world. Indeed, in the theology of Ritschl the kingdom of God is realized in this world through the love of neighbor and through fulfilling the duties of one's profession and state of life.[12] Weiss' book provided a much needed correction to the this-world orientation of Protestant liberal theology. World War One dealt the death blow to its optimism and near identification of nineteenth century bourgeois culture with the essence of Christianity.[13] This was the setting in which Barth's theology of crisis would see the light of day. Barth himself was not unmindful of the eschatological factor in Christianity: "Christentum das nicht ganz und gar und restlos Eschatologie ist, hat mit Christus ganz und gar und restlos nichts zu tun."[14]

Schweitzer illustrated the history of the "Leben-Jesu-Forschung" as the history of three great "either-ors":

> Bei Weiss gibt es keinen ausgeklügelten Weg: siehe, das Land liegt vor dir. Seine 'Predigt Jesu vom Reiche Gottes', 1892, hat in ihrer Art dieselbe Bedeutung wie das erste Leben-Jesu von Strauss. Er stellt das dritte grosse Entweder-Oder in der Leben-Jesu-Forschung. Das erste hatte Strauss gestellt: entweder rein geschichtlich oder rein übernatürlich; das zweite hatten die Tübinger und Holtzmann durchgekämpft: entweder synoptisch oder johanneisch; nun das dritte: entweder eschatologisch oder uneschatologisch."[15]

Schweitzer takes up where Weiss left off.

---

12. *Cf.* Christian Walther, *Typen des Reich-Gottes Verständnisses,* (München, 1961), pp. 137-155.
13. A good short description of the various currents in Protestant theology at this time is given by Heinz Zarnt, *Die Sache mit Gott,* (München, 1967), ch. 1, "Die grosse Wende," pp. 13-65.
14. *Römerbrief,* second edition, (München, 1922), p. 198.
15. Schweitzer, *op. cit.,* I, p. 254.

2. THE 'CONSEQUENT-ESCHATOLOGICAL' INTERPRETATION OF THE LIFE OF JESUS

Schweitzer agrees with Weiss' portrayal of the eschatological in understanding Jesus as far as it goes. Weiss and his followers related the eschatological only to the preaching of Jesus and to the "Messianitätsgeheimnis," but not to his public ministry. In doing just that 'consistent eschatology' is able to throw a more conclusive light on the "Zusammenhänge und Unzusammenhänge der Ereignisse" of Jesus' life.[16] For the 'dogmatic' element in Jesus' history began not just with his preaching of the kingdom of God, but in his understanding of this kingdom in relation to himself. "Eschatologie ist ja nichts anderes als dogmatische Geschichte, welche in die natürliche hineinragt und sie aufhebt. Ist es nicht schon a priori das einzig Denkbare, dass derjenige, der seine messianische Parusie in Bälde erwartet, in seinem Handeln nicht mehr von dem natürlichen Gang der Ereignisse, sondern nur von jener Erwartung bestimmt wird?"[17]

Jesus belonged to John the Baptist's movement of penance. He may have come to the consciousness of his messianic character and mission at the moment of his baptism by John. In any case, together with the Baptist he awaited the coming of the kingdom and the new state of things it would usher in. It was certainly to be presumed that both of them would have prominent places in this coming kingdom. Then the small of

---

16. This summary depends on the already cited works of Schweitzer, *Das Messianitäts- und Leidensgeheimnis, eine Skizze des Lebens Jesu,* and *Geschichte der Leben-Jesu-Forschung,* II, ch. 21, "Die Lösung der konsequenten Eschatologie," pp. 402-450, but primarily on the latter work. Whereas the former is longer, the latter represents Schweitzer's thought after the appearance of Wrede's *Das Messiasgeheimnis in den Evangelien.*
17. Schweitzer, *Geschichte,* II, p. 403.

this world would be great, and the great of this world would be small. "Also ist für ihn die theoretische Möglichkeit gegeben, dass auch der Höchste, der Messias-Menschensohn, aus einem natürlichen Menschenwesen hervorgehe."[18] In connection with Psalm 110 Jesus argued with the pharisees over the question as to how the Messiah could be David's son. It is therefore likely that he came to the solution that the Messiah would be born from David's lineage in the last generation,[19] and that by the breaking in of the kingdom he would be changed into the super-natural Son of Man.[20] Jesus was of the race of David .... Ergo!

With this stroke Schweitzer goes beyond Wrede, whose book seemed to establish from a literary standpoint that Jesus' messianism was an interpretation imposed subsequently on the confusing events of his life and death. No, Jesus had a messianic consciousness during his life. With a multitude of examples Schweitzer is able to corroborate this conclusion by illustrating that Jesus acted as though he were the Messiah throughout his public life. E.g., his consciousness of having power to forgive sins, his praising of those who suffer for his sake because he will remember them before his Father, etc.

Jesus thought that through his preaching and that of his followers the kingdom of God could be brought about. This was because they con-tinued the spirit of John the Baptist by urging the select group of the predestined to conversion and repentance. "But from the days of John the Baptist until now the kingdom of heaven has been enduring violent assault, and the violent have been seizing it by force" (Mt 11:12). With

---

18. *Ibidem*, p. 404.
19. *Cf*. Mk 12:35-37a; Mt 22:41-46; Lk 20:41-44.
20. Schweitzer gives in the *Skizze*, pp. 66-71, a discussion of the relationship of the Son of Man to Jesus' messianism.

this message of seizing the kingdom of heaven by force in the face of the coming judgment, Jesus sends his disciples to the four corners of the earth. He did not reckon on their coming back, but anticipated the parousia in the immediate future. This is evident from his words of dismissal in Mt 10:23: "When they persecute you in one town, flee to another. Amen I say to you, you will not have **gone** through the towns of Israel before the Son of Man comes."[21]

"Die natürliche Geschichte desavouierte die dogmatische, nach der Jesus gehandelt hatte,"[22] for his disciples came back, and the parousia of the Son of Man did not take place, "Das war für Jesus, der einzig in der dogmatischen Geschichte lebte, das erste 'geschichtliche Ereignis', das Zentralereignis, welches seine Tätigkeit nach rückwarts abschliesst, nach vorn neu orientiert."[23] Because the tribulation of those repenting had not brought in the kingdom, it only went to prove that "...noch eine Leistung fehlt und noch ein Gewalttätiger zu den Vergewaltigern des Reiches Gottes hinzutreten muss."[24] And what failed was the sacrifice of Jesus himself, on the model of Isaiah 53, and in the pattern of John's martyrdom. From then on Jesus planned his going up to Jerusalem as a challenge to the high priest and authorities to bring the messianic tribulation down upon himself.

Ehe das Reich kommen konnte, musste die Drangsal eintreffen.
Sie blief aber aus. Man musste sie also herbeiführen, um so das
Gottesreich herbeizunötigen. Busse und Knechtung der widergött-
lichen Macht thaten es nicht allein, sondern es musste noch ein
Stärkerer zu den Gewaltthätigen hinzutreten: der zukünftige

---

21. Cf. *Geschichte*, I, p. 416: "Dass seine Worte dies und nichts
     anderes besagen, dürfte klar sein. Es ist die Form, in der Jesus
     den Jüngern das Geheimnis des Reiches Gottes offenbart."
22. *Ibidem*, p. 416.
23. *Ibidem*.
24. *Ibidem*, p. 442.

Messias, der an sich die Enddrangsal heraufführte in der Form, wie sie sich schon an dem Elias erfüllt hatte. So geht das Geheimnis des Reiches Gottes in das Geheimnis des Leidensgedankens über.[25]

That is then in summary form the 'consistent eschatological' interpretation of the life of Jesus. Jesus' messianic consciousness was totally oriented to the bringing about of the kingdom of God which he considered to be something of the future, and in which he as the glorious Son of Man-Messiah would hold judgment and rule.

'Consistent eschatology' depends principally on one fact -- the "Parusieverzögerung." It is not only the turning point in the life of Jesus, it is also "das erste Datum in der 'Geschichte des Christentums', for "die ganze Geschichte des 'Christentums'," bis auf den heutigen Tag, die innere, wirkliche Geschichte desselben, beruht auf der 'Parusie- verzögerung': d.h. auf dem Nichteintreffen der Parusie, dem Aufgeben der Eschatologie, der damit verbundenen fortschreitenden und sich auswirk- enden Enteschatologisierung der Religion."[26]

The end result then of Jesus' life and mission was eschatology. His reputed failure to bring about the end time becomes the historical basis for his followers to construct something to fill the void -- dogma. This process is the subject of the following section.

25. *Skizze*, p. 88.
26. *Geschichte*, II, p. 417.

3. THE 'CONSISTENT ESCHATOLOGICAL' UNDERSTANDING OF THE FORMATION OF CHRISTIAN DOGMA

Martin Werner takes over Schweitzer's 'consistent eschatological' theology of Jesus' life and teaching and develops the "Parusieverzögerung" as the cause of the development of Christian dogma.[27] In Werner's *Die Entstehung des christlichen Dogmas* it is asserted that, "Der von Jesus selbst stammende Grundgedanke, der das apostolische Urchristentum beherrscht, dass durch seinen Tod und seine Auferstehung irgendwie der baldige Anbruch der Aeonenwende im Sinne der spätjudisch Apokalyptik veranlasst werde, dass demnach das Auftreten Jesu überhaupt ein Phanomen der anbrechenden Endzeit sei, klingt in den Schriften der nachapostolischen Zeit deutlich nach."[28] But because the parousia failed to take place soon after the resurrection, the eschatological significance of the latter gradually diminished and eventually disappeared completely.

In the early Christian cult the eucharist served the function of preserving the expectation of the soon-to-come world end. This is illustrated in the prayer for the parousia which the *Didache* shows belonged to this celebration. But as the first generation began dying out, the problem of the failure of the parousia to take place kept becoming ever more acute. This is witnessed to by the warning against false messiahs as found in Mk 13:22, and by the fact that a number of false messiahs did actually appear, such as Dositheus, Simon Magus, and Montanus. The *First Epistle of Clement* cites the tiring of the Christian expectation: "Dies haben wir auch schon in den Tagen unserer Väter

---

27. Besides Werner's *Entstehung* see also his *Der protestantische Weg des Glaubens*, (Bern, 1955).
28. *Entstehung*, p. 83.

gehört, und siehe, wir sind alt geworden, und nichts von all dem ist uns widerfahren."[29] Cyprian in the third century still believes in the parousia. He writes: "...illud enim primo in loco scire debes, senuisse iam saeculum."[30] Hippolytus is not so sure, and Origen believes the preaching of the closeness of the parousia an example of human ignorance. The apologists take up a new theme asserting that "Christianity preserves the world," and finally, in the fourth century, Eusebius identifies the age of Constantine with the messianic era of peace.[31] The Constantinian age represents then the end stage in the long process of reinterpretation which is, indeed, a radical change from the eschatological expectation of Jesus and the first Christians.

This long period of obscurity and doubt is the context in which the eschatological significance of the death and resurrection of Christ is reinterpreted, and in which, "Die 'Entstehung des christlichen Dogmas', das heisst der dogmengeschichtliche Prozess des voraugustinischen Zeit-alters ist nichts anderes als die Art und Weise, wie die hellenistisch-synkretistische Spätantike die Auseinandersetzung mit dem Urchristentum unter der objektiven Notwendigkeit der zwangsläufigen Enteschatologis-ierung dieses ursprünglichen eschatologischen Glaubens vollzogen hat."[32] The origin or beginning of Christian dogma depends in this system not on any primitive Christian teaching or objective fact, but upon the histori-cally necessitated reinterpretation of eschatological faith. "Die Eschatologie Jesu war gar nicht auf irdische Dauer eingestellt. Die irdische Dauer aber wurde Tatsache, folglich musste die ganze

---

29. *Ibidem*, p. 108.
30. *Ibidem*, p. 109, footnote 14.
31. *Ibidem*, p. 113.
32. *Ibidem*, p. 724.

überzeitlich eingestellte Religion Jesu auf das Geleise der Zeitlichkeit umgestellt werden."[33] This is the historical problem which forms the background and which shapes the ultimate solution, which is the beginning of Christian dogma.

Before taking up the discussion of Werner's representation of the formation of dogma it will be useful here to consider somewhat in detail what he judges to be the qualifications of the 'consistent eschatological' interpretation as presented in his own introduction.

The problem of the relationship between the early Catholic Church and primitive Christianity as the prime field of inquiry for the study of Christianity's dogmatic origins is basicly for Werner the same as it was for Harnack, that is, a problem of **transformation**. In fact, the presumed discontinuity between the two stages has been in Protestantism a constant feature in the interpretation of the historical reality.[34]

Despite the nature and degree of this transformation it must, however, be assumed that there was also an element of continuity in the process. This appears only to be stating the obvious, but for Werner it is an obvious which must be stated because other historians, notably Harnack and especially Loofs, saw the process almost exclusively from the side of Hellenization. Thus, Werner criticizes Harnack's pithy definition of dogma -- "eine Conception des griechischen Geistes auf dem Boden des Evangeliums" -- for almost completely neglecting the "auf dem Boden

<hr>

33. *Entstehung*, p. 25, quoting Walter Köhler, Dogmengeschichte als Geschichte des christlichen Selbstbewusstseins, (Zürich, 1938), p.32.
34. Werner admits that this judgment over the "apostasy" of the Catholic Church was more "dogmatic" than historical. This judgment is particularly evident in his evaluation of the relationship of the Church to the many heresies: "Diese Grosskirche ist die erfolgreichste Häresie."

des Evangeliums," and proposes to correct this by investigating the presuppositions on the side of Christianity to the formation of dogma.

Werner gives credit to Ferdinand Christian Baur for being the first to overcome the historical dilemma by setting up the principle: "Der Anfang der Dogmengeschichte kann nur der Anfang der Bewegung des Dogmas selbst sein."[35] This means that any investigation of the origin of dogma cannot begin without reference to the teaching of Jesus and the apostles. For Baur the history of dogma began with the affirmation that "Jesus is the Messiah." The process of dogmatic growth continued necessarily with this belief because it implied a new principle of salvation over against the law of Judaism, which principle was the substitution by Paul of the death of Christ in place of the law, and which enabled Christianity to become independent of Judaism.

Following Walter Köhler's line of thought reaching back to Baur, Werner also maintains that,

> 'Dogma als Ausdruck des denkenden christlichen Selbstbewusstseins tritt zuerst in Erscheinung in Jesus von Nazareth. Er ist der Uranfang.'[36] ....es wird anerkannt, dass die spätjüdische Eschatologie hier nun in der besondern Form der Naherwartung auftritt und dass in dieser Tatsache die eigentlichen, wesentlichen, sachlichen Bedingungen der nachher als innere Notwendigkeit sich durchsetzenden Hellenisierung des Urchristentums beschlossen liegen.[37]

In current New Testament scholarship the general acceptance of the "formgeschichtliche Methode" is practically without question. What must, however, be remembered of form criticism is that it is a method of literary, not of historical criticism. Its aim is the recreation of the Sitz-im-Leben in the original community or in the life of Jesus, the

---

35. *Cf.* footnote 1.
36. *Entstehung*, p. 24, quoting Walter Köhler, *op. cit.*, p. 6.
37. *Entstehung*, p. 25.

circumstances of which gave rise to the peculiar types of gospel tradition which today are found in the redactional framework of the synoptics, i.e., miracle stories, logia, controversial or instructional utterances, etc. "Zunächst muss doch gefragt werden, nicht: was ist als geschichtlich denkbar? sondern: was ist als christliche Gemeindetradition verständlich? Und dieser Frage ist die Frage nach dem geschichtlich Möglichen je nach dem einzelnen Fall ein- oder nachzuordnen."[38] Thus Bultmann. The results of this method of criticism could have been foreseen -- almost thoroughgoing skepticism relative to the historical Jesus. Bultmann's statements, "...dass wir vom Leben und der Persönlichkeit Jesu so gut wie nichts mehr wissen können," and that the gospels are "Kultlegenden," and "...von der Legende überwuchert," are well-known.[39] By reason of default of an adequate criterion of historicity within the school of form criticism, historical judgments are issued without consideration of the methodological question for a reliable criterion of historicity.

On the other hand, for Schweitzer the most urgent problem was precisely the question of a scientifically justifiable criterion of historicity, and to accuse him of naiveté on this point is to miss the mark completely. Werner tries to find this criterion insofar as the "facts" allow themselves to be ordered in a historically logical, if not immediately verifiable context: "Die einzelnen Daten der ältesten Überlieferung werden als geschichtlich glaubwurdig gesichert, soweit sie als sachlich notwendige Glieder eines folgerichtigen geschichtlichen

---

38. *Ibidem*, p. 54; quote is from Rudolf Bultmann, *Geschichte der synoptischen Tradition*, p. 291.
39. *Entstehung*, p. 53; quotes from Bultmann: *Jesus*, p. 12; *Geschichte der synoptischen Tradition*, p. 396; *Jesus*, p. 29.

Zusammenhanges ausschliesslich und eindeutig nach Massgabe eines rein objektiven Kriteriums sich durchführen lässt."[40]

'Consistent eschatology' as a criterion of historicity makes manifest what connected Jesus with the late Jewish apocalyptic and what separated him from it. It does this by pointing out that the synoptic texts represent Jesus after the pattern of the apocalyptic books of Daniel and of Enoch. In other words, Jesus is a phenomenon of the late Jewish apocalyptic ambient with its typical expectation of the reconstitution of this world which is awaited in eager urgency. In this way Jesus can be inserted into, or rather, interpreted within a logically consistent historical context. It will be found that this interpretation provides both a logical interpretation of the gospel tradition, and a high degree of trust in the historicity of the gospel narratives. Its objective character is certified by the fact that it is not imposed upon the texts, but derives from the texts themselves.[41]

Jesus' outlook was entirely oriented toward the future. He spoke of "entering into the kingdom," and of "sitting at table." In speaking of this "coming age" he used the categories of apocalyptic expectation: the messianic affliction, the parousia of the Son of Man, the general resurrection and judgment, etc. It is evident that for him the parousia meant the end of the present world order and the creation of a new one, but also in the form of a material existence. For Jesus the kingdom of God was no present reality but the future realization of an eschaton which stood in dire contrast to the present world and state of things. The kingdom was of the future, but its arrival was imminent.

---

40. *Entstehung*, p. 67.
41. *Cf. ibidem*, 67ff.

Denn Jesus lehrt nirgends, die Vorstellungen der apokalyptischen Eschatologie seien nur in uneigentlichen Sinne zu versthen,
und aus der Art und Weise, wie er sie selbst vertritt, lässt sich
eine solche Meinung auch nicht erschliessen. Die Behauptung, das
es sich fur Jesus irgendwie nur um Bilder und Symbole handle, ist
lediglich vom modernen Bewusstsein her eingetragen.
    Im Grunde bleibt als einzige Möglichkeit, eine klare und
grundsatzliche Scheidelinie zwischen Jesus und der spätjüdischen
Apokalyptik zu ziehen, nur das gewiss nicht neue Radikalmittel im
Rest, alle apokalyptisch-eschatologischen Aussagen Jesu als unecht
zu erklären.[42]

With these thoughts Werner believes 'consistent eschatology'

refutes those theories of eschatology which seek to interpret Jesus'

preaching of the kingdom as an "Entscheidung" (Bultmann) using only the

eschatological paraphernalia as a means, and those theories which inter-

pret it as God's rule in the present (Gloege and Wendland).[43]

    The criterion then for the acceptability and verity of 'consistent

eschatology' is that it itself provides an adequate criterion for histor-

icity. What it states is that the delay of the parousia after the death

of Jesus and the non-fulfillment of the eschatological expectation became

a problem which was conducive to the transformation of the original escha-

tological doctrine into the structure of church dogma. "Die Konstruktion

der konsequenten Eschatologie ist geschichtswissenschaftlich in Wahrheit

derart glänzend ausgewiesen und gerechtfertigt, dass sie als die endgül-

tige geschichtliche Lösung des Problems des historischen Jesus und des

Urchristentums anerkannt werden muss."[44] The Church was brought into

such a state of acute embarrassment through the failure of the parousia

---

42. *Ibidem*, pp. 42-43.
43. So Gerhard Gloege, *Reich Gottes und Kirche im Neuen Testament*, and
     H. D. Wendland, *Die Eschatologie des Reiches Gottes bei Jesus*.
     These two works are mentioned by Werner. Of course, one could add
     others such as: W. G. Kümmel, *Verheissung und Erfüllung*, (1935[2]),
     and C. H. Dodd, *The Parables of the Kingdom*, (1935).
44. *Entstehung*, p. 77.

to take place that it at last had to deal realistically with the fact of existence in unlimited terrestrial time, and so reinterpreted everything in the light of this fact. And this is the process of the formation of Christian dogma.

It is now time to take a look at how Werner applies the doctrine of late Jewish apocalyptic expectation to the New Testament. Paul has a differing estimation of the significance of the death of Jesus than the propitiatory view of the primitive Jewish-Christian community. For him the last age of the world has already begun with the death and resurrection of Jesus. This understanding is based on a rather one-sided interpretation of two statements of Paul in Galatians 1:4 and 6:14. We quote the second statement: "But as for me, God forbid that I should glory save in the cross of our Lord Jesus Christ, through whom the world is crucified to me, and I to the world." Instead of accepting the obvious interpretation of this sentence -- that it has to do with Paul's relationship to the world and the world to him since he has been confronted with the cross of Christ, Werner understands Paul to have meant the "end" of the world as it is already effective in the lives of the faithful.[45] From this a number of other primitive views receive a new interpretation through the death of Jesus: the lordship of those angelic powers opposed to God is broken; the Sinaitic law is no longer valid, since according to Jesus' teaching (Mt 5:18) the law loses its validity with the coming end of the world; the risen Christ has become the first among the risen from the dead and the period leading to the general resurrection is now opened; and the era of existence in the flesh is broken, so that

---

45. *Cf. ibidem*, p. 185ff.

believers may now live in the resurrection body of Christ. The first
great step in de-eschatologization was taken by the apostle Paul, now
looking backwards to Christ instead of forwards as Jesus had done.

As a result of his partial de-eschatologization of the views of
the Jewish-Christian community, Paul developed the notion that baptism
was a dying and rising with Christ through which the baptized passes from
the old eon to the eschatological state of being "in the body of Christ."
At the beginning of the second century this redemption concept was
further developed through the Johannine theology of being born again
(Jn 3:5), to the Hellenistic concept of "rebirth."[46] But for Paul it
meant that the flesh of those who are "risen" with Christ will also
"rise" after their deaths. "Die natürliche Fleischesleiblichkeit des
Menschen bleibt intakt.... Also kann die gegenwärtige Erlösung, sofern
sie nach Paulus eine Beziehung zur Auferstehung haben soll, nur den Sinn
haben, eben dieser natürlichen gegenwärtigen Fleischesleiblichkeit der
Gläubigen die zukünftige Auferstehung zum ewigen Leben zu garantieren."[47]

In other words, the redemption which was originally conceived as
eschatological is now being conceived as something of this world, which
can be personally appropriated in the sacraments. Another Hellenistic
concept which came into play at the same time is that of "divinization."
Eventually Irenaeus would argue that God had bestowed the redemption on
his creature because it was fitting once he had created it.[48]

The de-eschatologization of Paul also affected the meaning of the

---

46. *Cf. Der protestantische Weg des Glaubens*, I, p. 168ff.
47. *Cf. ibidem*, p. 168.
48. *Cf. ibidem*, p. 169. Werner refers to Irenaeus, *Adversus Haereses*,
    III, 6,1; 19,1; IV, 1,1; 38,4; 63,3; and also to Ps 81, 1.6 (LXX)
    and II Pet 1,4.

eucharist.[49] At first it had only signified a meal of thanksgiving and prayer oriented toward fellowship with Christ, who was soon to reappear in the parousia. Now it also became a guarantee for the faithful that they would share in the final resurrection of the dead. Irenaeus "hebt die Übereinstimmung der Lehre von der Eucharistie mit der Lehre von der Erlösung des Fleisches zum ewigen Leben hervor und erklärt: das eucharistische Brot sei, nachdem die Epiklese über ihm ausgesprochen ist, nicht mehr gewöhnliches Brot, sondern die aus zwei Bestandteilen ('Dingen'), nämlich einem Irdischen und einem Himmlischen, bestehende Eucharistie. Das Himmlische aber, das sich mit der irdischen Speise des Gemeindemahles verbindet, ist der Logos-Geist."[50]

Werner's teaching on the beginning and evolution of the God-man dogma has attracted the greatest attention to this thought; it is, however, only a part of his system and must be understood within the total context of that system. Through a one-sided selection of early Christian texts Werner believes that he successfully establishes that the primitive Christian community thought that the Son of Man -- and therefore, Christ -- had the nature of an angel.[51]

49.　*Cf.* Schweitzer, *Geschichte der paulinischen Forschung*, (Tübingen, 1911), p. 189: "Dass die gesteigerte eschatologische Erwartung zu sakramentalen Anschauungen gelangen kann, ist an sich begreiflich. Diejenigen, die unmittelbar vor der hereinbrechenden Herrlichkeit stehen, müssen ein Verlangen danach tragen, für ihre Person zur Gewissheit der Teilnahme an derselben zu kommen und sich greifbare Garantien für die 'Errettung' aus dem kommenden Gericht anzueignen. Der Begriff der 'Zeichnung' und 'Versiegelung' spielt in der Apokalyptik eine gewaltige Rolle. Entsprechende Veranstaltungen sind geradezu ein Produkt jeder intensiven Zukunftserwartung.
　　　Es ist also überaus wahrscheinlich, dass der Täufer und das Urchristentum eschatologische Sakramente geschaffen haben, die Paulus als bestehend und beglaubigt nur zu übernehmen hatte."
50.　*Weg*, p. 172, referring to Irenaeus, *Adversus Haereses*, IV, 18,5; 38, 1.2; V, 2,3.
51.　*Cf. Entstehung*, pp. 302-321, and *Weg*, pp. 173-183.

In support of the so-called "Engelchristologie" Werner adduces

several arguments and a number of Christian texts on the Son of Man.

Perhaps the most striking text is that of the apocalypse of *Enoch* where

the Son of Man is referred to as "one of the holy angels": "Ich sah dort

den, der ein betagtes Haupt hat, und sein Haupt war weiss wie Wolle; bei

ihm war ein anderer, dessen Antlitz war voll Anmut gleich eines von den

heiligen Engeln."[52] In conjunction with the Son of Man being called an

angel in *Enoch* is the place given him next to God -- at "the right hand

of God." This place is one of special election, which *Enoch* mentions

several times: "Denn der Auserwählte steht vor dem Herrn der Geister, und

seine Herrlichkeit ist von Ewigkeit zu Ewigkeit ...auserwählt ist er vor

dem Herrn der Geister nach seinem Wohlgefallen"; "Der Auserwählte wird in

jenen Tagen auf meinem Thron sitzen und alle Geheimnisse der Weisheit

werden aus dem Gedanken seines Mundes hervorkommen; denn der Herr der

Geister hat es ihm verliehen und hat ihn verherrlicht."[53]

Thus Werner sees the Son of Man as a creature with the nature of an

angel specially chosen by God over all other creatures to bring the dis-

cordant powers of evil into subjection.

The Son of Man is addressed as κύριος, as this was a common way of

addressing angels. The fourth book of *Esra* gives many examples of angels

being so addressed. A particularly striking text in the post-apostolic

---

52. *Enoch*, 46, 1; quoted from *Entstehung*, p. 304, footnote 9. As has
    been pointed out, Werner does not follow here the sense of the *Enoch*
    text since the Son of Man is there represented only as "like an
    angel." *Cf.* further Felix Flückiger, *Der Ursprung des christlichen
    Dogmas,* (Zürich, 1955), p. 68: "... er steht im Gegenteil hoch über
    den Engeln, die er gleich den Menschen richten wird. ·Ihm kommt, wie
    E. Sjöberg gezeigt hat, eine einzigartige Würde und Stellung zu, die
    ihn über alle himmlischen und irdischen Wesen erhebt und in beson-
    ders enger Beziehung zu Gott erscheinen lässt."
53. *Enoch*, 49, 2 and 51, 3; quoted from *Entstehung*, p. 303, footnote 8.

apocryphal literature is found in Hippolytus where the angel, Baruch, appears to the twelve year old Jesus as he watches sheep in a meadow. Even Jesus addresses the angel with the title, "Lord."[54] The same usage is found in Acts 10:3 and 10:13 where Cornelius and Peter both address angels as "Lord."

As Jesus is often addressed as "Lord" one comes naturally to the conclusion, according to Werner, that the earliest Christianity conceived him of being one of the angels, although as Son of Man the highest among them. So St. Paul in 1 Cor 8:5-6 speaks of the many gods and many lords and reminds Christians that they are to have to do only with the one Lord, Jesus, although there are many.

Added to this is the fact that the oldest gnostic theories which made use of Paul's teaching considered angelic natures to have been agents in the creation of the world, as Paul considered Christ to have been instrumental in the creation of the same. A negative argument is also given: "Hätte das Urchristentum bei der Übernahme der apokalyptischen Menschensohn-Dogmatik gerade die Engelnatur dieser himmlischen messianischen Gestalt abgelehnt und bereits durch die spätere Vergottung des Messias ersetzt, so müsste in der ältesten Überlieferung über die Lehre Jesu und den urapostolischen Glauben irgendwelche ausdrückliche und deutliche Polemik gegen diese apokalyptische Auffassung vom Messias konstatierbar sein. Dies ist jedoch keinesweges der Fall."[55]

The new theory of the redemption of the flesh to eternal life also made a divinization of Christ necessary, so that the more dominant opinion of Christ's angelic nature as maintained by the Arians yielded,

---

54. *Refut.* V, 26, 6; *cf. Entstehung*, p. 308.
55. *Weg*, pp. 176-177.

however, to the argument of Athanasius: "Das entscheidende Gegenargument des Athanasius gegen diese Engelchristologie der Arianer lautet, dass ein Engel die Erlösung des Menschen ebensowenig zustande zu bringen vermöchte wie ein Mensch. Der wirkliche Erlöser müss Gott sein, weil jetzt nach der neuen Lehre Erlösung 'Vergottung' ist."[56] Finally, the councils of Nicea and Chalcedon made the divinity of Jesus official dogma and thereby completely overturned the more original "Engelchristologie" and its eschatological framework for the factual world of Hellenism.

It is not unknown that in the early Church the Holy Spirit has also been referred to as an angel. In the *Ascension of Isaiah* he is called the second angel next to the angel Christ. Sometimes the Holy Spirit is conceived according to the Hebrew language as a feminine angel, as by the Elchasaites.[57] Yet before the Nicean-Constantinopolitan dogma of the Trinity could develop, these earlier variant forms had to be judged as erroneous and heretical.

Werner understands the doctrine of the trinity to have evolved in the Church through the reception of the homoousios notion from Valentinian gnosticism, which in the hands of the Church's theologians becomes a weapon against the Sabellians.[58] In *Adversus Haereses*, II, 17, Irenaeus pointed to the inconsistencies of Valentinian gnosticism. For at first its devotees maintain a homoousios relationship between the primeval Father and the higher gods generated by him, but then hold that there are essential differences between the primeval god and the emanations of the pleroma, thus impugning the reality of the homoousios.

---

56. *Weg*, p. 178, referring to Athanasius, *De Incarnatione*, 13, and *Oratio contra Arianos*, II, 70.
57. *Cf. Entstehung*, p. 338, and footnote 86.
58. *Cf. ibidem*, pp. 594-606.

Tertullian, Clement of Alexandria, Origen, etc. use the homoousios concept reverting to the original gnostic sense of the one nature. Finally, in the fourth century in the struggle with Sabellianism it becomes a part of the official Church vocabulary protecting monotheism but interpreting it in a Sabellian way! Thus, in moving from the Monas of God to the Trias, the Church was bending to polytheism, for "Trinitas bedeutet nicht eine 'Dreieinigkeit,' sondern eine 'Dreiheit'."[59]

> Dass ohne den Einfluss der gnostischen Pleromspekulation die nachapolstolische Kirchenlehre von sich aus sicher nicht auf den Einfall gekommen wäre, den Zahlbegriff der Trias == Trinitas zu einem theologischen Begriff zu prägen, ergibt sich deutlich aus der ganzen Entwicklung des christologischen Problems. In ihrer eigenen, ältesten, auf die apostolische Lehre zurückgehenden Tradition fand sie etwas Derartiges überhaupt nicht vor. Und zur Zeit des Aufblühens der gnostischen Systeme herrschte im Bereich der werdenden Grosskirche das Nebeneinander und Durcheinander von Engelchristologie, Logoslehre, naivem Modalismus und anderem. Dazu kommt, dass vor allem die kirchliche Auffassung vom heiligen Geiste längere Zeit zunächst noch unabgeklärt blieb. Es stand also noch gar nicht fest, welches überhaupt die drei Grössen seien, die allenfalls zu einer Trinitas zusammengefasst werden könnten.[60]

The dogma of the Trinity is then the Church's adaption of a limited polytheism through accepting a Trias, but not a Quinio, Septenatio or Octanatio. The multitude of the gnostic aeons are reduced to three, which make a goodly godly pleroma.

59. *Ibidem*, p. 598.
60. *Ibidem*, p. 599.

4. CRITICISM OF 'CONSEQUENT ESCHATOLOGY'

The designation ἄγγελος as a title for Christ is not found in the
New Testament. Nevertheless, the meaning of angel, "messenger," is fixed
as far back as Homer. "Der ἄγγελος ist der, der eine Botschaft uber-
bringt, der Bote."[61] Kittel, in his article on ἄγγελος, draws attention
to the fact that angels in the New Testament always have or serve a
function in relation to Jesus, who as Son has a much more excellent
position than they. He also sketches the relationship of Jesus to the
angels according to the New Testament:

> Jesus ist dem Urchristentum Gegenwart Gottes und seiner Herr-
> schaft. Es ist Ausdruck dieser Meinung, wenn die urchristliche
> Erzählung Jesu Geschichte von Engeln begleitet sein lässt. Sie
> erscheinen besonders in den Vor- und in den Auferstehungsgeschich-
> ten. In der sonstigen Erzählung von Jesus wird ihr Dienst nur in
> besonderen Augenblicken erwähnt (Versuchung Mt 4, 11 par; Gethsem-
> ane Lk 22, 43), jedoch stets für möglich gehalten (Mt 26, 53). Er
> ist für die Evangelisten Bestätigung und Ausdruck der Wesensart
> Jesu. .... Es versteht sich danach für das gesamte nt.liche Denken
> von selbst, dass jede Gleichordnung der Engel- mit der Christus-
> vorstellung ausgeschlossen ist.[62]

The Epistle to the Colossians is quite definite on the relative
place of the angelic powers and Christ in creation. So Col 1:15-16: ὅς
ἐστιν εἰκὼν τοῦ θεοῦ ἀοράτου, πρωτότοκος πάσης κτίσεως, ὅτι ἐν αὐτῷ
ἐκτίσθη τὰ πάντα ἐν τοῖς οὐρανοῖς καὶ ἐπὶ τῆς γῆς, τὰ ὁρατὰ καὶ τὰ ἀόρατα,
εἴτε θρόνοι εἴτε κυριότητες εἴτε ἀρχαὶ εἴτε ἐξουσίαν· τὰ πάντα δι'αὐτοῦ
καὶ εἰς αὐτὸν ἔκτισται· καὶ αὐτός ἐστιν πρὸ πάντων καὶ τὰ πάντα ἐν αὐτῷ
συνέστηκεν. This text leaves no doubt that while the canonical New Testament understood Jesus like the angels as an intermediary being between
God and the inferior creation, at least the author of this epistle also
unhesitatingly saw him as a being far superior to any of them in their

---

61. Kittel, *Theologisches Wörterbuch*, I, p. 72.
62. *Ibidem*, pp. 83-84.

myriad ranks.

In the same year as M. Werner published his *Die Entstehung des christlichen Dogmas*, i.e., in 1941, Joseph Barbel published his own *Christos Angelos* which handles exclusively the interpretation of Christ in early Christianity as an angel -- with, however, considerably different conclusions.[63] In 1957 in an article of the same title Barbel again took up the pen and reaccessed both his own conclusions and those of M. Werner.[64]

Strikingly, Barbel was able to expand considerably Werner's work by adducing and discussing even more texts on Christ as an angel. He believes both Methodius of Olymp (or Philippi) as well as Lactantius have at least come close to speaking of Christ as having the nature of an angel. He quotes Methodius in illustration: "... denn es war in höchstem Grade angemessen, dass der Älteste der Äonen und der erste der Erzengel, als er mit den Menschen in Verbindung treten wollte, in Adam, dem ersten Menschen der Gesamtmenschheit, Wohnung nahm."[65] A text from the apologete, Lactantius, is even more pointed: "Und obwohl (Gott) nachher unzählige Geister schuf, die wir Engel nennen, so hat er doch nur diesen Erstgeborenen, der sich väterlicher Macht und Majestät erfreut, mit der Bezeichnung göttlichen Namens ausgezeichnet."[66]

The text of an old Latin preacher is clearly an example of an

---

63. *Christos Angelos, die Anschauung von Christus als Bote und Engel in der gelehrten und volkstümlichen Literatur des christlichen Altertums*, (Bottrop i. W., 1941).
64. "Christos Angelos," die frühchristliche und patristische Engelchristologie im Lichte der neuen Forschung," in: *Liturgie und Monchtum*, 21 (1957), pp. 71-90.
65. *Symposion* 3, 4, (*Griech. christl. Schriftsteller*, p. 30); quoted from Barbel, *ibidem*, p. 72.
66. *Inst. div.* 4, 6, 3 (*Corpus Scriptorum Eccles.*, Lat. 19, 712; quoted from Barbel, *ibidem*, p. 72.

"Engelchristologie": "Als der Herr aus dem Feuer sieben Hauptengel schuf, machte er einen aus ihnen zu seinem Sohn und bestimmte, dass Isaias ihn als Herrn Sabaoth verkünden sollte."[67] Barbel adduces a number of other texts which tend to interpret Christ as an angel in relationship to Michael the archangel, at least insofar as both are commanders (ἀρχιστρά-τηγος) of the heavenly armies.[68] Some other texts suggest a relationship between Gabriel, angel of the annunciation, and the Logos. Thus the *Epistola Apostolorum* (Ethiopian version): "Damals (erschien ich) in der Gestalt des Erzengels Gabriel Maria und redete mit ihr... und ich, das Wort, ging in sie ein und ward Fleish, und ich selbst ward für mich selbst Diener und in der Gestalt eines Engelbilds."[69] But even in this text it is not exactly true to say that the Logos was an angel; rather that the Logos <u>appeared</u> as an angel. "Die Anschauung, dass der Logos sich selbst im Schosse seiner Mutter gebildet hat, besagt keine Gleichung zwischen Christus und Gabriel."[70]

Besides the decidedly one-sided angelic understanding of Christ put forward by Werner, a number of other judgments are possible about these texts. We collect here a few Barbel has arrived at in the course of his study. Of the old Latin preacher he says: "Er ist ein sehr primitiver Geist, der eine Menge disparater Vorstellungen aufgenommen hat, ohne sie zur Einheit fügen zu können."[71] In other words, in some levels of early popular Christian thought, Christ was seen as one more mediator or angel

---

67. Title given: "Von den dreierlei Früchten des christlichen Lebens; ed., R. Reitzenstein, *ZNW*, 15(1914), p. 216.
68. *Cf.* Barbel's book, *Christos Angelos*, p. 44.
69. H. Duensing, transl., (Berlin, 1925), p. 12f.; quoted from Barbel, *ibidem*, p. 46.
70. Barbel, *ibidem*, p. 71
71. *Ibidem*, p. 31.

between man and God. In itself this is not so strange, since at this early time gnosticism and Christianity were both systems of thought influencing one another, the canon of the New Testament was not yet fixed, and theology was an infant science. It was only in the course of these early times that the Church theologians could gradually separate those thought forms which were adequate tools for expressing the truths of revelation from those which were not. And when the New Testament canon was fixed those works favoring an "Engelchristologie" became part of the apocrypha.

The interpretation of Christ as angel is most frequently found among the fathers when they speak of the appearances of God in the Old Testament. Yet, Barbel finds that,

> Manche kirchlichen Schriftsteller gingen bei ihrer Deutung der Gotteserscheinungen auf den Logos anscheinend absichtlich der Engelbezeichnung aus dem Wege. Sie wollten keine falschen Auffassungen begünstigen. Unter dem ständig steigenden Druck der Schwierigkeiten, welche die bisherige Deutung der Gotteserscheinungen mit sich brachte, kam es allmählich zu einem Umschwung. Manche behielten zunächst die Deutung der Gotteserscheinungen auf den Logos bei, suchten sie aber fruchtbar zu machen für den Nachweis des ganzen und ungeschmälerten Gottheit des Sohnes. Das ist vor allem deutlich bei Athanasius, dem der Engelname als Bezeichnung des Sohnes zum Anlass wird, die Gleichwesentlichkeit des Sohnes mit dem Vater herauszustellen. Die Gotteserscheinungen in ihrer Deutung auf den Christos Angelos empfindet er dabei ganz deutlich mehr als Schwierigkeit denn als Hilfe bei der Darlegung der Gleichwesentlichkeit des Sohnes.[72]

The Ecclesia Catholica did not find the interpretation of Christ as angel congenial, and gradually excluded it by favoring a more theologically refined vocabulary for what it wanted to express.

Werner's greatest failure, and the one which clearly reveals the "dogmatic" way he has marshalled his sources, is that although the

---

72. Barbel, the article, "Christos Angelos," p. 82.

58

"Engelchristologie" has apparently represented one of the possible

interpretations of Christ in early Christianity, the sense of angel as

"messenger" has been consistently ignored by him. And indeed, Christ as

ἄγγελος is a messenger from God: Angelus quia nuntius. "Wenn man hier so

oft von einem Engel liest, so wird man förmlich gezwungen, über die je

verschiedene Bedeutung dieses merkwürdigen Schwebebegriffes nachzudenken.

Dabei drängt sich der Botensinn des Wortes in den meisten Fällen von

selbst auf."[73]

As for the "Engeltrinitätslehre" Barbel supports the conclusion of

Georg Kretschmar's *Studien zur frühchristlichen Trinitätstheologie*: that

the background of the oldest Trinitarian speculation is partly formed

through the late Jewish picture of two high intermediaries (paracletes)

before God.[74] Secondly, Barbel agrees with Jean Daniélou that when the

term Angelos is referred to Spirit and Logos (as it often is in these

times of early theology) it simply designates spiritual substances. That

is to say, Angelos is an early semitic way of designating what in the

later theology became "person."[75]

Only a very "dogmatic" handling of the early Christian sources such

as Werner practices, often preferring gnostic and other spurious writings

to the canonical Christian New Testament, could achieve his very one-

sided conclusions. For to maintain that early Christianity understood

Christ predominately as an angel is no less preposterous than his

teaching that the delay of the parousia was the only formative influence

---

73. *Ibidem*, p. 86.
74. *Ibidem*, p. 80, referring to Georg Kretschmar, *Studien zur frühchrist-
    lichen Trinitätstheologie*, (Tübingen, 1956), pp. 62-124, and 219.
75. Barbel, *op. cit.*, p. 88, referring to Daniélou, "Trinité et angél-
    ologie dans la theologie judéo-chrétienne," in: *Recherches de
    Science Religieuse*, 45 (1957), pp. 5-41.

to the beginning of dogma.

Werner's assertion that the belief in Jesus as Messiah was the first Christian doctrine which was transposed into the two-nature theory of Chalcedon through the "Engelchristologie" as completely ignores (without refuting) the more common understanding of the Kyrios title as does his assertion, "Dass ohne den Einfluss der gnostischen Pleromaspekulation die nachapostolische Kirchenlehre von sich aus sicher nicht auf den Einfall gekommen wäre, den Zahlbegriff der Trias == Trinitas zu einem theologischen Begriff zu prägen,"[76] completely ignores the triadic schemata in Paul, John, and the developing creedal formulae.

The Greek term κύριος was common in pre-Christian Judaism as it was in the world of Hellenistic culture. In the former it was the well-known Septuagint translation for the tetragrammaton, YHWH. Yet even in Judaism κύριε was also simply an honorific title, as a translation of the Aramaic מר,[77] or in the Greek text of Mt 7:21 and Mk 11:3. Thus, one may not immediately conclude from every occurrence of Kyrios in the New Testament that the septuagintal denotations of divinity are implied.

Even in the early Christian mission to Hellenistic Judaism the use of the Greek, "kyrios," does not immediately imply the divinity of Jesus. At this stage of development it seems that the title was simply used by the early Christians as a means of referring to Jesus some of those functions which formerly were ascribed exclusively to Yahweh.[78] Ferdinand Hahn mentions the function of "Weltenrichter" in connection

76. *Vd.* footnote 60.
77. *Cf.* Oscar Cullmann, *Die Christologie des Neuen Testaments*, (Tübingen, 1957)
78. *Cf.* Ferdinand Hahn, *Christologische Hoheitstitel*, (Göttingen, 1963), p. 117.

with the Old Testament "day of the Lord" as one of these. Jesus exercis-

ing God's judgment is clearly expressed in 2 Thess 1:7-10 (among other

texts).

Arthur W. Wainright develops at length from the New Testament two

other areas where Jesus performs functions which in previous Judaism were

reserved to God: creation and salvation.[79] It is not only the fourth

evangelist who develops the role of the Son, the Logos, in creation; this

agency of Jesus in the creation is also witnessed in Col 1:16, certainly

a document from the mission to Hellenistic Judaism.

The same is true of the divine function of saving, attributed

exclusively to God in the Old Testament. Thus Isaiah 43:11, "It is I, I

the Lord; there is no savior but me," becomes in Acts 2:21, "And it shall

be, that whosoever shall call on the name of the Lord shall be saved."

This gradual development from Kyrios as an honorific title in

Palestine (as elsewhere), through an ascribing of previously divine

functions to Jesus in the Hellenistic Jewish mission, to the full

confession of his divinity in the Hellenistic gentile mission, where

interest shifted from a "functional" Christology to an "ontological" one

is the natural development of the doctrine, as outlined by Cullmann, Hahn,

and Fuller.[80] Here finally on Hellenistic soil we find that the Kyrios

title in Hellenistic Judaism was the first full acknowledgment of Jesus as

divine. Thus the work of Bossuet in his *Kyrios Christos* of 1913 is borne

out, and Werner's doctrine that the Kyrios title signified an angel in the

earliest Christology is overturned. For here Jesus is given all the

79. Arthur W. Wainwright, *The Trinity in the New Testament*, (London,
     1962), pp. 130-170.
80. Reginald H. Fuller, *The Foundations of New Testament Christology*,
     (New York, 1965).

honors of divinity, the Kyrios texts of the Septuagint are applied to him without hesitation since in this world the LXX rather than the TM was the Christian bible, and here the divine name is transferred to Jesus "quite consciously (Phil 2:10f.) and with ontic implications."[81]

This development in christology as the Christian mission spread from Palestine to the Hellenistic Jews of the diaspora and finally to the Greeks also takes cognizance of the threefold early Christian experience of God, as Father and one in the Jewish monotheistic concept, as Son and Lord in the growing New Testament revelation, and as Spirit in the Church, comforting and carrying on Jesus' work, while being one with him and the Father. For the Spirit also exercies the divine functions of judgment (Jn 16:8-15) and of creation (Ps 33:6).[82] The doctrine of the trinity grew apace with christology, if not quite so quickly.

The ridiculousness of Werner's assertion that trinitarian thought could only have become a part of the apostolic kerygma through the gnostic pleroma speculation is patent to an unbiased reader of the New Testament, who sees in the many trinitarian formulae there, such as 1 Cor 12:4-6, 2 Cor 13:14, Rom 14:17-18, Mt 28:19, Gal 3:11-14, 1 Pet 1-2, etc., that Christian trinitarian thought was based on a threefold experience of God, and not on speculation apart from this experience.

J. N. D. Kelly writes:

A host of other passages stamped with the same lineaments might be quoted. In all of them there is no trace of fixity so far as their wording is concerned, and none of them constitutes as their wording is concerned, and none of them constitutes a creed in any ordinary sense of the term. Nevertheless the

81. *Cf. ibidem*, p. 186; on Phil 2:6-11, pp. 204-214.
82. *Cf*. Wainwright, *op. cit.*, pp. 199-234.

Trinitarian ground-plan obtrudes itself obstinately throughout, and its presence is all the more striking because more often than not there is nothing in the context to necessitate it. The impression inevitably conveyed is that the conception of the threefold manifestation of the Godhead was embedded deeply in Christian thinking from the start, and provided a ready-to-hand mould in which the ideas of the apostolic writers took shape. If Trinitarian creeds are rare, the Trinitarian pattern which was to dominate all later creeds was already part and parcel of the Christian tradition of doctrine.[83]

---

83. J. N. D. Kelly, *Early Christian Creeds*, (London, 1960), p. 23.

CHAPTER THREE

THE SUBSEQUENT DEBATE

1. FRIEDERICH LOOFS

Loofs criticizes Harnack's notion of dogma inasmuch as it is too
narrow and concentrates too much on the form of dogma of the four**th**
century.[1] When on grasps the "essence" of dogma the way Harnack does,
it is neither possible to find a dogmatic structure in every age, nor
are Church dogmas the determinations which have grown out of the knowledge and convictions of faith. Loofs therefore finds Harnack's
overstressing of the teaching aspect ("begrifflich ausgeprägte Lehrsätze") not pertinent to the total matter of what dogma is about, for
this style of 'dogmatic Christianity' is "gegenwärtig faktisch
antiquiert."[2]

Loofs takes up the notion of dogma earlier used by Engelhardt and
Gieseler according to which dogma represents the presence of an

---

1. *Leitfaden zum Studium der Dogmengeschichte*, (Halle, 1906[2]), p. 8:
    "Seine 'Kritik', ja seine gesamte Darstellung, 'gilt nicht dem all-
    gemeinen Genus Dogma, sondern der Species, nämlich dem bestimmten
    Dogma, wie es sich auf dem Boden der antiken Welt gebildet hat und,
    wenn auch unter Modifikationen, noch eine Macht ist'."
2. *Ibidem*, p. 6.

ecclesiastical teaching concept. "'Dogmen' sind diejenigen Glaubens-
sätze, deren Anerkennung eine kirchliche Gemeinschaft von ihren Gliedern,
oder wenigstens von ihren Lehrern, ausdrücklich fordert."[3] Such an
understanding of dogma presumes not only a church somehow organized, but
also "das Bewusstsein der Gemeinsamkeit einer Überzeugung sowie der
Notwendigkeit derselben zum Heile." Such a notion, he believes, corresponds to the actually predominant usage of the word dogma since the
fourth century, that is to say, as normative sentences of Christian
teaching.

Loofs admits his dependency on the work of Harnack. He adopts
Harnack's way of portraying (a) "das Werden der Dogmen im Zusammenhänge
mit der Entstehung und Abwandlung der Gesamtanschauungen vom Christentum,
aus denen sie ursprünglich hervorgewachsen sind," and (b) "geschichtlich
so darzustellen, dass sowohl den zeitgeschichtlichen, ja zufälligen
Faktoren der Entwickelung wie der 'Tenacität' des Dogmas ihr Recht
wird."[4] Loofs also admits his adherence to the Harnackian school of the
Hellenization of Christianity.

The world of the second century was marked in its philosophy and
religion by a strong syncretism. The highest expression of this
tendency was, of couse, Gnosticism. Within its dualism between spirit
and matter, cosmological speculations, and progressive emanations (Äonen)
from the highest God even to the touching of the same with matter there
was also a place for the "(umgedeutete) Evangelium von der Erlösung
durch Christus," indeed even a "zentrale Bedeutung."[5] In those circles

---

3. *Ibidem*, p. 9.
4. *Ibidem*, p. 5.
5. *Ibidem*, pp. 105-106.

which were excluded from the growing universal Church this Hellenization
was acute; with the Church it has remained, and is to be found first
among the Greek apologists of the second century.[6] Since the apologists
knew no difference between religious faith and philosophical truth, they
could take over the teachings of contemporary philosophy about God
without scruple. "Allein aus der Gemeindetradition erklärlich ist nur
die Aufnahmen des (den Dualismus prinzipiell ausschliessenden) Pradikäts
der Allmacht Gottes und die Behauptung der Schöpfung der Welt durch ihn.
Alle weiteren Angaben über Gottes Wesen haben in der platonisch-stoischen
Popularphilosophie der Zeit Parallelen."[7] This goes even for the
Church's monotheism, which always retained a certain heathen-philosophical, pluralistic coloring.

This strange coloring of the doctrine of God began with the taking
over of the heathen-philosophical notion of Logos which in the heathen
background had had a different meaning. In John's Gospel the Logos is
tied to the notions of "teacher" and "teaching";[8] in the philosophy of
that time it was, on the contrary, only one eon of the most high God.
It was in this last meaning that the apologetes read Philo's doctrine
of the Logos "into" the scriptures. As is taught in Pro 8:22ff., this
Logos is caused in time for the purpose of the creation of the world.
Its nature is to occupy a middle place between the pure spirituality of
God and the matter of the world. In the Logos' being caused one finds
the γεννηθῆναι, which is presumed by the notion of Son, and which is
clearly to be distinguished from κτισθῆναι. In this way Christian

6. *Cf. ibidem*, p. 114ff.
7. *Ibidem*, p. 119.
8. *Cf. ibidem*, p. 125, especially footnote 1.

doctrine approached the emanational thought that the Logos is eternal in God, although his having come forth is a thing of time.

A similar heathen-philosophical notion from the contemporary world served the apologists for bringing out the doctrine of the trinity, namely the σοφία of God which was so easily applied to the Holy Spirit. It is also something which existed before the world and was at the same time an ἀπόρροια of God. For so often that the πνεῦμα is brought into connection with the Father and Son, as in the baptismal formula, it is not an example of a trinitarian teaching, but "vielmehr ein Zeichen der heidnischphilosophischen Dehnbarkeit ihres Monotheismus."[9] In this way Loofs sees the development of the trinitarian dogma as joining the pluralistic monotheism of the apologists rather than the economic trinitarian way of thinking of Asia Minor (as for example, Ignatius of Antioch) which, in itself, would have also been possible.[10] "Und der pluralistische Sauerteig ist trotz vielfacher Bemühungen nie ganz ausgefegt worden."[11]

9. *Ibidem*, p. 126.
10. *Cf. ibidem*, p. 102 and p. 137ff.
11. *Ibidem*, p. 126.

2. REINHOLD SEEBERG

Reinhold Seeberg opens his *Lehrbuch der Dogmengeschichte* with a description of the essence of dogma, which is a "kirchlicher Lehrsatz oder das ganze Gefüge dieser Lehrsätze."[12] Yet not all "Aufstellungen" of theology or for that matter of the community faith deserve the title 'dogma.' Only those sentences which are "canonized" by a formal recognition of an organized church may be so denominated. Certainly this does not exclude the fact that other factors such as politics, a particular theological development, or the needs of piety may have also contributed to the formulation of dogmas.

A further factor of true dogmas is that they never have a purely theoretical character, but always have some relationship to salvation. This is especially so as regards Christianity because it represents, according to Seeberg, a redemption type of religion, and not one of the lower types such as do the religions of law or of mystery.

The final characteristic of a dogma is that it represents a cognitional expression of the truth of revelation. "Daher sind die Dogmen immer prinzipiell Erkenntnis der Offenbarungswahrheit, deshalb gehört auch zum Beweis der Wahrheit des Dogmas der Nachweis ihres schriftgemässen oder ihres apostolischen Charakters."[13] In testing individual dogmas it is then necessary to examine whether they sufficiently bring out the tendencies of a redemptive type of religion, such as Christianity is, or whether foreign elements have become a part of them. For this last mentioned state of affairs would be the corruption of the truths so interpreted.

---

12. Halle, 1906[2]; vol. 2, 1910[2].
13. *Ibidem*, vol. 1, p. 3.

68

Seeberg criticizes the view of two other historians of dogma, Thomasius and Harnack. Thomasius believed that the process of the history of dogma had followed a pattern, namely that each dogma stood in a relationship of dependence on the foregoing dogma in such wise that the entire process is always tending towards the more perfect expression of the truth. Seeberg rejects this view because it does not account for the accidental, which has also played a role in the real, historical growth of dogmas. A second reason for his rejection of this view is that each new dogma descries the area of Christian truth by modifying, deepening, extending the whole, without being a simple extension of what has gone before. His final judgment of Thomasius' view is that it is an "eigentlich nur aggregierende Anschauung von der Dogmengeschichte."[14]

Seeberg agrees with Harnack's view that the history of dogma is a process of Hellenization, but he criticizes Harnack for misinterpreting the place of dogmas within Protestantism. The Reformation did not do away with dogma as a principle of faith, but only with its infallibility. The dogma of the ancient Church remains "in der reformatorischen Kirchen fort, nicht nur als ein rudimentärer Annex, sondern als ein wirksames historisches Prinzip."[15] Harnack limited the task and extent of the history of dogma too much by concentrating on the basis of the ancient Weltanschauung, "die bemessen an dem Sprachgebrauch des Wortes Dogma wie an der geschichtlichen Wirksamkeit des Dogmas nicht also berechtigt anzusehen ist."[16]

And so the extent of the history of dogma is conceived in Seeberg's

---

14. *Ibidem*, p. 11.
15. *Ibidem*.
16. *Ibidem*; Seeberg mentions that Loofs also judges Harnack's view in a similar way: *cf*. Loofs, PRE IV[3], p. 760.

own fashion thus:

> Die Dogmengeschichte scheint einzetzen zu sollen bei dem
> ersten Dogma im strengen Sinn, d.i. dem Nicänum. Da nun aber die
> nicänische wie die spätere Dogmenbildung auf dem religiösen
> Verstandnis und der gemeinsamen Anschauung der altkatholischen Zeit
> ruhen, so hat die DG. zu beginnen mit dem nachapostolischen Zeit-
> alter. Sie schliesst mit den letzten Dogmen, die von den Kirchen
> produziert worden sind, d.h. mit dem 2. Konzil von Nicäa (787), mit
> dem vatikanischen Konzil (1870), mit der Konkordienformel (1580)
> und der Synode zu Dortrecht (1619). Dass diese Feststellungen
> allesamt den Charakter von Dogmen haben, **kann** nicht geleugnet
> werden.[17]

It is now clear that Seeberg views the task and reality of the

history of dogma differently, indeed in a wider and more true fashion

than did Harnack, because he understands dogma to be the expression of

the faith of the organized Church about the truth of salvation.

The notion of Christianity as being a type of redemption religion

is so strong in Seeberg's thought as to suggest that he seems to have a

feeling for the economy of salvation within the dogmatic factors of early

Christianity. An example of this is his adherence to the view that before

there was any dogma of the rinity, Christ was believe

so named.[18] He finds texts for this in Ignatius of Antioch (Sm. 1,1;

Trall. 7,1; Magn. 15, etc.). It was simply the peculiarity of Christ's

deed which made it necessary to refer to him as God. What was his

relationship to the Father? He stands "in" and "next to" God; he came

from the Father and went back to him; he is now with the Father. "Diese

Einheit schliesst aber den personlichen Unterschied nicht aus; wie die

Gemeinde mit Christus zur Einheit vermischt ist, so Christus mit dem

Vater (Ignat., Eph. **5**,1), vereinigt mit dem Vater tat er nichts ohne ihn,

wie die Gemeinde nichts ohne den Bischof tun soll (Magn. 7,1)."[19]

---

17. *Ibidem*, pp. 13-14.
18. *Cf. ibidem*, p. 90ff.
19. *Ibidem*, p. 90-91.

The case of the Spirit is similar. The traditional formula naming

the Father, Son and Holy Spirit confirms not a doctrine of the Trinity,

but the community's manner of experiencing the three. It was a distinc-

tive note of the new community that it experienced the possession and

movement of the Spirit. Although he represented no "begrifflich scharf

bestimmte Grösse," the Spirit witnessed the power of God, which in turn

carried on what Christ had begun.[20]

In contrast to Marcion and the gnostics the Fathers of the Church

insisted that the God of the redemption was not separate from the God of

the creation, and that the highest expression of his will was the

salvation of man.[21]

> Der trinitarische Gedanke sowie die energische Betonung der
> Identität des schöpferischen und erlösenden Gotteswillens und die
> bewusste Vereinigung von Allmacht, Liebe und sittlicher Gerechtig-
> keit in Gott haben konkrete Lebenszüge in den Gottesbegriff hinein-
> gebracht. Wie durch diese Erwägung der Eigenschaften und der Taten
> Gottes das Bewusstsein seiner Lebendigkeit gegenüber den abstrakten
> Formeln des griechischen Gottesbegriffes aufrecht erhalten wurde,
> so nötigte auch der Gekanke an den in Christus sich offenbarenden
> Gott zu einer religiösen Erfahrungserkenntnis Gottes.[22]

The dogmatic thinking on this level of the Christian consciousness was

certainly no empty speculation. Seeberg says, however, that this almost

ideal state could not withstand the force of the Greek spirit. With the

Cappadocians the doctrine of the Trinity came to a certain conclusion,

for they were able so to unite the unity and the threeness with one

another that afterwards this teaching was in the West hardly ever again

a problem. Through the introduction of the concepts ὑπόστασις and οὐσία

and the use of the expression μία οὐσία καὶ τρεῖς ὑποστάσεις, they were

---

20. Cf. ibidem, p. 108ff.
21. Cf. ibidem, p. 315.
22   Ibidem, p. 316

able to unfasten the thought of the Trinity "von dem Boden religiösen Erfahrung," and to turn it "in einen metaphysischen Lehrsatz."[23] The result of this process was the gradual hardening and petrification of the faith, for behind the whole stood "ein hilfloses Hin- und Herschwanken zwischen der Formel der Einheit und der Formel der Dreiheit, ein Rechnen mit Zahlen, die bald keine Zahlen sein sollen und dann doch wieder Zahlen sind."[24]

As with the ideas of Loofs, a critical discussion of Seeberg's explanation of the origin of dogma is undertaken below in connection with the necessity of dogma finding its expression in terms of particular thought forms.

3. ALFRED NORTH WHITEHEAD

For the sake of completeness we include here consideration of the thoughts offered by the philosopher, A. N. Whitehead, on the beginning of dogma.[25] Although not a scholar of the history of dogma in the usual sense, Whitehead has addressed himself in a well-known set of lectures to this problem. Without attempting an appraisal from the standpoint of more modern and empirical study on the history of religions, we limit ourselves to sketching his ideas on the origin of dogma.

At the heart of every great religious tradition is the "solitariness" of a great religious figure. For, "Religion is what the individual does with his own solitariness."[26] Religion is not to be confused with its trappings, such as ritual, collective enthusiasms,

---

23. *Ibidem*, vol. 2, pp. 138-139.
24. *Ibidem*, p. 124.
25. *Religion in the Making, the Lowell Lectures for 1926*, (Cambridge, 1926.
26. *Ibidem*, p. 16; *cf.* pp. 16-20.

moral codes, etc. In its genesis religion is based on a great primal experience of solitariness in relation to God. Examples of this are "Mahomet brooding in the desert, the meditations of the Buddha, the solitary Man on the cross."[27] However, on its doctrinal side religion can be described as "a system of general truths which have the effect of transforming character when they are sincerely held and vividly apprehended."[28] Therefore, the religion of every man is also that which is closest to his "solitariness."[29]

"The dogmas of religion are the attempts to formulate in precise terms the truths disclosed in the religious experience of mankind."[30] And again: "A dogma is the precise enunciation of a general truth, divested so far as possible from particular exemplification."[31] But dogma is based on the primary experience of a great and particular religious figure.

The step which logically follows such an experience is the "primary expression" of the direct intuition in the media of action, words, or art.[32] This, albeit in the experience of a single person, is the first stage in the process of forming a common expression of a direct intuition. But once expressed, "There is then a community of intuition by reason of the sacrament of expression proffered by one and received by the other.[33]

The expressive sign is not only interpretative of another's

27. *Ibidem*, p. 20.
28. *Ibidem*, p. 15.
29. *Cf. ibidem*, p. 60: "In its solitariness the spirit asks, What, in the way of value, is the attainment of life? And it can find no such value till it has merged its individual claim with that of the objective universe."
30. *Ibidem*, p. 58.
31. *Ibidem*, p. 126.
32. *Cf. ibidem*, pp. 131-139.
33. *Ibidem*, p. 132.

experience; it is also creative. For there is very little first-hand expression in the world. Most of the time, "expression is what may be termed responsive expression, namely, expression which expressed intuitions elicited by the expressions of others."[34] If the "primary expression" of the religious intuition fails to elicit a "responsive expression" in others it will die. Thus, in the particular expression of religious dogma there is also a return from "solitariness" to society. This third stage in the process toward the formation of dogma Whitehead names the "responsive expression."

The fourth and last stage in the process is the disengaging of the particular from the primary and secondary expressions of the original intuition, and its being rendered into precise formulations which will weather the transformations of history. "Such precise expression is in the long run a condition for vivid realization, for effectiveness, for apprehension of width of scope, and for survival."[35]

In summary there are then, according to Whitehead, four distinct stages in the process of the formation of dogma: "primary experience," "primary expression," "responsive expression," and "precise enunciation." Religion as a human institution depends ultimately on original intuition which is capable of being universalized in the form of dogma. Yet its ultimate criteria are not measurable in any precise sense, but depend on insight.[36] "Progress in truth of science and truth of religion is mainly a progress in the framing of concepts, in discarding artificial abstractions or partial metaphors, and in evolving notions which strike more

34. *Ibidem*, p. 133.
35. *Ibidem*, p. 126.
36. *Cf. ibidem*, pp. 66-67.

deeply into the root of reality."[37]

Whitehead's reflections on the formation of dogma have the value of throwing light on the fact that dogma is rooted in religious experience, and that its more precise formulation has validity insofar as the community to which it is introduced finds that expression a "re-kindling" of the original experience.

4. HANS JONAS

The phenomenological appearance and first grasping of a dogmatic truth has been most thoroughly described by H. Jonas in his excursus, "Über die hermeneutische Struktur des Dogmas," which first appeared in 1930 in his study, *Augustin und das paulinische Freiheitsproblem, eine philosophische Studie zum pelagianischen Streit.*[38] The Pelagian contro-versy was a struggle over the truth of dogmas -- specificially those of predestination and of original sin. Before it the Church had not speci-fically defined the dogma of original sin. The reality was, of course, already there in the Christian consciousness and, in particular, in the consciousness of Augustine. The Pelagian errors provided the occasion for the revealed truth to be firmly and formally grasped in propositional form.

Jonas represents this process of the realization of a dogmatic truth in the terminology of Heideggerian phenomenology: "Die formale Tatsache als solche nun: das Vertretensein der zum Austrag stehenden Existenzialphänomene durch theoretische Gebilde von dem Typus, wie ihn satzmässige metaphysische Dogmen darstellen, ist von entscheidender

---

37. *Ibidem*, p. 131.
38. Göttingen, 1930, 1965[2]. Citations are from the revised edition.

Bedeutung..."[39] The expression of dogmas in sentence form is an expres-

sion of existential phenomena, which are realized within the horizon of

faith. As such they are "hypostatizations" (Hypostasierungen) of the

experiences which have brought them about.

According to his phenomenological approach Jonas describes dogmas:

"Dogmen sind ihrer äusseren Form nach Sätze von der rationalien Struktur

des apophantischen (theoretischen) Subjekt-Prädikat-Satzes, und stellen

als solche ihren Aussagegehalt in den Bereich der in durchgängigem

logischen Zusammenhang stehenden Gegenstandlichkeiten hinein. Die

'Objekte' aber, anschauliche Grössen und Geschehnisse, eingeordnet in

einen einheitlich gegenständlichen Realitätshorizont, haben vertretenden

Symbolcharakter für die ursprünglichen innerexistenziellen Phänomene, die

so durch sie in der Weise Ding-analoger Tatsachen und Vorgänge verbild-

licht werden."[40] In the above description there are several salient

points: (1) Dogmas correspond to the rational structure of the human

spirit, expressing itself in sentences with subjects and predicates; (2)

as such the objects or happenings described are placed within the reality-

horizon of the speaking subject; (3) the words and happenings expressed

within this reality-horizon have a representative function for the exis-

tential phenomena, which originally caused them to be expressed in the

conceptuality of this particular reality-horizon.

The process in which dogmas come to be is precisely an objectifi-

cation in language of existential phenomena. This objectification takes

place through a transcending of the exigencies of the individual's

private experience by passing into the sphere of metaphysical or

---

39. *Ibidem*, p. 80.
40. *Ibidem*, pp. 80-81.

mythological language.[41] In this process there is a "fundamental onto-logical transformation of the phenomena," a "translation," that is, their hypostatization into another being,[42] in which the phenomena are for the first time imaginatively graspable.

This translation into concepts, which are communicable in order that existential phenomena be expressed, brings about a rationalization, or production of concepts, which are then able to be brought into logical relationship with other concepts in terms of correspondence and contra-diction.[43]

The use that can be made then of such communicable and rational expressions in forensic discussion is necessarily tied in with said expressions being torn from their original, dialectical balance with one another in the individual "Dasein." Jonas says that the hypostatization

---

41. *Cf. ibidem*, p. 81: "Der Grundakt also, der die Dogmatisierung möglich macht und trägt, ist eine Vergegenständlichung der in die Sprache drängenden Daseinsphänomene, eine fundamentale Selbst-objektivation des von sich bedrängten, sich auslegen wollenden Daseins; dies die formalste Charakteristik des Vorganges der Dogmen-bildung."

42. *Cf. ibidem*: "Für diesen [Erkenntniszusammenhang], im Sinne der Selbstexplikation jenes Daseins, das nicht dichten, sondern im Sich-Darstellen sein eigenstes Sein erkennen wollte (wie auch für unser nachträgliches hermeneutisches Interesse), ist das Entscheidende an dieser Transzendentalisierung und Symbolbildung, dass sie ein-schliest und voraussetzt eine fundamentale ontologische Transfor-mation der Phänomene, eine bis in die untersten Strukturen hinab-reichende 'Übersetzung' in ein anderes Sein: nämlich ihre Hypostas-ierung von nur existenzialen Vollziehbarkeiten zu quasi dinglichen Anschaulichkeiten -- analog dem Weltseinenden --, wodurch sie erst als gehaltlich eindeutige in eine imaginative Aussendimension einbeziehbar wurden."

43. *Cf. ibidem*, pp. 81-82: "Zur Objektivierung und transzendenten Hypos-tasierung tritt so in der Folge zwangsläufig die Rationalisierung, d.h.. die Abstraktion von diesem 'Anschauungs' -Felde in eine Frei-beweglichkeit des Begriffes, durch die das, was ursprünglich exis-tenziales Vollzugssein, nun aber objektiv 'bestehendes' An-sich-Sein ist, befähigt wird, in umfassenden theoretischen konstruktionen zu fungieren und sich dem Postulat einer abstrakten Einheit der Theorie (gemäss der Logik der Einstimmigkeit und Konsequenz) zu

into rational concepts which are subject to the laws of logic is the "Kehrseite" of the translation of the "Ursprungsphänomene" in their factual existence.

The above described process of the formation of dogma corresponds, Jonas maintains, to the fundamental character of the human spirit (Geist), in that its most essential character is to be "symbolic," expressing itself in formulae and symbols.[44] This process is necessary to the human spirit in its own self-realization. It must take this roundabout way through formulae and symbols, often loosing its way in their problems and coordinations, too often forgetting their representative function and their origin, and only after a long detour is the spirit once again able to return through them to the original phenomena from which they spring. Nevertheless, it is precisely in this long process of symbolization of existential experience (Daseinsbewegtheit), pushing towards the expression of itself, wherein the essential force in the process of the formation of dogma is to be found. The formation of dogmas is then, in Jonas' phrase, "Selbstobjektivation."[45]

---

unterstellen."
44. *Cf. ibidem*, p. 82: "All dies entspringt einer unausweichlichen Fundamentalstruktur des Geistes als solchen: Dass er sich in gegenständlichen Formeln und Symbolen auslegt, dass er 'symbolistisch' ist, ist Wesentlichstes des Geistes -- und Gefährlichstes zugleich. Um zu sich selbst zu kommen, nimmt er wessensmässig diesen Umweg über das Symbol, in dessen verlockender Problemwirrnis er sich, ferne vom symbolisch darin verwährten Ursprung und das Stellvertretende absolut nehmend, zu verlieren neigt -- und nur in einer langen Rückbildung, nach erschöpfender Durchmessung jenes Umweges, vermag ein entmythologisiertes Bewusstsein sich den in dieser Verkleidung versteckten Ursprungsphänomenen auch begrifflich direkt zu nähern..."
45. *Cf. ibidem*, p. 82: "In dieser notwendigen, nicht zufälligen und nicht vermeidbaren Daseinsbewegtheit der Selbstobjektivierung, die die ganze Selbsterfassung und -auslegung des Daseins bis in sein 'unmittelbarstes' Selbstbewusstsein hinein durchherrscht, ist das primäre existenzial-ontologische Motiv zur Dogmenbildung zu suchen. Im letzten Grunde sind die Dogmen also: Selbstobjektivationen."

There are, of course, other motives which in the formation of dogma also play a role, such as the satisfaction of certain theoretical interests, or the desire for explanatory or harmonizational constructions, all of which enable the individual to unify his experience within the metaphysic of his own factual being. In such a way dogma often provides the answer to rational antimonies which are included in the particular metaphysic of the individual being (Dasein).

Thus, Jonas explains the dogma of original sin as a mythological symbol which serves the purpose of giving a rational expression to the fact of human insufficiency before God. It also provides a way of explaining certain other difficulties and contradictions: the perversity of human nature in relation to the idea of a good creator: man's lack of freedom to do good acts in relation to his duty to perform them; the fact of grace together with man's ability to be his own master.

The phenomenology of the formation of dogma is sketched by Jonas in a more thoroughgoing way than by any other: dogmas are the sentential and symbolic expression of existential phenomena striving for rational expression and settlement within the reality-horizon of the person(s) first giving them expression. No one has sketched so completely the necessity of objectification in language of the phenomena which stand behind the making of dogma, that is, of the fact that also in this area thinking necessarily includes speech.

There is, however, in Jonas' description of the psychological formation of dogma too much emphasis on the fact of "Selbstobjektivation," and no mention at all of dogma's relation to revealed truth, much less any mention of the community's approval and acceptance of a dogma formed in the way he describes. It may well be that he presumes these two facts and considers an explicit reference to them as not germane to his excursus. If he really intends to explain Christian dogma as only something like "die Selbstauslegung des eigenen Daseins" he is no longer a Christian theologian.

5. GUSTAV AULÉN

G. Aulén presents his thoughts in *Die Dogmengeschichte in Licht der Lutherforschung* as a program for the fundamental revision of the task of the history of dogma.[46] The history of dogma is conceived as a search for "die Eigenart des Christentums." This would seem to be a search for the inner motifs which have shaped the intellectual grasp of Christianity, although Aulén does not expend the effort of clearly defining his terms.

Harnack is criticized for failing to grasp clearly the relationship between the "Hauptgedanke" of Christianity, which he sometimes characterizes as the victory of Christ over the devil and the forces of evil, sometimes as the melting together of Christianity and an idealistic theory of redemption.[47]

> Der christologische Hauptgedanke ist unfraglich der Inkarnationsgedanke. ...Die Inkarnationschristologie steht damit in einem doppelten Gegensatz zum antiken Idealismus: erstens gegen die rationale Gottesspekulation, zweitens gegen den idealistischen Erlösungsgedanken, für welchen es charakteristisch ist, dass der Erlösungsweg der Weg von unten nach oben, vom Menschen zu Gott ist. Wenn man aber das religiöse Motiv des Inkarnationsgedankens versteht, findet man, dass es sich hier um das vollständig Entgegengesetzte handelt. Von der Versöhnung heisst es: alles kommt von Gott. Der Erlösungsweg ist der Weg Gottes zum Menschen. Die Inkarnationschristologie zeigt sich dadurch als die Selbstverteidigung des Christentums gegen die hellenisierenden Tendenzen, die sonst in der alten Kirche unbestreitbar mächtig vorhanden sind.[48]

---

46. Guterslöh, 1932.
47. *Cf. ibidem*, p. 9ff. By idealism Aulén understands rationality
48. *Ibidem*, pp. 11-12.

Two opposing ways of approaching theology are represented by Thomas Aquinas and Luther. For Thomas the "Hauptbegriff" is fides caritate formata, which makes justification then into an ethical exercise. "Alles ist unter den Geschichtspunkt der Gnade gestellt, aber alles ist zugleich ganz rational gedacht. Dieser Erlösungsgedanke reprasentiert die höchste Blute der mittelalterlichen Theologie, er zeigt das Resultat der Synthese zwischen Idealismus und Christentum."[49]

Luther represents a more theocentric theology because he sees everything in Christianity stemming from the incarnation, which is God's work, and not man's speculation. "Man könnte die ganze reformatorische Tat Luthers darin zusammenfassen, dass er endlich wieder in die Tiefen der Liebe Gottes hat sehen dürfen, dass er endlich wieder die Art der Agape Gottes verstanden und zum Zentrum seiner Verkündigung gemacht hat."[50]

Our reaction to this type of foundation to the history of dogma is simply that Aulén is not working within the field of the history of dogma. At best his work is a type of "Motivforschung," and its relationship to church dogma is left unexplored.

6. WALTER KÖHLER

W. Köhler also attempts to establish a new foundation for the history of dogma in his *Dogmengeschichte als Geschichte des Christlichen Selbstbewusstseins*.[51] Just as the material of church history is usually wider than the history of the Christian church and usually represents rather the history of Christianity, so will Köhler expand the notion of

49. *Ibidem*, p. 27.
50. *Ibidem*, p. 32.
51. Zürich, 1938.

the history of dogma.

Since the church itself is only "eine historische Zufälligkeit," it seems incorrect to restrict the history of dogma to officially sanctioned teachings of faith, as R. Seeberg and F. Loofs did. For to ignore everything in the history of Christianity which is unchristian or "unchurchly" would be one-sided. "Nein, wir machen die Tore ganz weit auf und fassen die Dogmengeschichte als Geschichte des christlichen Bewusstseins, das zur Erkenntnis seiner selbst kommt. ....Es geht um die Geschichte des christlichen Gedankens im christlichen Denkens...."[52] Thus the history of dogma is conceived more as a phenomenology of Christian thought.

Aulén is criticized for conceiving Christianity as due to the absolute breaking in of God into history. For Köhler this would set the phenomenon of Christianity out of history. If Christianity is like any religion, only one possible form of human religiosity, it too must be understood within the context of history. Therein one can seek the dynamics and underlying structures, such as individual teachings, but it is wrong to separate these from the context of the total self-understanding and movement.

Thus, what Köhler offers is hardly a history of dogma. It could be more correctly described as a Hegelian description of the development of Christian thought. This is easily illustrated by citing several paragraphs:

> Dogmengeschichte, mag sie bestimmt werden wie sie will, ist heute eine Selbstverständlichkeit, ebenso wie Dogmatik als die begriffliche Vergegenwärtigung des Heilsbesitzes. Und die wissenschaftliche Grundlage für beides ist die Denkgrundlage der Wissenschaft überhaupt. Der Dogmenhistoriker und Dogmatiker

52. *Ibidem*, p. 3

denkt nicht anders als der Historiker und Jurist. M.e.W.: das Denken gehört zum unerbehrlichen christlichen Besitz.[53]

And on the trinity Köhler writes:

> Der Ansatzpunkt ist... die Göttlichkeit des Geistes. Daran schliesst sich allerlei Reflexion an. Sehr alt etwa ist die Vorstellung von der Präexistenz des Geistes, der als präexistenter über Jesus kommt. ...Die sich hier zeigende Vorstellung der Trias der göttlichen Offenbarung ist eine sehr alte. Naturgemäss: Gott hatte sich im Sohne manifestiert und manifestiert sich im heiligen Geiste. ....Nun ist es Origenes, ...der ganz ähnlich wie in der Christologie, auch bei der Pneumatologie in die gärenden Massen Ordnung heineinbringt. ....Unter den Dreien im göttlichen Kreise ist der heilige Geist der kleinste. Warum? An dem Vater hat alles Seiende sein Prinzip, der Sohn hat an dem Vernünftigen sein Gebiet, der heilige Geist an dem Geheiligten, d.h. an der Kirche. ....Die hat er zu durchwalten und zu vollenden. Die Heiden, sagt Origenes ganz folgerichtig, haben den Vater und den Sohn, den Logos, der ja auch die Weltvernunft ist, gekannt, aber nicht den heiligen Geist; der hat sein Ressort nur innerhalb des Christentums. Ins Moderne übersetzt, in die Sprache Hegels -- Origenes ist der Hegel der alten Dogmengeschichte -- heisst das: sinnvoll auf Erden ist alles, aber pneumatisch nur das Christliche.[54]

7. KARL BARTH

K. Barth takes exception to the Catholic notion of dogma as "veritas a Deo formaliter revelata et ab Ecclesia definita." "In den Dogmen redet die Kirche der Vergangenheit -- ehrwürdig, respektabel, massgeblich non sine Deo, wie es ihr zukommt -- aber die Kirche: sie definiert, d.h sie beschränkt in den Dogmen die offenbarte Wahrheit, das Wort Gottes. Und damit wird aus dem Wort Gottes Menschenwort, nicht unbeachtliches, sondern höchst beachtliches, aber Menschenwort. Das Wort Gottes ist über dem Dogma wie der Himmel über der Erde ist."[53]

Rather than allowing dogma to hold or to contain the truths of revelation, Barth sees in it only a "Beziehungsbegriff," a "concept of

53. *Ibidem*, p. 48.
54. *Ibidem*, pp. 264-266.
55. *Kirchliche Dogmatik*, I, (Zürich, 1947), pp. 281-282.

relation," which is oriented "toward" revelation. It cannot grasp revelation but remains always only oriented towards it, because the word of God is always beyond human grasping. "Um welche Beziehung es dabei geht, wissen wir schon: es handelt sich um die Beziehung der Überstimmung der kirchlichen Verkündigung mit der Bibel als dem Wort Gottes. Man kann also das Dogma definieren als die kirchliche Verkündigung, sofern sie mit der Bibel als dem Worte Gottes wirklich übereinstimmt."[56] The science and study of dogma never achieve this agreement between the preaching of the Church and the word of God, but they always aim at their own purification since "die veritas ab Ecclesia definita ist selber Frage nach dem Dogma."[57]

Barth takes further exception to the Catholic notion of dogma as teaching. He suggests that the development in the Catholic Church would have been closer to the biblical usage if the Church had retained in its usage of dogma the notion of "command" or "decree."[58] For even if the truth of revelation were contained in dogma, it would not be so much the truth of a teaching (Lehrsatz) as of a command.

> Ist Offenbarungswahrheit -- so müssen wir weiter ausholend
> fragen -- ....anderen Wahrheiten darin gleich, dass man sie als
> ἀλήθεια, d.h. als Enthülltsein eines verborgenen Eigentlichen in
> menschlichen Vorstellungen, Begriffen und Urteilen festlegen und
> in der so beschränkten und geprägten Form sozusagen konserviert,
> auch abgesehen von dem Ereignis ihres Enthülltwerdens als Wahrheit
> haben kann. So steht es offenbar mit der Wahrheit eines Lehrsatzes.
> Aber erträgt denn die Wahrheit der Offenbarung solche Versachlichung
> und Entpersönlichung? Kann man sie haben abstrahiert von der Person
> dessen, der sie offenbart und von dem offenbarenden Akt dieser
> Person zu vernehmen gibt? Kann das Haben dieser Wahrheit anders
> stattfinden als wiederum in einem Akt der sie vernehmenden Person,
> in einer Entscheidung, d.h. in einer Stellungnahme?[59]

A teaching can be confronted as mere theory, but a command must be obeyed

---

56. *Ibidem*, p. 283.
57. *Ibidem*, p. 282.
58. *Ibidem*, p. 285.
59. *Ibidem*, p. 283.

or ignored. And this according to Barth, if the meaning of dogma in
Catholicism were "command" instead of "teaching," would correspond a
little better to the demand of the word of God on men, inasmuch as it
would require obedience and decision.[60]

L. Scheffczyk points to several advantages to Barth's notion of
dogma as a concept of relation between scripture and the church's preaching: dogma is closely bound to scripture; it performs a serving function
for the task of announcing the word; its very movement keeps man in
constant conversation with the God of revelation. "Aber es bleibt dabei
unbefriedigend, dass dem Dogma kein strenger Verpflichtungscharakter
zuerkannt ist, dass es ferner letzlich der Kritik des einzelnen Theologen
ausgeliefert wird und dass das Gespräch, niemals zu einer endgültigen
Auskunft führend, schliesslich den Charakter eines Disputes um des Disputes willen annehmen kann."[61]

---

60. Werner Elert, Barth's opponent in Luther studies, allows dogma to
have the meaning of teaching insofar as dogma is a confession of
the truth of the gospel. "In der Bezeichnung des evangelischen
Dogmas als Bekenntnis kommt zum Ausdruck, dass seine Verbindlichkeit
nicht ursprünglich, sondern nur abgeleitet ist." *Der Christliche
Glaube*, (Hamburg, 1956[3]), p. 39.
   Thus Elert allows dogma to have a certain authority in the
church, which is more than Barth does. "Das Dogma bezeichnet das
Minimum des Sachgehalts, in dem alle offentliche Verkündigung über-
einzustimmen hat." *Ibidem*, p. 37. The church lends authority to
dogma, that is, to its confession (Bekenntnis) inasmuch as all
teaching must agree with it. Dogma does not, however, have authority for faith, as in Catholicism, but only for teaching and preaching, because faith is a personal matter.
61. "Dogmatik," in *Was ist Theologie?* (München, 1966), pp. 191-192.

8. BERHARD LOHSE

B. Lohse's *Epochen der Dogmengeschichte* is in no sense so preten-
tious as the more comprehensive works of Harnack and Loofs.[62] Lohse
views their attempts at giving definitions for dogma as too narrow,
particularly as their definitions imply infallible authority. For this
reason he finds the wider notion adopted by Walter Köhler and Martin
Werner -- "vorherrschener Ausdruck des Gemeindeglaubens hinsichtlich des
Sinngehalts der christlichen Offenbarung" -- more apropos. Such a category recognizes that official church sanction is not of the essence of
the matter. In fact, Lohse finds no example of dogma in the modern sense
in the ancient Church because he finds the claim of infallibility everywhere lacking. So, even the so-called 'dogma' of Nicea really is not a
dogma; it is a confession.

Basil the Great in the middle of the fourth century seems to be the
first to separate dogma from kerygma, which distinction was then later
adopted at Chalcedon, where that council proclaimed: "We teach that one
must confess...." It was then no accident when the reformers called their
teachings not "dogmas" but "confessional writings."[63] "Es ist daher
geraten, innerhalb der evangelischen Kirche, den einmal gebräuchlich
gewordenen Begriff der Dogmen im Sinne von Bekenntnissen oder auch Lehr-
bekenntnissen zu verstehen."[64] Consonantly, Lohse sees Peter's confession in Mt 16:15 as the first dogma. In that confession Peter expressed
his decision for Jesus and ever since there has never been a time in the
church when faith in Jesus has not been expressed in confession, which

---

62. Stuttgart, 1963.
63. *Cf. ibidem*, p. 15.
64. *Ibidem*, p. 16.

86

is dogma. In fact, the whole of the history of dogma is simply the growth in varying circumstances of the confession of Jesus.

While it is true that the simple equation of dogma and confession which Lohse makes enables him to treat the development of official teaching in the Protestant churches without accepting the notion of dogma, say in the Catholic Church, it is nevertheless also true that the church's role, an authoritative role in the actual historical development, comes off too short in this oversimplification.[65]

9. ALFRED ADAM

A. Adam's *Lehrbuch der Dogmengeschichte* avoids the pitfalls of the older German Protestant histories of dogma.[66] It has no idiosyncratically original viewpoint on the foundation of dogma to prove at the expense of balance and of truth. Thus, the notion of dogma employed is remarkably simple and unlabored: "Die Dogmen sind die grundlegenden Lehrentscheidungen der Vergangenheit, und sie in ihrem Werden, ihrem Sinn und ihren Auswirkungen als verbindlich gemeinte Lehre der Kirche zu verstehen, bleibt ein wichtiges Thema jeder Darstellung."[67]

Although Adam acknowledges that from the Protestant viewpoint no dogma can be regarded as infallible, since every formulation is constantly to be tested against the bible, this is seen not so much as a sign of the inherent fallibility of dogmatic expression as it is of the testimony of its own historicity. Thus, "Die hohen Dogmen des Glaubens, wie sie in der alten Kirche für die trinitarische Theologie und die Christologie

---

65. *Cf.* Peter Meinhold, *Geschichte der kirchlichen Historiographie*, (München, 1967), vol. 2, p. 536.
66. Vol. 1, Gutersloh, 1965; vol. 2, 1968.
67. Ibidem, vol. 1, p. 31.

formuliert und in der grossen Symbole aufgenommen sind, bleiben der

Gegenstand der alten Dogmengeschichte, dem sich auch die evangelische

Theologie verpflichtet weiss."[68]

As a consequence of this concern with genuine historicity Adam can

note a growing consensus on the task of the history of dogma between

Protestant and Catholic historians. He writes in understanding of the

Catholic effort:

> Im engeren Sinn ist das Dogma die von der Kirche formulierte
> Offenbarungslehre, deren Definitionen zum Teil punktuell sind, wie
> etwa in der Verwerfung häretischer Auffassungen, zum Teil einen
> breiten Ausschnitt der Lehre umfassen, wie vor allem in den Dekret-
> en des Tridentinums. Wenn auch an diesen Entscheidungen nicht
> gerüttelt wird, so macht sich doch eine Interpretation bemerkbar,·
> die den bisher üblichen Gesichtspunkt einer maximalistischen Aus-
> legung verlässt und jede dogmatische Definition nur im Rahmen ihrer
> Formulierung verstehen will. Auf diese Weise erlangt der geschicht-
> liche Ort jedes einzelnen Dogmas ein erhebliches Gewicht, so dass
> eine neue Dogmengeschichte als Möglichkeit am Horizont erscheint.[69]

Indeed, as the history of dogma becomes ever more historical theol-

ogy, and less the reading into history of a one-sided notion of dogma, as

with the classical historians of dogma, the way from the controversial

theology of the past to the ecumenical and common searching of founda-

tions of today is already being followed. Thus, Adam can write in praise

of the modern publication under Catholic auspices, the *Handbuch der*

Dogmengeschichte, that it attempts "die Beschreibung des geschichtlichen

Weges zu der heutigen katholischen Lehrverkündigung. ....Dabei ist das

Dogma im strengen Sinne nicht mehr das Hauptthema, sondern die Dogmen

sind als Knotenpunkte einer Gesamtentwicklung verstanden."[70]

It is in the spirit of the above that Adam develops his own history

---

68. *Ibidem.*
69. *Ibidem*, p. 25.
70. *Ibidem*, p. 26.

of dogma. For he sees its beginning in the experience of faith of the
resurrection of Jesus, the announcement of which assumed the authority
that the Saviour had previously claimed for himself.[71] In the announcing
that Jesus is the Christ, that is, the promised king of the end of time,
the kerygma became the beginning of all Christian theology. Immediately
the kerygma transformed itself into hymnic forms, many of which are found
in the New Testament. Adam underlines his perception of the dogmatic
significance of the early Christian hymns in speaking of the Didache:

> In der Apostellehre (Didache), die um 95 n. Chr. anzusetzen
> ist, wird überraschenderweise keine regula fidei geboten. Dafür
> erscheinen die wichtigsten Stücke des Kerygmas in den hymnischen
> Gebeten, die als Einleitung und Schluss der Agapenfeier am Sabbats-
> abend rezitiert werden sollen. Jesus wird als Knecht Gottes
> gepriesen, der das ewige Leben und die Erkenntnis des Heils verkün-
> digt hat; er ist der heilige Name Gottes, der in den Herzen der
> Gläubigen wohnt und ihnen Erkenntnis Gottes, errettenden Glauben
> und Unsterblichkeit der Person kundgetan hat; um des Sohnes Gottes
> willen ist die Schöpfung ins Leben gerufen, er aber hat die erwähl-
> ten Gläubigen auf den Weg der Erlösung geführt, so dass die Kirche
> einst vollendet wird, wenn das Ziel der Liebe erreicht sein wird
> in dem endgültigen Kommen der Gnade. -- Hier hat die Heilsbotschaft
> hymnischen Charakter und gehört zum Gottesdienst, genau wie in den
> Hymnen des urchristlichen Zeugnisses. Wenn also hier in der Doxo-
> logie die Grundlagen des späteren Dogmas in besonders deutlich aus-
> geprägter Gestalt vorliegen, so ist festzustellen: Für die Alte
> Kirche bestand kein Gegensatz zwischen liturgischem Gottes- und
> Christuslob auf der einen Seite und dem begrifflich formulierten
> Inhalt des Dogmas auf der andern Seite. Dieser Sachverhalt besagt:
> Das Dogma ist ursprünglich der Lobpreis Gottes auf dem Felde des
> Denkens.[72]

This is not a heterogeneous development, but the natural growth of a
vital force. "Im allgemeinen tritt die Botschaft Jesu als Lehre zurück;
sie wirkt sich vor allem in den paränetisch-katechetischen Stücken aus.
Dagegen wird die Person Jesu immer stärker betont, und alles, was mit den
Begriffen Menschensohn, Sohn Gottes, Messias, Davidssohn zusammenhing,
wird jetzt voll ausgeführt, wobei der Würdetitel 'Sohn Gottes' immer mehr

---

71. Cf. ibidem, p. 66ff.
72. Ibidem, pp. 83-84.

in den Mittelpunkt der Gedanken tritt. Daraus hat sich die erste Stufe
der Dogmenbildung erhoben."[73]

10. LESLIE DEWART

"The issue raised by Harnack is by no means closed in contemporary
theology."[74] This quotation from H.E.W. Turner's Bampton Lectures of 1954
may serve as an appropriate introduction to the rationale of our consideration to the charges of "Hellenization" brought forward by Leslie Dewart.
Although Dewart explicitly dissociates his interpretation of the
Hellenization process from that of Harnack (corruption),[75] both agree in
maintaining that modern Christianity must go beyond the Hellenic cultural
forms as in any way adequate for the continued representation and presentation of the central mysteries of Christianity. For Dewart the work of
the great councils of Nicea, Constantinople, and Chalcedon, while necessary in the Hellenic cultural world of the early centuries, represents
today only a "petrification;" since the expressions of Christian faith
have not developed beyond the cultural forms in which they were first
expressed.

Dewart's starting point is what he observes as the disjunctive
relationship prevalent today and existing between "contemporary experience" and Christian faith. "Contemporary experience" is described as
"...the mode of consciousness which mankind, if not as a whole at least
in respect of our own civilization constituting man's cultural vanguard,

---

73. *Ibidem*, p. 72.
74. H.E.W. Turner, *The Pattern of Christian Truth*: A Study in the
    Relations between Orthodoxy and Heresy in the Early Church, (London,
    1954), p. 495.
75. *Cf. The Future of Belief*, (New York, 1966), pp. 133-134, and *The
    Foundations of Belief*, (New York, 1969), *passim*.

has reached as a result of its historical and evolutionary development.[76] Whatever contemporary man's outlook is, it is scientific. That is, it maintains an underlying respect for the diffidence of science, for the scientist's readiness to change his mind. This attitude can only regard with suspicion the typically "Catholic" attitude, depending on the "long and honorable history of Scholasticism," which in a "fairly total and serene self-assurance" regards a great deal of truth to be found in an eternal and relatively unchanging body of doctrine.

To this disjunction between experience and faith one can respond by maintaining in relative isolation religious experience and world outlook. A less common alternative is the denial or rejection of the validity of contemporary experience. By far, however, the more common solution is the retention of the validity of contemporary experience, while at the same time rejecting to quite varying degrees the realism and moral validity of institutional religion.[77]

Dewart's book advances the notion that the solution to this dilemma is to be sought in an historically overdue process that would parallel Bultmann's demythologization of scripture, namely in the dehellenization of dogma: "...dehellenization may well be described, without a negative reference to the past, as the conscious historical self-fashioning of the cultural form which Christianity requires now for the sake of its future. In other words, dehellenization means, in positive terms, the conscious creation of the future of belief."[78]

Dewart believes that the fact that there has been a development of

76. Ibidem, p. 9.
77. Ibidem, p. 19.
78. Ibidem, p. 50.

Christian dogma is in some way related to the nature of human consciousness. A close examination of human consciousness should then throw a particular light on the process of dogmatic development.

Consciousness, or transcendence, as it is sometimes called, is that quality of the human psychic life which differentiates man from the objectifying, cognitional world of the beasts. It should be described not as man knowing himself, but as man's knowledge of himself in the act of knowing another. The act of knowledge which is consciousness -- being present to oneself -- does not represent a quantitative increase to the objects of knowledge since in this case, "...the supposed object of knowledge is already present as a whole in the first moment of consciousness."[79] That is to say, consciousness occurs only in the act of knowing some object, but consciousness itself is not that act of knowledge.

Since the object of consciousness (oneself) is present in every act of knowledge, consciousness cannot suffer a quantitative increase (as simple cognition can), but increases only in the manner of intensification.

> Any examples, since drawn from human experience, will of necessity argue circularly. As a light burns more brightly, without changing color, when a rheostat is turned, or as a broadcast is more clearly understood when one raises the volume of the same sound which at first was but with difficulty perceived, growth in consciousness typically comports the experience of knowing clearly now that which, as we "come to think about it," we had been aware of all along, even before we "reflected" on it, and yet had somehow managed not to notice.[80]

The study of doctrinal development has up to the present been hindered by the fact that faith has been understood as a type of actualization of man's intellect. Thus, although the acts of faith differ from

---

79. *Ibidem*, p. 83.
80. *Ibidem*, pp. 83-84.

the acts of the intellect by reason of their respective objects (as also by reason of the natural or supernatural quality of the faculty in which the habits of knowledge and faith reside) the truth of faith has remained the same as the truth of other acts of the intellect -- a <u>conformitas</u> <u>intellectus</u> <u>et</u> <u>rei</u>. According to the scholastic theory, knowledge, and therefore truth, can increase by reason of an intensification of its habit within the faculty in which it resides, or by reason of being extended to more objects.

Consequently, since the death of the last apostle and the closing of the objective body of revelation there has only been a <u>secundum</u> <u>quid</u> type of development possible -- that is, the raising to explicit consciousness of truths which have always been contained in the body of once and for all revealed truth.[81] In this sense St. Thomas noted that through the ages there has been a material increase in the number of <u>articuli</u> <u>fidei</u>.[82] But such a bringing to explicitness of what has always been implicit is, according to Dewart, no development at all. "The assumption which underlies this view is that any novelty not <u>totally</u> reducible to the original would imply a substantial divergence from -- and thus a corruption of -- the original."[83]

Such a view is inextricably bound up with the scholastic notion of truth and its implied eternal character. However, one can hardly say that the scholastic doctrine of truth is the only one under which one may consider Christian revelation. Dewart finds fault with the scholastic

81. There may also be, of course, a material development of the truths of faith in the life of the individual Christian inasmuch as he becomes progressively through time more conscious of truths which have <u>actually</u> been revealed.
82. II-II, q. 1, l. 7.
83. Dewart, <i>op. cit.</i>, p. 89.

inability to take account of true development principally on two grounds: in the first place, it fails to notice that human experience or the cultural context, which is the presupposition of Christian faith, has since the time of the early Church changed; and secondly, truth, in the wider sense, demands constant revision of itself.

Here we come to perhaps the most fundamental change of outlook in Dewart's book -- his notion of truth. Typifying his starting point is Dewart's taking over from modern philosophy the centrality of consciousness. "In contemporary thought (if abstraction is made from the differences of sects and schools), consciousness is understood as the typical and proper form of human psychism -- indeed, of human existence and life."[84] Man shares with the animals the "intussusception" of forms from the outside world. Man differentiates himself in the stream of psychic development through his self-consciousness, which is "the emergence of a self as it becomes present to itself by self-differentiating itself from the totality of being...."[85] Man is not constituted as a substance which would first exercise existence, but in consciousness itself, which is "the coming into being of mind, soul and man."[86]

"Consciousness develops," says Dewart, not as the perfection existing in the faculty of a being, "...rather, because it is in its nature to develop; unless it developed it would not exist at all. Its motto, as Marcel has said, is not _sum_, but _sursum_. This should serve to emphasize again that consciousness is not the _becoming_ (that is, the mental activity) of a _being_ (that is, mind, soul or man). It is the

84. _Ibidem_, p. 80.
85. _Ibidem_, p. 90.
86. _Ibidem_, p. 91.

coming-into-being of mind, soul and man."[87]

Truth is not the perfection of a faculty, but pertains to the very constitution of man's substance.

> Truth is not the adequacy of our representative operations, but the adequacy of our conscious existence. ....But since consciousness differentiates the self out of the totality of undifferentiated reality, the faithful, steadfast and continued development of the self can actually occur only to the degree that the world is objectified, that is, conceptualized, systematized, organized, lived with and made meaningful for our consciousness. ....It is the result of the mind coming-into-being through the self-differentiation of that-which-is into self and world.[88]

Dewart's plan for the dehellenization of dogma poses many problems. He states that it means "the conscious creation of the future of belief." His characterizations of Hellenic thought forms -- the equating of intelligibility and necessity (p. 44), and "the ideals of immutability, stability and impassibility" (p. 134) -- are very casual and noticeably take no notice of the serious work that has been done in this area by Claude Tresmontant and Thorlief Boman.

In calling for this "conscious creation of the future of belief" Dewart fails to see that one does not create new cultural forms. Thought categories are givens (data) in any particular culture. It is not the task of Christian theology actively to "dehellenize" dogma before a more viable cultural form has registered itself and proved as serviceable for the task as the culture and language once employed by the Greek speaking minds in the early formulation of Christian theology. The superseding of Greek theological expression will only come to be when western culture no longer depends on the heritage and legacy of the Greek language.

---

87. *Ibidem*.
88. *Ibidem*, pp. 92-93. In his later work, *The Foundations of Belief*, (New York, 1969), Dewart develops once again these ideas without noticeable advance. *Cf.* especially pp. 57-114.

However, so long as the post-Christian West, its languages and, therefore, its thought forms remain a direct descendant of the glory that was Greece and Rome, there is, it seems, no possibility for a radical "dehellenization of dogma."

Dewart rightly recognizes that translation involves at least a partial shift in meaning.[89] But so long as such a large percentage of the etymological origin of a modern language such as English comes directly or indirectly from the Greek, there is no possibility for the total "re-conceptualization of Christian dogma." The reason for this is, of course, that so many concepts in English, as also of so many other languages of the Christian West, are even less a translation from Greek roots as they are simply a transposition of Greek concepts into modern forms of expression. Thus, words such as ὕβρις, πολειτεία, ψυχή, πατήρ, κρινεῖν, εὐλογέω, πάθος, σωτηρία, γνῶσις, ἰδέα, ἴδιος, νεκρός, and a thousand others still carry their basic Greek meanings and colorings over into their English equivalents and derivations. The ultimate dehellenization of dogma can only come about when the mysteries of Christianity will be expressed in languages which have no relation to Greek. It could be an interesting project to pursue the question whether missionary activity in cultures such as those of China and Japan means the introduction of "new words" (of Greek and Latin origin), or whether the interests of more lasting and meaningful missionary activity would not mean the creation of a new and more indigenous theological vocabulary.

A second line of criticism must come from the fact that Dewart does not understand the complexity of processes which have contributed to the development of dogma. He reduces it unnecessarily to only one type of

---

89. *Cf. The Future of Belief*, pp. 108-109.

development, namely, the explication of the implicit in revelation. Thus Dewart: "The articles of faith increase in number because it is possible to express the same objective dogma, the same eternal and divine truth, in more explicit and thus in more complex human terms. The sense is, however, that the dogma itself does not in any real sense change, although its articulation becomes more complex."[90] And, "If Christian dogma can develop in no other sense of the word than that admitted by St. Thomas, ...it means that dogma does not develop at all." "The assumption which underlies this view is that any novelty not totally reducible to the original would imply a substantial divergence from -- and thus a corruption of -- the original."[91]

Dewart's understanding of the development of dogma as it has historically taken place is based exclusively on St. Thomas' article, "Utrum articuli fidei secundum successionem temporum creverint" (II-II-1-7). H. Hammans, in his study of the recent theories on the development of dogma,[92] draws attention to the fact that Thomas and the other medieval scholastics had no real theory for the development of dogma. "Thomas gibt also hier keine Theorie der Dogmenentwicklung, sondern der Offenbarungsentwicklung, wenn auch seine Formel für die Entwicklung der Offenbarung: explicatio fidei in analogem Sinn für die Dogmenentwicklung gebraucht werden kann."[93] Dewart shows then no understanding for the different types of theories -- the "intellectual," the "historical," and the "theological" -- such as Hammans, for example, names the various approaches to understanding the phenomenon of the development of dogma.

90. *Ibidem*, pp. 77-78.
91. *Ibidem*, p. 89.
92. *Die Neueren Katholischen Erklärungen der Dogmenentwicklung*, (Essen, 1965).
93. *Ibidem*, pp. 16-17.

In summary, Dewart naively supposes that the only alternative to an intellectual type explanation of the development of dogma is his own theory of the heightening of human consciousness.

A third line of criticism must come from the fact that Dewart rejects the traditional notion of truth as an **adaequatio intellectus et rei** or a fieri aliud in quantum aliud, and substitutes for it an adequacy of conscious existence in relationship to the exigencies of life:

> Although truth is not the adequation of the intellect to being (insofar as understanding consists in the assimilation of being by the formal mediation of concepts), truth might nevertheless be called an adequation of man to reality, in the sense that it is man's self-achievement within the requirements of a given situation. We can call it an adequation provided we keep in mind that since man as such has the reality of being, adequation is not the human substance's transition from non-being to being in the accidental order of cognition. In this context adequation would not connote conformity, correspondence, likeness or similarity. It would connote adjustment, usefulness, expediency, proficiency, sufficiency and adaption.[94]

Thus Dewart completely overturns that notion of truth which has ever made philosophy the seeking of truth for its own sake (propter seipsam solum). Truth for Dewart is subordinated to efficiency and to a dynamism the measure of which is what it produces.

In our opinion, this dynamic and efficient conception of truth excludes Dewart from any further discussion among men who seek truth for its own sake. The best that can be said for his work is that he reverts to a type of evolutionary Hegelianism: "...truth does not depend upon the conformity of experience to being by means of some determinate concept which uniquely represents the envisaged being. Rather, it would depend upon the realization (that is, the actual coming-into-being), of human experience precisely as human (that is, of consciousness), as

---

94. Dewart, *The Future of Belief*, p. 110.

consciousness differentiates itself from the world (that is, relates itself to itself and to an-other)."[95]

11. PETER MEINHOLD

P. Meinhold finds two grounds in modern theological research which, he believes, are directing Protestant theology toward a reconsideration of the foundations of the history of dogma.[96] These grounds are two conclusions generally accepted today as facts, namely the distance between the Jesus of history and the Jesus of faith, and the distance between the preaching of Jesus and the kerygma of earliest Christianity. These two presumptions seem to depend heavily on the work of Harnack.

Meinhold finds W. Köhler's attempt to locate the beginning of dogma in the teaching of Jesus praiseworthy. Yet his understanding of dogma as the "Selbstbewusstsein" of Christianity in relation to the problems facing any positive religion relegates any influence of the Church on the formation of dogma to the accidental. For him the history of dogma is rather the history of theology. And although he locates the beginning of dogma closer to Jesus than either Harnack or his immediate followers, Seeberg and Loofs, its inception represents the transformation of Jesus' eschatological thinking into the realm of temporality. Thus once again the link between Jesus and the beginning of dogma is only an indirect one.

Meinhold also finds fault with W. Elert's attempt to locate the

---

95. *Ibidem.* See also the passage quoted above from pp. 92-93. On p. 73 of *The Foundations of Belief* Dewart acknowledges his debt to Hegel.
96. *Cf.* the following works by Meinhold: "Zur Grundlegung der Dogmengeschichte," *Saeculum*, X(1960), pp. 1-20; "Der Ursprung des Dogmas in der Verkündigung Jesu," *ZKTh*, 89(1967), pp. 121-138; "Die Bemühungen um die Grundlegung der Dogmengeschichte," in *Geschichte der Kirchlichen Historiographie*, (München, 1967), pp. 515-544.

beginning of dogma in the kerygma of the apostles. "Ist das apostolische Kerygma nicht vielleicht seinerseits schon eine Explikation des in der Verkundigung Jesu angelegten 'Dogmas'?"[97]

Neither these nor the other attempts thus far made have been able to found the beginning of dogma in the preaching of Jesus. And therefore it is inevitable that these two "distances" should exist.

Meinhold maintains that he is able to span these two "distances" in the "dogmatic" claim of Jesus. "Ganz gewiss gibt es das Dogma nicht im Sinne eines Lehrsatzes oder einer expliziten Aussage bei Jesus. Aber es gibt einen dogmatischen Anspruch Jesu, der darin besteht, dass er selbst mit seiner Person, mit seinem Sein und Wirken, in das Evangelium hineingehört, ja, sich selbst zum Mittelpunkt des Evangeliums gemacht hat, das er verkündigt."[98] Before either the kerygma of the apostles or of the early Church lies the last reachable ground for the student of critical history -- Jesus' own "dogmatic" claim.

In announcing the coming of the kingdom of God lies the content of Jesus' "dogmatic" claim. It does not seem to disturb Meinhold that he thereby changes one of the primary meanings of the concept of dogma: "So ist 'das Dogma' nicht primär ein theoretischer oder kirchlicher Lehrsatz, sondern die besondere Form, in der sich die Stellung Jesu in der von ihm verkündeten Heilsbotschaft auspricht."[99] This about-face is strange since in the earlier part of his article the correction of Harnack's "Hellenisierung des Christentums" view to Loofs and Seeberg's "von der Kirche anerkannte Lehrsätze" view seemed to be portrayed with a definite favor.

---

97.   "Der Ursprung des Dogmas in der Verkündigung Jesu," p. 132.
98.   *Ibidem.*
99.   *Ibidem.*

Yet there is a further development to Meinhold's thesis. In Jesus' presentation of himself there is already the hint that connection with his own person is an integral part of the gospel of the reign of God. This is found in the fact that Jesus himself, and not the primitive community, characterized his mission as that of the "Son of Man" and of the "Servant of the Lord" (Ebed Yahweh).

It is not true to say that Jesus' whole consciousness was dominated by the eschatological and apocalyptic. He takes the "Son of Man" title from that world and forcefully asserts it in the present. And that title he colors with the other title of "Servant of the Lord," which is in the gospels the role that also describes his mission. It is precisely in the combination of these two roles, by himself, that Jesus gives rise to his "dogmatic claim": "Die irdische Mission des Menschensohnes ist nach dem Verständnis Jesu die des Gottesknechtes."[100]

This combination of titles, effected by Jesus himself, is the primary dogmatic fact of Christianity. In it are implicitly given all future dogmatic developments and interpretations effected by the Church according to the needs of the times.

This makes it impossible to speak then of an undogmatic beginning to Christianity, which only subsequently and at the expense of being unfaithful to its original thrust, expressed itself in doctrines and creeds. Jesus' claim to combine the two titles in himself is the dogma; from it flow the dogmas of the Church.

The hermeneutic root of this new foundation to the problem of the beginning of dogma Meinhold sees in the fact that no "factum historicum brutum et nudum" is ever available to us. Every historical fact is

---

100. *Ibidem*, p. 135.

always received within the guise of a particular interpretation. It is precisely the search for brute facts and for "wie es eigentlich gewesen" that has for too long steered the history of dogma in the wrong direction. Fact and interpretation belong as closely to one another as light and its source. One cannot understand the one without the other.

> So ergibt sich weiter die grundlegende Frage, ob nicht der historische Jesu selbst mit seiner Verkündigung eben die Deutung und Interpretation veranlasst hat, die diejenige des Kerygmas geworden ist. Mit anderen Worten: Ob nicht der Verkündiger sich selbst verkündigt und ob er nicht sich selbst so sehr in den Mittelpunkt seines Evangeliums gestellt hat, dass die Tradierung dieses Evangeliums immer beides zugleich umschliessen muss, das Faktum und die Deutung desselben, den Verkündiger und den Verkündigten, den Erwecker des Glaubens und ihn selbst als den Gegenstand des Glaubens.[101]

Our criticism of Meinhold's attempt to found the beginning of dogma in the preaching of Jesus runs along the lines we have already indicated, namely that to do this he must change the ordinary understanding of dogma in use in the churches -- an officially sanctioned teaching expressing the truth of revelation in non-biblical words and thought forms. Meinhold's attempt at reformulating the meaning of that concept is brought out clearly in an earlier article in which he offered the following definition of dogma: "Es ist -- und das bedeutet unsere Berufung auf den unableitbaren dogmatischen Anspruch Jesu -- die von Jesus selbst gegebene Auslegung seiner Person und seines Werkes. Somit ist das Dogma inhaltlich die in der Verkündigung Jesu begründete Auffassung seiner selbst, wobei es gerade das Zentrum des Evangeliums ausmacht, dass er seiner Person und seinem Werke die schlechthin heilsbedeutende Funktion für das Gegenwärtigwerden der Gottesherrschaft -- jetzt und einst -- zuschreibt."[102]

---

101. *Ibidem*, p. 138.
102. "Zur Grundlegung der Dogmengeschichte," p. 17.

We find Meinhold's attempt to refound the beginning of dogma strik-
intly original, and interesting insofar as he is able to bridge the great
"distances" common in Protestant thought between the Jesus of history and
the Christ of faith, between the gospel and the kerygma. However, we
believe that his sacrificing the usual understanding of dogma for the
claim of Jesus expressed in his self-consciousness to be an unnecessary
attempt to transcend the ambiguities of history. It is not the "dogma
of Jesus" (subjective genitive) the historian of dogma seeks but the
"dogma of Jesus" (objective genitive), the teaching of the Church.

12. Wolfhart Pannenberg

W. Pannenberg treats expressly the question, "Was ist eine dogmatische Aussage?" in his essay with that name.[103] He states that any
answer to this question can in the context of Protestant theology simply
not be assumed, inasmuch as the older liberal theology and some more
recent theologians such as Paul Tillich reject the notion of a Protestant
"Dogmatik" since, "Dogma als kirchlich sanktioniertes Lehrgesetz sei
etwas spezifisch Katholisches."[104] More recently, however, some theologians such as Pannenberg's teacher, Edmund Schlink, understand dogma as
"Antwort der Kirche auf die Offenbarung Gottes."[105] It is in the same
direction that Barth formulated his notion of dogma as the agreement of
the church's preaching with revelation as found in scripture. For, says
Pannenberg, "Das Gegenuber der Offenbarung als einer selbständigen,

---

103. *Grundfragen systematischer Theologie, Gesammelte Aufsatze,*
      (Göttingen, 1967), pp. 159-180.
104. *Ibidem,* p. 159.
105. Schlink, *KuD* 3(1957), pp. 252, 260. So also, as Pannenberg
      mentions: H. Vogel, *Gott in Christo,* (1951); G. Gloege, *RGG* II,
      222.

richterlichen Instanz zur Lehre und Bekündigung der Kirche ist für evangelishces Verständnis von Dogma und Dogmatik bezeichnend."[106]

Melanchthon, the first of Protestant dogmatic theologians, looked upon his work, *Loci Communes*, as a summary of the scriptures in which he sought points from which the whole of revelation finds it center. It was also Calvin's intention in his *Institutio Religionis Christianae* to write a summary of revelation. The Formula Concordiae also aimed at achieving such a summary of teaching. But if Protestant dogmatic theology understands itself as a summary of the apostolic preaching, then it can never become a norm of belief next to scripture, but must always remain revisable in its light. This doctrine rests, however, on the assumption that the scripture's content is clear on its own terms, and thus is the supreme judge of all dogmatic talk.

This inherent clearness of scripture was certainly Luther's teaching in the *Assertio Omnium Articulorum* of 1520: "per se certissima, apertissima, cui ipsius interpres, omnium omnia probans, iudicans et illuminans."[107] In the *De Servo Arbitrio* this teaching was expanded. There is not only an inner clearness to scripture, which is given by the Holy Spirit, and which makes one certain of salvation, there is also an external clearness which consists in the unequivocalness and incontradictableness of its essential contents. Luther sees here the res of scripture, i.e., that which in its clearness is revealed in such things as the incarnation, vicarious suffering, the heavenly army of Christ, and even in the Trinitarian and Christological dogmas, all of which are, however, concentrated in Christ. For he is the central content of

---

106. Pannenberg, *op. cit.*, p. 160.
107. WA 7, 97; quoted from Pannenberg, p. 163.

104

scripture, from which all its books are judged: "alle Bücher zu tadeln, wenn man sieht, ob sie Christum treiben oder nicht."[108]

It is precisely at and from this point -- Luther's doctrine of the external clearness of scripture -- that Pannenberg begins to go his own way. "Aus Luthers Lehre von der äusseren Klarheit der Schrift, dem Kernstück seiner Überzeugung von ihrer Selbstevidenz, ergibt sich also die unmittelbare dogmatische Bedeutung historisch-exegetischer Befunde: Der dogmatische Inhalt der Schrift muss sich durch die historische Argumentation aufweisen lassen."[109] But the question of scripture's clearness is not to be separated from the other question of its unity, and precisely this question is in recent times extremely disputed. Historical research has shown that the New Testament does not spring from a unity of teaching, but is more the product of differing theologies. Käsemann's words that the New Testament does not establish the unity of the Church, but is rather the ground for the diversity of the confessions is well-known.[110]

As a result Käsemann sought to find unity in the notion of justification, less in the sense of a teaching as "...im Sinne des gnadenhaften Charakters des Heilsgeschehens verstanden."[111] Hermann Diem proposed a "Verkündigungseinheit," by which, through the apostolic witnesses, Jesus proclaims himself.[112] The differences to be found in the apostolic witness he attributes to each context in which it was proclaimed. Pannenberg rightly points out that the matter at hand is

108. WA DB 7, 384; quoted from Pannenberg, p. 165.
109. Pannenberg, *op. cit.*, pp. 165-166.
110. "Begründet der nt. Kanon die Einheit der Kirche?" in *Ev Theol* 11 (1951-52), pp. 13-21.
111. *Vd.* Pannenberg, *op. cit.*, p. 168.
112. *Dogmatik*, p. 201.

rather to find the constant feature in each example of the apostolic witness and that, therefore, Diem really has not solved the problem. Indeed, since scripture can no longer be understood as a unity of teaching, there seem to be only two possibilities in achieving unity: either through a hermeneutical principle such as Käsemann's "der Rechtfertigungsglaube als Existenzhaltung zum Auslegungskanon," which exists, however, only in the mind of the interpreter and is therefore no longer an objective norm of unity; or, as Diem attempts, in the "Christusgeschehen," which must then be separated and distilled from each example of the original Christian witness.

Pannenberg maintains that one must go back beyond the kerygmatic expressions of the original Christian witnesses in a process of historically uncovering the "Christusgeschehen" which then, understood in its historical context, becomes the norm of unity in scripture from which all else is judged. But this "Christusgeschehen" can be norm of scripture and judge of all future church proclamation only in so far as it carries within itself its own significance. This, however, it does insofar as it is not understood as an "Einzelfaktum" without context, but on the background of the Jewish hopes and Old Testament expectation of the time. In this way Pannenberg believes that he is still working in the context of Luther's doctrine of the external clearness of scripture. Form criticism has only made it necessary to go back another step behind the literal meaning of the text to the historical sense, which we today must understand as something separate from the literal sense. The history of the tradition is seen then as simply the development of its (i.e., the "Christusgeschehen") inherent significance, which in turn can be evaluated in its light.

106

When the significance of Jesus then is revealed not first by dogmatics, but as the content of its historical expression, the unity of dogmatic and historical assertions becomes apparent.[113] For, dogmatic assertions are not primarily concerned with the individuality of an historical happening. They presume this and then seek to state the universal significance of the same. Historical assertions, on the other hand, always presume some type of universal "Bedeutungshorizont," that is, the particular "Vorverständnis" of the historian, in the light of which his research, understanding, and statements are conditioned. The "Dogmatiker" treads, however, the opposite road; he seeks universal significance working from one event, the history of Jesus. "Bdide Momente, die universale Bedeutung und die besondere Individualität des Weges Jesu, hängen so miteinander zusammen, dass der Erkenntnisvollzug immer wieder von einem zum andern übergehen muss: Die historische Individualität Jesu ist erst recht verstanden in Erkenntnis ihrer universalen Bedeutung -- letzlich sogar erst im persönlichen Vertrauen -- alle dogmatischen Aussagen über seine universale Bedeutung bedürfen immer wieder der Begründung und Bewährung aus der historischen Besonderheit der Botschaft, des Weges und der Gestalt Jesu."[114]

The universality of dogmatic statements comes from the fact that they have to do with the earthly way of Jesus, but in relationship to the action of God in him, who raised him from the dead. But assertions about God are universal assertions because they have to do with the God of universal reality. Thus the eschatological and universal character of his resurrection becomes particularly clear, because in it the God of the

113. *Cf.* Pannenberg, *Offenbarung als Geschichte*, (Göttingen, 1961).
114. Pannenberg, *Grundfragen*, p. 172.

Old Testament once again reveals himself as the God and Lord of all things.

The systematic character of dogmatics hangs from its universality. In the eschatological happening all things will fit together in unity, and this is the viewpoint from which dogmatics sees all of reality. Because dogmatics seeks to state the universal character of the eschatological happening in Christ, it only follows that it will make use of the language of philosophy, which also is concerned with universals.

In agreement with his teacher, Edmund Schlink, Pannenberg sees the doxological character as an essential structure element of the act of confession, and therefore of dogma itself. When one confesses, he is praising God for being the God he is, the one who reveals himself in the event of Jesus Christ.

Another element of dogmatic assertions is their proleptic character. In the resurrection of Jesus, or better, in his being raised by God (Auferweckung), is the end of the world and the rising of the dead manifested. And for this reason he can be addressed as "Son of Man," "Son of God," and "Lord." It is the nature of dogmatic assertions to speak of this end-state which in relation to us is not yet realized, but which in relation to Christ is already factual. But dogma itself never has the eschatological form of final truth; the authority of the confessions lies in the fact that they must be tested by every believer against revelation as found in scripture. Only insofar as they bring this to expression do they have authority.

Thus, Pannenberg's answer to the original question about the meaning of a dogmatic statement seems to be the following. The res of scripture is the Christ-happening known in the external clearness of

scripture. A dogmatic statement is this Christ-happening proving itself
through its historical uniqueness to have also a universal significance.
That is to day, the dogmatic part of a dogmatic statement is the universality of significance that comes to it through its proximity to the
"Christusgeschehen."

Pannenberg's answer to the original question is then idiosyncratic
to his whole theology. It has the advantage of calling attention to the
universal significance of God's single action in the historical Jesus.
Yet it also, like the other statements we have seen among the Protestant
theologians, recognizes only a very limited and derived authority in
dogmatic speech for the church.

13. JAROSLAV PELIKAN

The most recent history of dogma is that of J. Pelikan, *The Christian Tradition, A History of the Development of Doctrine*.[115] In our
evaluation of Harnack's overly narrow conception of the task of the
history of dogma we have already made reference to Pelikan's criticism of
Harnack and his own more expansive view: "What the church of Jesus Christ
believes, teaches, and confesses on the basis of the word of God: this is
Christian doctrine."[116] But, "the history of doctrine is not to be
equated with the history of theology or the history of Christian
thought."[117] For to do so would be to confuse the idiosyncratic
positions of not a few Christian thinkers with the Christian faith,
although it is also true that what the teachers of one age thought often

---

115. Vol. 1, *The Emergence of the Catholic Tradition (100-600)*, (Chicago,
1971); vol. 2, *The Spirit of Eastern Catholicism (600-1700)*,
(Chicago, 1974).
116. Vol. 1, p. 1.
117. *Ibidem*, p. 3.

became church doctrine in the next. "By relating what is confessed to what is believed and to what is taught," Pelikan "seeks to take account of how doctrines have developed."[118]

Thus, Pelikan sees the task of the history of dogma in a fashion similar to the way it is seen by Alfred Adam. And like Adam, Pelikan's position closely approaches the task of the history of dogma within Catholicism. For Pelikan, unlike classical Protestantism, can speak thus of tradition: "The form which Christian doctrine, so defined, has taken in history is tradition. Like the term 'doctrine,' the word 'tradition' refers simultaneously to the process of communication and to its content. Thus tradition means the handing down of Christian teaching during the course of the history of the church, but it also means that which was handed down."[119]

In the controversial theology of the past the assumption was entirely too common that one's own position represented the unchanging essence of eternal truth, while all opposing views were somehow shaped by history. Today it is recognized that the formulation of every Christian truth is shaped by its own historical context.

> Tradition without history has homogenized all the stages of development into one statically defined truth; history without tradition has produced a historicism that relativized the development of Christian doctrine in such a way as to make the distinction between authentic growth and cancerous aberration seem completely arbitrary. In this history we are attempting to avoid the pitfalls of both these methods. The history of Christian doctrine is the most effective means available of exposing the artificial theories of continuity that have often assumed normative status in the churches, and at the same time it is an avenue into the authentic continuity of Christian believing, teaching, and confessing. Tradition is the living faith of the dead; traditionalism is the dead faith of the living.[120]

---

118. *Ibidem*, p. 4.
119. *Ibidem*, p. 7.
120. *Ibidem*, p. 9.

110

In addressing himself thus to the problems of writing a history of doctrine Pelikan avoids determining what the more narrow concept of dogma would include.

14. JOSEF NOLTE

J. Nolte's *Dogma in Geschichte* is, according to the author's acknowledgment, inspired by Hans Küng's *Strukturen der Kirche* and his *Die Kirche*.[121] The tendentiously critical tone of the book leads one to believe that it is more thoroughly inspired by his mentor's *Unfehlbar? Eine Anfrage*.[122]

The constant theme of this work is that the dogmatic consciousness of the Church is now being confronted by the experience of historicity and its attendant mobility in all actual relationships. Dogmaticism (Dogmatismus) is the specter with which Nolte fences throughout. His program does not, he insists, imply the reduction of the Christian message or its challenge, nor even the destruction of the dogmatically fixed forms of faith but: "Der in Dogmatismus totalisierten Wirklichkeitsansicht steht somit die Geschichte gegenüber. These dieser Arbeit ist es: das dogmatische Bewusstsein ist ebenso wie das einzelne Dogma nicht über oder unter und auch nicht neben die Geschichte zu stellen, sondern der Dogmatismus ist in die Geschichte einzubringen und zurückzustellen und somit zugleich das Metadogmatische als der umgreifende Horizont zurückzugewinnen bzw. jeweils neu zu erfragen."[123] Nolte's newly coined word,

121. *Dogma in Geschichte, Ökumenische Forschungen,* eds., H. Küng, J. Moltmann, *et alii.* II. Soteriologische Abteilung, Band III, (Freiburg, 1971). *Cf. Strukturen der Kirche,* (Freiburg, 1961, p. 13, and especially *Die Kirche,* (Freiburg, 1967), p. 344ff.
122. Zürich, 1970.
123. Nolte, *op. cit.,* p. 17.

"metadogmatic," receives discussion further on.

An historical overview of the ancient use of the word, "dogma," reveals only a negative result for the present state of dogmaticism. The word is used precious little by the Fathers and then as often as not in a negative sense, as when Marcellus of Ancyra wrote, "The word **dogma** has to do with human willing and opining."[124] Since the Renaissance the word has found more common usage among theologians, but not yet in the determined manner of the dogmaticism common within the Church in modern times. Nolte maintains that both the Reform and the Counter-Reform preserved the ancient usage of the word. Thus he sees no particular weight in Luther's statement in his *Adversus Exsecrabilem Antichristi Bullam* of 1520 where he refers to his propositions condemned by Leo X as "dogmata catholica." A more affective usage of the word and, in particular, of "dogmaticism" is to be found first in Kant's *Kritik der Reinen Vernunft* of 1772, which pejorative usage is taken up by Fichte, Schelling and Nietzsche. This does not, however, explain the special development of the word in its various forms within the scope of the Catholic representation of faith in more modern times. This development and narrowing of the concept which proceeds through Veron, Gotti, Chrismann, and culminates in the "definition" of Vatican I as a "...definierter Glaubenssatz, unfehlbare Offenbarungswahrheit, absolute Glaubenspflicht und Heilsverbindlichkeit," cannot be explained either by the ancient or the Renaissance usage.[125] "Lediglich die Vorliebe der Neuscholastik für die sehr bequeme Traditionslehre des Vinzenz von Lérin könnte die Atmosphäre und den Kanal geschaffen haben, worin dessen 'Lieblingswort' Dogma aus dem christlichen

---

124. Fragment 86.
125. Nolte, *op. cit.*, p. 31.

Altertum herübergeflossen ist."[126]

Although the word, "dogma," can be used in a neutral sense, as when it denotes abbreviation, a short formula, a resume or a catchword, dogmaticism denotes uncritical self-assertion. "Der Grundzug des 'Dogmatischen' wäre dann auf die kürzeste Form geracht der Hang zum Undialektischen und Unkritischen bzw. die unbedachte Gewöhnheit. Dogmatisch reden hiesse dann: einseitig verabsolutieren."[127]

Even an examination of the New Testament reveals dogmatic speech in only the technical and legal form as in the "dogmatic" decrees of the Council of Jerusalem (Acts 15 where δόγμα is adequately translated as "decree"), and perhaps in the form of tradition attached to a particular school of thought, as in the various forms of conversion-oriented oratory, the handing on of particular teachings, and early theology. The attitude of consciousness peculiar to dogmaticism (Bewusstseinshaltung des Dogmatismus) is found in several areas of the New Testament. Inasmuch as this quantity is characterized by overweeningness, exaggeration, isolation, and undialectical absolutization,[128] it is to be found not in the preaching of Jesus, but rather in the hardened field of late, Jewish religiosity within which context Jesus preached a gospel of freedom. One finds it also in the legalistic and spiritualistic misinterpretations of Paul's message. Indeed, the preaching of both Jesus and Paul was pointedly directed toward the dissolution of the dogmaticism of their times.

It goes almost without saying that scholastic theology of recent times has looked upon the following text from Vatican I as a definition of dogma: "Porro fide divina et catholica ea omnia credenda sunt, quae in

126. *Ibidem*.
127. *Ibidem*, p. 43.
128. *Ibidem*, p. 71.

verbo Dei scripto vel tradito continentur et ab Ecclesia sive solemni iudicio sive ordinario et universali magisterio tamquam divinitus revelata credenda proponuntur."[129] However, the very fact that this "definition" is in the imperative mood proves that it was never intended to be regarded as such. Furthermore, historical analysis and textual criticism reveal the following points: (1) there is only an asyndetical relationship of this text with those which immediately precede and follow it; (2) there is no anathema clause corresponding to this text; (3) this paragraph was not prepared by the theological deputation (it is not to be found in the first schema); (4) Bishop Senestrey of Regensburg is responsible for its insertion, in all likelihood as a measure against the more conservative and conciliaristic standpoint of Döllinger, in order to assert the authority of pronouncements of the papal ordinary magisterium. Nolte's conclusion: "Der Satz richtet sich also gegen einen konziliaristischen Minimalismus, und es kann von daher gefragt werden, ob er überhaupt die ganze Kirche angehe."[130] In short, it is an imperative interjection of the aggressive infallibilists and less a definition than a "desire for a definitive statement at the same time regulating and crippling everything."[131]

At this point Nolte interjects a scathingly critical indictment of dogmaticism in the Church which he judges as mostly the fault of neo-scholasticism. It includes such remarks as:

> Ist der Katholizismus nicht ex termino Vermeidung von Extre-
> mismus? ....Ist der Katholizismus seinem wesentlich versöhnenden
> Zug entsprechend nicht von der Wurzel her immer schon gegen Über-
> treibung, Überforderung und Einseitigkeit, wie sie sich als

---

129. DS, 3011.
130. Nolte, *op. cit.*, p. 79.
131. "...wohl eher als Desiderat nach einer solchen alles regelnden, aber auch alles lähmenden Letztdefinition...", *ibidem*, p. 80.

Wesenszug des Dogmatismus zeigen? ....Dem Wunsch nach <u>Stabilität</u> sind Formen der Autoritätsbetonung, des Konformismus bis zum sacrificium intellectus verwandt. Dem korrespondiert die Tendenz zum undialektischen und thetischen Stil. Es fehlt die kritische Distanz. ....Diese Formen zielen auf eine deutliche (wenn auch meist unbewusst vollzogene) Ideologisierung des Glaubens. Es fehlt die freie Akzeptation der Wirklichkeit und die Entsprechung zur Geschichte.[132]

Yet Nolte sees the beginnings of dogmaticism's waning in the new style of representing the faith which was begun at Vatican II, in the documents of which no solemn dogmatic definitions were issued, no statements were made with the claim of infallibility, and a new consciousness of the relationship of reality to truth became evident -- in a word, where the leaders of the Church began to be aware of the historicity of even their own "dogmatic constitutions." These are the work of a pilgrim Church which is beginning to manifest what Nolte calls a "metadogmatic" (metadogmatisch) attitude.

Whereas the psychological basis of dogmaticism is to be found in the frenzied attempt to secure reality within well-determined limits, to overemphasize the chaotic in general experience, and to dam up the meaninglessness of the flux in life -- all through a process of fixated ideologization, it is the characteristic of the metadogmatic attitude to take the reality of history seriously -- as the transcendental horizon of extension, the essential quality of which is non-objectivication. History is not just the relation of what is past, but the conceptual abbreviation of all happening, the place of reality, field of being.[133]

The dogmatic thinking which has characterized the Catholic Church of modern times is not essential to Catholicism itself; nor does criticism

---

132. *Ibidem* pp. 87, 89, 90.
133. *Cf. ibidem*, p. 139.

of it in Nolte's opinion imply disagreement with the content of particular dogmas. Such criticism is aimed at the form and style in which the faith has been presented. As guide to its criticism Nolte finds Nietzsche's saying, "Das Vollkommene soll nicht geworden sein," congenial.[134]

A further characteristic of the more modern way of looking at dogma is to see it in its pragmatic, social function. This is not to consider it in a crudely utilitarian way, but as "regulation of speech [Karl Rahner's 'Sprachregelung'], as mode of communication, which is the Church's special speech, at once instrumental and operational."[135] This development follows the breakdown of universally accepted philosophical premises in the modern world, and their replacement with the historical and social sciences, as also with the philosophy of language and social psychology. But such a pragmatic foundation of dogma would allow its occurrence in situations of genuine crisis for the faith. When the crisis passes, however, so would such regulated speech give way to less-determined ways, as no expression is perfect. Thus, the metadogmatic would even correspond with one feature of modern philosophy -- the drive toward transcendence which manifests itself in the historical process.[136]

When one attempts to discern more precisely how Nolte conceives the metadogmatic in view of the question of whether it actually can replace the dogmatic ecclesial expressions, the answer is excessively abstract and (at least) to that extent unsatisfying. He speaks of a coincidence

---

134. Cf. ibidem, p. 198ff.; Fr. Nietzsche, Genealogie der Moral, Werke, II, edit. by K. Schlechta, (Stuttgart, 1964), p. 242.
135. "...nicht ...mit einem kruden Utilitarismus zu verwechseln ist, als Sprachregelung, als Kommunikationsermöglichung, als kirchliche Spezialsprache instrumental und operational begriffen." --Nolte, op. cit., p. 207.
136. Nolte identifies with Marcuse's use of the word, "transcendence." Cf. Nolte, op. cit., p. 214, footnote 3.

between the dialectic and metadogmatic forms of consciousness, of such abstractions as synthesis, reconciliation, and dissolution (Aufhebung) as the goal of both the dialectical process and of the metadogmatic form of consciousness.[137] He speaks of a coincidence between a transcending form of thought and of his projected metadogmatic form for dogma, which is ready to dare the changeover from usual horizons to a new field of work.[138] He speaks of the dialectic, specific quality of the metadogmatic impulse as change and changeability, whereby the invariability and unchangeability of dogmaticism is broken.[139] He speaks of the metadogmatic state of consciousness which remains in the balance between acceptance and distance as an alternative to the positing and negating of dogmaticism.[140] He calls functionality an expression of the appropriateness of the metadogmatic pose in the measure of collectedness and silence.

Assuredly this is a schizophrenic and uncommitted posture compared to the inexorable challenges of faith which the Church has felt justified in demanding in a very "dogmatic" manner of her followers all the way from the martyr's acclamation, "Jesus is Lord," to the schoolchild's reciting of the Creed which he as yet little grasps. But then Nolte explicitly denies dogmatic character to both such acclamations and to the early baptismal creeds.[141] In the attempt to take history with utter seriousness and to point to the lack of an historical sense as the crisis of dogmaticism and of dogma, Nolte has really failed to accept all the historical variability of the representations of faith as they have

137.   Cf. *ibidem*, p. 232.
138.   Cf. *ibidem*, p. 233.
139.   Cf. *ibidem*, p. 235.
140.   Cf. *ibidem*, p. 238-239.
141.   Cf. *ibidem*, p. 254.

factually occurred in history.

Historicity, even of the concept of dogma, does not simply explain everything away. It is possible that there may be a true evolution from the simple and undifferentiated toward the more complex and, to that extent, more useful function of the concept and word. The concept, dogma, has since the Reformation and the various doctrines of the reformers at least left no doubts in the minds of the faithful as to what was Catholic teaching and what was not. Therefore, it has at least served the process of clarification.

The highest qualification of a statement of faith, "de fide definita," might in the future pass into disuse; that remains to be seen. It will, however, have served its purpose in protecting and preserving and outlining the faith through some centuries of controversy.

Granted that there is room for such a science as the hermeneutics of dogma which in part seeks to clarify the meaning of a particular dogmatic pronouncement within its historical context, and others have begun this,[142] Nolte fails to take cognizance of the fact that at times the Church is obliged to speak forth its faith clearly, unmistakeably, and authoritatively. That is to say, with such authority that it absolutely requires assent as a condition of communion. This has happened too often in history to need recounting here. Thus the tone and occasionally also Nolte's expression is wrong, as when he categorically states: "Streng genommen fällt dann auch der sensus dogmatum nicht mit den dogmata und die fides nicht mit den dogmata fidei ineins. Es

---

142. *Cf.*, for example, the articles by J. P. Rudder, B. van Iersel, P. Schoonenberg, P. Fransen, W. C. H. Driessen, in Piet Schoonenberg, ed., *Die Interpretation des Dogmas*, (Düsseldorf, 1969).

entschärft die im Vulgärkatholizismus zumeist als sakrosankte Hypostasen dargestellten und gedachten Dogmen erheblich, wenn man sieht, dass sie nach der Lehre des Vatikanum I nur Ausdruck, nicht Sache des Glaubens sind."[143] From the very nature of language any expression can only be a particular expression of a dogma, but is that expression which is defined because only some such particular expression delimits some one aspect of the total truth, which then becomes not only 'expression' but also 'matter of faith.'

True, Nolte does give passing acknowledgment to the validity of previous credal and dogmatic formulae,[144] but his category of the meta-dogmatic and its supposed and asserted superiority to the purely dogmatic is unsatisfactory. It presumes some type of faith-life which cannot at all be asserted in propositional form. What this superior type of faith representation might be remains a mystery (Nolte gives no concrete examples) and will probably stay so since all truly human experience is representational in speech (propositional) forms albeit most imperfectly. Despite Nolte's unquestionable intellectual vigor, one senses the low church attitude that fellowship is more important than doctrine, particularly well thought-out and expressed doctrine.

Nolte's over-critical work does perhaps prove a service in calling attention to the lack of balance on the scholastic and manualistic side ("maximalists" he calls theologians of this ilk). Such theology has been too interested in placing as many propositions as possible under the

---

143. Nolte, *op. cit.*, p. 82. True, on p. 84 Nolte gives a more balanced description of dogma: "Die Dogmen könnten dann ...als die geschichtlich-notwendige und geschichtlich-kontingente Verwirklichung der auf anderer Ebene befindlichen Glaubens betrachtet werden..." Unfortunately the cutting edge of Nolte's criticism is more often expressed in statements such as the former.
144. *Cf. ibidem*, pp. 84, 257.

magisterial cloak of "de fide definita," and of raising other statements which somehow touch the faith to the highest possible dogmatic note. The "minimalist" position of Veron, Chrismann, and Döllinger has after all been sufficiently criticized elsewhere.

Obviously the truth lies somewhere between these two extremes in an attitude which accepts the dogmatic decisions of the Church for what they are -- historically conditioned teachings directed at historically conditioned crises of faith, to be accepted with the "submission of faith" on the precise questions to which they were addressed, but never as the totality of faith. Thomas Aquinas' definition of the articulus fidei, "Perceptio divinae veritatis tendens in ipsam,"[145] contains a valuable reminder for all dogma and dogmatic expression. It can only be a small "perception" of a many-splendored thing.

We do not here develop a criticism of Nolte's erroneous presumption that the early history of the word, "dogma," yields only a negative result. This will, however, be a theme of chapter four of this work.

---

145. II-II-1-6; *cf*. Walter Kasper, *Dogma unter dem Wort Gottes*, (Mainz, 1965), p. 105.

15.   CRITICAL DISCUSSION IN TERMS OF THOUGHT FORMS

According to the three historians of dogma, Harnack, Loofs, and
Seebert, the development of the Trinitarian dogma represents a Hellenization of the original content of revelation. According to Harnack this
is a corruption. Loofs views it as the camouflaged introduction of
polytheism into Christianity. Seeberg interprets the experiential
expression of the doctrine of the Trinity in early Christianity as a
"heilsökonomisch" matter until the conceptual formulation of the dogma
with the Cappadocians leaves "den Boden religiöser Erfahrung," and the
dogma becomes only another "metaphysischer Lehrsatz."

Behind each of these solutions looms the problem of thought forms,
i.e., the problem of whether individual thought forms are suitable or
not to bring out the truths of revelation. L. Scheffczyk interprets this
reality, "dass es sich bei der Denkform um ein formales, das Denken des
Menschen strukturierendes Prinzip handelt, das als Gestaltgesetz den
Gedanken ihre eigentümliche Pragung, ihren Stil und Rhythmus verleiht."[146]
Because thought forms are original modes of experience they are not in
themselves imaginable without some content. They are not shells in which
is to be found a kernel of truth. They are rather the peculiarity of a
whole world-outlook, the determinations of which stamp the general
directions, main ideas and general truths of that Weltanschauung. They
correspond to the ingenuous and indigenuous experience of self and of
world in a particular culture.

It is not to be overlooked that not every type of thought form is
without further qualification suitable as a means of expression for the

---

146.   "Die Einheit des Dogmas und die Vielheit der Denkformen," *MThZ*,
1966 (17), p. 259.

truths of revelation. Subsequent to the study of a thought form there arises the question as to whether it represents a viable possibility for the "dynamics" of a particular part of revelation. For example, it seems to this author doubtful that the personalistic thought form, the I-Thou relationship as popularized by Martin Buber is a suitable means for representing the relationship between man and God in the Jewish-Christian tradition. The reason for this is that it in no way suggests the infinite expanse between man and God.

A thought form is suitable to give expression to a particular dogma when it is able to bring out the "grundlegenden Sinn des Dogmas." "Dieser Sinn ist die geistige Mitte, die jede Glaubensaussage besitzt und die dem gläubigen Denken prinzipiell greifbar sein muss, sei es in der betreffenden Aussage selbst, sei es im Hinblick auf den Zusammenhang mit anderen Glaubenswahrheiten auf Grund der analogia fidei."[147]

Certainly it is true to say that a Hellenization has taken place in the ancient Church. Yet the right question is whether this process was a corruption, or to what extent it was justified. When the Council of Nicea used the word "homoousios" to give expression to Jesus' relationship to his Father, a word was introduced into the vocabulary of orthodoxy which was not biblical. The discussion at that time necessitated the use of such a concept so utterly foreign to the biblical revelation in order to clear up the question in dispute. Arias and Athanasius had held differing views of the place of Jesus in relation to God, and both claimed to base their positions on the scriptures. It was then no longer sufficient simply to repeat the formulations which can be found in scripture. In order that the truth of revelation could be preserved it was unavoidably

147. *Ibidem*, p. 240.

necessary to use a word which unambiguously expressed the sense of the scriptures.

In a sense the process leading to the making of this dogma through the official introduction of a certain term represents what Karl Rahner has called a "Sprachregelung," a "regulation of speech."[148] In regulating the manner that man should talk about the mystery orthodoxy determined how man addresses himself to the mystery. The regulation of speech character of this process is especially clear from the fact that a council of Antioch in 268 had condemned Paul of Samosata for his use of the same word, "homoousios," in an unorthodox sense. Paul had, of course, used the word in a sense different from that adopted at Nicea. Although the details of his argumentation at that council at Antioch can no longer be ascertained with clarity, the best interpretation of his thought is given by Basil of Ancyra, according to which Paul is said to have understood the word, "homoousios," in the sense that Father and Son had only one being (solitarium atque unicum sibi esse patrem et filium praedicabat).[149]

It is possible to judge the introduction of Greek concepts into Christianity as a corruption, as Harnack and Loofs do or, with greater justification one can agree with R. Seeberg's words: "Nicht die Hellenisierung', Romanisierung oder Germanisierung an sich korrumpieren das Christentum, diese Formen bezeugen an sich nur, dass die christliche Religion in den betreffenden Epochen selbständig durchdacht und angeeignet worden und dass sie Bestandteil der Kultur der Völker geworden

---

48.   "Was ist eine dogmatische Aussage?" in *Schriften zur Theologie*, V, (Köln, 1964), p. 68.
49. *Cf.* J. N. D. Kelly, *Early Christian Creeds*, (London, 1960[2]), p. 247ff.

ist."[150]

If one were to insist that the essence of the Christian message can
only be preserved in the expression of the bible (Harnack sees the
Hellenization process beginning already with the apostle Paul!), it would
always be illegitimate to speak the biblical message in words other than
biblical terms. (If a person were logical with this argumentation, one
would even have to preach the gospel in the language of its inspiration
-- koiné Greek.) Therefore, it is legitimate to translate the original
language and expression of revelation into the notions of other languages
and cultures.

Since every language carries its own outlook on reality, every
translation will perforce represent at least a partial deformation. What
is expressed in one language can never be completely and sufficiently
translated into another language. A clear example of this inadequacy of
expression in translation is the place in the Vulgate, Eph 5:32, where
the word μυστήριον is translated into Latin as "sacramentum." In this
case there simply was no corresponding Latin word for the Greek μυστήριον
and all its attendant denotations. Indeed, the basic meaning of
"sacramentum" which is "oath," does not even correspond to the basic
meaning of μυστήριον, which is "secret rite."

Apart from basic meanings every language is rich in its own
connotations. Therefore, every translation, even the most perfect,
remains only an approximation.

On the other hand it is completely impossible to grasp intellectually some spiritual reality without at the same time giving expression
to it in the terms of some language. So Martin Heidegger writes: "Nur

---
150. Seeberg, *op. cit.*, vol. 1, p. 3.

insofern der Mensch spricht, denkt er."[151] And no language can exhaust
the reality about which it speaks except perhaps mathematics in which the
definition of a certain geometric figure is the perfect expression of its
being. When on the contrary a certain concrete reality is given
expression, such as even the relationship of Christ to his Father, no
single word, not even the word, "Son," can bring out the totality of
Jesus' relationship to his Father.

Consequently, when the bishops at Nicea decided for the word,
"homoousios," to express the relationship between Father and Son and
to preserve the true sense of the Catholic faith, there was also to some
extent a disfiguration of the biblical thought forms. For this Greek
expression omits the narrative concreteness and vividness of the bible.

Nevertheless, it is biased and unjustified to suppose that every
such translation of biblical thought forms represents a corruption. Such
a translation represents rather a plus factor insofar as now the scriptural data assumed a degree of philosophical exactness which was lacking
in the original expression. The homoousios brought clearly to expression
what was only implied in the scriptures. The word points to the fullness
of the biblical content which until then was not universally recognized.

One can characterize further the differences between the Hebrew and
Greek ways of thinking. So it is sometimes said that the Hebrew or
biblical way is historical, existential, personal, dynamic, concrete,
oriented towards happenings; the Greek way on the contrary is substantial,
essential, logical, static, abstract, a-historical, cosmic.

Thorlief Boman points more cogently to the differences as stemming
from the fact that place is the more usual thought form of the Greek way,

151. *Was heisst Denken?*, (Tübingen, 1954), p. 51.

whereas time is the more usual thought form of the Hebrew way:

> Wie der Raum die gegebene Denkform für die Griechen ist, so die
> Zeit für die Hebräer. Nun ist aber die Zeit, wie sogar Kant sagt,
> nichts anderes als die Form des inneren Sinnes, d.i. des Anschauens
> unserer selbst und unseres inneren Zustandes.... Daraus folgt,
> dass das Denken der Hebräer notwendig psychologisch wurde, denn
> Psychologie befasst sich ja gerade mit uns selbst und unseren
> inneren Zuständen und Vorstellungen. Dann ist aber ebenso notwen-
> dig gegeben, dass das griechische Denken logisch geprägt wurde,
> denn die logische Gesetzmassigkeit steht äusserlich (objektiv)
> fest, unabhängig von unseren seelischen Zuständen....
> Die entscheidende Realität der Erfarungswelt war für die Hebräer
> das Wort, für die Griechen das Ding. Doch hatte das Wort auch für
> die Griechen wegen seines Sinnes grosse Bedeutung. Der Sinn ist
> aber zum grossen Teil von dem Wort als gesprochene und synamische
> Realität unabhängig.... Das Ding (hatte) grosse Bedeutung auch für
> die Hebräer, nicht wegen Form, Gestalt und Aussehen, sondern teils
> als Gerät, d.h. als Mittel zum Handeln, teils wegen seines
> inhärierenden Sinnes.... Im ersten Fall wurde das Ding als dynam-
> ische Realität, im zweiten Fall als eine qualitative, inhaltlich
> bestimmte Einheit erfasst.
> .... Weil die Griechen überwiegend visuell, die Hebräer überwie-
> gend auditiv veranlagt waren, gestaltete sich allmählich die
> Wirklichkeitsauffassung der beiden Völker so verschieden.
> .... Wie unsere beiden Hauptsinne, Gesicht und Gehör, ihre
> erstaunlichen Leistungen mit dem Preise einer ausgeprägten Einseit-
> igkeit haben bezahlen müssen, haben auch die beiden hochstehenden
> Altertumsvölker, Hellas und Israel, ihre erhabenen Beiträge zur
> Weltkultur nur wegen ihrer Einseitigkeit leisten können. Wir, ihre
> geistigen Nachkommen und Erben, können sie nicht höher ehren, als
> beider Erbschaften gleich zu achten und zu bewahren und, wenn
> möglich, ihre Synthese zu finden.[152]

At the end of his long study, "Hellenisierung -- Judaisierung des

Christentums," A. Grillmeier asks himself the question which thought form

is the more suitable to bring to expression the truth of the gospel. In

answer he states, "dass hier nur von den vortheologischen Haltungen

beider Völker die Rede ist. Wenn wir nun rein auf das Volkstum und die

natürlichen Vorgegebenheiten bei Israel und Hellas sehen, so scheint es

erlaubt zu sein, zu sagen: sie standen -- aufs Wesentliche gesehen --

beide dem Evangelium gleich nah und gleich fern. Genauso wie die

---

152. *Das Hebräische Denken im Vergleich mit dem Griechischen*,
      (Göttingen, 1954), pp. 166-168.

Offenbarung in Israel nur eine beschränkte irdische Form fand und notwendig finden musste, um darin erstmals der Menschheit gegeben zu werden, so konnte sie in Hellas und Rom und kann sie in jeder Kultur unter der Rücksicht der Form neue Möglichkeiten der Verkündigung und Deutung finden."[153]

If this is so, then the judgment of Harnack, that the expression of the basic truths of Christianity in the speech and thought forms of Greek philosophy was a corruption is not only one-sided, it is a position of genuine prejudice. Harnack lacked the balance of judgment necessary to see that every transmission into another cultural form represents a certain plus factor as well as a disfigurement. Moreover, not every expression of what is in the gospel can bring to the fore all that is in the gospel.

It is remarkable that Nicea did not make use of the logos concept since this concept is already to be found in the Gospel of John. One would think that this biblical use of this Greek term would have prejudiced the fathers of Nicea to prefer it to the non-biblical homoousios. But this is not what happened, for the logos concept could also be interpreted in an Arian sense as well as in the genuine biblical sense. Therefore, the Council had to find a word which would exclude the adoptionism of Arias.

The suggestion of Loofs that the original monotheism obtained a light economic-trinitarian color through the introduction of the eons of vulgar paganism and gnosticism does not explain why there was expansion only to three persons. If Christianity was uncritically assimilating

---

153. *Scholastik* 33 (1958), p. 557.

elements from these other movements in the spirit of syncretism, it would have been consonant to expand its theology to other intermediary beings, as was common in polytheism. But the triad had a foundation in the cannonical scriptures which represented a certain boundary to any Hellenization process. Thus, the Councils of Nicea and Constantinople were able to set the proper boundaries between the genuine Christian tradition and polytheistic movements of the time. It would, however, have been a complete Hellenization if Christianity had accepted the eons and melted into the syncretistic stream of the times.

In conclusion it may fairly be said that to represent the growth of the Trinitarian dogma as a Hellenization in a depreciatory sense demonstrates lack of understanding for an historical process which has until now not found its equal. This is so because even to this twentieth century no other thought form has been able to displace the Greek, which is still determinative for the greater part of the Christian churches.

PART TWO

HISTORICAL STAGES IN THE DEVELOPMENT OF THE CATHOLIC
UNDERSTANDING OF DOGMA IN RELATIONSHIP TO THE QUESTION
OF ITS BEGINNING

CHAPTER FOUR

THE CONCEPT OF DOGMA IN HISTORY AND THOUGHT

1. INTRODUCTION

In the introduction to his essay, "Der Begriff des Dogmas in der
Alten Kirche,"[1] Martin Elze maintains, quoting W. Elert,[2] that, "Eine
einfache Wortanalyse mit Hilfe des antiken Sprachgebrauchs, von der
hierbei gewöhnlich ausgegangen wird, kann nicht zum Ziel führen. Denn
was haben die Dogmata, die Seneca als solche bezeichnet, mit dem Dogma
der christlichen Kirche zu tun? ....Wir haben hier auch ein erstes
Beispiel dafür, dass man die in der Theologie notwendigen Begriffe nicht
einfach nach ihrem 'biblischem' Gebrauch definieren kann." The articles
on dogma by O. Weber,[3] A. Deneffe,[4] J. Ranft,[5] (among others) cannot
possibly, Elze declares, achieve their goal because the usage of "dogma"
in the churches today "als Antwort der Kirche auf die Offenbarung
Gottes," that is, "Bekenntnis,"[6] is so very different than its usage in

1. *ZThk* 61 (1964), pp. 421-438; quote p. 421.
2. *Der christliche Glaube*, (1956³), p. 35f.
3. *Grundlagen der Dogmatik*, I, (1955), p. 44.
4. *Scholastik* 6 (1931), pp. 381-400, 505-538.
5. *RAC*, III, (1957), cols. 1257-1260.

the ancient Church. Elze even implies that J. R. Geiselmann's article,

"Dogma," in the *Handbuch Theologischer Grundbegriffe*,[7] is guilty of the

following dislocation: [Die historische Fragestellung] "darf aber ...

nicht in der Weise zum Auge gebracht werden, dass man in den Begriff ohne

weiteres schon bei seinem anfänglichen Vorkommen die Definitionselemente

seines modernen Gebrauches hineinlegt und seine Bedeutungsgeschichte dann

eben nur noch als deren Explication verstehen kann."[8]

More recently Walter Kasper also points to the disparity between

current church usage of the notion of dogma and that of former times:

"Wir stehen also vor dem zunächst überraschenden Tatbestand, dass ein

für das heutige Denken in der katholischen Kirche so zentraler Begriff

wie Dogma erst seit dem achtzehnten Jahrhundert in der katholischen

Theologie und erst seit dem neunzehnten Jahrhundert im offiziellen

Sprachgebrauch der Kirche im heute üblichen Sinn verwendet wird."[9]

Elze maintains that, corresponding to the transitive meaning of

dogma -- "glauben, meinen," and the intransitive meaning -- "'(gut)

scheinen' woraus die Bedeutung 'beschliessen,'" there were likewise two

specific and independent usages of the concept.

> Δόγμα als 'Meinung' wird zum Ausdruck für eine Lehrmeinung im
> Sprachgebrauch der Philosophie, δόγμα als 'Beschluss' wird im
> Sprachgebrauch des Rechtes zum Ausdruck für eine öffentlich
> erlassene verbindliche Verordnung. Man hat sich diesen Sachverhalt
> ähnlich vorzustellen wie beispielsweise bei dem deutschen Wort
> Urteil, das sowohl im Sinn des logischen Urteils wie in dem des
> Gerichtsurteils zum stehenden Begriff innerhalb der philosophischen
> und der Rechtssprache geworden ist. Beide Bedeutungssphären stehen
> unverbunden nebeneinander. So ist bei anderweitigem Vorkommen des
> Wortes jeweils zu fragen, an welche dieser beiden Bedeutungen

---

6. *Cf.* W. Pannenberg, "Was ist eine dogmatische Aussage?" in *KuD* 8
   (1962), p. 81.
7. Vol. I, (1962), pp. 225-241.
8. Elze, *op. cit.*, p. 422.
9. *Dogma unter dem Wort Gottes*, (Mainz, 1965), p. 37.

angeknüpft wird. Eine besondere religiöse Verwendung des Begriffs δόγμα tritt daneben auf griechischem Boden nicht ein und ist dort auch nicht denkbar.[10]

We find it necessary to pose two questions: namely, whether Elze's opinion that there is a certain exclusivity between the philosophical and legal meanings of δόγμα is conclusive, and whether a religious use of the concept in Greek is not also demonstrable. We do agree with Elze that a simple consideration of the word's etymology and biblical usage will not unfold the meaning of the concept as it has been used in historical Christianity. However, there is a thread of meaning and sense of the word which ties its earliest etymology and biblical usage with modern church history, and which we believe enhances its meaning and gives cause for a meaningful usage of the word today.

2. DOGMA IN ITS "SECULAR" MEANING

Kittel gives as the most fundamental meaning of the noun, δόγμα: "τὰ δεδογμένα (μοι) was als richtig erschienen ist."[11] Then he lists five usages: (a) "opinion"; (b) the special philosophical meaning of "opinion," "tenet," or "principle," "teaching"; (c) what has been determined, the decision of a single person or of a group; (d) usually the emphasis lies upon the fact of publication of a decision as, for example, from a king or ruler: (e) in Hellenistic Judaism the divine institution of the mosaic law, as in 3 Mac 1:3. The closeness of this usage to that of (b), "teaching," is evident. So, the Torah may be compared to the "dogmas" of philosophy as a system of the holy teachings of a divine

---

10. Elze, *op. cit.*, pp. 422-423.
11. "Δόγμα, δογματίζω," in *Theologisches Wörterbuch zum Neuen Testament*, II, pp. 233-235.

philosophy, as Josephus does.[12]

The verb, δογματίζω, corresponds completely to the meanings of the noun.

Joseph Ranft summarizes nicely: "Δόγμα kommt von δοκέω, meinen, glauben, wähnen, scheinen, beschliessen. Dies Verbum drückt also zunächst die subjektive Überzeugung aus, dann aber auch die daraus erwachsende objektive Festsetzung."[13]

Plato speaks of "dogmas of the rulers": τοῖσ τῶν ἀρχόντων δόγματι.[14] He speaks also of the state as a place to live for a grouping of men who have common "dogmas": πόλις οἴκησις πλήθους ἀνθρώπων κοινοῖς δόγμασι χρωμένων.[15]

In an inscription from Halasarnae on the the island of Kos from about 200 B.C. the "determinations of the people's assembly" is mentioned: τοῖς δόγμασιν τᾶς ἐκκλησίας.[16]

Aristotle speaks of the "so-called unwritten dogmas" of Plato: ἐν τοῖς λεγεμένοις ἀγράφοις δόγμασιν.[17]

Justin Martyr remarks in this connection: "If we say that everything is ordered and has come to be from God, we shall give the impression of repeating a dogma of Plato": Πλάτωνος δόξομεν λέγειν δόγμα.[18]

Irenaeus writes: "Omnes a Simone haeretici initia sumentes, impia

---

12. *Antiquities*, 15, 136.
13. "Dogma," in *Reallexikon für Antike und Christentum*, (Stuttgart, 1957), III, col. 1257.
14. *Politics*
15. *Definitions*, p.415, C; quoted in Deneffe, *ibidem*.
16. Dittenberger, *Sylloge Inscript. Graec.*, II³, n. 569, 18, p. 67; quoted by Deneffe, *op. cit.*, p. 388.
17. *Physics*, 4, 2; quoted in Deneffe, *op. cit.*, p. 390.
18. *Apology*, 1, 20, 4 (MG 6, 357C); quoted in Deneffe, *ibidem*.

et irreligiosa dogmata induxerunt in hanc vitam."[19]

Another apologist, Athenagoras of Athens speaks also of the "dogmas of the philosophers": τὰ δόγματα τῶν φιλοσόφων.[20]

The usage of "dogma" in a somewhat derogatory tone for the teachings of the philosophers or other teachings not in particular harmony with Christianity is common among Christian writers. For example, Jerome writes: "Confer huiusmodi doctrinam [evangelicam] dogmatibus philosophorum."[21] And Augustine writes: "Quicumque dogmatizat et affirmat humanum sibi ad vincenda peccata et Dei mandata facienda sufficere posse naturam.... anathema sit."[22]

Even in Thomas Aquinas we find: "Et ad hoc quidem Apollinaris Laodicensis tria dogmata posuit, ut Leo Papa dicit in epistola quadam ad Constantinopolitanos.... In qua quidem dogmate Appolinaris secutus est Arium. ....Unde propter haec dogmata damnatus est Apollinaris in Concilio Constantinopolitano; et Eutyches, qui eius tertium dogma secutus est, in Concilio Chalcedonensi."[23] But Aquinas can also write: "Sed pestifera dogmata non sunt, nisi illa quae opponuntur dogmatibus fidei...."[24]

Deneffe mentions that in the book entitled, *De Historia Philosophia*, and which was falsely attributed to Galenus, four directions are to be found among the philosophers: the dogmatic, the skeptic, the eristic, and the mixed. This does not, however, prevent each group

19. *Adv. Haer.*, 2 praef. 1; quoted in Deneffe, *ibidem*.
20. *Leg. pro Christi*, 6 (MG 6, 902A); quoted in Deneffe, p. 388.
21. *Comm. in Evang.*, Mt 1, 2, c. 13 vers. 32 (ML 26, 90B); quoted in Deneffe, p. 389.
22. *Epist.*, 175, 6 (ML 33, 762); quoted in Deneffe, p. 397.
23. De Unione Verbi Incarnati, in *Quaestiones Disputatae*, I, corpus.
24. II-II, q. 11, a. 2, sed contra.

from having its own "dogmas."[25]

Deneffe mentions further that, "Das II. allgemeine Konzil von Konstantinopel 553 wirft dem Theodor von Mopsuestia vor, das er Christus mit Plato, Epikur, Marcion vergleiche und sage, wie jeder von diesen sein Dogma erfunden und seine Schüler nach seinem Namen habe benennen lassen, so habe auch Christus sein Dogma aufgestellt": ὥσπερ ἐκείνων ἕκαστος εὑράμενον οἰκεῖον δόγμα.[26]

Finally, even Pope Leo XIII used "dogma" in this deragotory way: "Tanta est inter eorum [Socialistarum] prava dogmata et purissimam Christi doctrinam dissensio, ut nulla maior existat."[27]

3. DOGMA IN SCRIPTURE

The word "dogma" occurs in the Greek or Latin translations of the Old Testament a varying number of times, depending on which translation is being consulted. For example, Swete's edition of Theodotion's translation it occurs twelve times,[28] always with the meaning of "order," "dispensation," or "law"; whereas in the Septuagint (also in Swete's edition), the word is only used once, namely in Daniel 6:12 & 13.[29] Δογματίζω occurs in this translation twice, namely in Dan 2:13 and 2:15. In both cases it means "to order."

The variance in usage is also illustrated in Theodotion's reading of Dan 2:13: καὶ τὸ δόγμα ἐξῆλθε. The Aramaic has אֲזָת. The Vulgate

---

25. Diels, *Doxographi Graeci*, (Berlin, 1879), p. 604, 5; 604, 2; quoted in Deneffe, *op. cit.*, p. 389.
26. Canon 12, Denzinger-Schönmetzer, *Enchiridion Symbolorum*, 435; quote is from Deneffe, *op. cit.*, **p.** 390.
27. *Quod Apostolici* from December 28, 1878, (*AAS* 11 (1878), 372; quoted from Deneffe, *op. cit.*, p. 400.
28. Cambridge, 1905.
29. *Cf.* Deneffe, *op. cit.*, p. 383.

reads: "et egressa sententia." Yet Jerome uses δόγμα in other places in the Vulgate, for example, in Esth 4:3 and in Job 13:4. In Esther it means "order," in Job "teaching." Again, what in Theodotians"s reading of Dan 6:15, τὸ δόγμα Μήδοις καὶ Πέρσαις, and in Aramaic is דת, is in the Vulgate, "lex Medorum atque Persarum."

The word δόγμα is found in the New Testament five times: in Lk 2:1, Eph 2:15, Col 2:14, and in Acts 16:4 and 17:7. Alexandrinus has it also in Heb 11:23: οὐκ ἐφοβήθησαν τὸ δόγμα τοῦ βασιλέως. However, Nestle-Aland and seemingly all others today read here the hapaxlegomenon διάταγμα.[30] In either case the meaning is clear and the same: "the edict (order) of the king." The same is true of Lk 2:1: ἐξῆλθεν δόγμα παρὰ Καίσαρος Αὐγούστου.

The places in the epistles and Acts where δόγμα occurs give rise to more speculation regarding its meaning. Kittel even says that here, "Einen besonderen Ton gewinnen Nomen und Verbum."[31] His reference is to the practice in Hellenistic Judaism of referring to the mosaic law and its requirements as δόγματα.

Although there is some room for excluding τοῖς δόγμασιν from Col 2:14, which reads, ἐξαλείψας τὸ καθ'ἡμῖν χειρόγραφον τοῖς δόγμασιν ὃ ἦν ὑπεναντίον ἡμῖν, and of excluding ἐν δόγμασιν from Eph 2:15a, which reads, τὸν νόμον τῶν ἐντολῶν ἐν δόγμασιν καταργήσας,[32] the authorities for said exclusions are very weak. It is, of course, more reasonable to follow the lectio difficilior, although said exclusion for the Colossians passage would certainly make it grammatically easier. For τοῖς δόγμασιν

---

30. E.g., Wettstein, (Amsterdam, 1752); Tischendorf, (Leipzig, 1872); Merk, (Rome, 1964).
31. *Theologisches Wörterbuch*, II, p. 234, under δόγμα.
32. *Cf.* the footnotes to the two passages in Nestle-Aland, *Novum Testamentum Graece et Latine*, (Stuttgart, 1963²⁵).

is most easily understood as a dative of instrument.[33] But then the
passage would have to be translated in somewhat the following fashion:
"He has done away with the document of guilt against us by his dogmas
(teachings)."

Kittel rejects such an understanding (i.e., instrumental dative)
because of the contextual relationship with Col 2:20, 'where the verbal
form, δογματίζεσθε is used and where the word obviously has reference to
the "regulations" of the mosaic law. Thus, the usual way of trans-
lating this text understands a dative of reference instead of the
instrumental dative, and the text relates logically to the stipulations
of the mosaic law. So, for example, the Kleist-Lilly translation of
Col 2:14 (with verse 13): "At that time when death had come to you from
your sins and your lack of physical circumcision, God brought you to
life with Jesus, when he forgave you all your sins, and canceled the
bond with its decrees that was against us."[34]

It seems that we can add yet another reason for rejecting an
interpretation (*i.e.*, translation) supposing a dative of instrument --
the context, at least in meaning with Eph 2:14b-15a, ἐν τῇ σαρκὶ αὐτοῦ
τῶν νόμον τῶν ἐντολῶν ἐν δόγμασιν καταργήσας, since it is here obviously
said that Christ did not "remove the law of ordinances by dogmas
(teachings)," but that he "removed the law of ordinances in 'stipulations' in his flesh." The real "in the flesh" (ἐν σαρκί) conception
Paul has of Christ precludes any pseudophilosophical or docetic manner
of expression when speaking of the redemption and physical reality of
Jesus.[35]

---

33. Kittel, *op. cit.*, p. 234.
34. *The New Testament*, (Milwaukee, 1956).
35. *Cf.* Rom 1:3, 8:3, 9:5; 1 Tim 3:16.

138

Nevertheless, Chrysostom understands this passage of Colossians as a dative of means and writes, τοῖς δόγμασι, φησί. Ποίοις δόγμασι; τῆ πίστει.[36] Theodoret understands the passage in the same way: ἔδωκε δὲ ἡμῖν τὰ εὐαγγελικὰ δόγματα, ἐν τῆ τουτῶν φθλακῆ τὴν σωτηρίαν ἡμῖν ἐπαγγειλάμενος.[37]

These two ecclesiastical writers of the school of Antioch agree once again in this interpretation of Eph 2:15, but here Chrysostom is undecided over the correct understanding. He writes: ἢ τὴν πίστιν οὐκ φησι, δόγμα αὐτὴν καλῶν· ἀπὸ γὰρ πίστεως μόνης ἔσωσεν· ἢ τὴν παραγγελίαν, καθὼς ἔλεγεν ὁ Χριστός· ἐγὼ δὲ λέγω ὑμῖν, μηδὲ ὀργισθῆναι ὅλως.[38] Theodoret writes to the same text of Ephesians: δόγματα δὲ τὴν εὐαγγελικὴν διδασκαλίαν ἐκάλεσιν.[39] We must, however, on the basis of the internal reasoning from the text (context) , and from the physical and real mode in which Paul habitually expresses himself, conclude that the interpretations of these two eminent ecclesiastical writers relative to the respective texts are incorrect and that they do not represent the literal sense of the texts.

The two passages in Acts in which δόγμα appears are also easily translated with "order," "ordinance," or "decree." So Acts 17:7: καὶ οὗτοι πάντες ἀπέναντι των δογμάτων Καίσαρος πράσσουσιν. So also Acts 16:4: Ὡς δὲ διεπορευοντο τας πολεις παρεδίδοσαν αὐτοῖς φθλασσειν τὰ δόγματα τὰ κεκριμένα ὑπὸ τῶν ἀποστόλων καὶ πρεσβθτέρων τῶν ἐν

---

36. *Hom. in Eph.*, 5, (MG 62, 340); quoted by Deneffe, *op. cit.*, p. 385. *Cf.* footnote number 5 to Kittel's article in *ThW*, p. 234: "Bengel zu kol 2,14: haec sunt decreta gratiae; zu Eph 2, 14: per quae proponebatur misericordia in omnes...."
37. *Interpretatio Epis. ad Coloss.*, (MG 82, 612b); quoted in Deneffe, *op. cit.*, p. 385.
38. *Op. cit.*, (MG 62, 39); quoted in Deneffe, *op. cit.*, p. 385.
39. *Op. cit.*, (MG 82, 524b); quoted in Deneffe, *ibidem.*

Ἱεροσολύμοις.

In these two passages from Acts there is, of course, no question
of the apostles in Jerusalem making a statement as to what the faith of
the Church is. Their concern is a practical one, namely, under what
conditions would converts from paganism be admitted to the community of
the faithful.[40] Nevertheless, W. Kasper points out that although it is
true that the point at issue here is not one of faith, the decision
taken is not without importance to subsequent development. "Trotzdem
ist der lukanische Bericht indirekt nicht ohne Bedeutung für eine
neutestamentliche Begründung dogmatischer Entscheidungen in der Kirche.
Er verweist uns auf eine Urentscheidung in der apostolischen Kirche, die
konstitutiv für das Sein und die Einheit der Kirche war."[41] J. R.
Geiselmann even calls it the "Urtyp des Dogmas," because it has to do
with a "Glaubensfrage," namely, whether the gentiles could be accepted
into the Church without being subjected to the Jewish ceremonial law.[42]
Kasper continues his thought: "Diese Urentscheidung zur Kirche aus Juden
und Heiden, die Entscheidung über das Verhältnis von Gesetz und Evangelium zeigt, dass zur Kirche vollmächtige Entscheidung im Heiligen Geist
und damit Dogma gehört."[43] Yet, we must also add that in so far as the
word, δόγματα, itself is used in Acts 16:4, "decisions" suffices as a
fully adequate translation. For the "decisions" are those "which were
decreed by the apostles and elders in Jerusalem."[44]

By way of conclusion it can be therefore said that δόγμα as used

---

40. *Cf.* Acts 15:1-29.
41. Kasper, *op. cit.*, p. 29.
42. Geiselmann, *op. cit.*, p. 226.
43. Kasper, *op. cit.*, p. 30.
44. The decretal action of the Council of Jerusalem is more often
     expressed by the cognate verb, δοκέω; *cf.* Acts 15:22 & 28.

in the scriptures always means "order," "ordinance," "decision,"
"decree," or "stipulation," with the one exception of the Vulgate Job
13:4, where it certainly means "teaching." Eph 2:15 and Col 2:14 which
might seem to support a popular usage of the concept of dogma are seen
from the literal meanings of the texts to be inconclusive in this regard,
and that although Chrysostom and Theodoret both used them in this way.
Their interpretations reflect not the literal meanings of the texts, but
very probably the already incipient usage of the term with the Church
for teachings of faith.

4. DOGMA IN RELIGIOUS USAGE THROUGH THE THIRD CENTURY.

Although it is true that in earliest Christianity "dogma" seems to
have been often used for moral commandments, the falsity of Elze's contention that a special religious usage of the word is not to be found in
Greek becomes patent through a simple listing of some of the texts
collected by Deneffe.

Among the Apostolic Fathers a rigid line of demarcation between
moral and doctrinal prescriptions is not made. Both are included under
the δόγματα Χριστοῦ. Such a theological demarcation is without doubt a
later development. Yet its elements, in both moral and doctrinal
teaching, are already witnessed from the earliest times in connection
with the word, "dogma."

Ignatius of Antioch writes to the Magnesians: Σπουδάσατε οὖν
βεβαιωθῆναι ἐν τοῖς δόγμασι τοῦ Κυρίου καὶ τῶν ἀποστόλων, ἵνα πάντα,
ὅσα ποιεῖτε, κατευοδωθῇσηται, σαρκί τε καὶ πνεύματι, πίστει καὶ ἀγάπη.[45]
This is the earliest example of the appearance of "dogma" where it
_____
45. _Ad Magnesios_, 13, 1 (MG 5, 776A).

141

clearly means both moral and doctrinal teaching. J. R. Geiselmann

obviously goes too far when he denys that the text refers to moral

prescriptions at all.[46] This is clear from the context in which Ignatius

immediately beforehand speaks of humbling oneself, as did Abraham and

Job, and because he points to the two ways of πίστις and of ἀγάπη. This

form of dividing the apostolic teaching is also found in his letter to

the Ephesians (9, 1), and seems to be an incipient line of demarcation

between revealed moral and doctrinal traditions.[47]

Athenagoras speaks of the "dogmas taught and spoken by God": δὲ

αὐτῶν τῶν δογμάτων οἷς προσέχουεν, οὐκ ἀνυρωπικοῖς οὖσιν, ἀλλὰ θεοφάτους

καὶ θεοδιδάκτους, πεῖσαι ὑμᾶς μὴ ὡς περὶ ἀθέων ἔχειν δυνάμεθα.[48] An

example of such a divine dogma Athenagoras gives in Christ's saying, "I

say to you, 'Love your enemies.'" Once again, no sharp demarcation is

made between moral and dogmatic teaching.

Clement of Alexandria continues this usage when he mentions the

Christian gnostic, who "has grown old in the scriptures, living according

to the apostolic and ecclesiastical correctness of the dogmas":

'Ογνωστικὸς ἄρα ἡμῖν μόνος, ἐν αὐταῖς καταγρηράσας ταῖς Τραφαῖς, τὴν

ἀποστολικὴν καὶ ἐκκλησιαστικὴν σῴζων ὀρθοτομίαν τῶν δογμάτων, κατὰ τὸ

Εὐαγγέλιον ὀρθότατα Βιοῖ.[49] This whole body of teaching, which Deneffe

sees as the "Gesamtheit der geoffenbarten Glaubens- und Sittenlehre,

vielleicht mit Einbeziehung der rein kirchlichen Lehre,"[50] "is

---

46. Geiselmann, *op. cit.*, p. 226.
47. *Cf.* Deneffe, *op. cit.*, p. 505: "Die Apostel aber predigten sowohl
    Glaubenslehren als geoffenbarte Sittenlehren. Daher wird das ἐν
    τοῖς δόγμασιν ....mit Recht übersetzt: 'in den Lehren', nämlich in
    den Glaubenslehren und den geoffenbarten Sittenlehren."
48. *Suppl. pro Christ.*, 11, 1; quoted from Deneffe, *op. cit.*, p. 506.
49. *Strom.* 7, 16, (MG 9, 544AB).
50. Deneffe, *op. cit.*, pp. 506-507.

preserved," Clement says, "by the Gnostic who lives entirely according to the gospel."

Origen continues this usage when, for example, comparing Christ, the founder of the "saving dogmas," with Moses, the lawgiver of the Hebrews: περὶ Μωσέως καὶ Ἰησοῦ Χριστοῦ, τοῦ νομοθέτου τῶν Ἑβραίων, καὶ τοῦ εἰσηγητοῦ τῶν κατὰ Χριστιανισμὸν σωτηρίων δογμάτων.[51] Deneffe mentions also other places in Origen where dogma is used in a wider sense as, for example, for the whole gospel: τί δὲ ἄτοπον τὸ ἀρχὴν τοῦ ἡμετέρου δόγματος, τουτέστι τοῦ εὐαγγελίου, εἶναι τὸν νόμον.[52]

5. SOME FURTHER OCCURRENCES OF DOGMA BEFORE THE SIXTEENTH CENTURY

In the fourth and fifth centuries the same general lack of distinction between teachings of faith and of morals continues with Eusebius (+ 340), the historian. He speaks of the εὐσεβείας δόγμασιν which determine the lives of Christians,[53] and also of the ἐκκλησιαστικὸν δόγμα in reference to the teachings of immortality and of the resurrection of the dead: τὰ περὶ ψυχῆς ἀθανασίας καὶ νεκρῶν ἀναστάσεως ἐκκλησιαστικὰ δόγματα.[54] Eusebius uses the latter phrase also for decrees of a purely ecclesiastical nature: πάντες τε μιᾷ γνώμῃ δὲ ἐπιστολῶν ἐκκλησιαστικὸν δόγμα τοῖς πανταχόσε διετυποῦντο, ὡς ἂν μηδ᾽ ἐν ἄλλῃ ποτὲ τῆς Κυριακῆς ἡμέρα τὸ τῆς ἐκ νεκρῶν ἀναστάσεως ἐπιτελοῖτο τοῦ Κυρίου μυστήριον.[55]

---

51. *De Princ.*, 4, 1 (MG 11, 344A).
52. *Contra Celsus*, 2, 4 (MG 11, 802B); *cf.* Deneffe, *op. cit.*, pp. 507-508.
53. *Hist. Eccl.*, 1, 4, 4 (MG 20, 77B).
54. *Ibidem*, 3, 26, 4 (MG 20, 272C).
55. *Ibidem*, 5, 23, 2 (MG 20, 492A).

Cyrill of Jerusalem entitles the fourth book of his Catechesis,
Περὶ τῶν δέκα δογμάτων.[56] The first of these has to do with God: Πρῶτον
τοίνυν ὑμῖν τῇ ψυχῇ τεθεμελιώσθω δόγμα τὸ περὶ θεοῦ, ὅτι ὁ θεὸς εἷς ἐστι
μόνος, ἀγέννητος, ἄναρχος, ἄτρεπτος, ἀναλλοίωτος.[57]

Gregory of Nyssa distinguishes clearly between dogmas of faith and
moral doctrine: Διαιρῶν γὰρ εἰς δύο τὴω τῶν Χριστιανῶν πολιτείαν, εἷς τε
τὸ ἠθικὸν μέρος καὶ εἰσ τὴν δογμάτων ἀκρίβειαν, τὸ μὲν σωτήριον δόγμα ἐν
τῇ τοῦ βαπτίσματος παραδόσει κατησφαλίσατο· τὸν δὲ βίον ἡμῖν διὰ τῆς
τηρήσεως τῶν ἐντολῶν αὐτοῦ κατορθοῦσθαι κελεύει.[58]

Cyrill of Alexandria is also conscious of this distinction: Μυρία
γὰρ ὅσα ἐννοῆσαι τις ἄν διὰ τῆς τοῦ Σωτῆρος ἡμῶν ἰσχύος πεπληρῶσθαι
θαύματα· γεγράφασί γε μὴν τῶν Εὐαγγελίων οἱ κήρυκες τὰ ἐν τοῖς γεγονόσι
λαμπρότερα, κατά γε τὸ εἰκὸς, καὶ δι᾽ ὧν ἦν μάλιστα τοὺς ἀκροωμένους
δύνασθαι βεβαιοῦσθαι πρὸς πίστιν τὴν ἀπαράφθορον, καὶ παίδευσιν ἔχειν
ἠθικήν τε καὶ δογματικήν, ἵνα πίστει μὲν ὀρθῇ διαπρέποντες, ἔργοις δε
τοῖς εἰς εὐσέβειαν βλέπουσι πολυτρόπως ἠγλαισμένοι.[59]

To Jerome's use of dogma in a derogatory sense we have already
referred. He also uses the expression in a positive sense, as in
referring to some works of Origen: "Quid ibi de dogmatibus ecclesiae
dicitur? Quid de Patre et Filio et Spiritu Santo? Quid de carnis
resurrectione? Quid de animae statu atque substantia? ....Nihil ibi de
fide, nihil de dogmatibus comprehensum est. Moralis tantum tractatur
locus et allegoriae nubilum serena expositione discuitur."[60]

---

56. MG 33, 453.
57. *Ibidem*, 4, 4 (MG 33, 457B).
58. *Epist.*, 24 (MG 46, 1089A).
59. *In Joan.*, 21, 25 (MG 74, 756C).
60. CV 55, 121, 13ff. (ML 22, 744); quoted from Deneffe, *op. cit.*,
    p. 514.

Vincent of Lérin's (c. 434) equating dogma with the depositum fidei is well-known: "Crescat igitur oportet et multum vehementerque proficiat tam singulorum quam omnium, tam unius hominis quam totius ecclesiae, aetatum ac saeculorum gradibus, intelligentia scientia sapientia, sed in suo dumtaxat genere, in eodem scilicet dogmate, eodem sensu eademque sententia."[61] And, "Christi vero Ecclesia, sedula et cauta depositorum apud se dogmatum custos, nihil in his unquam permutat, nihil minuit, nihil addit."[62]

The semi-pelagian, Gennadius of Marseilles (+ c. 500) authored a work entitled, *De Ecclesiasticis Dogmatibus*.[63] It is a summary of doctrine and treats of the trinity, the homoousion, the resurrection of the dead, immortality, original sin, the sacraments, etc. The word, "dogma," does not seem to occur in the text.

For the period from the 8th to the 15th century Deneffe lists examples for the use of the concept of dogma, but they are not illustrative of any significant change.[64] So from the Spanish adoptionist bishops of the 8th century: "Nos igitur e contrario secundum sanctorum venerabilium patrum Hilarii, Ambrosii, Augustini ...et ceterorum orthodoxorum atque catholicorum dogmata confitemur et credimus Deum Dei filium ante omnia tempora sine initio ex patre genitum, coaeternum et consimilem et consubstantialem, non adoptione, sed genere."[65]

The scholastics use the word very little. Bonaventure apparently never uses it. We have already quoted Thomas Aquinas using it in both a

---

61. *Commonitorium*, 23 (ML 50, 668A).
62. *Ibidem*, (ML 50, 669C).
63. *Corpus Haereseologici*, I, edit., Franciscus Oehler, (Berlin, 1856).
64. *Cf*. Deneffe, *op. cit.*, pp. 517-519.
65. Letter of 792 or 793; *Mon. Germ. Conc.*, II, 111, 32; (ML 101, 1322D); quoted from Deneffe, *op. cit.*, p. 517.

derogatory and a positive way. Thomas also opposes dogma to heresy: "Haeresis est infidelitatis species, pertinens ad eos, qui fidem Christi profitentur, sed eius dogmata corrumpunt."[66] And in his hymn, "Lauda Sion": "Dogma datur christianis, Quod in carnem transit panis, Et vinum in sanguinem." Obviously dogma did not just denote the teaching of faith to Thomas, and it certainly was not tied to authoritative definition. Deneffe says in reference to Thomas: "Es bezeichnet einen Gattungsbegriff und ist durch Zusätze näher zu bestimmen. So braucht es auch der hl. Bernhard, wenn er in einem Brief (*Epist.* 189, 4 (ML 182, 355C) an Papst Innozenz II. schreibt, es sei Aufgabe der Bischofe, über die Dogmen zu erteilen: 'quorum esset ministerii, de dogmatibus iudicare.'"[67] One must, however, in this connection study the medieval concept of articulus fidei.

6. ARTICULUS FIDEI

Although the word, "dogma," was used occasionally by the medieval theologians in the general sense of "doctrine,"[68] it was not restricted to a revealed doctrine which has to be believed. The medievals used another expression, the "articulus fidei," which seems to a great extent to have taken the place of the modern notion of dogma.[69] The Apostles'

---

66. II-II, 11, a. 1.
67. Deneffe, *op. cit.*, p. 519.
68. *Cf.* J. M. Parent's remark relative to St. Thomas' usage in I-II, q. 11, a. 1: "Haeresis est infidelitatis species, pertinens ad eos qui fidem Christi profitentur, sed ejus dogmata corrumpunt": "C'est l'usage le plus typique, car c'est précisément son rapprochement avec la notion d''hérésie' qui entraînera le mot, dans son évolution sémantique, vers un sens ecclésiastique." -- "La Notion de dogme au XIIIe Siècle," in *Études d'Histoire Littéraire et Doctrinale du XIIIe Siècle*, (Ottawa, 1932), p. 141, footnote 1.
69. "Posé en termes généraux, le problem de l'articulus fidei n'est autre que celui des rapports entre l'Ecriture Sainte et le dogme

Creed served as a summary of the faith. Its individual propositions were known as the "articuli fidei." In his article, "Articulus Fidei. Eine begriffsgeschichtliche Arbeit," Ludwig Hödl sketches from his study of many unpublished medieval manuscripts the broad lines of thought surrounding this notion, and which await a more thorough investigation.[70]

Two derivations are given for the concept, "articulus." Praepositinus, chancellor of the University of Paris from 1206 until 1209, is the first author mentioned by Hödl to have used this notion: "...translatum est enim hoc nomen articulus ab articulis digitorum."[71] For him, as for his successor, Philip le Chancelier (+ 1236), it denoted the smallest unit that could be grasped by a finger joint, and hence the smallest unit -- "minimum in suo genere," which could be treated in any faculty. So Philip: "Articulus dicitur secundum proportionem eorum que inveniuntur in aliis facultatibus; utitur enim hoc nomine grammatica, rethorica, phisica. Sed in unaquaque facultate articulus docitur minimum in suo genere. Ergo minimum in credibilibus erit articulus."[72] Others, as for example, Alexander of Hales, sought to derive the notion from the Latin "arctare," "to force" or "to coerce," because the articuli fidei coerce one to believe.[73] In addition to these two possible derivations of the articuli fidei, Philip lists two other meanings: "Magister Hugo de

---

.... L'article de foi se trouve à l'interférence de ces deux données de fait: les innombrables énoncés de l'Écriture et les vérités délimitées par les symboles." -- J. M. Parent, *op. cit.*, p. 142. *Cf.* St. Thomas, II-II, 1, 9, "Utrum convenienter articuli fidei in symbolo ponantur."

70. In: *Einsicht und Glaube, Gottlieb Sohngen zum 70. Geburtstag*, edits., J. Ratzinger and H. Fries, (Freiburg, 1962), pp. 358-376.
71. *Summa Theol.*, p. III, Cod. lat. 65, Todi, fol. 110 va; quoted by Hödl, *op. cit.*, p. 348, footnote 3.
72. *Summa*, Paris, Nat. lat. 15749, fol. 85^c; quoted from Parent, *op. cit.*, pp. 156-157, footnote 6.
73. *Cf.* Parent, *op. cit.*, p. 153, and Hödl, *op. cit.*, pp. 367-369.

Sancto Victore definit sic: Articulus est natura cum gratia. Item

aliter: articulus ist praeceptio veritatis divinae tendens in ipsum."[74]

Hugo's definition, Philip says, can claim no general validity. It

reflects the theological program of the Victorines, seeking to illustrate

the relationship of God's grace manifesting its uniform self in the

creation and in the redemption.

Philip attributes to the definition of articulus fidei as,

"perceptio veritatis divinae tendens in ipsum," a greater validity. It

points to the teaching function as well as the virtue (theological)

function of the articles of faith. Not every truth about God is,

however, an articulus fidei. Philip gives as an example for one that is

the scholastic thesis, "Christum esse aliquid secundum homo," which

"Quaestio" denoted the incarnation. The favorite derivation from

"arctare" points to the obliging character of the articles, which

depends not on their translucence to human reason, i.e., to philosophy

or to historical facticity, but to the fact that they are revelation,

communication of divine truth, teaching handed on from the apostles.

So, the individual members of the Apostles' Creed are known as the

"articuli fidei." As such they are the first principles of the science

of faith, of theology.

Hödl summarizes the thinking of the early scholastics:

> 1. Der articulus fidei ist eine unteilbare Grösse der Glaubens-
> lehre, eine Bedeutungseinheit der fides, welche Prinzipien-
> Charakter hat, und zwar sowohl für den Glauben der Väter wie für
> unseren Glauben. 2. Der articulus fidei ist seinem Wesen nach
> Unterweisung, Offenbarung der Wahrheit; als solcher hat er den
> Charakter der doctrina. 3. Der Glaubensartikel verpflichtet zum
> Glauben, und zwar so, dass sich diese Glaubenspflicht auch auf das

---

74. *Summa de Bono,* Cod. Lat. 192, Toulouse, fol. 80rb. Cod. Lat. 66,
     Oxford, Magd. Coll., fol. 118ra. Quoted from Hödl, *op. cit.,* p. 367.

erstreckt, was in den _articuli_ _fidei_ miteingeschlossen ist.[75]

Transcending the analyses, etymologies, and definitions his predecessors had made of the articulus fidei, St. Thomas is the first to
distinguish it according to its particular difficulty, i.e., its "ratio
specialis."[76] "Illud quod habet specialem difficultatem in fide, et
cujus suppositio non dependet ab alio supposito, proprie dicitur
articulus fidei."[77] In the _Summa_ Thomas explains more at length how the
articles are distinguished by reason of their objects:

> Et ideo ubi occurrit aliquid speciali ratione non visum, ibi
> est specialis articulus: ubi autem multa secundum eandem rationem
> sunt incognita, ibi non sunt articuli distinguendi. Sicut aliam
> difficultatem habet ad videndum quod Deus sit passus, et aliam
> quod mortuus resurrexit: et ideo distinguitur articulus resurrecti-
> onis ab articulo passionis. Sed quod sit passus, mortuus et
> sepultus, unam et eandem difficultatem habent, ita quod, uno
> suscepto, non est difficile alia suscipere: et propter hoc omnia
> haec pertinent ad unum articulum.[78]

"Mais le dogme ne s'adresse d'abord à l'intelligence que pour
mieux engager tout l'homme."[79] And it is Thomas' peculiar genius to call
attention to the religious character of the articuli fidei in showing
how they situate man in relation to his last end and the eschatological
hope of Christianity. Considering in general the object of faith
(Quaestio 1 of the II-II), and addressing himself in particular to the
question as to whether those things to be believed should be distinguished in certain articles (articuli), he writes: "Quia vero fides
principaliter est de his quae videnda speramus in patria, secundum illud
Heb. 11, 1: 'Fides est substantia sperandarum rerum'; ideo per se ad

75. Hödl, _op. cit._, p. 370.
76. It is Parent who says that Thomas is the first. _Vd._ Parent, _op._
    cit., p. 158.
77. _III Sent._, d. 25, q. 1, a. 2, ad 6.
78. II-II, 1, 6, corpus.
79. Parent, _op. cit._, p. 158.

fidem pertinent illa quae directe nos ordinant ad vitam aeternam: sicut
sunt tres Personae, omnipotentia Dei, mysterium incarnationis Christi, et
alia huiusmodi. Et secundum ista distinguuntur articuli fidei."[80]

In Thomas' thought human life is ordained toward the attainment of
happiness, which reveals itself as the contemplation of the divine.
Therefore, the articuli fidei, insofar as they relate man in faith to
his last end, are really the "substantia sperandarum rerum." "Illud
proprie et per se pertinet ad objectum fidei per quod homo beatitudinem
consequitur."[81] They are not only an anticipation of the final state of
man in the eschatological end-time, they are also the principles of
Christian wisdom. To quote J. M. Parent once again: "Parce qu'ils
ordonnent la vie humaine à la 'fruition divine', les dogmes commandent
l'orientation de notre activité entière vers la béatitude, et, à ce
titre, ils sont, dit saint Thomas, les principes de la sagesse chrétienne,
de cette 'sagesse' qui dirige la vie non seulement selon les raisons
humaines, mais aussi selon les raisons divines: 'Initium sapientiae
secundum ejus essentiam sunt prima principia, quae sunt articuli
fidei'."[82]

The above quote demonstrates that Parent believes he establishes
the equivalence of dogma and articulus fidei. His work is indeed
characterized by the effort to reconcile the rather modern notion of
dogma and the medieval notion of articulus fidei employed by St. Thomas.
In this we must point out that his essay in harmonization falls short of
the truth because he has not sufficiently taken into account the fact
that the status quaestionis considered by St. Thomas differs considerably

80. II-II, q. 1, a. 6.
81. II-II, q. 2, a. 7.
82. Parent, *op. cit.*, p. 159. Quote from Thomas: II-II, q. 19, a. 7.

from that of 1932.

The difference in the status quaestionis is perhaps most easily
demonstrated by listing the three summary points of A. Lang in his
consideration of the notion of articulus fidei in St. Thomas, with
particular attention to the last point.[83] In short, according to Lang:

1. Sicherlich muss der Glaubens artikel eine <u>unmittelbar</u>
formell von Gott geoffenbarte Wahrheit sein. Dieses Moment wird
von Thomas, wenn auch nicht mit ausdrücklichen Worten hervorgehoben,
so doch als selbstverständlich vorausgesetzt.... Dass besagt
eindeutig, dass nur Offenbarungswahrheiten zu den Glaubensartikeln
oder direkt zum Glauben gehören können,[84] dass aber nicht <u>alle</u>
Offenbarungswahrheiten daher zu rechnen sind.
2. Der volle Begriff des Glaubensartikels erfordert ein zweites
Moment, die fundamentale Bedeutssamkeit des Inhalts für den Glauben
und das Glaubensleben.... Da die in der Glaubenserkenntnis
begonnene übernaturliche Lebensbewegung in der Visio ihre Vollen-
dung und ihren Abschluss findet, so lässt sich vom Inhalt der
seligen Schau der wesenswichtige Inhalt des irdischen Glaubens
gewinnen.... Faktisch sind es die Geheimniswahrheiten, die sich
mit Gott und den Geheimnissen Gottes beschäftigen, die allein den
Inhalt der prima credibilia ausmachen können....
3. Aber nicht jede Offenbarungswahrheit, auch nicht jede
Glaubenswahrheit von Bedeutung, ist schon ohne weiteres ein
Glaubensartikel.... Dazu ist noch ein drittes Moment notwendig,
die Aufnahme in ein <u>Symbolum</u>. Die Glaubensartikel stehen beim hl.
Thomas noch in einem ganz innigen Verhältnis zu den kirchlichen
Symbola. Deshalb werden die Offenbarungslehren über die Eucharistie, die Sakramente, die Vorsehung nicht als articuli betrachtet
und die diesbezüglichen Einwände, die auf die Wichtigkeit dieser
Wahrheiten hinweisen, zu entkräften gesucht. In den Symbol-
wahrheiten, die durch die Aufnahme ins Symbolum in besonders feier-
licher und von keinem Gläubigen übersehbaren Weise von der Kirche
zum Glauben vorgelegt werden, sind alle heilswichtigen und für alle
glaubenspflichtigen Wahrheiten enthalten....[85]

---

83. "Die Gliederung und Reichweite des Glaubens nach Thomas von Aquin
und den Thomisten," in *Divus Thomas* (Fribourg), 20 (1942), pp. 207-
236, 335-346; 21 (1943), pp. 79-97.
84. As Lang points out, the articuli are a selection from the many
revealed truths which is necessary for the simple to obtain a grasp
of those truths which are necessary for the life of faith: "Veritas
fidei in sacra Scriptura diffuse continetur, et variis modis, et in
quibusdam obscure; ita quid ad eliciendum fidei veritatem ex sacra
Scriptura requiritur longum studium et exercitium ad quod non
possunt pervenire omnes illi quibus necessarium est cognoscere fidei
veritatem: quorum plerique aliis negotiis occupati studio vacare non
possunt. Et ideo fuit necessarium ut ex sententiis sacrae Scripturae

151

Revelation, importance, and reception into a creed -- these are the three qualities of the articuli fidei. From Lang's analysis it becomes clear that if there are subsequent dogmas, such as those which pertain to the sacraments,[86] which are not contained in the Apostles' Creed, then it is not correct to assume that the modern notion of dogma is equivalent to Thomas' notion of articulus fidei, which designated the individual members of that Creed. To do so is to misjudge Thomas' status quaestionis, for we have already seen his more common usage of dogma which is not in the refined sense of an articulus.[87]

Thomas' doctrine leaves, of course, room for the increase of the material object of faith either through decision of the supreme pontiff, "ad illius auctoritatem pertinet sententialiter determinare ea quae sun fidei,"[88] or through a council, which he calls a "synodus generalis."[89]

---

aliquid manifestum summarie colligeretur, quod proponeretur omnibus ad credendum; quod quidem non est additum sacrae Scripturae, sed potius ex sacra Scriptura sumptum." -- II-II, q. 1, a. 9, ad 1. To this text Lang states: "Für die Aufstellung der Glaubensartikel sind eben neben der Glaubensgewissheit didaktische Fragen und systematische Gesichtspunkte massgebend. Darnach geschah ihre Auswahl aus den Offenbarungswahrheiten." *Cf.* Lang, *op. cit.*, p. 220, footnote 4.

85. Lang, *op. cit.*, pp. 220-222.
86. *Cf.* H. R. Schlette, "Dogmengeschichte und Geschichtlichtigkeit des Dogmas," in *Geschichtlichkeit und Offenbarungswahrheit*, (München, 1964), p. 74: "Die theologischen Aussagen uber die Sakramentenlehre sind nicht in die bekannten Glaubensbekenntnisse (Symbola) eingegangen, so dass es keinen 'articulus fidei' gibt, der von den Sakramenten spricht. Hieraus ist zu schliessen, dass Dogmengeschichte mehr ist als die Geschichte der 'Glaubensartikel' und dass es verbindliche kirchliche Lehren gibt und geben kann, die im Wortlaut des Credo nicht erscheinen."
87. *Cf.* "Dogma," in *A Lexicon of St. Thomas Aquinas*, (Washington, 1948), pp. 337-338.
88. II-II, q. 1, a. 10, Leonine Edition. Earlier editions of the *Summa* have read "finaliter" in this passage instead of "sententialiter."
89. II-II, q. 1, a. 10.

7. DOGMA AS USED BY THEOLOGIANS FROM THE SIXTEENTH CENTURY
UNTIL THE PRESENT CENTURY

From the sixteenth century on there have been many theological works written and printed which use the word, "dogma," in their titles or in the course of their exposition. The majority of these works do not, however, attempt to define or delineate in any explicit fashion, precise or even descriptive, what their authors understood by this concept.

Careful study reveals, nevertheless, that there was a definite and traceable shift in the use and understanding of this term. In the following pages we shall survey some of the theologians, beginning in the sixteenth century, to illustrate how and why this change took place. The inclusion of a considerable number of Latin quotes in the text seems necessary in order that the reader may judge for himself the validity of our conclusions.

a. Ruard Tapper (1487-1559)

Ruard Tapper published in 1555-1557 his great work in controversial theology, *Explicationis Articulorum Venerandae Facultatis Sacrae Theologiae Generalis Studii Lovaniensis Circa Dogmata Ecclesiastica Ab Annis Triginta Quattuor Controversa, Una Cum Responsione Ad Argumenta Adversariorum*.[90] The perusal of this work shows that Tapper, indeed, one of the more notable theologians at the Council of Trent,[91] attached no special

---

90. Louvain, 1555-1557.
91. *Cf.* J. Mercier, "Tapper," in *DThC*, 15, cols. 52-54.

meaning to the word, "dogma," beyond that of Church doctrine in contro-
verted matters. That there is no special definition or solemnity to a
dogma at this time is evident from his discussion of the Tridentine
decree on the number of the sacraments where the word, "dogma," does not
even appear, although the later, more specialized meaning is clearly
intended. The decree in question is that first one of the Council on the
sacraments,[92] which later theologians would use as their principle "proof
text" in demonstrating that it is a dogma of divine faith that there are
seven sacraments.[93] Tapper writes:

> Et ne ulla in futurum de Fidei veritate apud Armenos fieret
> hesitatio, ut Acta testantur, sub quodam compendio, sacrosancto ·
> approbante concilio, Eugenius tradit orthodoxae Fidei veritate, et
> ita definit quidem firma Fide de Sacramentis credendum esse, et
> concilium Tridentum dicit anathema his, qui docent non esse septem
> Sacramenta gratiam conferentia, vel non habere virtutem sanctifi-
> candi ex opere operato, et quae Augustinus, et Patres de Sacra-
> mentis docent, ipsi in Ecclesia catholica prius didicerant, et
> ideo non suam, sed Ecclesiae tradunt doctrinam, quae columna est
> et fundamentum veritatis.[94]

A usage which Tapper occasionally employs and which demonstrates
that he attached no particular significance to the word, "dogma," is his
using it in referring to the opinions of the reformers. Thus: "Et
adversus impugnationem Martini Lutheri suum hoc dogma defendens, repetit,
quod originalis ista contagio non tale peccatum fit, quod culpam propter
peccatum ab Adamo admissum nobis adhaerere solet."[95]

    b. John Driedo (1480-1535)

One searches in vain in John Driedo's *De Ecclesiasticis Scripturis*

---

92.   *Vd.* Denzinger-Schönmetzer, *op. cit.*, 1601.
93.   *Cf.*, for example, Ludwig Ott, *Grundriss der Dogmatik*, (Freiburg,
      1963), p. 405f.
94.   Tapper, *Explicationis Articulorum*, articulus primus, p. 41.
95.   *Ibidem*, articulus secundus, p. 61.

et Dogmatibus,[96] so important for the Tridentine teaching on tradition,[97] for an explicit handling of the notion of dogma. At the beginning of the fourth book of this work, Driedo announces his theme: "In hoc libro disserendum est de dogmatibus, et traditionibus Ecclesiae, et conciliorum, de canonibus, constitutionibus et decretis pontificum et de libris sanctorum et doctorum patrum doctrinis, extra canonem scripturae sacrae constitutis, quam vim, efficaciam, et autoritatem habeant, an apocryphum fit, quicquid est extra canonem scripturae sacrae."[98]

In speaking of the various Church fathers and ecclesiastical writers, Driedo writes of their opinions (dogmata) as providing a precious commentary on the scriptures:

> Sed omnium horum dogmata sunt distinguenda ab auctoritate sacrarum literarum. Non enim sic scripta sunt, tanquam ex eis testimonium proferatur, ut aut dissentire, aut suspicari, aut dubitare non liceat, nec idcirco vera sunt ea, quia ipsi autores ita sentiunt, aut quia in eorum libris leguntur. Nam et ipsi tradiderunt quaedam, non tanquam sententias, quas ipsi firma fide crederent, sed tanquam pias opiniones, aut probabiles, aut versimiles, aut non contumaciter reiiciendas, quibus necessitati fidei impertinentes, aliquod tamen si vera supponantur, ad intellectum sacrarum literarum facientes.[99]

It is quite evident from this passage that Driedo uses the word, "dogma," in the general sense of doctrine, and in no way restricts it to matters of revealed faith.

---

96. Louvain, 1533.
97. *Cf.* J. L. Murphy, *The Notion of Tradition in Driedo*, (Milwaukee, 1959).
      J. Lodrioor in "La Notion de Tradition chez Driedo," in *EThL* 26 (1950), p. 41, gives this interpretation to tradition in Driedo: "Quant à la question de savoir si le terme traditiones recouvre adéquatement les dogmata extra canonem constituta, les vérités et les coutumes extra-scriptuaires, nous croyons pouvoir répondre par l'affirmative."
98. Driedo, *op. cit.*, p. 477.
99. *Ibidem*, Bk. 4, 1, p. 490. (This is the actual page. According to the erroneous pagination in the editio princeps the page on which this passage occurs is 496.)

Several other occurrences of "dogma" in the fourth book, which
depend on St. Basil's usage (*De Spiritu Sancto*, 27, 66), support this
conclusion.[100] For example: "Dogmata quae in ecclesia praedicantur,
quaedam habemus e doctrina scripto prodita, quaedam rursus ex Apostolorum
traditione in mysterio, id est, in occulto tradita recipimus, quorum
utraque parem vim habent ad pietatem, nec in his quisquam contradicit,
quisquis sane vel tenuitur expertus est."[101]

Driedo can, however, also use the word, "dogma," when he is speaking
of revealed truths: "...non enim omnia Christianae religionis dogmata
evidenter et dilucidae sunt in canonicis libris expressa, sed quaedam
clarius, quaedam autem obscurius." This is said in reference to the
heretics misinterpreting the scriptures: "Sic Arriani omnes scripturas
indicantes Christum esse verum Deum et hominem, et Novatiani omnes
scripturas indicantes post baptismum relapsis dandum esse reconciliati-
onis sacramentum, maligna interpretatione depravabant...."[102]

Driedo uses dogma then both for the general doctrine of the fathers
and of the Church, and at times for revealed truth; for him it is
important only that such dogma, or doctrine, be in the Church's tradition.

c. Melchior Cano (1509-1560)

Despite the theme of his work, *De Locis Theologicis*,[103] Melchior
Cano offers no systematic treatment of the notion of dogma. We can,

---

100.　Driedo quotes Basil: "Aliud autem est dogma, aliud edictum, nam
　　　dogmata silentur, edicta publicantur. Est enim silentii obscuritas,
　　　qua utitur scriptura, mentem ad contemplationem dogmatum inhabilem
　　　exercens, idquam ad utilitatem versantium in scripturis." -- *De
　　　Spiritu Sancto*, 27, 66.
101.　Driedo, *op. cit.*, Bk. 4, 5, p. 611.
102.　*Ibidem*, Bk. 4, 6, p. 629.
103.　Salamanca, 1563.

however, derive his understanding of dogma from the way he uses the word.

Dogmas are revealed: "Nam dogmata fidei sive Christus ipse per se Aposto-
is reuelarit, seu Spiritus sanctus post Christi Ascensionem in caelum,
mutari non possunt: sed firma haec in veritate manent perinde atque illa,
quae Christi sunt ore prodita."[104]

In discussing the function of ecumenical councils Cano clearly
distinguishes disciplinary decrees from matters of faith: "...non statim
si quicquam iuris Canonici volumine continetur, fidei dogma esse credendum."[103] And, "Id dicimus, nec omnia quae aut iuris aut conciliorum
volumina continent, doctrinae Christianae esse iudicia nec omnia rursum
doctrinae iudicia, fidei censuras esse. Multa siquidem ad sanam
ecclesiae disciplinam attinent, quae fidei decreta non sunt."[106]

Cano seems to make only two explicit statements on the dogmata
fidei. They must be apostolic: "Si quod fidei dogma patres ab initio
secundum suorum temporum successionem concordissime tenuerunt, huiusque;
contrarium ut haereticum refutarunt, quod tamen e sacris literis non
habetur, id nimirum per Apostolicam traditionem habet ecclesia.... Omnia
siquidem fidei dogmata ab Apostolis accepit Ecclesia, vel scripto, vel
verbo."[107] And, they are usually defined by council and pope, or by pope
alone, or are at least the expression of the constant and peacefully held
belief of the faithful: "Quodcumque dogma fidei vel ecclesia habuerit vel
concilium auctoritate Pontificis roboratum, vel etiam summus ipse Ponti-
fex fidelibus praescripserit, vel certe sancti omnes concordissime
constantissimeque tenuerint, ita nobis illud pro catholica veritate

---

104. *Ibidem*, 3, 5; p. 111.
105. *Ibidem*, 5, 5; p. 189.
106. *Ibidem*.
107. *Ibidem*, 3, 4; p. 109.

habendum est, ut contrarium sententiam haereticum sentiamus, quanvis nec aperte nec obscure in scriptura sacra contineatur."[108]

Cano understands dogma as a revealed truth, deriving from Christ or the Holy Spirit, which has always been held by the fathers in the vocal or written tradition of the Church,[109] and which has been defined by a general council or by the supreme pontiff. He who would hold the contrary opinion must be adjudged as a heretic.[110] This doctrine of Cano on the dogma fidei seems to be the earliest expression of the teaching on dogma which was adopted by the First Vatican Council.

Probably the explanation of why Cano does not offer a special treatment of the notion of dogma is that he was perhaps the first to use 'dogma' in this restricted sense, and the reflex thinking on his own thought process, which would be necessary for a special treatment, never occurred to him. Or, perhaps he was not conscious of accomplishing a shift in meaning significant enough from the earlier practice to merit a particular justification.

In any case, the changes from the wider, medieval notion of dogma as simply doctrine, and from heresy as any opposition to Church doctrine and discipline to the narrower concept of pertinacious opposition to revealed dogma, have taken place in Cano's thought. It is even possible

---

108. *Ibidem*, 12, 7; p. 416.
109. Cano is often listed as one of the strongest and first supporters of the two source theory (*i.e.*, of scripture and tradition as the two sources of revelation). This view seems to be short-sighted, for Cano does speak of the traditions of the Church thus: "At non sunt istae, ut diximus, scripturae additiones, sed interpretationes." *Cf.* Ulrich Horst, "Das Verhältnis von Schrift und Tradition nach Melchior Cano," *TThZ* 69 (1960), pp. 207-223.
110. *Cf.* Cano, *op. cit.*, 12, 9; p. 431: "Qua ex re intelligitur, pertinaciam eam, que hereticum facit, semper solumque in eo inveniri, quod dogma aliquod tenere pergit, cui cognoscit catholicam sententiam adversari."

158

in the controversial theological world, in which he lived and taught,
that these shifts took place unconsciously. The ground for this
assertion is that A. Lang has been able to establish that the wider,
medieval status quaestionis on matters of divine faith still reigned at
the Council of Trent, and this although Cano was a participant and
contributor to that Council.[111]

The *De Locis Theologicis* exercised a decisive influence on the
counter-reformation theology,[112] which was so clearly controversially
oriented and, to that extent, not always emphasized the more normally
central elements of Christian theology. That Cano's thought moved in
this arena of controversy is quite clear, for now dogma is a matter to
be defined by the Church: "Cum ergo is dubitaverit de uno quolibet
dogmate, quod in Scripturis invenitur vel ab Ecclesia definitum est, si
illi ostendas aut Ecclesiae definitionem aut Scripturae apertum dogma,

---

111. *Cf.* Lang, "Der Bedeutungswandel der Begriffe 'fides' und 'haeresis'
und die dogmatische Wertung der Konzilsentscheidungen von Vienne
und Trient," in *MThZ* 4 (1953), p. 142: "Diese Texte lassen erkennen,
dass die Synode einerseits bei den Offenbarungswahrheiten, die sie
beschäftigen, durchaus nicht ihren Glaubenscharakter (als fides
divina) eigens betonen will, dass sie andererseits sich nicht auf
das Gebiet des formell Geoffenbarten beschränken, sondern die ganze
Fülle des katholischen Glaubenslebens erfassen will."
112. Bertholdo Vogl discusses the "theological places" in his *Prolegomenon Sacrae Theologiae Seu Introductio In Theologiam Scholastico-
Dogmaticam,* (Salzburg, 1743), and illustrates how these 'places'
become the sources not only of explaining the faith, but also of
those arguments useful against the doctrines of the reform. So he
says (p. 54) that the locus theologicus "...esse sedem quasi, in
qua principia theologica conquiescunt, vel si mavis fontem, e quo
tanquam rivuli argumenta ebulliunt, ...tum, qua fidem explicare,
tum qua dogmata regulasque morum ponere, tum qua utrumque tueri
contra heterodoxorum assultus necesse habet. ....Nunc duo gener-
atim ponimus I. SACRAM SCRIPTURAM II. TRADITIONEM DIVINO-APOSTOLI-
CAM deinde tria subjungimus I. DECRETA CONCILIORUM OECUMENICORUM
II. DEFINITIONES ROMANORUM PONTIFICIUM III. UNIVERSALEM ECCLESIAE
ATQUE UNANIMEM SS. PP. CONSENSUM. ...."

necesse est illum aut dubium abiicere, aut credere, Ecclesiae Scripturas-
que testimonia incerta esse."[113]

d. Gabriel Vasquez (1549-1604)

Gabriel Vasquez discusses in his *Commentariorum Ac Disputationum*
In Sanctam Thomam the question whether it is necessary to confess after
committing a mortal sin before receiving the Eucharist: "...etiam ab
initio Ecclesiae necessariam ex praecepto semper fuisse confessionem
peccati mortalis commissi ante Eucharistiam praemittere. Deinde hoc
praeceptum non esse solum Eucharisticum, sed Divinum, simul cum ipsa
Sacramenti institutione a Christo traditum. Priorem partem huius senten-
tiae, quam in hoc capite confirmabo, non solum veram existimo, sed etiam
expresse definitam ut dogma fidei a Concilio Tridentin. sess. 17. cap.
illo 7. et cannone 11. ita ut, qui contrarium sentiret, aut doceret, non
solum excommunicatus, sed etiam haereticus esset."[114]

One sees in the above passage how the interest of theology has
swung in discussing the "veritates credendae" from the obligation to
believe to the question of a particular proposition's degree of
certainty.[115]

e. Francis Veron (1578-1649)

in the unsigned preface to the 1702 edition of Francis Veron's
(Veronius) *De Regula Fidei Catholicae Seu De Fide Catholica* there are
two interesting statements.[116] The first illustrates the now current

---

113. Cano, *op. cit.*, 12, 9; p. 429.
114. London, 1631. Quote: tertia pars, disputatio 207, caput 3.
115. *Cf.* Lang, *op. cit.*, p. 134ff.
116. Louvain, 1702. First edition: Paris, 1646, under **the** title, *Règle*

thinking on definition as being the usual complement to truths which must be held: "Sane fatendum est, hanc regulam eruditam admodum esse et accuratam, in qua et singulari diligentia et exactissima cura discernuntur ea, quae Fide Catholica tenenda sunt ab iis, quae tantam in Ecclesia auctoritatem nondum meruerunt." Immediately following is the other statement which encourages the reader to learn the difference between those teachings of faith which must be held, and those teachings for which a certain amount of liberty is still left to the individual believer: "Ea itaque utere, Lector benevole, et ex illa disce Ecclesiae Fidem, quam contra haereticos propugnare debes. Disce pariter, quae sint dogmata, quae hactenus non definivit Ecclesia."

These two statements from the pen of an unknown theologian of the eighteenth century witness to a stricter understanding of the notion of faith and of heresy than A. Lang was able to establish for the time of the Council of Trent, and to a correspondingly stricter notion of dogma than we have been able to establish before the time of the same Council. Here it is clearly implied that dogmas have to do with divine faith and not merely Church doctrine in the wider sense. The changing of the notion of heresy, i.e., the restricting of it to matters of divine faith is also evident here.

What is affirmed in the preface of the *De Regula Fidei Catholicae* is also Veron's teaching from the time of the first French edition of 1646. Because of it Veron has often been accused of Gallicanism and of minimalism in matters of faith.

Gen. De La Foy Cath. Separée De Toutes Autres Doctrines, Contenant Le Moyen Efficace Pour La Réduction Et Réunion De Ceux De La Religion Prétendue Réformée À L'Église Catholique. We cite the Latin edition of 1702.

Illud omne et solum est de Fide Catholica quod est revelatum in verbo Dei, et prepositum omnibus ab Ecclesia Catholica, Fide divina credendum. Neque refert, an illa propositio emanet ex Concilio aliquo universali, ex ejus decreto, et definitione; an ex sensu fidelium omnium.

Complectitur haec Regula verbum Dei: Nam fides ex auditu, auditus autem per verbum Christi. Complecitus et Ecclesiam docentem, in Concilio Catholico, hoc est universali, expresse aliquid definientem, aut enunciantem; vel ex sensu omnium tum Pastorum, tum fidelium velut practice eloquentem.[117]

It is certain that Veron's motivation in setting up the aforegoing rule in matters of faith was to make the Catholic Church and its teaching as palatable as possible to prospective converts.

Somewhat further in his text Veron expresses his belief that a doctrine of faith cannot be taught by the pope alone:

Nullae Decretales Romanorum Pontificum contentae in corpore Juris Canonici, sive in sex libris Decretalium, sive in Clementinis, sive in Extravagantibus, nullae Bullae posteriorum, qui in sede Petri sederunt, sufficientes sunt fundando articulo Fidei Catholicae: seu nulla doctrina est de Fide, quae continetur in istis Decretalibus aut diplomatibus. Probatur, quia Papa quocumque modo loquens, etiam ex Cathedra, non est universalis Ecclesia; ergo quod ab eo proponitur, non proponitur ab Ecclesia universali; ergo non est doctrina Fidei Catholicae.[118]

The narrower, modern notion of heresy is adopted by Veron: "...non esse de Fide Catholica, seu non esse doctrinam, quam omnes, quo sint Catholici tenere debeant, tanquam de Fide, cujusque contrarium sit haereticum, et removens a gremio Ecclesiae."[119]

Veron does not use the word, "dogma," in his definition of what is to be held as of Catholic faith, as did Melchior Cano. Yet the fact that he equated what is strictly of Catholic faith with dogma is evident from further reading:

Sed non inde sequitur, Ecclesiam per talem praxin proponere tanquam credendum de Fide Catholica aliquod dogma, sufficit praxin

---

117. Veron, *op. cit.*, pp. 1-2.
118. *Ibidem*, pp. 16-17.
119. *Ibidem*, p. 20.

162

proponere tanquam credendum de Fide Catholica aliquod dogma,
sufficit praxin essen bonam, cui bonitate satis est, quod fundetur
in opinione probabili; hinc, ut jam notatum tot praxes suas etiam
universales Ecclesia mutare potest. Praxes enim sunt variabiles,
utpote praecepta, nullo autem modo dogmata fidei, variari possunt,
quippe veritas invariabilis est.[120]

Veron quotes Vasquez and Bellarmine at length in support of the

theme of his opus -- the conscious restriction of the teaching and

binding authority of the pope to the essentials of faith. He also

teaches that the pope is not above a general council. As a controver-

sialist whose lifelong task was to persuade Christians away from the

churches of the reform, Veron's method of reducing the power of the

papacy to essentials is a most conciliatory attitude for a theologian

of the Counter-Reform.

     f. Philip Neri Chrismann (1751-1810)

    Philip Neri Chrismann continued the tradition of Francis Veron in

his *Regula Fidei Catholicae et Collectio Dogmatum Credendorum*, first

published in 1792.[121] That is to say, he also sought, out of regard for

the controversial situation of his day, to reduce the extent of the

Church's infallibility to the minimum. It was evidently for this reason

that his book was placed on the Index of Forbidden Books on January 20,

1869. The various editions of this book in the eighteenth century

witness to its popularity.[122] Chrismann's definition of dogma resembles

that of Veron: "...dogma fidei nil aliud fit, quam doctrina, et veritas

divinitus revelata, quae publico Ecclesiae iudicio fide divina credenda

---

120. *Ibidem*, p. 27.
121. Kempten, 1792.
122. Migne included the *Regula* in the *Theologiae Cursus Completus*,
     (Paris, 1841), vol. 6, cols. 877-1070. Spindler published it in
     Augsburg in 1844 and in 1846, and again in Würzburg in 1854. *Cf.*
     E. Mangenot, "Chrismann," in *DThC*, IIb, col. 2415.

ita proponitur, ut contraria ab Ecclesia tanquam haeretica doctrina damnetur."[123]

That a teaching may be proposed by the Church as dogma, it must be clearly revealed: "Ut igitur doctrina aliqua fit fidei catholicae dogma, seu articulus, necesse inprimis est, ut fit revelata a Deo per Christum, Prophetas, Apostolos, seu Auctores canonicos; sola enim revelatio fidem divinam fundat, ...omnem scilicet fidei divinae articulum Dei revelantis auctoritate pernecessario inniti."[124]

Miracles and visions after the time of the apostles which might be adduced as authority for believing particular doctrines with divine faith are explicitly rejected, as are also papal and conciliar authority. They would all lack the infallible revelation of God through his Son and the canonical authors. But is is a different thing for these authorities, particularly a council, merely to declare what has already been revealed, and must therefore be believed with divine faith as a catholic dogma: "Alterum igitur dogmatis catholici requisitum est, ut fit ab Ecclesia universa, vel in Conciliis generalibus repraesentata, vel in orbe disper-sa omnibus propositum fide divina credendum."[125] Here there is no question of a "new" doctrine, but only of the Church witnessing in an official way (even through her universal but ordinary teaching activity) to what is already revealed. Chrisman's notion of dogma is the common one since Vatican I. In his own time it was, however, regarded as minimalistic since he emphasizes the necessity of formal definition for dogma, and neglects the ordinary magisterium even more than Veron did. In the *Syllabus Errorum* Pius IX condemned a proposition which expressed

---

123. Chrismann, *op. cit.*, #5, p. 2.
124. *Ibidem*, #6, p. 3.
125. *Ibidem*, #9, p. 7. *Cf.* #12, #13, #14, pp. 10-14.

the tendency of both Veron and Chrismann's *Regulae*: "Obligatio, qua
catholici magistri et scriptores omnino adstringuntur, coarctatur iis
tantum, quae ab infallibili Ecclesiae iudicio veluti fidei dogmata ab
omnibus credenda proponuntur."[126]

g. Joseph Kleutgen (1811-1883)

Joseph Kleutgen, the theologian who was in part responsible for the
final version of the dogmatic constitution, *Dei Filius*, at the first
Vatican Council, had previously made his views on the subject of divine
faith clear in his work, *Die Theologie der Vorzeit*.[127] This work was
written as an attempt to restate the ancient faith against the opinions
of Hermes, Hirscher, and Günther. The first tract is entitled, "Von der
Glaubensnorm," and is in great part a critique of the minimalism of
Chrismann's *De Regula Fidei Catholicae*.

In this spirit Kleutgen writes: "Wenn nichts zum Glauben gehört,
als was die Kirche durch ausdrückliche Entscheidung festgesetzt hat; so
konnte man viele Jahrhunderte lang über die wichtigsten Geheimnisse und
Sittenlehren der Religion keinen Glaubensact erwecken, und jeder 'der
Ansicht folgen, die ihm nun eben die richtigste zu sein schien'."[128]

The heart of Kleutgen's argument against Chrismann is that he
limits too severely the ordinary magisterium of the Church. To the
contrary, all that is the object of faith which is recognized as revealed
by God.[129] However, not every truth which is revealed has also been
declared a dogma by the Church. In this way the Church does not make a

---

126. Denzinger-Schönmetzer, *op. cit.*, 2922.
127. Münster, 1853-1870, 3 vols.; 1867-1874², 5 vols.
128. *Ibidem*, vol. 1, (1867), p. 103.
129. *Cf. ibidem*, p. 106: Gegenstand des religiösen Glaubens überhaupt
     ist alles, was als von Gott geoffenbarte Wahrheit erkannt wird."

dogma, but can only declare as dogma what is already contained in revelation. Thus, there is much in revelation which is not dogma quoad nos, but no declared dogma which is not in revelation.

Indeed, there are many other truths of faith which are proclaimed in the Church as such, and which therefore have the qualities of dogmatic teaching and must be believed, although they have never been explicitly and precisely formulated.[130] For there have been many dogmatic teachings of great importance which were taught and believed for centuries before they were finally defined. Examples are teachings on the eucharist and other sacraments, on predestination and justification, on the necessity of good works, etc., which were first judged as dogma in a formal and judicial fashion at the Council of Trent. "Und eben weil dies niemand läugnen kann, ohne die katholische Kirche selbst zu läugnen, muss man auch zugeben, dass eine Lehre, die zu welcher Zeit es immer sei, als eine geoffenbarte allgemein gelehrt wird, für uns bloss hiedurch und abgesehen von aller kirchlichen Entscheidung zum Dogma wird."[131]

As a result, Chrismann's effort to reconcile those he considered heretics by minimalizing the content of faith, although praiseworthy in intention, must be rejected. It insufficiently reduces the object of

---

130. *Cf. ibidem*, pp. 106-107: "Alle Lehren, welche in der Kirche allgemein als Glaubenswahrheiten verkündigt werden, erhalten hiedurch, ganz abgesehen davon, ob wir auf anderem Wege sie als geoffenbarte und der Kirche überlieferte Lehren erkennen können oder nicht, die Eigenschaft dogmatischer Lehren. Wenn die Hirten der Kirche, sei es nun durch die Unterweisung, die sie selbst ertheilen, sei es durch jene, die in ihrem Namen und unter ihrer Aufsicht von der Geistlichkeit ertheilt wird, allgemein eine Lehre als Glaubenslehre verkündigen; so haben wir hierin ein thatsächliches Zeugnis der allgemeinen Kirche, dass diese Lehre in der ihr überlieferten Offenbarung, dem depositum fidei, enthalten ist, und es wäre reine Willkür dieses Zeugnis nur unter der Bedingung, dass es zugleich urkundlich von der Kirche formulirt sei, als vollgültig anerkennen wollen."
131. *Ibidem*, p. 108.

faith to controversial matters, and neglects the richness of dogmatic truth to be found in catechisms, in homiletic and ascetical works, and in instruction.[132]

8. DOGMA AS USED BY HISTORIANS UNTIL THE PRESENT CENTURY

a. The Tübinger Schule

1. Introduction

In this section we are concerned with the first formulation of dogmatic truth in its psychological relationship to revelation. Here there is no question of the authoritative or "Church moment" of dogma, but of its "phenomenological moment." By "phenomenological moment" we understand that first perception of a dogmatic truth in relation to and dependent on revelation. The "phenomenological moment" of dogma does not include revelation itself. Revelation is the act of God; dogmatic expression is the act of the human spirit. The question of the beginning of dogma is not only a question of the Church teaching in an authoritative way. It is also a question of the first perception of a truth in relation to revelation, which only subsequently can be grasped by the teaching Church as an expression of its constitutional inheritance.

It may seem strange to treat of the theologians of Tübingen in this section on the psychological origin of dogma. However, the school of Tübingen has one important contribution to make concerning the psychological beginning of dogma. It has consistently called attention to the "Gemeingeist" or "Gesamtsinn" in the body of the faithful as a principle factor in the development of dogma. This consciousness of

---

132. *Cf. ibidem*, p. 115.

revealed truth in the minds of the faithful and the perception of it as
a truth of revelation are completely necessary steps in the genesis of
that process which results in an authoritative pronouncement of the
teaching Church.

J. H. Walgrave remarks on the unbridgeable hiatus between theologians of such differing types as Marin-Sola and Newman. It is not only
the difference of outlook between the scholastic method of theology and
an historical viewpoint on the development of dogma; it is also the
difference between "the psychology of concrete, spontaneous knowledge,
and the scientific analysis applied to this knowledge afterwards."[133]
Practically the same could be said of the theologians of Tübingen, whose
characteristic it is to see in the problem of dogma's development the
historical forces in dialectical process with one another. Newman's
peculiar gift was to perceive even more deeply than the Tübinger
theologians the psychological moments involved in the development of
dogma.

It is perhaps meaningful to mention once again that, although
theologians like Möhler and Newman were primarily concerned with the
general problem of the development of dogma from the original depositum
fidei, they were not completely unaware of the other question -- the
development of dogma in the sense of its beginning. This problem they
treated only in a subordinate way.

When we speak here of the theologians of Tübingen we are certainly
not concerned with all of them, but with Johann Adam Möhler (1796-1838),
Johann Evangelist Kuhn (1806-1887), and Franz Anton Staudenmaier (1800-

---

133. *Newman the Theologian: The Nature of Belief and Doctrine as Exemplified in His Life and Works,* (London, 1960), p. 302.

1856).[134] Characteristic of the Tübinger Schule are certain fundamental

points of view which distinguish it clearly from scholastic theology:

(1) The Reality of dogmatic development is an historical process, and

not a purely logical one;[135] (2) The Church is looked upon as a living

organism which has a tradition which has developed, as an organism does

without changing its identity, in the course of time;[136] (3) This

development of the tradition takes place in the dialectic of historical

---

134. *Cf.* H. Fries, "Tübinger Schule," in *LThK* 10, cols. 390-392; and J.
      R. Geiselmann, *Die katholische Tübinger Schule: ihre theologische
      Eigenart*, (Freiburg, 1964).
135. *Cf.* J. S. Drey, "Vom Geist und Wesen des Katholizismus," in *Geist
      des Christentums und des Katholizismus: ausgewählte Schriften
      Katholischer Theologie im Zeitalter des Deutschen Idealismus und
      der Romantik*, edit. by J. R. Geiselmann, (Mainz, 1940), p. 195:
      "Das Christentum als eine positive göttliche Religion ist eine
      zeitlich Erscheinung, eine Tatsache. Als solche hat es eine Zeit,
      da es entstand, eine Zeit da, und eine Gestalt, in der es als
      göttliche Offenbarung gegeben ward. Aber keine Tatsache überhaupt
      ist momentan, d.h. keine erlischt und verschwindet in dem Augen-
      blick wieder, in dem sie entstand; sie greift vielmehr ein in die
      Reihe und das Zusammenwirken aller übrigen, breitet sich aus und
      hemmt oder beschleunigt, oder ändert ab ihre gemeinsame Wirkung in
      engeren oder weiteren Kreisen; dadurch erlangt sie ihre eigene
      Geschichte."
136. The notion of society as an organic structure with a life of its
      own is, of course, taken from the romanticism of the time. *Cf.*
      J. R. Geiselmann, *Lebendiger Glaube aus geheiligter Überlieferung:
      der Grundgedanke der Theologie Johann Adam Möhlers und der Kathol-
      ischen Tübinger Schule*, (Freiburg, 1966), pp. 124-125, quoting
      Franz Schultz, *Klassik und Romantik der Deutschen* I (1935), II
      (1940), (no page given): "Grundlegend ist für die Theologie des
      Grunders der Katholischen Tübinger Schule die Idee des Lebens. Sie
      ist der romantische Zentralbegriff. Denn 'was als zentralstes
      Gesetz Gangart alles philosophischen und menschlichen Suchens
      bestimmte, was man als ureigenstes Merkmal gegenüber Denken und
      Schaffen der Aufklärung empfand, ist in der deutschen Romantik die
      Idee des Lebens. Leben, die universalste Idee der Romantik, ist
      für sie aber nicht nur Strukturgesetz, nicht nur innere Form ihrer
      Weltanschauung, aus der sich Gestalt und Wesen der mannigfaltigen
      Wertgebiete von Kunst, Wissenschaft, Natur, Religion, Volk, Staat,
      entfächern, sie ist zugleich Mitte, an der als sinngebender Einheit
      die Mannigfaltigkeit der übrigen Ideenwelt in ihrem Umschwung
      zentripetale Attraktion findet.'"

process, i.e., usually through the appearance of the opposite teaching --
heresy;[137] (4) The life that is in the Church as an organism is the Holy
Spirit, who manifests himself in the body of the faithful. That is to
say, when there is a question of dogmatic growth, it will manifest itself
where the Holy Spirit and the life are -- in the body of the faithful and
in their consciousness or "Gesamtsinn."[138]

2. Johann Adam Mohler (1796-1838)

In a few words Mohler sketches his conception of the relationship
between formulas, dogmas, etc., and the inner life of Christianity. He
emphasizes the inadequacy of sentences and words which, although necessary, represent only poorly the life that Christianity is.

> Das Christenthum besteht nicht in Ausdrücken, Formeln und
> Redensarten, es ist ein inneres Leben, eine heilige Kraft, und
> alle Lehrbegriffe und Dogmen haben nur in so fern einen Werth, als
> sie das Innere ausdrücken, welches mithin als vorausgesetzt wird.
> Ja als Begriff, der immer beschränkt ist, umfasst und erschöpft er
> das Leben, das unaussprechliche, nicht und ist immer mangelhaft;
> aber als Leben ist es auch nicht mittheilbar, und kann nicht
> fixirt werden; das geschieht durch Darstellungen in Begriffen,
> durch Ausdrücke. Da aber die Lehrbegriffe, Dogmen u.s.w. Dar-
> stellungen eines bestimmten innern Lebens sind, und dieses selbst
> durch sie fixirt werden soll, so sind sie nicht gleichgültig,

---

137. Cf. J. R. Geiselmann, *Die katholische Tübinger Schule*, p. 60,
quoting J. S. Drey, *Kurze Einleitung in das Studium der Theologie*,
(Tübingen, 1819), #244, p. 163: "Das oportet et haereses esse (I
Kor. 11, 19) ist also eine dialektische Notwendigkeit, 'weil nach
einem allgemeinen menschlichen Gesetz die Wahrheit vollkommen nur
durch die Gegenüberstellung der Gegensätze erkannt wird. Damit ist
das verkündete bzw. das durch feierliches Urteil bestimmte Dogma
mit Bezug auf die nicht deutlich ausgesprochenen Offenbarungswahrheiten das Endstadium eines dialektischen Progresses bzw. einer
Entwicklung, hervorgerufen durch die realen Bewegungen von Ortho-
doxie und Häresie.'" *Cf.* J. A. Möhler, *Die Einheit in der Kirche*,
(Tübingen, 1825), #46, pp. 173-179.
138. *Cf.* Möhler, *ibidem*, #49, pp. 193-199, and Geiselmann, *Lebendiger
Glaube aus geheiligter Überlieferung*, p. 344ff.

sondern höchst wichtig."[139]

Möhler is certainly right in stating that Christianity and its reality is something more than its conceptual expression. Today it is even difficult to imagine how certain "intellectualist" tendencies could give such an impression. Today the contrast between life itself and its various expressions is so widely realized that his statement seems even perhaps a bit unnecessary. "...Aber als Leben ist es auch nicht mittheilbar, und kann nicht fixirt werden; das geschieht durch Darstellungen in Begriffen, durch Ausdrücke." The life itself, he says, is not communicable; its fixation, however, occurs in the various forms of speech in which it is expressed. These speech-forms are indeed necessary because they establish the norms of this inner life. "....die Lehrbegriffe, Dogmen u.s.w. Darstellungen eines bestimmten innern Lebens sind, und dieses selbst durch sie fixirt werden soll...."[140] It is seen then that Möhler has not really grasped the inner and completely necessary connection between perception and experience of the Word, and communication of life. This criticisim will, though, only become clear somewhat further on.

Möhler does not really put his finger on the phenomenology of the appearance of dogmatic formulas. His interest is rather in showing that the inner life of Christianity, a life brought about through the preaching of the gospel and the activity of the Holy Spirit, is something that cannot be completely grasped in formulas which, nevertheless, are expressions of that life and which tend toward its maintenance.

---

139. *Die Einheit in der Kirche, oder das Princip des Katholicismus,* (Tübingen, 1825), pp. 46-47.
140. *Ibidem,* p. 47.

In his *Symbolik* Möhler describes the process of dogma's becoming.[141]
It is the coming to clear consciousness of what has always been taught in
the Church, and this occurs through the appearance of the dogma-to-be's
antithesis. So it was Luther's teaching that justification comes about
through faith alone which occasioned the bishops collected at the Council
of Trent to consider in detail what the traditional teaching from St.
Paul and the fathers was. Without the antitheses (Gegensätze) provided
by Luther and the reformers, the clearer doctrinal definitions of Trent
would not have come to be.

This process of dialectic occurs in the living tradition of the
Church. What the individual teaches on his own must be weighed and
balanced against the common understanding in the social body that the
Church is.[142] For, "Die Kirche ist der Leib des Herrn, sie ist in ihrer
Gesammtheit seine sichtbare Gestalt, seine bleibende, ewig sich verjüng-
ende Menschheit, seine ewige Offenbarung."[143] And it is the "Gesammt-
verständnis," or "ecclesiastical consciousness," of this body which
constitutes tradition.[144]

This understanding cannot be separated from its contents. It is
the living Word in the hearts of the faithful. Yet there is a distinction between the teaching of scripture and the teaching of the Church.
They are one but they have differing forms.[145] Thus, one can also affirm

---

141. *Symbolik, oder Darstellung der dogmatischen Gegensätze der Katholiken und Protestanten nach ihren öffentlichen Bekenntnisschriften,*
(Mainz, 1832, 1838²), p. 149.
142. *Cf. ibidem*, #38, especially p. 361ff: "Das Gesamtverständnis ent-
scheidet gegen das des Einzelen, das Urteil der Kirche gegen das
des Individuums: die Kirche erklärt die heilige Schrift."
143. *Ibidem.*
144. *Ibidem:* "Dies Gesamtverständnis, dies kirchliche Bewusstsein ist
die Tradition im subjectiven Sinne des Wortes."
145. *Cf. ibidem*, #40, p. 374ff.

that the teaching of the Church is the same as the teaching of the

scriptures. This teaching or dogma receives through denial a development

and verification that it did not yet possess in the early Church.

Between the apostolic tradition and the teaching of the Church in suc-

cessive ages there is only a "formal difference" occasioned by expressing

in another and in a contemporary terminology the ancient truth.

Möhler even writes that the Nicean Creed is, in itself, as a some-

time meaningful expression of the apostolic faith, expendable: "Die Ent-

stehung der nicänischen Formel gibt hierüber den besten Aufschluss.

Diese Form ist das Menschliche, Zeitliche, an sich Vergängliche, und

könnte wohl gegen hundert andere ausgetauscht werden."[146]

So the appearance of error and heresy enables us to go further than

the previous ages of the Church in the perception of divine truth (i.e.,

tradition in Möhler's "subjective" sense), and this is the work of

theology.[147]

Möhler then explains how it is possible to regard all dogmatic

progress or development as a deviation from the original, apostolic

faith, as happens with some Protestants, who have denied the authorita-

tive character of tradition. Where scripture is looked upon as the only

source and means of knowing the salvation offered in the gospel ("die

einzige Quelle und Norm der Erkenntnis der evangelischen Heilsanstalt...

---

146. *Ibidem*, p. 376.
147. *Cf. ibidem*, p. 375f.: "Indem die Kirche die ursprüngliche Glaubens-
lehre in der eben entwickelten Weise Entstellungen gegenüber
erklärt und sicherstellt, geht nothwendig auch der apostolische
Ausdruck in einen anderen über, welcher gerade am geeignetsten ist,
den bestimmten, zeitlichen Irrthum recht kenntlich darzustellen und
zugleich abzuweisen."
Cf. also #42, p. 382ff.: "Ueber das Verhältnis der kirchlichen
Auslegung der heiligen Schrift zur gelehrt-wissenschaftlichen.
Patristische Auctorität und freie Forschung."

..."), without acknowledging the necessity of tradition and of a living authority, then the scripture has no meaning, because it can have any and all meanings. This fact explains, for example, how Protestants who differ from one another as much as Harnack and Barth can, nevertheless, share the opinion that all dogma is a deviation and degradation of the gospel.

To insist on the one and only sense of scripture which has always been held in the Church we could call, although Möhler dosen't use this terminology, "the dogmatic task of the Church."

In conclusion it must be stated that while Möhler's understanding of dogma as an expression of the inner life of the Church is a valuable insight, his failure to state their necessary inner connection is regretable. For it is simply not possible to have any type of life of faith without believing in something "dogmatically." Perhaps his inability to state succintly the relationship between dogma and the inner life of the Church is due to his suggestion that the beginning of dogma is occasioned by the appearance of heresy, an observation which is inadequate, yet in keeping with the polemic tone of his *Symbolik*.

3. Johann Evangelist Kuhn (1806-1887)

With the rationalism of his day J. E. Kuhn held that the truth of revelation is developed in the reason of man, but differed from the rationalists by maintaining that this development is not to be understood in the sense of the human spirit (Geist) coming to a substantial perfection of itself. When the revealed truth is referred to as "faith" Kuhn does not mean the subjective consciousness (Bewusstsein) of revelation, but the "Offenbarung in ihrem An-sich."[148]

Moreover, the recogniton (Erkenntnis) of revelation is not the act of the spirit (Geist) coming to itself, but the pedagogy (Erziehung) of the divine teacher raising human consciousness to a higher stage of development by the communication of a new truth.[149] This does not mean the increase of revelation itself, but the ever-increasing human expressions of it. As soon as the Christian truth entered the world it came into vital contact with the spiritual (geistigen) forces of that time. But by reason of the energy natural to it, this truth soon became the "Mittelpunkt" of the history surrounding it.[150]

This truth of revelation and of the apostolic kerygma is carried on through the living tradition of the Church,[151] a tradition which was at first oral and subsequently written down. Thus, dogma has its source in the Word of God, partly written down, partly handed on by word of mouth.[152] There is in dogma a divine element, and a human element of the Church. The divine element has its foundation in the Logos of God. It is communicated and realized in the individual by the work of the Holy Spirit, and preserved in the living tradition of the Church. The Church's moment in dogma comes more to notice when it is first of all recalled that only the Church can, and has decided which books in its tradition

---

148.   *Cf.* J. R. Geiselmann, *Die lebendige Überlieferung als Norm des christlichen Glaubens dargestellt in Geiste der Traditionslehre* Johannes Ev. Kuhns, (Freiburg, 1958), p. 84. This is true in the second edition (1859) of Kuhn's *Einleitung in die katholische Dogmatik.* In the first edition (1846) his concept of faith seems to have been more influenced by Schleiermacher's subjective notion of faith.
149.   *Cf.* Geiselmann, *op. cit.,* p. 84.
150.   Kuhn, *op. cit.,* (Tübingen, 1859[2]), p. 149.
151.   By living Tradition (lebendige Überlieferung) Geiselmann understands "nicht mehr wie für den Theologen der Erweckungsbewegung, Johann Michael Sailer, das Ergriffensein in Herz und Gemut..., sondern die wache Helle des Geistes." *Op. cit.,* p. 204.
152.   *Cf.* Geiselmann, *op. cit.,* p. 49ff.

175

are divinely inspired. The gospel is the Word of God about salvation, but it belongs to the Church to recognize it, to define it, to proclaim it. For she was founded by the Logos and is guided by the Holy Spirit for this purpose.

Kuhn retains the principle of dialectic in the process of the development of Christian truth.[153] It is not a dialectic of content, however, but a dialectic of differing concepts and ideas (Begriffe und Vorstellungen) springing from the once and final fact of revelation. These differing conceptions are not the results of a process of logical deduction, but of the dialectic of the living tradition in opposition to and in conjunction with historical process and event. Here one sees a distinct difference between Möhler and Kuhn. Möhler understood Christianity and its revelation more in terms of life and the Spirit's communication of life. Kuhn's thought is centered on revelation as the communication of truth, where spirit meets spirit in open dialectic.[154]

The bearer (Träger) of revelation is not just the Spirit of God but, in their own subordinate way, also the Church and its preachers and teachers. Thus, the Church as a whole is the subject or agent of development. The Spirit of God dwells in the whole body of the faithful which, as community in the Spirit, is a higher thing than the individual's partaking of the Spirit.[155]

It is not enough merely to repeat the ideas and concepts of scripture. Where there is life there is real dialectic. From time to time the historical process requires the Church to issue new proclamations of the old truth in the form of dogma. "Der Fortschritt und die

---

153. Cf. ibidem, p. 211ff.
154. Cf. ibidem, p. 204.
155. Cf. ibidem, p. 207.

Entwicklung der christlichen Offenbarung vollzieht sich aber in der

Bildung der Dogmen. Diese haben eine Geschichte. Wo aber Geschichte ist,

da ist auch Veränderung."[156]

In his *Einleitung in die katholische Dogmatik*, Kuhn treats the

notion of dogma and thoroughly defines it in the following way: "Der

allgemeine Begriff des Dogma, wie er aus den angeführten verschiedenen

Bedeutungen des Wortes resultirt, ist also der einer Lehre oder Satzung,

welche von einer (relativ oder absolut) geltenden Auctorität ausgeht und

für den Kreis ihrer Geltung und Wirksamkeit gleichmässig verbindende und

insofern diesen Kreis zur Einheit zusammenschliessende oder vereinigende

Kraft hat."[157]

The highest authority upon which dogma depends is that of God

himself, mediately it is that of Christ and the apostles. This action of

the Church is spoken of as a δογματίζειν. Like the action of the Council

of Jerusalem -- ἔδοξε τῷ ἁγίων πνεύματι καὶ ἡμῖν -- it is not a "making"

of something new, but a declaration -- δόγματι κρίνειν -- of what is

already there. Even less is this δογματίζειν a logical analysis or

explication of the primary expression of the Christian truth, or a

scientific expansion of the same. It is "die objective Dialectik seines

Inhalts."[158]

Kuhn's definition of dogma does not clearly bring out its

dependence on revelation. The context of his *Einleitung* would, however,

---

156. Geiselmann, *op. cit.*, p. 207.
157. Tübingen, 1859[2], p. 187.
158. The whole passage in question is: "Was die Kirche auf solche Weise
     und nach diesen Richtungen thut, ist keine bloss logische Analyse
     oder Explication des ursprünglichen Ausdrucks der christlichen
     Wahrheit, noch eine subjectiv wissenschaftliche Erweiterung
     desselben, sondern die objective Dialectik seines Inhalts." Kuhn,
     op. cit., p. 193.

imply such a dependence. Moreover, when he speaks of the "objective Dialectik seines Inhalts" one wonders whether the dialectic is between different parts of revelation, or between revelation in the living tradition and the wider historical process. The latter seems to be what Kuhn intended.[159]

From the historical standpoint it is much easier, Kuhn says, to consider what is and what is not de fide. He chides those theologians of a more speculative bent who spend many pages on distinctions over theological notes and then, in the end, are not able to agree among themselves.[160] "De fide ist die christliche Wahrheit, die die Kirche zu der Zeit, von der es sich handelt, ausspricht."[161] The believer must hold fast to the stand in faith that the Church of his time takes. If he were to hold on to an anachronistic orthodoxy, he would not be in contact with the living tradition of his own time and, to that extent, his faith would be untrue. So, after the condemnation of Arius' doctrine and the proclamation at Nicea of the homoousion, it was no longer enough merely to repeat the old formulas of faith. They could be understood in an orthodox or in an Arian way. The dialectic over the object of faith which the Arians caused challenged the Church to express its belief in a new way which could not be misunderstood, and which was a genuine growth in dogma.

---

159. Cf. Kuhn, op. cit., p. 194: "Der kirchliche Geist setzt die Wahrheit voraus, sie ist ihm durch Christus und die Apostel gegeben; in diese Wahrheit leitet und führt er die Menschen ein, indem er sie jeder Zeit so darbietet, wie Christus selbst und seine Apostel sie ihrer Zeit dargeboten haben, d.h. mit Rücksicht auf die Bedürfnisse der Zeit, ihre geistigen Strömungen und Gegensätze."
160. Cf. ibidem, p. 195, footnote 1.
161. Ibidem, pp. 195-201.

4. F. A. Staudenmaier (1800-1865)

For F. A. Staudenmaier the problem of the origen of dogma is intimately linked with the origen of dogmatics, the science of Church
teaching. Indeed, one cannot separate the two because both manifest
themselves as moments of the spirit developing itself.[162]

Staudenmaier sees the origen of dogma in the developing consciousness of the Church. This consciousness is, however, the tradition.
Within the Church there is through the medium of the eternally living
Word the eternally living Gospel. "Damit aber haben wir die Tradition
beschrieben; denn das zu allen Zeiten lebendig durch die Kirche hindurch-
gehende göttliche Wort, das nie alternde Selbstbewusstsein der Kirche ist
als ihr göttlich gewirktes Bewusstsein -- die Tradition."[163]

Revelation rests on the living Word of God, as it was preached by
Christ and the apostles. The preaching of the living Word has then a
priority to the written Word, the New Testament, not only in a chrono-
logical sense, but also theologically as the type from which the written
Word comes. In Staudenmaier's estimation the Church is even more
important than the scriptures: "Die Kirche umfasst Alles; sie selbst ist,
wie oben schon bemerkt worden, die lebendige Tradition, in welche die
heilige Schrift nur aufgenommen ist, wie ein Theil in das Ganze. Durch
diese Tradition ist die christliche Lehre nichts Stehendes, Starres,
sondern ein ewig frisch ausgesprochenes Wort Gottes."[164]

---

162. *Cf. Die Christliche Dogmatik*, vol. 1, (Freiburg, 1844), p. 142:
"Die Dogmatik ist vorläufig zu definiren als die aus den Elementen
der göttlichen Offenbarung sich erzeugende, in und durch sich
selber zusammenhängende, und sich auf sich selbst beziehende
Wissenschaft des Glaubens. Diese Wissenschaft ist der christliche
Lehrbegriff. Die Gestaltung des Lehrbegriffs nimmt ihren ersten
Anfang schon mit der Gestaltung des Dogma."
163. *Ibidem*, p. 20.
164. *Ibidem*, pp. 22-23.

It is, however, possible that when the individual draws a truth from his own consciousness of the tradition that he may err. This possibility of erring is avoided if he draws the truth, or "dogma," from the self-consciousness of the entire Church: "...denn das Dogma, das ein Wahrheit durch und von Gott, so wie eine Wahrheit von Allen für Alle ist, kann nur aus dem gottgewirkten Gesamtbewusstsein der Kirche hervorgehen."[165] Such a truth of revelation must always be interpreted in light of the tradition which formed it and out of which it has been drawn.

Dogma is formally defined as "...eine aus der göttlichen Offenbarung abstammende und durch das Bewusstsein der allgemeinen Kirche bezeugte Glaubenswahrheit."[166] It can be considered both subjectively and objectively. Subjectively, it is an inner certainty or conviction.[167] Objectively, it is through the just mentioned subjective moment already in process toward becoming a Church decree or conciliar determination.[168] As such it has the quality of absolute certainty, for dogmas are eternal and divine truths, because they stem out of the truth of God himself.[169]

---

165. *Ibidem*, p. 32.
166. *Ibidem*, p. 124.
167. *Ibidem*, p. 125: "...eine innere Gewissheit, eine fest innige Ueberzeugung, eine bestimmte Geltung, die für das betreffende Individuum mit keiner Willkür verbunden ist."
168. *Ibidem*, pp. 124-126: "Mit dieser innern Bestimmtheit und Gewissheit ist es schon im Uebergang begriffen zum Objectiven, dessen Kraft und Bedeutung sich in gegenwärtigem Falle dadurch geltend macht, dass das Wort Dogma, indem es ein Decret, ein kirchliches, auf Sittlichkeit Bezug habendes Gebot, einen conciliarischen Beschluss bezeichnet, eine allgemeine Bestimmung für Alle enthält auf welche es sich bezieht."
169. *Ibidem*, pp. 126-127: "Nach weiterer Bestimmung sind die Dogmen Glaubenslehren, die in der christlichen Kirche als allgemein geltend und an sich gewiss angenommen sind; die Geltung und Gewissheit, die an ihnen erkannt wird, ist keine bloss subjective, sondern eine schlechthin objective, absolute. Der allgemeine Charakter des Dogma ist daher; das absolut Gewisse, Zuverlässige;

For this reason no dogma has a purely private character as, for example, belonging only to a particular church.

As a completely finished teaching dogma has not always been present in the Church.[170] It is the result of development and of growing consciousness of the Church's spirit, which is in union with the divine. It was certainly in view of this development that St. Basil made his famous distinction between preaching and teaching, that is, between kerygma and dogma. The dogmas are kept silent, not in the sense of a disciplina arcani, but because they require more penetration and study. The kerygma is preached everywhere, because it is the more simple teaching of faith which is oriented toward practice, and which is immediately grasped even by the simple minded.[171] Staudenmaier approves this distinction.

Even as Basil saw the reality of the teaching of faith under two headings according to the degree of individual penetration, so can Stauddemaier grasp the reality of faith under two headings. In the first place, dogma is the immediate consciousness of the content of divine revelation. In the second place, it is a further, mediated consciousness of the same reality through the continuing determination of the Church's spirit (Geist).[172] What was in the first consciousness of the Church,

die Dogmen sind ewige und göttliche Wahrheiten, denn nur das Wahre ist das Gewisse. Die Dogmen ruhen auf keinem Wahrscheinen, sondern auf dem Wahrsein. Was sie wahr macht, ist nicht eine empirische, historische, zeitliche Wahrheit, sondern die aus dem göttlichen Urbewusstsein stammende ewige Wahrheit."

170. Cf. ibidem, p. 127: "Als Lehrbestimmung ist aber das Dogma nicht schon ursprünglich in der Kirche als ein formell absolut fertiger Begriff vorhanden gewesen, sondern es hat sich, die wir oben gesehen haben, in der Kirche dazu entwickelt und gestaltet."
171. Cf. ibidem, p. 127, and especially footnote 2.
172. Cf. ibidem, p. 128: "Das Dogma kann somit von einer zweifachen Seite angesehen werden, einmal so, wie das in ihm wohnende

even, as for example, what is in the scriptures, that is, the kerygma, becomes the premisses for the widening knowledge of faith (dogma, in Basil's sense) developing through history.

Against Schliermacher's subjectivism Staudenmaier maintains that dogmas cannot be simply the registrations of various feelings, even of a religiously moved consciousness. For this would lead to the preposterous state of affairs that something may be true in one church but not in another. Dogmas, however, have an absolute and objective character, because they are founded on the eternal truth of God, which is beyond the subjectivity of all feelings: "Die Dogmen müssen einen bestimmten und in dieser Bestimmtheit festen, unwandelbaren Charakter haben. Sie enthalten somit objective Wahrheit, und in dieser eine absolute Geltung für Alle, die in der Kirche sind. So haben sie den Charakter des Normativen, Gesetzlichen, noch mehr, des Constitutiven....."[173]

The process of the formation of dogma is, as mentioned above, simultaneous with the formation of dogmatics.[174] Revelation is both deed and proclamation. But deed is in one sense already proclamation, because it immediately resolves itself into a word. The proclamation may have enough determination about it to become immediately the stuff of dogma, or it may transpire in figurative imagery, as is common in poetic and rhetorical expression.

Bewusstsein unmittelbares Bewusstsein vom Inhalte der göttlichen Offenbarung ist; dann aber auch so, wie dieses anfänglich unmittelbare Bewusstsein durch die weitere Selbstbestimmung des kirchlichen Geistes zu einem vermittelten geworden ist. Was im Urbewusstsein der Kirche, in der Tradition, die Schrift mit eingerechnet, gegeben war, das verhält sich zum Dogma, d.h. zum vermittelten Dogma, wie die Prämisse zum Schluss."
173. *Ibidem*, p. 141.
174. *Cf. ibidem*, p. 142.

So, the language of the Bible usually makes use of imagery and metaphor in order to express what is deep, important, many-sided, infinite. Because of this there is need of a transposition into the more pure form of concept. "Aus dieser lebendigen und ewig frischen Quelle schöpft das Bewusstsein, indem es fortwährend den Inhalt in den entsprechenden Gedanken, Satz, umbildet, woraus der Lehrsatz entsteht."[175]

In the genesis of dogma there is an analytical and a synthetic process. The analytical moment is that process by which a truth of revelation is derived from other truths of revelation already known. The synthetic moment is seen in the several truths leading to another expression of one truth. Staudenmaier names this twofold process the dialectical character of dogma. Its essence is certainly not speculative construction, but speculatively to follow the forces of real dialectic which have been at work in the factual, life development of Christianity. This difficult thought is best represented by giving Staudenmaier's own words:

> Das Wesen des Dialektischen besteht auf dem Boden des Speculativen überhaupt in diesem Zweifachen, in der Analysis und in der Synthesis, welche beide in Vereinigung mit einander dahin wirken, die objective lebendige Ordnung der dogmatischen Begriffe zu erkennen. Denn da die dogmatische Wissenschaft eine speculative und keine a priori construirende ist, so kann es sich in ihr nicht darum handeln, ein System zu construiren, sondern nur nachzuconstruiren, folglich darum, das geistig zu wiederholen, was der göttliche Urheber der Offenbarung und ihrer Begriffe, und der Werkmeister des Systems heiliger und ewiger Wahrheiten in seinem Verstande construirt hat. Die ganze in Anwendung kommende Dialektik der geoffenbarten göttlichen Wahrheit Enthaltene zu erkennen. Denn die Darstellung des Erkannten in einem Systeme ist der systematisirende Thätigkeit vorbehalten.[176]

According to this method the only way to represent dogmatic truths is as the results of that dialectical development through which they have

---

176. *Ibidem*, pp. 170-171.

come to be expressed at the end of their particular historical course.

b. John Henry Newman (1801-1890)

It would be wrong to think of Newman as representing a theory of dogmatic origins.[177] Indeed, the *Essay on the Development of Christian Doctrine* established his place in the elaboration of the general theory of dogmatic development.[178] His concern in this work was not to justify the evolution of particular dogmas, but to show how the development of doctrine throughout the centuries and as a process of the unfolding of the "Idea" of Christianity was to be expected.[179]

Corresponding to the fact of development of dogma in the body of the Church is the problem of identity, that is, of the identity of the body of doctrine which the Church of Newman's day taught with the tradition of the apostolic Church. This identity should be conceived,

---

177. Because Newman nowhere treats the problem of dogma systematically we have thought it better to study his works thematically rather than chronologically.

178. Westminster, Md., 1968. First published in 1878.

179. *Cf. ibidem*, pp. 55-57: "If Christianity is a fact, and impresses an idea of itself on our minds and is a subject-matter of exercises of the reason, that idea will in course of time expand into a multitude of ideas, and aspects of ideas connected and harmonious with one another, and in themselves determinate and immutable, as is the objective fact itself which is thus represented.... It may be objected that its inspired documents at once determine the limits of its mission without further trouble; but ideas are in the writer and reader of the revelation, not the inspired text itself: and the question is whether those ideas which the latter conveys from writer to reader reach the reader at once in their completeness and accuracy on his first perception of them, or whether they open out in his intellect and grow to perfection in the course of time...... Unless then some special ground of exception can be assigned, it is as evident that Christianity, as a doctrine and worship, will develop in the minds of recipients, as that it conforms in other respects, in its external propagation or its political framework, to the general methods by which the course of things is carried forward."

not as if there were no difference between the depositum and the present

state of Catholic doctrine, because that would destroy the fact of

development, but in such a way as the one is understood as the natural

development of the other, in the complete understanding of which it is

already implied. This identity Newman proves through two sets of

arguments which J. H. Walgrave calls respectively, "The Historico-

Religious Solugion," and "Historical-Philosophical Solution."[180]

The "Historico-Religious Solution" Walgrave summarizes under three

sentences, the first of which is: "A true and faithful development of

doctrine is to be expected."[181] God has revealed a "definite and change-

less supernatural truth," but the wealth implied by any idea can only be

appreciated through a highly complex process of reflection and develop-

ment. The second sentence: "An infallible governing authority is to be

expected."[182] As in the area of natural religion the infallible guide

is personal conscience, which must be obeyed, so it is to be expected

that in the realm of supernatural religion a similar guide of an

infallible nature will be found.[183]

The third sentence is: "Both these expectations are fulfilled in

the Catholic Church alone."[184] Given the two facts that revelation will

develop, and that there is need for an infallible interpretative

---

180. *Newman the Theologian, the Nature of Belief and Doctrine as
      Exemplified in His Life and Works*, (London, 1960).
181. *Cf.* the *Essay*, pp. 55-98. We list Walgrave's paraphrases instead
      of Newman's original three sentences since the former are more
      descriptive of the realities involved. Newman's sentences are: 1.
      "Developments to be expected"; 2. "An infallible Developing Author-
      ity to be expected"; 3. "The existing Developments of Doctrine the
      probable Fulfilment of that Expectation."
182. Walgrave, *op. cit.*, p. 250.
183. *Cf.* Newman, *op. cit.*, p. 86.
184. Walgrave, *op. cit.*, p. 257.

authority, it is evident that the Catholic Church is the only body in the history of Christianity which has a body of developed doctrine in prominence and permanent possession, and an infallible authority to interpret it.

It is evident that not every development will be consonant with its origin. There exists also the possibility of corruptions coming in, such as heresies. Newman devotes the second and greater part of the *Essay* to a discussion of seven types of criteria by which corruptions may be distinguished from legitimate developments of the original idea. These seven arguments Walgrave lists under the title: "The Historical-Philosophical Solution."[185] These criteria are not meant to justify the evolution of particular dogmas. Their function is rather to describe, in a phenomenological way, the psychological processes of intellectual development of a basic intuition in a social body.[186]

These criteria or "notes," as Newman calls them, are best given in his own words.[187] 1. "First Note of a genuine Development of an Idea: Preservation of its Type." This means that the essential idea at the basis of the intuition must pervade all its true manifestations. Otherwise what appears to be a manifestation is a corruption. 2. "Second Note: Continuity of its Principles." This means that the principles upon which an idea is based and has developed remain the same throughout that development. 3. "Third Note: Its Power of Assimilation." This means that the controlling and developing idea absorbs opinions and institutions from the world in which it finds itself, but changes their significance in doing so. 4. "Fourth Note: Its Logical Sequence." This

185.   *Ibidem*, pp. 259-277.
186.   *Cf. ibidem*, pp. 259-262.
187.   *Cf.* Newman, *op. cit.*, p. 169ff.

means that in looking back on the process of the development of ideas one can see a certain logical progression which, although unconscious or barely reflected on in the social body, has been, nevertheless, at work. 5. "Fifth Note: Anticipation of its Future." This means that true development does not always occur at one time, but that there are often earlier intimations of the same, because the total process is ruled by the one basic idea. 6. "Sixth Note: Conservative Action upon its Past." This means that a true development does not obscure its past, but preserves it as indicative of the course which has lead to itself. 7. "Seventh Note: Its Chronic Vigour." This means that corruptions will not last or will at least decay, whereas true developments endure in power.

Throughout the *Essay* Newman presumes the existence of a dogmatic deposit. There is here no question of the beginning of dogma. As we see, the question which is discussed at such great length in the *Essay* is rather dogma's subsequent development from its original idea, which is revelation.

Newman touches our problem in the following passage: "It seems, then, that we have to deal with a case something like the following: Certain doctrines come to us, professing to be Apostolic, and possessed of such high antiquity that, though we are only able to assign the date of their formal establishment to the fourth, or the fifth, or the eighth, or the thirteenth century, as it may happen, yet their substance may, for what appears, be coeval with the Apostles, and be expressed or implied in texts of Scripture."[188] But this is only to restate the problem of dogma's development, not to consider the problem of its origin.

---

188. *Ibidem*, p. 99.

In his earlier work, *The Arians of the Fourth Century*, Newman does treat the problem of the beginning of dogma.[189] Here he believed "that freedom from symbols and articles is abstractedly the highest state of Christian communion."[190] In the earliest times there was no need for formulas of faith since it was kept alive in the tradition of those who had witnessed the life of Jesus. However, it was inevitable that "technicality" and "formalism" would come in when the need for public confessions arose, and this need manifested itself when heretics such as Paul of Samosata and Arias began to propagate their errant views among the faithful.

Up until this time the mysteries of Christian faith had been kept hidden in the "bosom of the Church" and were only gradually released to those who were "prepared to profit from them."[191] Newman is, of course, speaking of the process of instructing those prepared to believe and of the disciplina arcani. The heretics, on the other hand, made the confessions of faith as public and approved declarations necessary because they did not restrict their declarations to an initiate, but proclaimed them to the crowds and to the unprepared, who at once then became controversialists in the matter.[192] Newman quotes Tertullian here in his support:

> It is uncertain who among them is catechumen, who believer. They meet alike, they hear alike, they pray alike; nay, though the heathen should drop in, they will cast holy things to dogs, and their pearls, false jewels as they are, to swine. This overthrow of order they call simplicity, and our attention to it they call meretricious embellishment. They communicate with all men promiscuously; it being nothing to them in what they differ from them,

189. Westminster, Md., 1968. First published in 1833.
190. *Ibidem*, p. 36.
191. *Cf. ibidem*, p. 37.
192. *Cf. ibidem*, p. 138ff.

provided they join with them for the destruction of the truth. They are all high-minded, all make pretence of knowledge. Their catechumens are perfect in the faith before they are fully taught.[193]

In the face of this onslaught of irregular teaching proclaimed in an irregular way, the Catholic Church, "defenseless from the very sacredness and refinement of its discipline" was now forced to pass authoritative judgment on the dispute. The question at issue in the Arian crisis was the interpretation of the words of scripture, and indeed, regarding the understanding of the doctrine of the Trinity. Newman does not here distinguish between the actual question of the Arian dispute -- the creaturehood or divinity of the Son -- and the larger question, as it subsequently developed in the history of dogma, of the divinity of the Holy Spirit and of the Trinity. For his way of thinking, the "object" of faith is simply God, who manifests himself as Father, as Son, and as Holy Spirit. "Let it be observed then, that as regards the doctrine of the Trinity, the mere text of scripture is not calculated either to satisfy the intellect or to ascertain the temper of those who profess to accept it as a rule of faith."[194]

Newman believed that even the untrained mind acquiesces, through its religious training, to belief in the Trinity. It assents easily to the implicit acknowledgment of the divinity of each of the three persons. As the mind becomes cultivated it seeks to express in words something of the object which is the center of its affections and of its veneration. But to say anything of this divine object the mind must use words derived from its more common experience.

---
193. *De Praescr. Haeret.*, 41.
194. Newman, *op cit.*, p. 143.

Thus the systematic doctrine of the Trinity may be considered as the shadow, projected for the contemplation of the intellect, of the Object of scripturally-informed piety: a representation, economical; necessarily imperfect, as being exhibited in a foreign medium, and therefore involving apparent inconsistencies or mysteries; given to the Church by tradition contemporaneously with those apostolic writings, which are addressed more directly to the heart; kept in the background in the infancy of Christianity, when faith and obedience were vigorous, and brought forward at a time when, reason being disproportionately developed and aiming at sovereignty in the province of religion, its presence became necessary to expel an usurping idol from the house of God.[195]

Creeds serve then the purpose of tranquilizing the mind, whereas the text of scripture has primarily a religious character, being addressed in the first place to the affections. The creeds also serve the purpose of preserving the unity of faith by insisting on a certain formulary of words. But often these words are drawn from the scriptures and from early writings, and so they do not seem so strange when used by authority as the test for communion with would-be heretics.

The above represents what Newman calls "the abstract principle on which ecclesiastical confessions rest."[196] It is clear that he only takes up the question in *The Arians* in connection with the appearance of heresy. Placing the origin of dogma in the fourth century as he does is, however, not just a question of the topical nature of the work. For "... the temper of the Ante-Nicene Church was opposed to the imposition of doctrinal tests upon her members ...such a measure became necessary in proportion as the cogency of Apostolic Tradition was weakened by lapse of time."[197]

In one place in *The Arians* Newman does acknowledge the existence of a dogmatic deposit before the Church began to struggle with the

---

195.   *Ibidem*, p. 145.
196.   *Ibidem*, p. 149.
197.   *Ibidem*, p. 133.

heretics, and this is just a passing reference to the Apostles' Creed as the "chief source of instruction" for the catechumens in the primitive age.[198] While it is true that the fact of deviant teaching, or "heresy" as it is subsequently called when once recognized and condemned, has very often been the occasion for dogmatic development, the insufficiency of the fact of heresy to explain the totality of dogma and, in particular, its origin, is patent from the fact that the Church had a depositum fidei with which catechumens were instructed, even before the rise of the heresies.

Insofar as Newman in *The Arians* views the origin of dogma in connection with conciliar definition he comes close to Harnack who fails to perceive the "dogmatic" flavor of Christianity since the first proclaimers of the kerygma were sent "to Jerusalem, to Judea, and even to the ends of the earth." With Harnack it is more a question of the simple denial of dogma's existence before the fourth century; with Newman the point of emphasis is more the problem of how the rarefied intellectual formulas of the councils can be derived from the apostolic understanding of revelation. For dogma is not necessarily the result of conciliar definition, although it historically has often been so, as heresy has also played a great part in dogma's articulation. Below and beyond the level of the great councils in history there has always been the substratum of dogmatic truth, that is, the Church's consensus in matters of divine faith, which it has proclaimed as necessarily to be accepted and believed -- such as Jesus' divinity, the sacrificial character of his death, the truth of his resurrection, etc. The fact of the Church's consensus on such things even from the earliest times

198. *Ibidem*, p. 135.

approaches Newman's notion of the "idea" that Christianity from the beginning was, and which could develop in the course of time. It cannot, however, be said that the two are equivocal notions. Authoritative consensus is not so broad a notion as "idea."

Newman's conception of dogma, which, despite his lifelong interest in the study of its development was then, in one sense, too dependent on the controversial, conciliar experience, and too little refined to go expressly beyond the controversial arena of the councils in which he studied it.

As a matter of fact, Newman seldom attempted to define dogma. The definition given in *An Essay in Aid of a Grammar of Assent* is: "A dogma is a proposition; it stands for a notion or for a thing; and to believe it is to give the assent of the mind to it, as it stands for one or for the other."[199] This is obviously a psychological definition rather than a theological one, since it says nothing about the necessity of the proposition's being divinely revealed or of its being authoritatively proclaimed by the Church. But in the *Grammar of Assent* Newman is concerned with the psychology of faith rather than its theology.

Newman's conception of dogma is too little refined to envelop the dogma of the first three centuries, too little refined to exhaust adequately the reality of dogma. In this respect F. C. Baur's statement that, "Der Anfang der Dogmengeschichte kann nur der Anfang der Bewegung des Dogmas selbst sein,"[200] with which Martin Werner criticized Harnack, can also be applied to Newman. But the fact that it can be applied to Newman is without any doubt to be attributed to the occasional nature of

---

199. London, 1947. First published in 1870. Quote: p. 75.
200. See chapter II, footnote 1.

Newman's writings.

In his work, *On Consulting the Faithful in Matters of Doctrine*,[201] Newman shows how the voice of the laity can be, and actually has been, one of the infallible witnesses for the truth of revealed faith. He does not attribute to the laity a function similar to that of the teaching magisterium of the Church, that is, of judging, distinguishing, defining, and preaching the truth of faith. Nor is it necessary to ask their advice before the magisterium makes the official proclamation of a dogmatic decision. But the faith of the laity should be considered, as one of those witnesses of the apostolic tradition on the basis of which any dogma must depend before it can be defined.

The apostolic tradition has been entrusted to the entire Church with its various organs and offices per modum unius. At times in the history of the Church one witness to the tradition will come to the fore, at times another. Sometimes the voice of the bishops is more in evidence, sometimes that of the fathers or theologians, sometimes that of the faithful. In other instances it is the liturgy and traditional usages which give testimony to the faith of the Church. This witness can also be called forth by controversies, happenings, and movements of history. As a result none of these various channels of tradition should be neglected.

Much of this opusculum of Newman is simply the diary of his conversations with P. Perrone, the Roman theologian of the last century, and quotes from Perrone's work on the dogma of the Immaculate Conception. Newman quotes Perrone at length and shows how his own thought depends on

201. Edited by John Coulson, (London, 1961). First published in *The Rambler*, July, 1859.

that of Perrone. From his own prodigious knowledge of Church history
he lists a number of examples of how the Nicean faith was preserved
intact by the "consensus fidelium" at a time when not only did the
functions of the teaching Church cease to exist, but the bishops as a
whole were unfaithful to the confession of faith for a period of some
sixty years. At that critical time following the Council of Nicea it
was not the voice of the official Church, but the "consensus fidelium"
which, although usually dependent on the voice of the official Church
for direction in matters of faith, was in this instance determinative
for preserving the true, Nicean faith.

Newman treats expressly the phenomenology of dogmatic development
considered in its beginnings in his Fifteenth Oxford Sermon.[202] In his
own words, his aim is "to investigate the connexion between Faith and
Dogmatic Confession."[203] In this sermon which is more a lecture he
offers a definition of dogma which situates it as a congeries of judgments dependent on mental impressions received from elsewhere:

> Theological dogmas are propositions expressive of the judgments
> which the mind forms, or the impressions which it receives, of
> Revealed Truth. Revelation sets before it certain supernatural
> facts and actions, beings and principles; these make a certain
> impression or image upon it; and this impression spontaneously,
> or even necessarily, becomes the subject of reflection on the part
> of the mind itself, which proceeds to investigate it, and to draw
> it forth in successive and distinct sentences. Thus the Catholic
> doctrine of Original Sin, or of Sin after Baptism, or of the
> Eucharist, or of Justification, is but the expression of the inward
> belief of Catholics on these several points, formed upon an
> analysis of that belief.[204]

In several paragraphs Newman explains how this "inward idea of

202. "The Theory of Developments in Religious Doctrine," in *Fifteen
     Sermons Preached before the University of Oxford*, (Westminster,
     Md., 1966), pp. 312-351. First published in 1843.
203. *Ibidem*, #9, p. 319.
204. *Ibidem*, #10, p. 320.

divine truth" may be possessed without being explicitly an object of reflection. So, a peasant may have such a true impression but be completely unable to give an intelligible account of it. So also do entirely normal people have unperceived impressions which influence their actions, views, prejudices. Today we would speak of "unconscious factors" which exert an influence on conscious thinking and activity. "Now, it is important to insist on this circumstance, because it suggests the reality and permanence of inward knowledge, as distinct from explicit confession. The absence, or partial absence, or incompleteness of dogmatic statements is no proof of the absence of impressions or implicit judgments in the mind of the Church. Even centuries might pass without the formal expression of a truth, which had been all along the secret life of millions of faithful souls."[205]

Underlying Newman's thought in this Fifteenth Sermon is his doctrine of the distinction between "explicit and implicit reason."[206] To simplify Newman's thought somewhat, reason is "a living spontaneous energy within us," that faculty by which knowledge is gained without direct perception, that activity by which from a small beginning a world of ideas is built up, that unconscious series of mental connections which can even result in a system, but in an unreflective way. This is really his doctrine of "implicit reason." "Explicit reason," on the other hand, is the exercise by which the mind begins to analyze its various processes and to discover the principles and order by which it acts. It is, "the process of investigating our reasonings." All men

---

205. *Ibidem*, #13, p. 323.
206. *Cf*. Sermon XIII, "Implicit and Explicit Reason," in *Fifteen Sermons*, pp. 251-277, but especially pp. 256-259.

reason (implicit reason), but not all men reflect upon their reasoning (explicit reason). Explicit reason is an activity of the mind that follows implicit reason and which draws out that which is contained therein, but up till now not appreciated. The science of logic is explicit reason in its most comprehensive state.[207]

Like reason, faith is complete without reflection. It too is described by Newman as a process of reasoning: "Thus Faith is the reasoning of a religious mind, or of what Scripture calls a right or renewed heart, which acts upon presumptions rather than evidence, which speculates and ventures on the future when it cannot make sure of it."[208] Faith then is a reasoning process based on a person's basic presumptions. So Byrne concludes: "Faith in this latter sense is the same as Implicit Reason, it seems to us, save that it accepts 'presumptions' as the basis of its reasoning; whereas, Implicit Reason demands sensible or rational evidence."[209] When faith reasons upon its presumptions, it explicates itself in terms of creeds. The theme of the Thirteenth Sermon, "Implicit and Explicit Reason," are the words of 1 Pet 3:15: "...be ready always to give an answer to every man that asketh you a reason of the hope that is in you...." It is this exercise of explicit reason in faith which draws out intellectual and dogmatic formulae.

In further paragraphs of the Fifteenth Sermon Newman uses other expressions for the perception of the fact of revelation before its formulation. So, for example: "sacred ideas," and "the impression of

207.   Cf. Walgrave, op. cit., p. 96ff; and J. J. Byrne, "Newman's
       Anglican Notion of Doctrinal Development," EThL 14 (1937), p. 256ff.
208.   Sermon XI, "The Nature of Faith in Relation to Reason," in Fifteen
       Sermons, p. 203.
209.   Byrne, op. cit., p. 260.

Divine Verities." Because the human mind can reflect only piecemeal on the great reality or impression, and that by resolving it into a series of aspects and relations, creeds and dogmas become necessary but always inadequate expressions of the richness of the original idea. "Catholic dogmas are, after all, but symbols of a Divine fact, which, far from being compassed by those very propositions, would not be exhausted, nor fathomed, by a thousand."[210]

Newman says that at the basis of every dogma is an "impression" of the Object of divine faith,[211] which then is reflected upon and becomes a dogma when this impression is expressed in words, for "Theological dogmas are propositions expressive of the judgments which the mind forms, or the impressions which it receives, of Revealed Truth."[212]

At this point George Tyrrell's criticism of Newman in *Through Scylla and Charybdis* becomes pertinent.[213] Walgrave describes this criticism: "There seems, however, to be a contradiction between intuitive knowledge by faith and Newman's principle of dogma, according to which the Christian religion derives from a definite revelation of certain truths, given at a particular moment in time."[214] What is the warrant of our present beliefs? Is it a dogmatic deposit or the Church's contemporary vision of faith? The Fifteenth Oxford Sermon represents the latter view, *An Essay on the Development of Christian Doctrine* the former view. Tyrrell believed Newman did not grasp the incompatibility of the two views.

---

210. Newman, Sermon XV, *op. cit.*, #23, pp. 331-332.
211. *Cf. ibidem*, p. 323.
212. *Ibidem*, p. 320.
213. London, 1907.
214. Walgrave, *op. cit.*, p. 130.

Walgrave sees a way through this impasse in the following way. It is certain that Newman always held to the dogmatic principle of the depositum. On the other hand, it is "almost equally certain that he invariably held faith to be a quasi-vision of supernatural realities."[215] But the vision is always qualified by dogmatic teaching. In itself, the vision is not normative. The vision arises through contact with that devotional book, the Bible, or perhaps through preaching or other contacts with dogmatic theology.[216] There is no direct and independent intuition of faith. Walgrave's conclusion is: "Nowhere, not even in the Oxford sermon, does Newman represent the intuition of faith as a contact with supernatural realities, independent of verbal revelation."[217]

We can accept Walgrave's conclusion that Newman nowhere teaches a vision of the realities of faith independent of the dogmatic tradition and of "verbal revelation," if the following corrective is kept in mind. Newman says that at the basis of every dogma is an "impression" of the Object of divine faith. We would say, at the basis of every dogma is the Word of revelation which is grasped not as mere impression, but as

215. Walgrave, *op. cit.*, p. 131.
216. *Cf.* Sermon XV, p. 333: "The senses are direct, immediate and ordinary informants, but no such faculties have been given us, as far as we know, for realizing the objects of faith. The secondary and intelligible means by which we receive the impression of Divine Verities are such as the habitual and devout perusal of Scripture, the study of Dogmatic Theology."
217. Walgrave, *op. cit.*, p. 135; *cf.* Walgrave further: This intuition "is arrived at by degrees through Revelation as manifested in Scripture, the Creeds and the liturgy. Such a manifestation is itself, in a manner, notional and is bound to be if it is to reach us. This is a consequence of Newman's whole doctrine, according to which only what is notional can be communicated in words, and the experience of perceiving concrete reality is always inexpressible." So, in the *Grammar of Assent*, pp. 83-87; *cf.* p. 83: "Real assents are of a personal character; notional apprehension is, in itself, an ordinary act of our common nature."

word, and which is -- as dogma -- usually expressed in other words, although at times the original words of revelation are retained in the dogmatic expression.

The starting point of all dogma is revelation which is, concretely, the Word of God.[218] It is the character of a word not to be merely a natural or material sign, pointing arbitrarily at some reality beyond itself, but a formal sign, that is, something the very nature of which is to reveal another reality of which it partakes. Hence, the genesis of dogma is not, as Newman would have it -- Object, impression, words, dogma. The genesis of dogma follows rather the pattern -- Word of revelation, words of apprehender (at least mental words), dogma.

Revelation is a closed body of truth. The psychological beginning of dogma is at that point where the Word of revelation is simultaneously grasped and expressed by the human mind. For it is the nature of mind to express in words that which it in any way grasps. Newman's insertion of "impressions" dependent on a more or less unspecified "Object" seems to be wholly gratuitous.[219] We do not have "impressions of Revealed Truth" before we have the words in which it is expressed.

---

218. This is not to deny that revelation was a matter of deeds as well as words. But every deed, when apprehended by the human mind is expressed in a mental word.

219. *Cf.* Byrne's criticism, *op. cit.*, p. 285: "We would wish to know, for instance, what he means by 'objects of Faith'. They cannot signify -- we think -- the 'ideas' of those truths, because it is precisely the 'objects' which impress the 'ideas' on the mind. The 'objects' have a certain reality but the nature of that reality is not clear to us. A notion of their nature becomes even more difficult to grasp when we realize that men receive an impression of them in very different ways, e.g. from the Creeds, from a strong Faith, from a 'round of devotion', etc. Then too, how many 'objects' are there? Is there one for every religious truth or are there only the two that he names? If Christianity is not an 'object' how can it impress an 'idea' of itself on the mind?"

We believe there is, however, something to be said for Newman's notion of "impressions" which become the key to subsequent doctrinal development. After the closing of revelation and the establishment of the deposit of faith, the impressions these various truths of the deposit make in conjunction with one another have often been the basis for the subsequent growth in doctrine.[220] But this is simply to restate the principle of the analogy of faith.

Only in the *Grammar of Assent* does Newman address himself explicitly to this difficulty, and there only in a few words:

> Without a proposition or thesis there can be no assent, no belief, at all; any more than there can be an inference without a conclusion. The proposition that there is One Personal and Present God may be held in either way; either as a theological truth, or as a religious fact or reality. The notion and the reality assented to are represented by one and the same proposition, but serve as distinct interpretations of it. When the proposition is apprehended for the purposes of proof, analysis, comparison, and the like intellectual exercises, it is used as the expression of a notion; when for the purposes of devotion, it is the image of a reality....
> ....The propositions may and must be used, and can easily be used, as the expression of facts, not notions, and they are necessary to the mind in the same way that language is ever necessary for denoting facts, both for ourselves as individuals, and for our intercourse with others. Again they are useful in their dogmatic aspect as ascertaining and making clear for us the truths on which the religious imagination has to rest.[221]

In this passage Newman seems to recognize the fact that intellectual apprehension is essentially related to language. Yet he must have written these lines without grasping their full import for his doctrine in the earlier Fifteenth Sermon. For, although the *Grammar of Assent* was written later, it does not fully account for the disjunction between language and thought in his earlier work.

---

220. *Cf.* Sermon XIII, pp. 274-275.
221. *A Grammar of Assent*, pp. 90-91.

The psychological assumption underlying Newman's approach to the beginning of dogma in his earlier work is his disjunction of language and thought. "Language is a sort of analysis of thought." And, on the other hand, "...ideas are infinite, and infinitely combined, and infinitely modified, whereas language is a method definite and limited, and confined to an arbitrary selection of a certain number of these innumerable materials...."[222] From this and the above it is clear that Newman did not effectively grasp the inner and completely necessary connection between language and thought. His implied disjunction between the two is too exclusive. "Theological dogmas are propositions expressive of the judgments which the mind forms, or the impressions which it receives, of Revealed Truth."[223] For Newman "theological dogmas" are only derived from the experience of faith. He does not give adequate expression to the intrinsically related perception and expression of truth.

According to modern thinking on the philosophy of speech, thinking and speaking are so intimately related that a person can hardly accomplish the one without the assistance of the other.[224] Martin Heidegger even states: "Nur insofern der Mensch spricht, denkt er."[225] In his phenomenological method speech is of its nature a manifestation of the mystery of Being.[226] So, for example, the theme of his work on speech

222. Sermon XV, #34, p. 341.
223. See above, footnote 78.
224. *Cf.* the long discussion of this problem in Leo Scheffczyk, *Von der Heilsmacht des Wortes, Grundzüge einer Theologie des Wortes*, (München, 1966), p. 27ff.
225. *Was Heisst Denken?*, (Tübingen, 1954), p. 51.
226. *Cf.* Heidegger, *Unterwegs zur Sprache*, (Pullingen, 1959), p. 237: "Das Wort hebt an zu leuchten als die Versammlung, die Anwesendes erst in sein Anwesen bringt. Das älteste Wort für das so gedachte Walten des Wortes, für das Sagen, heisst Λόγος: die Sage, die zeigend Seiendes in sein es ist erscheinen lässt. Das selbe Wort Λόγος ist aber als Wort für das Sagen zugleich das Wort für das

is: "Das Wesen der Sprache: Die Sprache des Wesens."[227] Man is more a listener than a speaker, one who listens to the disclosure of Being through speech.

In conclusion it must be said that Newman's contribution to the explication of the problem of the beginning of dogma is sorely lacking. His concern in the *Essay on the Development of Christian Doctrine* is rather with the principles of the subsequent development of dogma; in *The Arians of the Fourth Century* he finds it nearly impossible to acknowledge the existence of dogma before the fourth century; in *An Essay in Aid of a Grammar of Assent* he is concerned with dogma as it is part of the psychological experience of faith.

Even the Fifteenth Oxford Sermon, which attempts an etiology of dogmatic propositions, must be deemed inadequate for our problem. For the theory which forms the basis for Newman's explanation of the appearance of dogma is his distinction between implicit and explicit reason, and its corollary, his separation of thought from the production of even mental words.

This explanation, impossible as it is, clarifies why Newman, like Harnack, could place the beginning of dogma in approximately the fourth century. His single statement in the *Grammar of Assent* that "without a proposition or thesis there can be no assent, no belief, at all," does not negate his more habitual way of regarding faith as a wordless "quasi-vision of supernatural realities."

---

227. Sein, d.h. für das Anwesen des Anwesenden. Sage und Sein, Wort und Ding gehören in einer verhüllten, kaum bedachten und unausdenkbaren Weise zueinander."
227. *Cf. ibidem*, p. 200, *et passim*.

c. Joseph Schwane (1824-1892)

More typical among Catholic theologians of the use of dogma in recent times than either the school of Tübingen or of J. H. Newman would be, for example, the historian of the subject, Joseph Schwane. Although neo-scholastic in personal outlook, he is the first Catholic theologian to succeed in producing a history of dogma akin to the not insubstantial works of this nature produced by Protestant historians.

In the Catholic tradition there are two types of decisions of the Church in matters of faith which deserve the titel "dogma." Both types are usually expressed in propositional form. In the first place, there are those decisions which are made with special formality such as on the occasion of an ecumenical council or special papal pronouncement. Thus, the Nicean Creed is Church dogma because it was formally approved and taught by the assembled bishops at that famous gathering and because an ecumenical council, being the most representative body of the Church, has ultimate and decisive authority in questions of faith. This is, however, not to exclude the pope, whose agreement to the work of such a council is necessary to give its decisions the final dimension of ecumenical authority.

In the second place, dogma or divinely revealed propositions of faith are also to be found in the ordinary day-to-day teaching and preaching and catechetical work which is done in harmony with the Church.[228]

---

228. On the distinction between dogma and doctrine, J. Tixeront writes in his *Histoire des Dogmes*, (Paris, 1909[5]), vol. 1, p. 2: "A prendre les choses à la rigueur, le dogme chrétien se distingue de la doctrine chrétienne. Le premier suppose une intervention explicite de l'Église se prononcant sur un point déterminé de la doctrine; la seconde embrasse un champ un peu plus vaste: elle

The fact of divine revelation, that is, presence in the sources of revelation -- scripture and the way the tradition has understood it -- is also always implied. One finds dogma then also on a less-noticeable level than in the formal decision of an ecumenical council or papal pronouncement declaring a particular truth to be revealed doctrine and therefore dogma. One finds dogma in the daily practice of the Church exercising its teaching mission.[229] Usually this level is referred to as the exercise of the ordinary teaching office of the Church, i.e., the "ordinary magisterium."

There are then two elements wholly necessary to every dogma in the Catholic understanding: content in divine revelation, and proposal by the Church to be believed. These elements of the "Catholic definition" are found in the thought of Joseph Schwane,[230] as they are also mentioned in the decrees of the First Vatican Council: "...fide divina et catholica ea omnia credenda sunt, quae in verbo Dei scripto vel tradito continentur et ab Ecclesia sive solemni iudicio sive ordinario et universali magisterio tamquam divinitus revelata credenda proponuntur."[231]

The first type of dogmatic truths, that is, those decided and then proclaimed by the Church with a greater degree of formality, such as has usually been done in the face of particular and threatening heresies,

---

comprehend non seulement les dogmes définis, mais de plus les enseignements qui sont d'une prédication ordinaire et courante, avec l'approbation certaine du magistère."

229. The Catholic historian of dogma Joseph Kleutgen, *Die Theologie der Vorzeit*, (Münster, 1867), vol. 1, pp. 119-121, lists as examples of undefined dogmas which are taught by the Church's ordinary magisterium: the infinity of God's nature; that he is all-good; all-knowing; that God has created the world in complete freedom; that his providence reaches to everything; that the fallen angels are damned; that those in purgatory grow in neither virtue nor merit.

230. *Dogmengeschichte*. 4 vols. Freiburg, 1862-1890; 1892-1905[2].

231. DB, 3011.

are called by Schwane "dogmata definitione ecclesiae declarata," or more frequently, "de fide divina et definita."[232] The second type of dogmatic decision, those truths always believed by the Church but for which no particular denial or heresy has ever made it necessary to proclaim formally, and which surround and fill out the formally proclaimed creeds and dogmas in the Church's life of faith, Schwane calls "dogmata communi ecclesiae magisterio proposita." More frequently, Schwane states, they are simply referred to as "de fide divina et catholica."

The "problem of the origin of dogma" has been for Catholic theology hardly a problem at all because according to Catholic theology those truths which have the status of dogma did not have their origin anywhere else but in scripture and the faith-consciousness of the Church insofar as this consciousness has found expression in the Church's official teaching. Accordance with scripture according to the mind of the Church is the absolute norm for all dogma because scripture is the authoritative distillate of the apostolic college and Church fulfilling its commission to proclaim the gospel. Thus Schwane, as Catholic historians of dogma in general, gives no more attention to a "problem of the origin of dogma" than the following statement: "Die Dogmen haben eine Lehre der göttlichen Offenbarung zum Inhalte, wie sie in der Heiligen Schrift und in der mündlichen apostolischen Überlieferung der Kirche niedergelegt ist; sie sind also ihrem Ursprung und ihrem Inhalt nach göttlich und zugleich in den öffentlichen, d.h. für alle Menschen bestimmten Urkunden der göttlichen Offenbarung oder in der kirchlichen Tradition enthalten."[233]

---

232. Schwane, *op. cit.*, vol. 1, pp. 4-5.
233. *Ibidem*, pp. 1-2.

9. THE TWENTIETH CENTURY DISCUSSION

a. Michael Schmaus

M. Schmaus is one Catholic theologian who in his studies of
Catholic dogma gives the "problem of the origin" of dogma a special
treatment.[234] For Schmaus dogma's relationship to scripture is clear
from the beginning: "Zu Dogmen werden die in der Heiligen Schrift oder
in den ungeschriebenen Überlieferungen in einer zeitgebundenen Vorstell-
ungs- und Sprechweise bezeugten Selbstmitteilungen Gottes dadurch, dass
sie sich in einer neuen, geschichtlich bedingten, von der Kirche gewirk-
ten Sprachform verleiblichen."[235] Apparently in order to preclude any
possible misunderstanding of the source of dogma based on a misconception
of the "two source" theory as stemming from the Council of Trent, his
expression in a later work is even more pointed in stating the scriptural
foundation of all dogma: "Grundlegend ist die Schriftgemässheit des
Dogmas. Es ist nichts anders als das Schriftzeugnis in einer entfalteten
Form."[236]

Dogma is revelation in the garment of other words, revelation
clothed in the words and forms of human expression appropriate and common
to history and culture subsequent to that of the Bible. It is God's
communication of himself (Selbstmitteilung Gottes) expressed in a way
certain to meet the questioning and perhaps erroneous opinions in
questions of faith of a particular time and place. As such, dogma
never does nor can express the whole of the truth of revelation. It is
the reflection of the total mystery and truth of Christ in a particular

---

234. *Katholische Dogmatik, I*, (München, 1960[6]), pp. 96-98; *Der Glaube
     der Kirche, Handbuch katholischer Dogmatik, I*, (München, 1969),
     pp. 194-197.
235. *Katholische Dogmatik, I*, p. 73.
236. *Der Glaube der Kirche, I*, pp. 187-188.

clime and time. Occasioned by particular circumstances it may not even
reflect the central or most important aspects of the truth in question,
but its divine origin in the corpus or depositum of revelation is
decisive. Without this foundation nothing can be raised to or declared
a dogma. But included under this foundation in revelation are also those
historical facts which revelation implies as necessary to its truth. So,
for example, the truth of Jesus' historical death on the cross is part of
revelation; the historical facticity of the existence of the Old Testament figure, Job, is not a part of revelation, since this question
prescinds from the truth contained in the Book of Job.

As has usually been the case, dogma has been occasioned by doubt.
First there has usually been ardent discussion, if not the crossfire of
contradictory assertion. So it was, for example, at the time of the
Reformation relative to the existence of a priethood separately ordained
from the common priesthood of the faithful. The reformers denied that
the ordination of priests was a separate sacrament. So the Church
decided at Trent, as decide she must with the body of revelation entrusted to her, what the truth of the matter is, and incorporated it in a
solemn declaration.[237] This declaration is a decision of the Church in
a matter of divine faith of what must be believed by the faithful. Such
a decision, once carried out, has the nature of dogma. For when the
Church decides what is determinative for the life of faith and what is
the truth of revelation which must be taught and believed she decides
irrevocably. If to a later age this irrevocable character of dogma
appears strange, it must be remembered that the dogma was occasioned by

237. DB, 1767ff.

a particular set of historical circumstances which perhaps are not duplicated in our contemporary world. But in the historical context of a dogma's definition the Church of that time decided that such a decision was determinative and necessary to its life of faith, because of its presence in the body of revelation. This brings up the question of the hermeneutic of dogmatic expression.[238]

J. S. von Drey of the Tübingen school was of the opinion that it is a general law of human knowledge that the truth can only be fully known by contrast with its opposite.[239] Augustine voiced a similar thought in one of his sermons: "Illi turbati quaerunt; qui autem norunt et didicerunt, quia scrutati sunt, et aperuit illis pulsantibus Deus, aperiunt et ipsi turbatis. Et sic fit ut illi sint utiles ad inveniendam veritatem, dum calumniantur ad seducendum in errorem. Negligentius enim veritas quaereretur, si mandaces adversarios non haberet."[240]

Schmaus sees this dialectic between heresy and orthodoxy as the usual way for a truth of revelation to pass into that stage of reflection in which it is eventually seen as a certain and necessary component of revelation. Beforehand such a truth is a part of the faith, but in a more or less unreflective way, much the way a healthy person possesses health, hardly ever thinking on it. When, however, the truth is actively reflected upon, it is possible for doubt to arise. And it is even possible to deny the truth. Usually heresy takes the form of affirming so strongly one aspect of truth, which should be held in constant

---

238. *Cf.* for example Piet Schoonenberg, ed., *Die Interpretation des Dogmas*, (Düsseldorf, 1969).
239. *Cf.* J. S. Drey, *Kurze Einleitung in das Studium der Theologie*, (Tübingen, 1819).
240. Ser. 51, 11; PL 38, 339.

dialectic with other truths, that it denies those other truths.

Then it is necessary for the Church with her teaching authority to
step in and to decide and to declare what is error and what is dogma.
Even St. Paul seemed to sense the need of this dialectic for the clarification of the truth: "For there must be factions (αἱρέσεις) among you,
so that those of proven worth may easily be recognized" (1 Cor 11:19).

So, Schmaus mentions, St. Paul's teaching on faith and the power
of the gospel were occasioned by the Jews' errors on the saving power of
the law by itself. St. Paul's teaching on the structure and life of the
Church were occasioned by the divisive factions in the Church at Corinth.
In similar fashion we owe Augustine's teaching on the sovereignty of
grace which became Church dogma to the Pelagian controversy.

Finally there are, according to Schmaus, two other factors which
have historically contributed to the origin of dogma. Not on every
occasion has a very specific error been the reason for proclaiming a
dogma. A general situation inimical to faith (glaubensfeindliche Gesamt-
situation) can also be that reason, as it was for example, at the proclamation of Mary's bodily Assumption which was pronounced in the context
of a world in which the atheistic interpretation of human life and the
ultimacy of dialectical materialism were doctrines subscribed to by
millions. The proclamation of such a dogma is then a reassertion of the
ethical and religious dimensions to human life.

In the proclamation of the Immaculate Conception and of the
Assumption of Mary there is also a second factor at play -- the piety
of the Church. For the faithful, meditating on the scriptures, have
long believed these dogmas before the moment of their formal declaration
by the Church. "Das Dogma wird zwar von den Trägern des kirchlichen

Lehramtes verkündet, aber in ihm wird der Glaube des ganzen Gottesvolkes ausgesprochen... so verkündigen sie doch nicht einen neuen Glauben, sondern den vom ganzen Gottesvolk reflex oder unreflex vollzogenen und gelebten Glauben. Sie sagen nichts anderes, als bisher geglaubt wurde. Aber sie sagen das bisher Geglaubte, das alte Wahre, anders."[241]

Schmaus also calls attention to the doxological aspect of dogma. In the announcing of dogmas the Church proclaims its orientation to and glorification of the Lord who speaks to her. It is an accomplishment of faith and answer to the word of revelation. "Das doxologische Element lässt sich vom Dogma nicht trennen. So kommt man zu der These, dass im Dogma Gott selbst wirkt. Im Dogma ereignet sich die Selbstzusage Gottes an den Menschen..... Im Dogma kommt daher die in Jesus Christus eine für allemal geschehene Selbsterschliessung Gottes im konkreten Hier und Jetzt zur Geltung."[242] For this reason every dogma is a confession, and all confessions or creeds have dogmatic character.

As is now clear, Schmaus envisions "die Entstehung des Dogmas" not simply as a problem of dogma's origin in the sense of its first appearance, but as the ongoing confession of the Church to the truth of revelation in dogma. As such one crosses the borderline between the problem of dogma's first appearance into the problem of the development of dogma.

---

241. Schmaus, *Der Glaube der Kirche*, I, p. 196.
242. *Ibidem.*

b. Karl Rahner

Within the many theological essays of K. Rahner there are several

insights which seem to us to be of importance for understanding the

problem of the beginning of dogma. Some of these insights crop up

several times in differing contexts.

The first such (logically first) insight of significance for our

purposes is the idea that revelation is not simply or even primarily a

communication of truths from God to man. Much more is revelation a

process, indeed in Rahner's word, a "dialogue" between God and man in

which something happens -- namely salvation.

> Aber eben dieses Offenbarwerden der göttlichen Heilswahrheit ist
> nicht eine Verkündigung, die primar in Lehrsätzen oder in Katechis-
> mustexten, sondern die in Ereignissen geschieht. Denn dasjenige,
> was im Christentum verkündet wird, ist nicht eine allgemeine,
> notwendige, abastrakte Wahrheit, die man von jedem Punkt der
> Geschichte aus gleichmässig erreichen könnte, weil sie in ewiger
> Selbigkeit und Klarheit gleichsam am Himmel der Ideen steht,
> sondern das Christentum ist primär das Ereignis, in dem Gott in
> seiner Gnade an uns handelt. ...Offenbarung im eigentlichen,
> ursprünglichen Sinn ist Offenbarungstat Gottes in geschichtlicher
> Raum-Zeitlichkeit, was nicht aus-, sondern einschliesst, dass das
> Wort zu den konstitutiven Elementen der Offenbarungstat selbst
> gehört.[243]

Revelation is not just a communication of sentences, but first of

all a dialogue in history between God and man, which is as much a "doing"

as a "speaking."[244] It is something which includes words, but which may

never be identified with them.

We can elucidate Rahner's idea of revelation as not being entirely

an intellectualistic affair by pointing to the parallel notion of revel-

ation being deed as well as word in the Hebraic conception of דבר,

---

243. "Heilige Schrift und Tradition," in *Schriften zur Theologie, VI,*
      (Einsiedeln, 1965), p. 123.
244. *Cf.* "Kirchliche Christologie zwischen Exegese und Dogmatik," in
      Schriften, IX, (Einsiedeln, 1970), p. 204f., and footnote 7.

'dabar.' If one looks upon God's word solely from the aspect of the communication of truth, one ignores the real richness of the biblical concept. For 'dabar' means "deed" as well as "word," and the one implies the other. To over-intellectualize revelation and to consider it only as the communication of truths is to denature the fullness of the biblical reality.[245]

A second significant insight of Rahner's is that whereas revelation only occurs within the context of the limitations of human existence and is therefore only to be expressed in human sentences, the revelation itself is not limited to these sentences.

> Einfach darum, weil es eine höhere Form der Offenbarung.... als die Selbstmitteilung Gottes in der Gnade grundsätzlich per definitionem gar nicht geben kann, so dass diese auch der üblich so genannten Offenbarung zugrunde liegen muss, die dann freilich ein Moment der amtlichen Objektivation, der begrifflichen Vorstellung und Gerichtetheit an alle von verpflichtender Kraft, eine Ausdehnung auf alle Dimensionen des menschlichen Daseins (individueller und gesellschaftlicher Art) bei sich hat, wie sie dieser Grundoffenbarung durch die Gnade in der Tiefe des menschlichen Wesens als solcher nicht auch schon zukommt. Ist dem aber so, so ist leicht zu verstehen, dass dieser ursprüngliche Offenbarungsvorgang, der auch in der Schrift vor der Theologie liegt, nicht einfach schlechthin in Identität mit einer bestimmten Objektivation in ausgewählten Sätzen des Neuen Testamentes gesucht werden kann. Er liegt diesen zugrunde, ist aber nicht mit bestimmten begrifflich objektivierenden Sätzen identisch, auch wenn diese die absolut verpflichtende und richtig vermittelnde Objektivation des ursprünglichen Offenbarungsvorgangs für uns sind.[246]

The above is stated in an essay on the theology already to be found within the New Testament. If then revelation itself is not to be identified with particular words or sentences of the scriptures, a fortiori neither are the dogmas already to be found in the New Testament to be

---

245. *Cf.* Carroll Stuhlmueller, "The Prophet and the Word of God," *The Thomist* 28(1964), pp. 133-173.
246. "Theologie im Neuen Testament," *Schriften, V,* (Einsiedeln, 1964), pp. 52-53.

identified with the words in which they are here for the first time expressed.

Rahner's third insight is consequently that dogma, indeed Church dogma, is already to be found in the New Testament. This is part and parcel of his thinking on theology in the New Testament. Every sentence of the New Testament does not represent a separate act of revelation. Rather do we observe within the confines of the New Testament the various authors working through problems which were presented in their times by referring back to previous revelation and reasoning on it. Such a "conclusion-type" theology does not do away with the necessity of revelation; it rather demonstrates, for example, how the nuances between sayings of the historical Jesus and the early community theology balance in the biblical expression, which we take to be the word of God itself. Thus the differences between Paul and the synoptics or John are not always, or perhaps even most of the time, to be attributed to separate and successive acts of revelation on God's part. They attest rather to the historicality of faith which is, with the change time implies, repeatedly to be expressed in different forms.

So one can safely say, "weil es im NT schon Theologie gibt, die dennoch Dogma ist, kann es solche Theologie auch in der späteren Kirche geben."[247] To use the word 'dogma' in this context necessitates our also indicating in what sense Rahner understands the word.

In at least two places Rahner gives descriptive "definitions" of dogma.[248] He states: "Kein katholischer Theologe wird bestreiten, dass

247. *Ibidem*, p. 40.
248. *Cf.* also Rahner's articles "Dogma," *LThK*, III, 438-441, 443-446; and "Dogma" and "History of Dogma," *Sacramentum Mundi*, II, (New York, 1968), pp. 95-98, 102-107.

es in der Kirche Dogmen gibt, die als solche wahre Aussage der Offenbarung sind, also mit göttlichem und nicht bloss mit kirchlichem Glauben geglaubt werden können und müssen -- und doch nicht als sie selber einem unmittelbaren Offenbarungsvorgang entspringen, sondern aus einem oder mehreren Sätzen ursprünglicher oder ursprünglicherer Offenbarung abgeleitet, expliziert sind."[249] Another "definition" brings out other elements common to the Catholic understanding of the reality: "Es ist zwar für jeden katholischen Theologen selbstverständlich, dass, wenn das aktuelle heutige Glaubensbewusstsein der Kirche eine Wahrheit als wirklich mit göttlichem Glauben geglaubt und als apostolische Überlieferung bezeugt, festhält und erklärt in einem unfehlbaren Spruch eines Papstes oder eines Konzils, diese Überzeugung kraft der Indefektibilität des Glaubens der Kirche auch wahr sein muss, also wirklich apostolische Überlieferung bedeutet, auch dann, wenn der einzelne Theologe oder Gläubige diese Tatsache noch nicht historisch nachgewiesen und ausdrücklich gemacht hat."[250]

A fourth insight of Rahner's which we find meaningful for our theme is the way he perceives the human side in the perception of revelation. He speaks of a global, unreflex, and pre-sentential experience of revelation. Even in the natural and profane experience of the human spirit there are many such global perceptions of a total reality which is too rich for immediate translation into human words, e.g., a mother's love, patriotism, etc. One knows exactly what those concepts mean, but one cannot express them forthwith in words.

One must have this global and unreflex knowledge of any reality

---

249. "Theologie im Neuen Testament," p. 35.
250. "Heilige Schrift und Tradition," p. 134.

before it is analyzable into logically separate but interrelated propositions. "Wir sehen: ursprüngliches, satzloses, unreflexes wissendes Haben einer Wirklichkeit und reflexes (satzhaftes), artikuliertes Wissen um dieses ursprüngliche Wissen sind keine sich Konkurrenz machenden Gegensätze, sondern sich gegenseitig bedingende Momente iner einzigen Erfahrung, die notwendig ihre Geschichte hat. .... Das reflexe Wissen hat immer seine Wurzeln in einer vorausliegenden, wissenden Inbesitznahme der Sache selbst."[251]

It is this preliminary unreflex possession of a matter of faith which is the principium inprincipiatum of every dogmatic development, whether within the continuum of historical time of the Church's existence after the appearance of the New Testament, or even before the appearance of the same when theology and dogma had already made their debut.

What then is a dogmatic statement? This question is the title of an essay in which Rahner attempts to formulate the conditions of an adequate answer.[252] He does this in terms of five propositions, reflecting at length on each proposition.

Raher's first proposition is that a dogmatic statement is a statement which professes to be true in the sense that any other statement of daily life is true. Naturally included then in this assertion are the following: "Verhältnis zum Aussagenden, Logik, Geschichtlichkeit der Begriffselement, Eingebettetheit der Aussage in einen geschichtlichen und gesellschaftlichen Zusammenhang, Verschiedenheit der literarischen Genera, unreflektierte Gemeinsamkeiten zwischen Hörendem und Redendem,

---

251. "Zur Frage der Dogmenentwicklung," *Schriften, I,* (Einsiedeln, 1964), p. 77.
252. "Was ist eine dogmatische Aussage," *Schriften, V,* (Einsiedeln, 1964), pp. 54-81.

ohne die eine Verständigungsmoglichkeit gar nicht gegeben wäre."[253]

A dogmatic statement is meant to be true then in the sense that any human statement is true, and this despite the de facto state of fallen human nature. It attempts to express a determined content which is not simply the externalization of a subjective state of the speaker, but which denotes an objectivity existing apart from him. This is carried out, however, in terms of analogy and the positive representations on which man is necessarily dependent when attempting to express the supersensible. Thus even a dogmatic statement presupposes the claim of truth not to be equally true and false, as it were, if dependent solely on the state of the speaker (as in absolute existentialism or modernism), but rather in the sense that one can objectively posit the question of its trueness.

Rahner's second proposition is that a dogmatic statement is a statement of faith, and indeed not in the sense that it simply says something about faith, but in the sense that in its very assertion faith is accomplished. A dogmatic statement involves not only the fides quae creditur, but also the fides qua creditur.

That is to say that the hearing of the word of God always involves the concrete man, and in his very hearing of that word a hearkening (or rejection), which implies a certain amount of theological reflection. Theology in the narrower sense, and thereby dogmatic statements, are only refinements of this reflexion. Thus a real dogmatic statement can never be completely separated from the act of faith itself. There is then an immense difference between the statement of a mere professor of religion and that of a believer, albeit both might discourse with similar or

253. *Ibidem*, p. 56.

identical words about the same faith objects.

Rahner's third proposition is that a dogmatic statement is always
an ecclesial statement. The reason for this is that the Church "das
Subjekt der erlösenden Heilstat Gottes und des Glaubens selbst ist, da
dieser wesentlich vom Hören kommt und von der Bezeugung der Botschaft
Christi abhängig bleibt, diese aber in der Gemeinde der Glaubenden, von
ihr und für sie geschieht."[254] Believing, confessing, praising are not
the only activities that take place in the Church; it is also the place
where theology (reflection on faith) produces a genuinely dogmatic statement. Although theology would undoubtedly exist if revelation were
individual, a "churchly" theology exists because revelation is eph'hap̓ax,"
and therefore communal and historical. Thus, when the Church theologizes
in an authoritative way, and it must be able to do this, it dogmatizes
or gives rise to what Rahner calls a "Sprachregelung."

The exercise of such a 'regulation of speech' about a certain
matter of faith does not mean that the matter can be expressed only in
this way. Neither does it mean that such an authoritative formulation is
absolutely the best expression of this matter of faith for all time.
It does, however, signify that at a particular time in its history and on
a particular occasion the Church becomes conscious of its faith in a
particular word, which then becomes a guiding line for all time.

An example of such 'regulation of speech' which is not completely
satisfying is that part of the Church dogma of original sin which asserts
that man is in the state of sin from Adam, i.e., a sinner from his origin.
One might think that there would be a better way of expressing this
reality. Nevertheless, the previous course of the history of dogma and

---
254. *Ibidem*, p. 65.

its terminology will always influence the discussion of this matter.

A theological statement points to the mystery. This is the fourth proposition. It leads to mystery in the same way a kerygmatic statement does, although in a dogmatic statement the moment of human reflexion is more prominent, while a kerygmatic statement remains that original statement upon which all later dogmatic reflexion must relate itself.

The conceptuality of the statement always points towards transcendance. Even when in the accomplishment of a dogmatic statement man is moved by the Spirit and grace of God, one may never assume that to have at one's disposal the conceptuality is the same as having that towards which it points. The dogmatic remains a part, a hint, a direction towards, a coming close to the reality itself.

Rahner's fifth proposition is that a dogmatic statement is not identical with the original word of revelation, i.e., the original expression of faith. The difference between the two does not consist in the fact that the one is the pure word of God, the other simply human reflexion upon it. For as soon as the word of God is grasped and believed by men, already there is reflexion upon it and hence also theology. Indeed, the two are already discoverable in the New Testament. The difference between the two is rather to be seen therein that the word of revelation consists in happenings and statements, "die die bleibende und unüberholbare norma normans, non normata für alle späteren dogmatischen Aussagen bilden, eben diese ursprünglichen Aussagen."[255]

And so the original expression of revelation (of which the scriptures are the prototype) will always retain a certain preeminence over all subsequent expression of even the same revelation, even when

---

255. *Ibidem*, p. 77.

issued in an authoritative way. For that original expression consists
in the sayings and happenings of the original historical event of
salvation upon which all later preaching and theology must base itself.
It is moreover necessary that the original **ex**pressions of revelation be
translated by the Church into differing forms at various times in order
that the original message may even be heard. And **rather** than a merely
historical investigation, the guarantee for hearing the original message
is always the faith of the actual Church.

It is also worth calling attention to the fact that one may not
point to the scriptures as the pure form of revelation, contrasting it
with the admixture of later times which involves theology and reflexion.
The reason for this is, as already stated, that in the early tradition
we already find reflexion, theology, unbinding theologumena, human
opinions, even errors. The task of refining the essential from that
tradition is the function of the teaching Church working under the
guidance **of** the Spirit, whose assistance has been promised to it.

Still to distinguish would be the dogmatic declaration of the
Church in its ordinary and extraordinary teaching functions from the
dogmatic word of private theologians which, while not of itself having
binding force, will nevertheless insofar as it truly is a 'dogmatic'
word -- i.e., reflecting or pointing to the faith-consciousness of the
Church -- direct the hearer toward the normal faith of the Church in its
everyday teaching authority. The borders between these various types of
dogmatic statements will not always be clear, particularly when the
private theologian offers something which might seem to be a sententia
libera, whereas in fact it attempts, insofar as it is truly theological,
to make the grasping and assimilation of the statements of faith by

others more comprehensible. For, "die theologisch entscheidende Funktion der theologisch freien dogmatischen Aussage ist doch gewiss die, das wirklich Geglaubte besser zu sehen und zu bekennen, Hilfe also für den Glauben selbst zu sein."[256]

Further also to distinguish would be the first confessional relating of oneself in verbal form to the matter of faith itself from that consecutive reality, the first reflexion upon the same, even within the context of the same verbal expression. These two types of dogmatic statement -- the one respecting the reflection on the possession of the matter of faith, the other respecting the matter of faith itself -- are never completely separable, since human knowledge is ever both immediate and reflex.

It is striking how Rahner's reflexions on the dogmatic statement as global experience and dogmatic statement as reflexive perception parallels Cardinal Newman's distinction between notional and real apprehension as applied to dogma. Indeed, Rahner's elaboration needs the explication that that distinction affords.

In conclusion it must be said that Rahner's reflections on the nature of revelation, the characteristics of a dogmatic statement, and in particular the relationship between the two, help clarify the nature of the problem of the beginning of dogma, already a reality in the time of the New Testament.

---

256. *Ibidem*, p. 81.

c. Aloys Grillmeier

In the first part of his work, *Christ in Christian Tradition, From the Apostolic Age to Chalcedon (451)*,[257] which is a comprehensive study of the growth of the Christological dogma from its beginnings in scripture until its formulation at Chalcedon, A. Grillmeier makes the point that the most influential of all New Testament texts on the growth of Christology is Jn 1:14. It is, he says, "the most penetrating description of the career of Jesus Christ that has been written."[258] In it "Christ appears as the definitive word of God to man, as the unique and absolute revealer, transcending all prophets." He is more than Moses, a lawgiver, for he brings grace and truth. In the many "I am" sayings of John's Gospel he is "Light" and "Life" of the world; thus he himself is a part of the message that is revealed. For it is the incarnation itself which best expresses the center of this Gospel, and this mystery is expressed in the tension built into the Logos-sarx concept.

The Logos in John is first of all 'revealer'; he has the same office as the Logos of Apo 19:11-16, i.e., divine ambassador. The message of this 'revealer' is intimately linked with who he is. So in 1 Jn 1:1-3 it is impossible to separate the teaching of the Logos from his person.

The notion of Logos as spoken word rather than reason seems to predominate in John. The two associated expressions θεός and μονογενής deepen and clarify the Johannine concept. All three terms "imply one and the same subject who is to be understood as preexistent, beyond time

---

257. New York, 1965. This is the extensively revised version of the article which appeared in *Das Konzil von Chalkedon*, (Würzburg, 1962³).
258. *Cf. ibidem*, p. 27ff.

and beyond the world. The Logos is God in God, mediator of creation and
bringer of revelation -- and this in the full sense by virtue of his
appearance in the flesh. He 'is' the Word of God in the flesh."[259]

Undoubtedly the first source for this doctrine is the Old Testament
theology of the word of God. But the wisdom tradition in Israel is also
a part of it, for the resemblance of John's prologue to Pro 8 and Eccl 24
is too close to be accidental. An additional influence may be the
already formed Pauline traditions of Christ being the "effulgence" and
"image" of God, as in Col 1:15, 2 Cor 4:4, and Heb 1:3.

It would be entirely misguided then to seek the source of the
Johannine Logos concept exclusively in the Hellenistic world. Yet if the
Evangelist choose this particular word and concept already so fraught
with meaning in the world of Greek learning, he must have done it with
conscious purpose. Its usage in John is then a witness of the encounter
of these two different worlds at an early date.

Grillmeier says of the prologue:

> It stands apart, like a Greek facade to the Jewish-Christian
> building that is behind -- the Gospel. .... The analogy should
> not be pressed, for the facade too is essentially of the Old
> Testament, and Christian, even though Hellenistic influence is
> unmistakable. This Logos concept is certainly more than mere
> frontage, put up on the outside; it is intrinsically bound up
> with the Gospel. But at the same time it represents a real accep-
> tance of ideas from the Greeks, even though the content assigned
> to them by John gives back to the Greeks infinitely more than
> they were able to bring to him. The Greek view of the Logos is
> in itself by no means sufficient explanation of the Johannine
> concept. While Heraclitus and the Stoics make the Logos the
> principle governing the cosmos, they allow that it is immanent.
> The Logos of the Prologue, on the other hand, is at the same time
> both personal and transcendent.[260]

The pecularly Johannine antithesis of logos and sarx together with

259. *Ibidem*, p. 30.
260. *Ibidem*, pp. 32-33.

their "depth of synthesis" is what makes the theology of the prologue so much less a "Hellenization" than a "Christianization." For nowhere in Hellenic thought is the logos at once personal, transcendent, and so uniquely immanent.

The work of the fathers of Chalcedon was clearly 'dogmatic' in intent and fact, i.e., in the sense of teaching officially what was the truth of Christian faith in opposition to the variant opinions of Nestorius and Eutyches. Grillmeier is nevertheless at pains in the latter part of his book to show that this work was not 'dogmatic' in the sense of setting up a new formula which in any way departed from the faith and tradition of the Church. Grillmeier does not even believe that any of the fathers of that council could have produced a philosophic definition of the concepts employed. "This had the disadvantage of leaving much unclear, but at the same time the advantage -- in view of the worldwide sifnificance of the statement -- of leaving open the expression of much about which the fathers could not as yet think explicitly."[261] "Even though the concepts of hypostasis and prosopon have not yet been defined, the sense of the dogma of Chalcedon is quite clear. The fathers mean to say that while there is a real distinction between the natures of Godhead and manhood, Christ is still to be described as 'one,' as 'one person or hypostasis.'"[262]

In a very real sense Chalcedon is then, as Karl Rahner has said, less an end than a beginning.[263] It is for the identical reason that the appearance of the Christological dogma is not a problem for

261.   *Ibidem*, p. 483.
262.   *Ibidem*, p. 486.
263.   *Cf*. "Chalkedon -- Ende oder Anfang?" in *Das Konzil von Chalkedon, III*, pp. 3-49.

Grillmeier in this extensive work on Chalcedon. For the Church's adoption of the dogma in the formula of Chalcedon is in no way the assertion of an arbitrarily adopted opinion; it is simply the reaffirmation of the constant tradition of the scriptures and earlier councils. This is seen in the wider usage of homoousion at Chalcedon, which word had already been employed at Nicea.[264] In no sense then is Chalcedon a "new" dogma.

> The Chalcedonian unity of person in the distinciton of the natures provides the dogmatic basis for the preservation of the divine transcendence, which must always be a feature of the Christian concept of God. But it also shows the possibility of a complete immanence of God in our history, an immanence on which the biblical doctrine of the economy of salvation rests. The Chalcedonian definition may seem to have a static-ontic ring, but it is not meant to do away with the salvation-historical aspect of biblical christology, for which, in fact, it provides a foundation and deeper insights.[265]

d. Georg Söll

In a sober and objective way Georg Söll takes up the historical usage and development of the notion, "dogma," in his work, *Dogma und Dogmenentwicklung*.[266] In so doing he is able to point to the continuity in development from the ancient usage of the term to its increasingly theological acceptance within the stream of Christian tradition. On the basis of the biblical evidence he even states, and in this we cannot agree,[267] the following: Da Lukas nur berichtet und Paulus δόγμα als Bezeichnung für religiose Wahrheiten auch in Eph 2, 15 u. Kol 2, 14 gebraucht, hat also der Dogmenbegriff bereits innerhalb der apostolischen

---

264. *Cf.* Grillmeier, *op. cit.*, pp. 484-485.
265. *Ibidem*, p. 491.
266. *Handbuch der Dogmengeschichte*, eds., M. Schmaus, A. Grillmeier, L. Scheffczyk, vol. I, (Freiburg, 1971).
267. *Cf. infra*, section 2 of this chapter, pp. 133- 136.

Zeit durch Paulus, wenn nicht durch das beschlussfassende Apostelkonzil, eine neue, und zwar die entscheidende christlich Bedeutungsvariante empfangen. Es ist Sammelbezeichnung für eine verbindliche Weisung in Glaubens- und Sittenfragen."[268] Indeed, the wholesale acceptance of this word for Christian usage was by no means accomplished in New Testament times. Although it is true that the Fathers of the Church were not always comfortable with this word, many of them did not hesitate to use it in a positive and ecclesiastical way. Söll sees its ecclesiastical usefullness founded on two factors: "Einmal wegen seines Charakters als Lehrsatz, d. h. als prägnante Zusammenfassung eines zur Annahme vorgelegten Lehrgegenstandes, zum zweiten wegen des damit erhobenen Anspruchs auf Gültigkeit und Verbindlichkeit."[269] The high point of this adaptation is to be found in the early centuries in Vincent of Lérin's *Commonitorium* in which the whole tradition of Christian teaching is referred to as "dogma," and in Gennadius' *Liber Ecclesiasticorum Dogmatum*. The former remained practically unknown for a thousand years, and the latter was for a long time improperly attributed to Augustine.[270] Despite the negative connotations of the term, and of which we treat at length earlier in this work, there was also a concurrent positive ecclesiastical usage, as when St. Bernard of Clairvaux writes that, "It is the affair of the pope to judge about dogmas."[271] It is Söll's merit that he rightly points to this continuity and developing aspect of the concept. Thus he corrects the erroneous impression given by Nolte, that the ancient use of the word would only point to a negative yield for the use of the word

---

268. Söll, *op. cit.*, p. 4.
269. *Ibidem*, p. 11.
270. *Cf. ibidem*, pp. 11-12.
271. Ep. 189, 5 (PL 182, 355C).

within the Church.

Consonant with the scope of his work, Söll traces the development
of the concept of dogma in its relationship to the question of the
development of dogma.[272] To the work of Melchior Cano in the development
of this concept he attributes only "einen beachtlichen Fortschritt," and
does not clearly grasp what we were able in an earlier chapter to prove,
namely that it is (apparently) first in Cano's *De Locis Theologicis* that
the clear, conceptual change from the ancient usage of the concept of
dogma to the modern ecclesiastical notion finds its original literary
expression.[273]

Söll attributes a greater weight in the precising of the notion to
Vincent Gotti (1664-1742). This is, however, not entirely correct since
the notion of dogma as a revealed truth, deriving from Christ or the Holy
Spirit, which has been held by the fathers in either the vocal or written
tradition of the Church, and which has been defined by a general council
or by a supreme pontiff, in other words, the notion of dogma which is
identified with the teaching of Vatican I, is already to be found in

---

272. *Cf.* Söll, *op. cit.*, p. 13: "...der Dogmenbegriff reflektiert den
DE-Prozess, aber nicht in dem Sinn, als ob seine Grundelemente
einer wesentlichen Veränderung unterlägen oder ihm neue entscheidende Begriffselemente zugewachsen wären, sondern nur insoweit,
als die grundsätzliche Möglichkeit und erweisebare Tatsächlichkeit
neuer dogmatischer Definitionen und somit eines quantitativen
Wachstums der Glaubenslehre im Laufe der DG im Dogmenbegriff
selbst einen Niederschlag finden musste, wenn anders er für alle
Phasen der historischen Entwicklung zutreffend und verbindlich
sein sollte. Es ist also sehr wohl ein Unterschied, ob man sagt,
es sei das Schicksal des Dogmas, immer wieder der DG anheimzu-
fallen (Chr. Baur), oder ob man einräumt, dass die DE klärend und
präzisierend auf den Dogmenbegriff eingewirkt hat."

273. The "noticeable progression" which Söll finds in Cano he mentions
on p. 12. The question of the definability of theological conclusions in Cano he treats on pp. 152-160. The proof of our
position on Cano is developed in this chapter, part 7, section c,
pp. 156-160.

Cano's *De Locis Theologicis* of 1563 at least a century before the time of Gotti.

Making the distinction between what is de fide -- that which is revealed by God, and what is de fide tenenda -- that which is revealed by God and which is presented by the Church to be believed, Gotti is simply interested in what Soll calls the "Art seiner [d. h., Dogmas] Festellung."[274] So Gotti in his *Theologia Scholastico-Dogmatica* from 1727-1735: "Aliquod dogma fidei dici potest, vel immediate, quia nimirum in Verbo Dei scripto vel tradito continetur, vel mediate, quia ex Verbo Dei huiusmodi necessaria infertur et colligitur. ...Quid sit, quidque requiratur, ut aliquid fiat dogma fidei? Dico primo: illud omne et solum est de fide divina in se, quod est revelatum in Dei verbo. Dico secundo: ut aliqua veritas tenenda a nobis sit tamquam de fide et ut a Deo revelata, requiritur ulterius, ut ab Ecclesia Catholica sit omnibus proposita tamquam a Deo revelata et ut fide divina credenda."[275] In opposition then to Söll, we find the decisive step in the evolution of the concept of dogma between Vincent of Lérin and the First Vatican Council not in the work of Vincent Gotti, but in that of Melchior Cano. For Cano clearly couples definition by pope or council with the authoritative ecclesiastical moment of dogma.[276]

In his further discussion of the development of the concept of dogma, Söll points to the fact that Vatican I was less interested in a "definition" (Begriffsbestimmung), than in delimiting what must be believed with divine and ecclesiastical faith in opposition to contrary

---

274. Söll, *op. cit.*
275. *Trac. Isag.*, dub. 4., vol. 1, 25; quoted from Soll, *ibidem.*
276. *Cf.* the same quote from Cano, above on pp. 157-158.

opinions. Therefore, much of the discussion of dogma has had to do with its juridical nature, and less often with its truth value.

By way of conclusion Söll offers his own definition of dogma: "Das Dogma ist also durch die Entwicklung des Begriffs wie durch Festellung der Kirche selbst ausgewiesen als eine vom kirchlichen Lehramt im Lauf der Geschichte unfehlbar und verbindlich vorgelegte Offenbarungswahrheit."[277] He lists five essential elements to dogma: "Das Dogma ist nämlich 1. seinem Inhalt nach eine Offenbarungswahrheit, 2. seiner Form nach ein Lehrsatz, 3. seiner objektiven Gültigkeit nach eine unfehlbare Glaubensaussage, 4. seinem subjektiven Geltungsanspruch nach eine jeden Gläubigen der Kirche im Gewissen verpflichtende Richtschnur und 5. seinem Werdegang nach eine im Lauf der Geschichte durch die Kirche vorgenommene Festellung."[278]

In his chapter, "Der Dogmenbegriff in seinen Äquivalenten," Söll considers two areas which are of interest to us here, the relationships between dogma and kerygma, and between dogma and teaching.

Söll places dogma and kerygma in relation to one another not because he envisages the one taking the place of the other, but by way of contrast. The difference between the living, primitive Christian preaching and a system of theologically explicated propositions is too evident to need further discussion. Nevertheless, Söll finds himself in agreement enough with H. Schlier's programatic essay which we shall discuss in chapter five, to declare: "Da es heute die Exegese innerhalb und ausserhalb der katholischen Kirche anerkennt, dass sich in den ntl. Schriften mehrmals bei bedeutenden Glaubensaussagen vorevangelische bzw.

---

277. Söll, *op. cit.*, p. 22
278. *Ibidem*, p. 20.

quasiliturgische Formulierungen finden, kommt der im Hinblick auf die spätere DE zu verstehenden Präexistenz eines unantastbaren, normativen und artikulierten, d. h. in klare Sätze und Präsymbola fixierten Glaubensgutes als ntl. Begründung des Dogmas tiefgreifende Bedeutung zu, und die Bewertung des so gemeinten Kerygmas als Äquivalent für Dogma ist daher durchaus vollziehbar."[279] Söll qualifies his agreement with the reservation: "Äquivalenz ist nicht Identität." However, one cannot cover over the fact that many of the essential qualities of dogma (Weseneigenschaften) are to be found in these primeval forms of the kerygma: factual identity with the truth of revelation, proclamation by the Church, the claim of infallible validity with the corresponding responsibility of obedient acceptance. This equivalence but non-identity Söll moderates with the following sentence: "Gleichwohl ist anzuerkennen, dass die Urform des Kerygmas die Weseneigenschaften des Dogmas in sich barg: sachliche Identität mit Offenbarungswahrheit, wobei die Wortoffenbarung darin ebenso aufgehoben im Sinn von aufbewahrt ist wie die Tatoffenbarung ('Christus ist erstanden!' und andere kerygmatische Niederschläge im Symbolum), Proklamation durch die Kirche, Anspruch auf unfehlbare Gültigkeit und Verpflichtung zu gehorsamer Annahme."[280] It would seem then that Söll sees a substantial identity between kerygma and dogma. The only one of his five above discussed essential qualities of dogma which may be lacking here is that kerygma is not always, if only seldom, expressed as a teaching (Lehrsatz). But this is a somewhat minor consideration, since religion is always dependent on words and consequently, on the communication of teaching as the next paragraphs will demonstrate.

---

279. *Ibidem*, pp. 25-26.
280. *Ibidem*, p. 26.

Dogma has an intimate relationship to teaching because, "die Offenbarung selbst ein intellektualistisches Gepräge hat."[281] Although variant understandings of revelation might well disagree with the above statement, they would be difficult to bring into harmony with the following facts of Christian tradition. Jesus identified himself as "the way, the truth, and the life" (Jn 14:6). He spoke of his Father's word as the "truth" (Jn 17:17), and he spoke of his own mission in life as being the manifestation of this truth or of "words" of the Father (Jn 17:7-8). Furthermore, if revelation is simply the unveiling of an existent state of affairs, it at least takes place through the communication of knowledge. Neither grace nor enthusiasm can completely explain the Christian message; it must at least also be explained as the communication of words: "For the Law was given through Moses; grace and truth through Jesus Christ" (Jn 1:17).

It is easy to multiply examples from the fathers of the Church which illustrate that they not only identified dogma with teaching, but were also quite conscious of the intellectual nature of the Christian kerygma. So, for example, Ignatius of Antioch: "Be assiduous to become strong in the dogmas of the Lord" (*Magn.* 13); and Irenaeus: "For if there were in reality neither good nor bad, but only this or that would be valid according to the opinion of men, then he (Christ) would not have spoken as a dogmatist" (*Adv. Haereses*, 2, 32). Söll points finally to the fact that the medieval way of identifying scripture and theology with the expressions, "sacra pagina," or "sacra doctrina," exemplify the then traditional way of looking at revelation as much as theology and dogma

---

281. *Ibidem*, p. 27.

as teaching.[282]

Yet the tendency to identify dogma with teaching was not without its problems. On the one hand, this terminology tended to emphasize the manner of presentation rather than the content, and on the other hand, dogma began to denote an unduly wide amount of material as it became "allgemeinste Bezeichnung für das katholische Glaubensgut." Linked thereto were the ideas that dogma could only be expressed in precisely determined formulae, and that these formulae always represented some type of logical connection with revelation.

In part these effects must be attributed to the exclusively intellectual outlook of scholasticism, which disregarded the intuitive and affective elements of dogma. This was, of course, the ground not only for Luther's criticism of dogma, but also for that of Romanticism and of Modernism. At the end of his historical overview of the equivalents for dogma Söll insists that this ecclesiastical reality is also a limited quantity which may not be stretched beyond the limits set for it by the First Vatican Council. "Was mit diesen 5 Komponenten: 1. Offenbarungswahrheit, 2. kirchliche Vorlage, 3. unfehlbares Lehrurteil, 4. verbindliche Glaubenspflicht, 5. Geschichtlichkeit nicht ausgesagt ist, darf füglich nicht vom Dogmenbegriff verlangt werden. Das Dogma darf also nicht mit 'Wesen des Christentums identifiziert werden."[283]

Söll's final words to the problem of the beginning of dogma are found in his chapter, "Die Entwicklung der christlichen Lehre im Licht des NTs." The question of the development of dogma is inextricably tied up with the question of dogma's beginning. For what the Church

---

282. *Ibidem*, p. 29.
283. *Ibidem*, p. 45.

understands under dogma -- an infallibly binding proposition of revealed truth taught by the Church in some one or other historical form -- has existed right from the beginning of Christianity itself, and therefore before that particular and very historically conditioned designation, "dogma," obtained a special Christian usage.

Although the fact of revelation came to a close with the death of the last apostle, revelation and its dogmatic presentation were already in process of development. So, Söll finds himself in agreement with K. Rahner and K. Lehmann in their following statement: "So sehr alles, was in der Schrift steht, für uns 'Dogma' und nicht bloss diskutable Theo-logie ist, so wahr ist es auch, dass vieles in diesem Dogma der Schrift, das für uns die Qualität der irrtumsfreien Aussage der Offenbarung hat, selbst abgeleitete Theologie ist im Bezug auf eine ursprünglichere Aussage der Offenbarung."[284]

Explicitly then, Soll identifies himself with the position that dogma begins already on the level of the New Testament, and at that moment of separation from the historical Jesus when faith, reflecting on its experience, begins to express itself in "dogmatic" teachings.

> Nichts widerlegt die Auffassung jener Dogmenhistoriker, die die apostolische Zeit aus der Darstellungen der DE ausklammern wollen, gründlicher als diese 'Theologen des NT' im engsten und besten Sinn des Wortes [d. h., die Apostel].
> Sowenig das NT auf den ersten Blick zur Theorie und zu den Prob-lemen der DE zu sagen scheint, so unanfechtbar sicher ist durch sein eigenes Zeugnis, dass die Entwicklung der christlichen Lehre, näherhin ihre Ausprägung in Form von Dogmen, in ihm selbst begon-nen hat. Dabei ist nicht entscheidend, ob man das Osterereignis und den dadurch in den Aposteln und in der ganzen jungen Kirche vollzogenen Wandel in Glauben und Glaubenseinsicht als Ausgangs-punkt betrachtet oder, was innerlich als begründeter erscheint, die Himmelfahrt des Herrn, d. h. den Augenblick, da die Apostel

---

284. *Mysterium Salutis*, I, pp. 738-741, (Einsiedeln, 1965); *cf*. Söll, *op. cit.*, p. 68, footnote 27.

232

und die Kirche nun nicht mehr mit ihrem Herrn, sondern nur noch über ihn sprechen und nachsinnen konnten. Die raum-zeitliche Trennung vom historischen Jesus erweist sich als der gemeinsame Beginn sowohl der gläubigen Reflexion über die durch Christus verkörperte und verkündete Offenbarung, d. h. der christlichen Theologie, wie der mit ihr unlösbar verbundenen Dogmen, d. h. der Hilfe der Glaubenswissenschaft aus der Offenbarung erhobenen Lehrsätze.[285]

In this statement of position on the beginning of dogma Söll shows himself to be in agreement with two Protestant theologians, who also see the beginning of dogma in the New Testament. W. Schneemelcher writes: "Es genügt die Feststellung, dass die Dogmenbildung mit der ersten Predigt nach Ostern einsetzt."[286]

The other Protestant with whom Söll finds himself in agreement is the historian of dogma, Peter Meinhold, who finds the beginning of dogma in the New Testament, but at an even lower level than the New Testament text itself, namely in the dogmatic claim of Jesus.[287]

Das Dogma ist also eine Aussage über die Bedeutung der Person und des Werkes Jesu für das von ihm verkündete Evangelium. In ihm ist impliziert die gesamte spätere dogmengeschichtliche Entwicklung enthalten. Indem Jesus beansprucht, die eschatologische Heils-gestalt zu sein, die die Gottesherrschaft schon jetzt wirklich werden lässt, ist die Aufgabe vorgegeben, das Verhältnis von 'Göttlichem' und 'Menschlichem' an seiner Person auszudrücken. Und indem der Himmelsmensch sein Werk durch Verwerfung und Tod hindurch vollenden kann, ist die andere Aufgabe vorgegeben, den Sinn seines Werkes in bezug auf die Menschheit festzuhalten. In dem dogmatischen Anspruch Jesu selbst ist deshalb vorgebildet, was im Laufe der Geschichte in Christologie und Soteriologie zu voller Entfaltung kommt. Wir werden deshalb nicht mehr von einem undogmatischen Christentum, das an den Anfängen unserer Religion gestanden hatte, sprechen können. Es genügt auch nicht, das Kerygma der Apostel bzw. der Urgemeinde oder urgemeindliche und spätere Bekenntnisse als den Grund des Dogmas anzusprechen; denn sie setzen es ja immer schon voraus, knüpfen daran an oder legen es aus. Demgegenüber gilt es festzuhalten, dass das Dogma seinen

---

285. Söll, *op. cit.*, p. 63.
286. "Das Problem der DG," in *ZThK* 48 (1951), p. 83. *Cf.* Söll, *op. cit.*, p. 63.
287. *Cf.* above the section on Meinhold, pp. 99-103.

Ursprung bei Jesus selbst hat und in seiner Selbstaussage verwurzelt ist, durch die er sich selbst in das Zentrum seines Evangeliums gerückt hat. Keimartig ist in diesem Anspruch die spätere Entwicklung zu den kirchlichen Bekenntnissen und zu den christlichen Lehren und Dogmen angelegt.[288]

Although Meinhold seems to have a somewhat fluid notion of dogma, "...eine Aussage über die Bedeutung der Person und des Werkes Jesu für das von ihm verkündete Evangelium," the fact that Söll finds himself in substantial agreement with him in finding the beginning of dogma at least on the level of the New Testament, if not in the dogmatic claim of Jesus himself, is more than noteworthy. It demonstrates that the traditional and antagonistic positions of those finding the beginning of dogma in "early Catholicism" versus those who would see the beginning of dogma and of every dogma in scripture may be coming to an end. "Da es erwiesen ist, dass sich im NT zugleich theologische Reflexion über die dort berichteten Heilslehren und Heilstatsachen findet und die Bibel als Ganzes Ausdruck und Zeugnis des urchristlichen Glaubensbewusstseins ist, erscheinen Bibel und Dogma auch unter diesem Aspekt als unlösbar miteinander verbunden."[289]

e. Jan Hendrik Walgrave

The most complete description of the psychological process of the beginning of dogma from a Catholic viewpoint is given by J. H. Walgrave in his book, *Unfolding Revelation, The Nature of Doctrinal Development.*[290] Ostensibly this book is a study of the notion of development in Christian tradition. After studying this concept in the patristic era and in

288. "Der Ursprung des Dogmas in der Verkundigung Jesu," *ZkTh* 89 (1967), p. 137; *cf.* Söll, *op. cit.*, p. 68.
289. Söll, *op. cit.*, p. 68.
290. Philadelphia, 1972.

medieval theology, Walgrave divides the modern theories on the development of dogma into three categories: logical, transformistic, theological.

The logical theories are those which center around a propositional
theory of truth and of revelation. These theories view the development
of dogma simply as a logical and syllogistic process. Marín-Sola is
their chief exponent. The transformistic theory is really not one theory
at all, but all those theories outside Catholicism which teach a dogmatic
relativism. Another way of stating the common feature of these theories
is that they (e.g., J. S. Semler, F. Schleiermacher, A. Harnack, P. Van
Buren) believe the bible is to be interpreted not by the objective rule
established for centuries in Christian life and experience, but according
o private judgment.

The theological theories are principally those of the Tübingen
school (especially J. A. Möhler) and of J. H. Newman which understand
doctrinal development as the progressive and various forms of a living
theological tradition in history, the ultimate criterion of which is
always the consensus of the magisterial Church.

There are several presuppositions to Walgrave's own theological
reflections. Although these presuppositions are well enough known, they
perhaps bear repeating here for the sake of setting the context for
further reflection.

The first is what Newman called "the principle of dogma, that is,
supernatural truths irrevocably committed to human language, imperfect
because it is human, but definitive and necessary because given from
above."[291] The second presupposition is that objective revelation has
een closed with the end of the apostolic age, which principle orthodox

---

1. *Cf. ibidem*, p. 8; Newman, *Development*, p. 179.

Christianity generally admits. Without this principle there is no development of dogma; with it there arises the duty and problem of reconciling the truth of dogma with the historicity of human thought and language. Since dogmas are "such propositions about revealed truth as are generally accepted by the consensus of the Church or consecrated by a definition of its highest authority in matters of doctrine,"[292] the distinction between _dogma_ and _dogmas_ is important. A dogma or the religious truth affirmed in such a proposition may be stated in various ways with relative degrees of accuracy and suitability in historical existence. Therefore, the propositions' themselves, the _dogmas_, are always subject to revision although the _dogma_ itself is not.

In his own attempt at a 'comparative synthesis' of the theological theories Walgrave reverts to this distinction. Faith comes from hearing. It is therefore something given by God, a knowledge and an expression which, nevertheless, is never adequately expressed in the articulation of human language. Therefore, the propositions themselves are not properly the object of faith. This is to say that the material object of faith differs from the propositional forms in which it is expressed. "Man's inner perception goes beyond them and reaches the real itself, the Dogma."[293]

Yet how can man possibly perceive the two (the real as well as the propositional) within the one formula? This is accomplished _per modum unius_ through the fact that God reveals himself in this way and, on the human side, through the distinction made by Newman between real and notional apprehension. Indeed, much of Walgrave's originality lies in

---

292. _Ibidem_, p. 38.
293. _Ibidem_, p. 330.

his elaboration of Newman's distinction.

Even within the theological theory of development it is possible to conceive the relationship of logic to intuition in several different ways:

> Is that process to be conceived of as a strictly supernatural clarification and articulation of a dim comprehensive intuition, impressed by God upon the mind of the Church through the grace of faith? Or is it, in the main and with due qualifications, still to be conceived of as an inferential process starting from propositions?
> Three types of answers are possible: (1) development of doctrine is a supernatural process in which there is no place for logical operation, although theology may find afterward a kind of logical connection between its results; (2) development of doctrine is basiclly a process of human reason, although in practice led and sustained by the light of faith; (3) development of doctrine essentially participates in the nature of both a supernatural process and a logical operation.[294]

The first position is attributed to de Lubac, von Balthasar, and H. D. Köster. For these authors the development of dogma is, strictly speaking, not a logical process at all. It is rather a process of faith discerning directly in its supernatural object various aspects which need not be justified either logically or historically.

The second position is that of C. Dillenschneider which was further elaborated by E. Dhanis. Both authors maintain that the development of dogma must begin from a formulated truth by way of discursive reasoning. Dillenschneider emphasizes that this process cannot, however, be reduced to a mere logic since there is within the Church a contact with the revealed reality which is directed by a certain type of the sense of faith. Sometimes this activity of the sense of faith is referred to as a 'divine logic.' This subjective contact with the divine reality is described by Walgrave quoting Dillenschneider as "the intuitive

---

294. *Ibidem*, p. 344.

supernatural sense of the believer, grounded in the power of his faith and the gifts of the Holy Spirit. By that sense he is able to discern, in communion with the Church, the potentialities of the deposit of revelation, objectively presented to him by the doctrinal authority."[295]

Walgrave finds Dillenschneider's "divine logic" inappropriate and would substitute something such as "divine rule" since the processes being described are no longer of a strictly inferential nature. He also notes that the sense of faith in this regard is a type of 'illative sense.'

A more satisfying form of the theological solution is that of E. Dhanis. This author emphasizes that faith is not only an assent to propositions but is also moved by a dim awareness of the God who reveals himself through them. Thus, the believer is moved by the witness within the propositions to a more comprehensive type of response than would be warranted by logic alone.

This is not to say that logic is not present; it is, but the type of logic is not one that depends exclusively on the sources for a given dogmatic statement. Logic will point to the presence of a truth in the sources, yet its certitude depends on the magisterium which is the guarantor of revelation. This resembles the normal growth of human knowledge from a preliminary undifferentiated experience of the whole toward a subsequent conceptual analysis. It differs, however, from ordinary logical processes because the object (God) which is believed can only become known (in this way) through his self-communication, and because the Holy Spirit is himself active in the process of clarification.

---

295. *Ibidem*, and C. Dillenschneider, *Le Sens da la Foi et le Progrès Dogmatique du Mystère Marial*, (Rome, 1964), p. 327.

Walgrave comments on Dhanis' theory:

> Perhaps Dhanis did not sufficiently penetrate his own profound view of attraction of faith. If God, in His effective attraction, immediately communicates Himself to the individual believer as the source of the message, it is not clear how He can make Himself felt as actually attracting without including a dim knowledge of that which attracts. A dim knowledge of God as attracting must imply a dim apprehension of His attracting reality. An awareness of God as actually inviting man to belief must be accompanied by an awareness of that to which He invites and attracts man. A direct affective experience of the formal object of faith cannot be separated from an affective experience of its material object.[296]

Therefore, Walgrave prefers the third position, that of Rahner and Schillebeeckx. This position acknowledges the logical and supernatural factors in dogmatic development as complementary. The science of theology in its logical processes is active in discovering the logic in thinking which is or has gone on, as it is active in furthering the process itself. Yet the whole process in the genesis of dogma is one that is supernatural. "The living process... is, as a whole, a concrete vital growth of self-differentiating apprehension guided by an inner principle that is light and life."[297] For the supernatural qualification of the magisterium is the ultimate criterion for every true development.

It is at this point that the validity of Newman's distinction between notional and real assent for the process of dogmatic development becomes essential.[298] Real ideas are present to the mind as objects of direct experience. Because they are rooted in experience, ideas are the object and term of real apprehension. Thus, the name of a town is the object of real apprehension only if one has a variety of impressions and

---

296. *Ibidem*, pp. 346-347.
297. *Ibidem*, p. 347; on the position of Rahner and Schillebeeckx see also p. 340.
298. *Cf. ibidem*, p. 299ff.

associations which accompany that name. If one has simply heard or read of that town he has only notional apprehension of it. Thus both types of apprehension are dimensions of human knowledge. They may even exist simultaneously regarding the same idea.

The object of faith is a real apprehension because it is rooted in the experiential knowledge of God. Theology may work out this experience into its notional aspects, i.e., propositions and dogmas aiming at conceptual clarity. They can, however, never take the place of the real and more primary apprehension.[299]

Walgrave believes that F. von Baader completes the above elaboration in Newman's thought through his explanation of the two senses of abstraction.[300] Abstract knowledge corresponds to notional apprehension: both depart somewhat from real experience for the sake of conceptual clarity. Real apprehension is the more primary and original form of knowledge; it is also the beginning of intellectual reflection. Yet the former type of abstraction is necessary to communicate one's knowledge.

---

299. *Cf. ibidem*, p. 305: "Faith, then, is an assent ot dogma, but an assent grounded in a real apprehension of the heavenly things to which the human forms of dogmatic language point. As such, the object of assent is the real, apprehended in the notional; and assent itself, beyond its being an intellectual acceptance, is in the first place a subjection to a reality. The development of dogma is not so much a logical working out of first propositions, as propositional clarification of a knowledge that, through the medium of these propositions, communicates with the real. Thus the point of departure of the development is not merely propositional. It is a comprehensive awareness of the real -- and the real is always the whole -- through a propositional expression that may be very partial and always remains inadequate. The comprehensive intuitive awareness of the whole and the propositional expression cannot be separated, but the former always exceeds the latter: one could not know a friend on that deeper level where 'heart speaks to heart,' if one did not see and hear him. In the same way faith could not attain to its real object on the level of supernatural communion without the mediation of dogma."
300. *Cf. ibidem*, p. 351f.

This is not to denigrate from symbols, which are also a powerful way of communicating truth. Symbols are indirect forms of communication which

> disclose a cosmic or all-comprehensive meaning in one flash of intuition. ....The symbolic expression is more directly related to the original appearance of meaning, being the first, more spontaneous, and more congenial mode of expressive activity. In a certain sense true symbols are not created by man. They are revealed to him in the very act of rising to consciousness as expressions of what shines through their transparent selves.[301]

"The development of doctrine begins in the Christian revelation, exteriorly presented by the message of Christ, interiorly assimilated through the working of the Spirit of Truth, and appearing against the background of general revelation."[302] Walgrave locates then the beginning of dogma in the premediated correspondence of revelation and faith, which is the appearance of existential Christian truth in real apprehension, and which issues in dogmatic (propositional or conceptual) forms as soon as the human subject seeks to clarify his own experience. It does this in a process that is both logical and supernatural. Once man is possessed by the truth of immediate experience he moves toward conceptual elaboration. "In Christian thought, as generally in human thought, conceptualizing reflection is an endeavor to embrace with intellectual consciousness what embraces us in its pre-intellectual appearance."[303]

This process of clarification takes place through language, either symbolic or conceptual. Symbolic expression is the more primitive expression in humanity as a whole. This is because images are the more direct way of focusing human consciousness on meaning. Indeed, images are revelatory of their very meaning in a transparent way. Conceptual

---

301. *Ibidem*, p. 353.
302. *Ibidem*, p. 372.
303. *Ibidem*, p. 373.

thought is the later and more sophisticated elaboration of symbolic expression. Dogmatic expression exists on the level of conceptual thought.

We regard Walgrave's treatment of the beginning of dogma, as elaborated above, as the most complete psychological description of this process. His dependence on Newman is obvious and acknowledged. Although all dogmatic expression is linguistic expression, the different moments of real and notional apprehension elucidate the exact focus of the beginning of dogma not precisely in either the magisterium or in the mind of an individual, but in the psychological processes of the believing Church.

10. DOGMA IN OFFICIAL CHURCH USAGE

That the word, 'dogma,' had in the early part of the sixteenth century not yet attained the precision it would at the First Vatican Council is easily illustrated from official Church usage. It and its variant, "dogmatizare," are both found in the acts of the Fifth Lateran Council from the years 1512-1517.

The first occurence speaks of "dogmatizing" against those who teach the mortality of the intellectual soul: "Cumque verum vero minime contradicat, omnem assertionem veritati illuminatae fidei contrariam, omnino falsam esse definimus, et ut aliter dogmatizare non liceat, districtius inhibemus...."[304]

The second occurence in the acts of that council has to do with the printing of books in Latin translated from various languages and which

---

304. Sessio VII, 17 iun., 1513, *Conciliorum Oecumenicorum Decreta*, eds., J. Alberigo, P. P. Joannou, etc., (Freiburg in B., 1962), p. 581.

teach false dogmas: "...nonnulli huius artis imprimendi magistri, in diversis mundi partibus libros tam Graecae, Hebraicae, Arabicae et Chaldeae linguarum in latinum translatos, quam alios, latino ac vulgari sermone editos, errores etiam in fide, ac perniciosa dogmata etiam religioni christianiae contraria...."[305]

Deneffe found only two usages of the word in the acts of the Council of Trent. So the following text: "Omnes itaque intelligant, quo ordine et via ipsa Synodus, post iactum fidei confessionis fundamentum sit progressura, et quibus potissimum testimoniis ac praesidiis in confirmandis dogmatibus et instaurandis in Ecclesia moribus, sit usura."[306] Deneffe thinks the council's usage of the word shows that it thereby signifies only the revealed truth of faith.[307] This seems unlikely since in the other place where he found the word to be used it means doctrine and, indeed, false doctrine: "...prorsus aboleri sancta Synodus vehementer cupit, ita ut nullae falsi dogmatis imagines et rudibus periculosi erroris occasionem praebentes statuantur."[308]

Besides the examples found by Deneffe, we have located the following two quotes which have to do with the doctrinal work of the council: "...ut congruentius maiorique cum deliberatione omnia procedant, nempe ut dogmata cum iis, quae ad reformationem spectant, simul tractentur et sanciantur: ea, quae statuenda videbuntur, tam de reformatione quam de dogmatibus..."; and: "Si vero opportunum videbitur, et tempus patietur, poterit etiam de nonnullis dogmatibus tractari, prout suo tempore in congregationibus proponentur."[309]

---

305. Sessio X, 4 maii, 1515, *ibidem*, p. 608.
306. Sessio XXV, 3-4 dec., 1563, *ibidem*, p. 751.
307. Deneffe, *op. cit.*, p. 520.
308. Sessio IV, 8 apr., 1546, *COeD*, p. 640.

All these passages reveal that, although dogma was becoming more closely associated with the truth of faith in the defensive position that the Church at this time assumed, it was not yet restricted to a revealed and clearly defined truth of faith, since it could in the same assembly still be used in the traditional sense of just "doctrine." Perhaps we should say, the word was .becoming the characteristic expression for doctrine in the defensive position. Thus, a number of theological works which appeared at this time began to use it in their titles: Franciscus Turrianus, *Liber Dogmaticus de Electione Divina et Liber Dogmaticus de Justificatione*, Rome, 1551; Jacobus Sirmondus, *Opuscula Dogmatica Veterum V Scriptorum, qui ante annos MCC claruerunt*, Paris, 1629. Even Petavius' work, *De Dogmatibus Theologicis*, Paris, 1644, offers no treatment of dogma as such. In other words, Petavius, as the Council of Trent a hundred years before, still attached no special meaning to the word beyond that of general doctrine.

If dogma was becoming the characteristic word for doctrine in the defensive position from the sixteenth century on, it gradually became tied to the ideas of formal and solemn definition in the nineteenth. This was, however, not yet the case in *Ineffabilis Deus* in 1854 although the "stuff" of dogma is certainly in this decreee:

> ....Ad honorem sanctae et individuae Trinitatis, ad decus et ornamentum Virginis Deiparae, ad exaltationem fidei catholicae et christianae religionis augmentum, auctoritate Domini nostri Iesu Christi, beatorum Apostolorum Petri et Pauli ac Nostra declaramus, pronuntiamus et definimus, doctrinam, quae tenet, beatissimam Virginem Mariam in primo instanti suae conceptionis fuisse singul- ari omnipotentis Dei gratia et privilegio, intuitu meritorum Christi Iesu Salvatoris humani generis, ab omni originalis culpae

309. Sessio XX, 4 iunii, 1562, *COeD*, p. 701, and Sessio XXIV, 11 nov., 1563, *COeD*, p. 750.

labe praeservatam immunem, esse a Deo revelatam atque idcirco ab omnibus fidelibus firmiter constanterque credendam.[310]

In that part of *Pastor Aeternus* which treats of papal infallibility the word, "dogma," comes to the fore: "....sacro approbante Concilio, docemus et divinitus revelatum dogma esse definimus."[311] Dogma is noticeably tied in this document of the First Vatican Council to the notion of defining, as it is in the following paragraph where the pope's dogmatic authority is spelled out:

> Porro fide divina et catholica ea omnia credenda sunt, quae in verbo Dei scripto vel tradito continentur et ab Ecclesia sive solemni iudicio sive ordinario et universali magisterio tamquam divinitus revelata credenda proponuntur.[312]

Here the ordinary teaching office of the Church also plays a role in determining the object of faith, as it factually does in preaching and teaching. Unfortunately, however, the notion of dogma being something solemnly defined has so often been tied to the notion of dogma in the time since Vatican I that it has been easy to lose sight of the fact that most moments of the life of faith have little to do with solemnly defined propositions. The Church at Vatican I, as history points out, was in an attitude of definse, and dogmatic definitions in opposition to errors of faith also come to be in an attitude of defense.

Vatican I determined finally the evolution of the word, "dogma." In the polemical atmosphere of the Counter-Reformation it declared dogma to be those parts of ordinary and revealed doctrine which receive particular definition. This often happens in the face of error and of heresy, that is, through accidents of history. It is true that the definition of dogma given in the constitution on faith extends also to

---

310. DB, 2803.
311. DB, 3073.
312. DB, 3011.

the ordinary magisterium, but this has often been overlooked. In any case, the word, "dogma," is not officially attached in the words of the First Vatican Council to this definition, although the usage of this quote in defining dogma is common among theologians.

Therefore the word, "dogma," as it is commonly used today is a concept heavily laden with polemicism, although it is not so always, nor need it be so.

11. CONCLUSIONS

There are six conclusions to be drawn from the material assembled in this chapter on the history and usage of the word, "dogma."

(1) Martin Elze and Werner Elert's opinion that there is a certain exclusivity or lack of continuity between the ancient use of this word and its religious usage is not true because, in the first place, it is easy to illustrate a "religious" usage of the word along with its "secular" usage among a number of the fathers of the Church. We have illustrated this from the works of Ignatius of Antioch, Athenagoras, Clement of Alexandria, Gregory of Nyssa, etc.

Elze and Elert's opinion points out the disparity between the ancient world's usage of the term as "edict" or "determination" and the Christian world's usage of it as "revealed doctrine." It is also true that one can not derive the meaning of dogma in historical Christianity from its usage in sacred scripture. But is it not much more true to see a degree of univocity in these various meanings inasmuch as they all can be understood under the notions of "decision" and "determination"? Plato spoke of the state as a place where men live together who have common "determinations." Caesar Augustus sent out a "decision" that the whole

246

world should be enrolled. The Vatican Council "determined" in a doctrinal "decision" what pertained to revealed truth. Before a doctrine can be proclaimed as dogma it is necessary that the Church reach a "decision" regarding its definability. Thus, there is a line of meaning in the notion of dogma -- decision, or determination -- which reaches from antiquity even to the present ecclesiastical usage.

(2) It is not correct to equate our modern notion of dogma with the medieval articulus fidei. That notion refers to the individual propositions of the creed. Moreover, the modern notion of dogma as revealed truth defined by the Church was not associated with the word in medieval times. At that time dogma meant simply "doctrine," as it does in Thomas Aquinas.

(3) Philip Neri Chrismann is not, as Walter Kasper maintains, the first to introduce the modern notion of dogma which was adopted by the First Vatican Council.[313] Moreover, Kasper's statement, "Wir stehen also vor dem zunächst überraschenden Tatbestand, dass ein für das heutige Denken in der katholischen Kirche so zentraler Begriff wie Dogma erst seit dem achtzehnten Jahrhundert in der katholischen Theologie .... im heute üblichen Sinn verwendet wird,"[314] is not exactly true. We have been able to establish that this notion is already to be found in Melchior Cano's De Locis Theologicis, published in 1563. The controversial notion of dogma as a revealed truth officially defined by the Church is also to be found in Francis Veron's De Regula Fidei Catholicae of 1646.

(4) The notion of dogma we have inherited from Vatican I is controversially oriented and stems from the embattled situation of the

---

313. Kasper, op. cit., p. 36.
314. Ibidem, p. 37.

Catholic Counter-Reformation. In the work of Melchior Cano it was used, almost unconsciously, to distinguish revealed truth from the teachings of the reformers (heretics). In the *Regulae* of Veron and Chrismann the term received more scientific precision inasmuch as it designated the minimum of what these two Gallican theologians judged as necessary to the Catholic faith.

(5) In general, in Protestantism dogma means "confession," that is, what the church confesses as the content of revelation. Within this act of confession is the act of glorifying God (Schlink and Pannenberg). Its most typical place is the liturgy. But such confessions, or dogma, never contain the substantial truth of revelation, which is as high above the word of man as heaven above the earth (Barth). In Catholic thought dogma, through the act of definition and proclamation by the post-apostolic teaching authority within the Church, expresses the truth of revelation not perfectly or exhaustively, but nevertheless the truth revealed by God which must be held and believed within the particular contingencies of time, space, and history in which the Church finds itself. In Catholicism dogma is, "eine neue Formulierung des ursprüng-lichen Offenbarungswortes im Glaubensbewusstsein einer bestimmten Zeit."[315] In Protestantism dogma remains "Antwort der Kirche auf die Offenbarung Gottes" (Schlink). These two differing notions are intimate-ly related to the question of the teaching authority within the Church.

(6) In the course of our survey we have examined many notions of dogma. The eschatological element of dogma is today particularly emphas-ized by Pannenberg, as St. Thomas once emphasized the eschatological note

---

315. Leo Scheffczyk, "Die Auslegung der Hl. Schrift als dogmatische Aufgabe," *MThZ*, 15 (1964), p. 191.

of the articulus fidei, arguing that it was a "participatio veritatis divinae tendens in ipsam," and that the "actus credentis non terminatur ad enunciable, sed ad rem."

Recently Walter Kasper has sought to emphasize once again the eschatological and prophetic character of dogma. He writes: "Ein Dogma ist das vorläufige Ereigniswerden der eschatologisch-endgültigen Wahrheit Christi."[316] And again: "Entsprechend der heilsgeschichtlichen Stellung der Kirche ist die dem Dogma eigene Wahrheit begründet in den eschatolog- ischen Ereignissen der Auferstehung und Erhöhung Christi als definitivem Sieg des Lichts über die Finsternis und in der noch ausstehenden escha- tologischen Volloffenbarung der Herrschaft Gottes, durch die die Botschaft der Kirche von der Auferstehung und dem neuen Leben erst verifiziert werden wird."[317] Kasper says that when one speaks of dogma one must not think exclusively of the Greek notion of truth (adaequatio intellectus et rei), but also of the existential notion of truth as ἀλήθεια, "Unverborgenheit," and of the biblical notion of truth as אמת which denotes subsequent verification through fulfillment of promise. According to this conception, that is true which proves itself as effective, or which works what it promises.

We find this dynamic notion of truth lacking in appropriateness, first of all because through its application Kasper wants to explain the notion of Church dogma biblically, although as we have seen, the biblical usage of dogma as "order" or "determination" has no particular religious significance. We demonstrated above that "determination" or "decree" suffice completely for the translation of δόγμα as used in scripture.

---

316. Kasper, *op. cit.*, p. 128.
317. *Ibidem*, p. 126.

Further, if one sacrifices the notion of truth as "adaequatio intellectus et rei" -- the fact that this formula may have been first formally expressed in the context of Greek philosophy is of no account -- the road is open to endless subjectivism. If men can no longer communicate in words which have a similar truth value in relation to the reality "out there," but only within the subjectivity of intra-personal experience, there will in the end be no room for the confessional unity of believers ("bekenntnisartige Gemeinschaft") in the community which is the Church. Each party will have its own confession professing what speaks to it in a dynamic way, and in that very transposition the notion of Church, as a community of believers professing the same faith, is destroyed.

We do not thereby exclude the possibility of ecumenical reunion through the mutual acknowledgment or peaceful acceptance of two differing creeds from differing ecclesial bodies. We simply affirm that the primary truth relationship of every dogma and creed is to the existent, to "id, quod est," and not to the dynamic effectiveness of a particular proposition in the lives of the faithful.

PART THREE

THE JOINING OF DOGMA AND SCRIPTURE IN RECENT THEOLOGY

CHAPTER FIVE

HEINRICH SCHLIER'S SUGGESTIONS TOWARDS THE
BEGINNING OF CHRISTIAN DOGMA

1. IS THE BEGINNING OF CHRISTIAN DOGMA TO BE FOUND IN
    THE NEW TESTAMENT?

The essay, "Kerygma und Sophia," by Heinrich Schlier has as its
subtitle: "Zur neutestamentlichen Grundlegung des Dogmas."[1] Although our
interest centers on examining his thoughts on the foundations of dogma in
the New Testament, it will be helpful to indicate first, in summary
fashion, his exegetical reflections to the First Epistle to the Corinthians, principally as found in the above mentioned essay. Schlier's
discussion on kerygma and dogma begins, however, in the essay, "Über das
Hauptanliegen des 1. Briefes an die Korinther," which appeared some years
earlier.[2]

During his lifetime, the apostle Paul carried on two great theological debates. The first was, of course, with the theology of Judaism and

---

1. *Die Zeit der Kirche*, (Freiburg, 1966), pp. 206-232; first published
    in *Evangelische Theologie* 11 (1950/51).
2. *Ibidem*, pp. 147-159.

had to do with grace and mercy, belief and works. The second took place with the Greeks, to whom he had preached the word of God. It had to do with kerygma and wisdom, belief and gnosis.

In the first chapters of First Corinthians Paul clearly addresses himself to the problems of the Corinthian Church which threatened and, certainly to some extent already had, compromised its unity. "Es wird ihm bewusst, dass der tieferliegende Grund der dortigen Zerwürfnisse und die eigentliche Gefahr für die korinthische Gemeinde ...sind: das Falsche Verständnis dessen, was 'Evangelium' ist, die bei Griechen freilich nicht überraschende Vorstellung, dass man es bei ihm prinzipiell mit so etwas wie einem philosophischen Logos zu tun habe und dass es eine Abart von griechischer Sophia oder Philosophia sei."[3] Paul contrasts as strongly as possible the manner of his preaching and the logos that he had delivered to the Corinthians with the way they understood sophia. For to understand the gospel in the manner of worldly wisdom, that is, only as another example of the "wisdom of the word" (sophia logou, 1 Cor 1:17), meant to the apostle the "emptying" of the power of the cross of Christ.

How did Paul understand that logos, which to him provided such a devastating understanding of the logos staurou? Schlier answers this question by listing five characteristics of this world's wisdom. In the first place, it is characterized by suzatein.[4] "Darin ist zwerlei enthalten: das Miteinander-Fragen mit dem Ziel der Aufdeckung beweisbarer Wahrheit und der prinzipiell unendliche Fortgang dieser gemeinsamen Suche. Ζυζητεῖν ist im neutestamentlichen Bereich ein bezeichnendes Wort für das Disputieren der Juden und Häretiker."[5]

---

3. From "Kerygma und Sophia," in *Die Zeit der Kirche*, p. 207.
4. *Cf. ibidem*, p. 208, and 1 Cor 1:20.
5. *Ibidem*. Schlier's understanding of this word is taken to task by:

Secondly, this wisdom is characterized by the use of proof and logical argument. Its aim is to convince by bringing forth reasonable grounds. From Colossians 2:8 Schlier says that the third mark of this wisdom, or philosophy, is that it is, in the last analysis, only a tradition of this world's elements. Fourthly, the wisdom of those against whom Paul turns himself is that of those who consider themselves wise and engage themselves with gnosis (1 Cor 1:5; 8:1f.; 12:8).[6] Schlier believes that although the exegesis of the scriptures played with such people a large role, their aim, nevertheless, remained that of attaining to wisdom, to which they attributed an excessive value. In any case, in 1 Cor 1:22 Paul names such Jews as seek signs in the same breath with the Greeks who seek wisdom and in contradistinction to himself and those who preach the kerygma of the crucified Christ.

The fifth and final characteristic of this wisdom is that it is always only a "human wisdom" (2:3), a "wisdom of this world" (1:28), a "wisdom of this eon" (2:6). "....auf solchem Wege gelangen sie alle jeweils und im ganzen immer nur zu der Weisheit, die nichts anderes ist als das Selbstbewusstsein und Selbstverständnis der Welt und der sie durchherrschenden Kräfte. Diese Weisheit ist immer und von vornherein das Ergebnis einer Selbsterfahrung und Selbstauslegung des Menschen und der Welt."[7]

It is clear that Paul will not have the gospel that he has preached equated with such a dialectical process of analysis of human and worldly

---

Hermann Diem, *Dogmatik*, vol. II, München, 1955), p. 43; Ulrich Wilkens, "Kreuz und Weisheit," in *Kerygma und Dogma*, 3 (1957), p. 78, footnote 4; Walter Fürst, *Kirche oder Gnosis?*, (München, 1961, p. 24.
6. *Cf*. Schlier, *ibidem*, p. 208.
7. *Ibidem*, p. 209.

wisdom.[8] As a matter of fact, he even adds that he has not announced the gospel in the manner of "wisdom" since now, in the present age, God has turned the wisdom of the world to toolishness. Although the way of wisdom had originally been a way of achieving to the knowledge of God, inasmuch as it has factually failed, the kerygma has taken its place. Philosophy, says Schlier, is today an anachronism.[9] And while worldly wisdom has missed its opportunity, God has made it into foolishness. For God created the world in wisdom ("Paulus denkt hier offenbar in den ihm bekannten hellenistischen Vorstellungen von der Rolle der Weisheit bei der Schöpfung."[10]), and the creature should have recognized the creator in the reflection of his wisdom in the world. "Erkennen ist hier nichts anderes als ein verstehendes Inne-werden Gottes durch die lichte Weisung des Seienden aus dem Sein selbst."[11] Instead, the recognition of the true God through the creation has, for the most part, been factually slight. Romans 1:20 indicates that such perception is not only possible, but also that it happens. Factually, however, the wisdom that character-izes human thinking, as it has and does manifest itself in the course of history, sets and judges the cross of Christ only as one more possibility of the interpretation of this world. That is to say, it evaluates it

---

8. "Das Kerygma, dessen Kern die apostolische Paradosis ist, steht als die grundlegende Norm, die jede echte Gnosis fundiert, an der sich jede Gnosis ausrichtet, die jede auf sich selbst gestellte, in sich selbst gegründete Gnosis als σοφία τοῦ κόσμου τούτου entlarvt, unan-greifbar richtend da. Es ist das -- und Paulus betont das sehr stark -- 'törichte' Kerygma, töricht nicht nur durch seinen Inhalt, den sich auch eine Gnosis weithin aneignen, zum mindesten angleichen konnte, sondern auch durch seine Form: ist es doch im Kern und dann von daher seiner Struktur nach Tatsachenmitteilung und nicht Dialek-tik und Existenzanalyse." --Schlier, "Das Hauptanliegen des 1. Briefes an die Korinther," p. 151.
9. *Cf.* "Sophia und Kerygma," p. 210.
10. *Ibidem.*
11. *Ibidem.*

only as one more "mythical quantity" among many.[12]

Against the whole tradition of worldly disquisition seeking a hardly achievable wisdom, Paul places as opposing and contrasting concept the kerygma of the cross of Christ. It is also apparently a _logos_ since he speaks of a _logos_ _tou_ _starou_, and it is also a _sophia_ since it has put the wisdom of this world out of course, but it is hardly a wisdom or a word in the sense of human possibilities.

The general features of the kerygma can easily be sketched.[13] Kerygma is "eine Kundgabe," "eine Mitteilung, die den Hörenden angeht. Es ist oft die Wiedergabe einer aufgetragenen oder auch einer aus der Sache sich eindeutig ergebenden Mitteilung und erfolgt daher oft in authentischer Formulierung."[14] A _keryx_ or herald is a person authorized to be the voice of him whom he represents. He stands between the person having the authority to speak and the public which is, through the act of the herald, addressed. "Und so ist sein Kerygma schon von hier aus als eine authentische, die Öffentlichkeit angehende, zur Formulierung neigende Kund- und Wiedergabe einer Mitteilung zu verstehen." But in this case the message to be proclaimed is that of a person and of what has happened to this person.

> Der Apostel proklamiert Jesus, den Christus, Christus Jesus, Christus Jesus Kyrios! Er proklamiert 'Christus gekreuzigt', 'Christus Jesus und diesen gekreuzigt'. Der Kyrios Christus Jesus wird also proklamiert und dies, indem seine geschehene und fortwirkende Kreuzigung verkündigt wird. Das wird dadurch bestätigt und ergänzt, dass Paulus auch sagt: Christus wird proklamiert: er ist von den Toten auferstanden. Demnach ist das Kerygma die

---

12. _Cf. ibidem_, pp. 209-214.
13. The most basic of twentieth-century studies on the kerygma is, of course, that of C. H. Dodd, _The Apostolic Preaching and its Developments_, (London, 1936). _Cf._ also Claude H. Thomlson, _Theology of the Kerygma, A Study in Primitive Preaching_, (Englewood Cliffs, N. J., 1962).
14. _Cf._ Schlier, "Kerygma und Sophia," p. 214.

Proklamation der geschehenen und fortwirkenden Ereignisse des
Todes und der Auferweckung Christi Jesu.[15]

To put it in definition form, the kerygma is: "die öffentliche, sich in
eine Formel zuspitzende Kundgabe Jesu Christi als des Kyrios und des ihn
als solchen erweisenden Geschehens seines Kreuzes und seiner Auferweckung
von den Toten -- durch den Apostel."[16]

From the kerygma as Paul represents it to the Corinthian community
in 1 Cor 15:1-11 Schlier can draw four conclusions. The first is that
the content of the kerygma is the happening (Ereignis) that God has
raised Jesus from the dead. Secondly, the resurrection of Jesus was
witnessed by a group which gives witness to the fact as though he had
appeared to them, and this group gives witness to his resurrection in
this way. Thirdly, the witness given in turn by the witnesses to
Christ's witness of himself necessitates the use of speech. "So muss man
sagen, dass die Selbstbezeugung des Auferstandenen in seiner Erscheinung
ein Eingehen und Offenbarwerden in die Sprache und in das Wort der Zeugen
hinein wird. Der Auferstandene überliefert sich durch seine Erscheinung
vor den Zeugen an das Wort und damit an die Sprache und an den Satz."[17]
In this way the revelation itself came "zur Sprache," and "zu Wort."
Fourthly, as the authentic word of revelation this logos carries within
itself the tendency towards formulation. It is therefore, "....von dem
Geschehen her ein einheitlicher und dashalb auch zu einheitlicher Formulierung drängender Logos verschiedener und verschiedenartiger Zeugen und
Zeugnisse."[18] As the unified word of various witnesses this logos is
determinative both for the gospel and its preaching as it is for the

15. *Ibidem*.
16. *Ibidem*.
17. *Ibidem*, p. 215.
18. *Ibidem*.

faith which it calls forth.

The paradosis which Paul announced to the Corinthians and which he in chapter 15 calls back to their memory is the gospel, indeed it is the heart of the gospel. For, "Das Kerygma in diesem Sinn und also das daraus erwachsende Symbol ist nicht ein aus dem 'lebendigen' Evangelium zu einer Formel zusammengedrängter und erstarrter sekundärer Auszug aus dem Evangelium, es ist nicht, wie meist behauptet wird, ein Extrakt des Evangeliums oder gar der Schrift, sondern es entlässt vielmehr selbst aus sich das Evangelium, das seinerseits als Verkündigung das Kerygma und damit die in ihm zu Wort gekommene Offenbarung entfaltet."[19]

Only when the kerygma is so understood, that is, as the revelatory word (logos) about the resurrection of Jesus Christ, tending toward a unified expression, although preached and (first) experienced by different apostles, can one fully appreciate the force of contrast between this logos and the logos of worldly wisdom.

For our purposes it will be necessary here to examine closely what Schlier chose to treat in a long and explanatory footnote. "Die sogen-annten Glaubensformeln, in denen das Kerygma fixiert ist, sind also der Sache nach im wörtlichen Sinn hervorgerufen durch die Selbstbezeugung des Auferstandenen vor den Zeugen."[20] Because Christ appeared to the apostles after his resurrection and thereby gave them the commission to give witness to his rising again (this commission is explicitly mentioned by Matthew 28:10, 19, and Luke 24:46-48), one must say that the "prae-symbola" and the creedal formulae represent the self-revelation of the risen Christ. Schlier quotes Heidegger here on the nature of causality:

---

19. *Ibidem*, p. 216.
20. *Ibidem*.

"Ursprung bedeutet hier jenes, von woher und wodurch eine Sache ist, was sie ist und wie sie ist,"[21] which he implies exists between Christ's revelatory action and the origin of the "praesymbola." But another factor comes also here into play and that is that the "witness of the witnesses" was adopted by the Church as its own, and the "praesymbola" could be preached in the assurance of the Holy Spirit. Perhaps the prime example of this is the "Kyrios-Jesus" acclamation which expresses the completeness of God's saving action in Christ.

Schlier sees then three moments in the formation of the "prae-symbola": the self-revelation of the risen Christ to a select group of witnesses, the witnesses themselves offering testimony to what they have seen and heard, and the Church adopting, repeating, preaching, in the conviction of the Holy Spirit, their testimony as its own. It is, therefore, correct to speak of the "praesymbola" as "articles of revel-ation" (Offenbarungssätzen). Their unity is due to a double cause. On the one hand they are the logoi of the risen one settling down in usage. On the other hand, in relation to what they announce, they are guaranteed by the Spirit. These logoi then are not only of apostolic origin, but also are logoi of revelation. They depend on the revelation of Christ himself. He is, through his act of self-revelation, in a very real sense, their cause.[22] To understand them only from the confessional standpoint is to overlook their revelational character. Nor could it be

---

21. *Ibidem*, p. 216, footnote 17, quoting *Holzwege* (1949), p. 7.
22. So, for example, Rom 10:17: "Faith then depends on hearing (ἀκοή), and hearing on the word (ῥῆμα) of Christ." *Cf.* Michel's commentary: "[Paulus] spricht daher vom ῥῆμα τῆς πίστεως, d.h. vom Wort, das vom Glauben handelt und Glauben erfordert. ῥῆμα Χριστοῦ könnte an sich das von Christus herrührende Wort sein; es muss sich von ἀκοή (= Botschaft, in bestimmter Weise unterscheiden." --*Der Brief an die Römer*, (Gottingen, 1966[12]), p. 262, footnote 3.

correct to look upon them as mere summaries of revelation. They are much more "der ursprüngliche Wesenskern des Kerygma."[23]

The kerygma is then, in the wide sense, the written or verbal preaching and tradition from the apostles. In a narrower sense, one can say that it is the heart of the whole kerygma, and that part of it which in dependence on the risen one's revelation of himself, is the "presentation" of the whole in authentic and normative precision. In this sense it can be found in the gradually forming confessions of the Church. It is true that they (the confessional formulae) are to be found here and there in the scriptures, but they are also to be found in express decisions of the Church, especially when it came to disputed questions.

It is Schlier's contention that such cases, that is, when a decision of the Church becomes regulative for the tradition, are not limited to the post-apostolic or, as some would say, "Hellenized" Church, but that our case in point, the logos of the gospel as it was preached by Paul in 1 Cor 15:1ff. is an example in the scriptures of the same.[24] When one examines what then is here layed out as unalterable determination, he finds according to the nature of the affair what the later theology would call dogma. For one finds here the two essential notes of such dogma as it is later defined, "die veritates a Deo revelatae et ab ecclesia propositae." And so one can name equally well this kerygma "dogma" as this dogma "kerygma." For the two can equally be defined through the same middle term: "veritates a Deo revelatae et ab ecclesia propositae."

_____

It is certainly possible that the difference between ῥῆμα and ἀκοή is to be located in just who it is that is transferring the message (Christ or an apostle); for both retain a common content.

23. Schlier, *op. cit.*, p. 217.
24. *Ibidem*, p. 230.

With these considerations we come to the end of our treatment of
Schlier's essay in so far as it relates to our interest here -- the
foundation of dogma in the New Testament. We thereby exclude from our
consideration other factors taken up explicitly by Schlier in the essay,
such as further considerations of the nature of Paul's gnostic adversar-
ies, and the relation of philosophy and theology.[25]

2. "AUSEINANDERSETZUNGEN" WITH SCHLIER

a. Hermann Diem

Introducing the chapter on "Dogmatische und Biblische Theologie" in
his *Dogmatik*, Diem discusses the Catholic position and Schlier's understanding of it.[26] Diem claims that the Catholic Church does not acknowledge the cleft between dogmatic and biblical theology and, therefore, the
parallelism (Zweigleisigkeit) between dogma and exegesis. He bases this
observation on the acknowledgement of Vatican I's founding the rule of
faith on tradition as well as on scripture,[27] which interpreted, Diem
maintains, that dogmatic statements deal with an historical happening,
the revelatory action of God. There is then from the viewpoint of
Catholic theology a traceable and continuous line in the tradition of the
Church of the revelatory action of God through the agency of the scriptures and through the primitive forms of the creeds, dependent on the
apostles themselves, reaching immediately to the history of Jesus. From
time to time the teaching authority of the Church will bring to explicit
consciousness results of this historical development inasmuch as it

---

25. *Cf.* on this last point especially *ibidem*, pp. 231-232.
26. *Dogmatik*, II, (München, 1955), pp. 40-49, 98ff.
27. Diem refers here to Denzinger, *Enchiridion Symbolorum*, 1792; *vd.* in
    the newer editions: 3011.

raises to "dogmas of faith" truths which so far were believed only
"implicitly" or "virtually."

The attitude of this relationship between history and dogma forbids
that a dogmatic statement be put in question through historical criticism.
And it makes no difference whether that criticism has to do with the
establishment of a determined historical event, or the interpretation
derived from such an event. "Der Begriff der veritas revelata umfasst
die Wahrheitsfrage in beiderlei Sinn."[28] But this does not mean any fear
of historical criticism in the Catholic Church. The holding to its
tradition is, through the apostolic succession, completely unembarrassed.
To the contrary, historical criticism can only provide a broader background in history for the Church's dogmatic statements.

Diem admits that this attitude of dogmatic-historical unity precludes the ever-increasing embarrassment of Evangelical theology relative
to the contention that there exists an insurmountable chasm between
scripture and the beginning of the history of dogma. But beneath it
lies also the danger of projecting a later development into an earlier
time, and of interpreting the earlier from the viewpoint of the subsequent. But such erroneous judgments, he is quick to add, if they are
provable at all, would also be rendered harmless through the (above
discussed) dogmatic presuppositions. By this he apparently means that a
supposed immutability on the part of Catholic dogmatic positions would
preclude their possibly being revised in view of later historical
research. Diem allows that in the working out of its dogmas the Catholic
Church has always made use of the methods of historical research. "Wenn
auch die historischen Forschungsergebnisse keine Beweislast zu tragen

---

28. Diem, *op. cit.*, p. 41.

haben, so ist die Kirche trotzdem daran interessiert, wenigstens für die
Voraussetzungen und Grundsätze ihrer Lehrentscheidungen die Begründung
möglichst weit in die Geschichte hinaufzurücken...."[29]

The important feature here, though, which Diem sees in the
relationship of dogmatic and biblical theology from the Catholic viewpoint is the continuity (Kontinuität). Dogma can never be just a commentary or historically conditioned and limited restatement of what happened
once. It is the proclamation of the event itself stated in language that
reaches back in a line of historical continuity to Jesus himself, and to
God's action in him.

Decisive for the Catholic standpoint (according to Diem) is what
the priority of position of the 'praesymbola,' as "Wesenskern" of the
gospel, does for the relationship of scripture and dogma.

> Durch die Identifizierung des Kerygmas mit dem Symbol, das von
> der Offenbarung in seiner wörtlichen Formulierung hervorgerufen
> ist, hat Schlier den frühest möglichen historischen Ort für die
> Entstehung des Dogmas erreicht, der noch vor der schriftlichen
> Fixierung des Evangeliums liegt. Damit ist aber von vornherein
> auch sachlich das Dogma als die Norm der Schrift dieser über-
> geordnet. Das Dogma ist nichts anderes als Kerygma in späterer
> Gestalt.[30]

The scriptures as the oldest witness to the tradition of the Church
retain a most special role but, "Eine normative Bedeutung für die Entwicklung des Dogmas kann sie aber nie bekommen. Es muss vielmehr bei der
umgekehrten Ordnung bleiben; und die mit der Entfaltung des Schriftkanons
parallel gehende Ausformung der regula fidei will keineswegs nur eine
summarische Zusammenfassung des Schriftinhalts zu pädagogischen, mission-
arischen und liturgischen Zwecken, sondern eine bindende Norm für die
Schriftauslegung geben."[31] Insinuating that the scriptures can never

---

29. *Ibidem.*
30. *Ibidem*, p. 45.

264

occupy a determinative role for the development of dogma over against the role of dogma itself is certainly to misunderstand Catholic theology. As Karl Rahner has said, even in Catholic thought scripture occupies in relationship to dogma the position of the "norma normans non normata."[32]

At first glance it seems very difficult to imagine how Diem derives the lack of a "Zweigleisigkeit" from the teaching of Vatican I. The text in question, "Porro fide divina et catholica ea omnia credenda sunt, quae in verbo Dei scripto vel tradito continentur et ab Ecclesia sive solemni iudicio sive ordinario et universali magisterio tamquam divinitus revelata credenda proponuntur,"[33] seems much more to support the "two source theory," as it developed in the post-tridentine theology and, as a matter of fact, in which sense this text has often been interpreted. If, on the other hand, Diem's observation means that there is in Catholic theology no such thing as a cleft between dogmatic theology and biblical theology, between dogma and exegesis, then it simply would not be true. The ongoing clashes between these two sciences is well-known to those working in them.[34] The real problem in this area in Protestant as well

---

31. *Ibidem.*
32. *Cf.* "Was ist eine Dogmatische Aussage," in *Schriften*, V, (Einsiedeln, 1964), p. 77.
33. Denzinger-Schonmetzer, *Enchiridion Symbolorum*, 3011.
34. *Cf.* Karl Rahner, "An die Exegeten, ein Wort des Dogmatikers," in *Exegese und Dogmatik*, edit., H. Vorgrimler, (Mainz, 1962), pp. 28-35. and the other essays in this collection. Rahner's essay appears also in *Schriften*, V, pp. 82-111. The following quote is taken from the latter, p. 82: "Dieser Aufsatz ist ...aus dem Eindruck entstanden, dass innerhalb der katholischen Theologie eine gewisse Entfremdung zwischen den Vertretern dieser beiden Disziplinen obwaltet. ... Die Dogmatiker scheinen da und dort den Eindruck zu haben, als kümmerten sich die Exegeten herzlich wenig um jene Theologie, an die sich der Dogmatiker gebunden weiss und die auch uber jene Fragen Aussagen macht, die den Gegenstand der Exegese (im weitesten Sinn des Wortes) bilden. Die Exegeten ihrerseits scheinen da und dort der Meinung zu sein, dass die Dogmatiker ihnen Bindungen auferlegen wollen, die von der Sache her nicht gerechtfertigt sind, weil die

as Catholic theology is the relationship between the two sciences. And the cleft here seems not to follow confessional lines, but rather the differing lines of the theological disciplines.

It seems then that the only sense in which Diem's statement about there being no parallelism or "Zweigleisigkeit" between these disciplines in Catholic theology can be understood is that it makes no difference how a dogmatic truth is derived from the source of revelation -- scripture, in the witness of the tradition --, since in Catholic thought the tradition is apparently as binding as the scripture itself.

If Schlier's shifting of emphasis for the beginning of dogma (Ansatzpunkt) to the dogmatic tradition at a level below the New Testament were to receive more general acceptance, not because it represents a "Catholic position" but on the basis of its own factuality, it would not tend to place dogma on yet a higher judge's stool over scripture, but it could help clarify the relationship of the two realities to one another. And it would factually, as Diem points out, contribute to solving the problem of an insurmountable chasm between scripture and dogma.

What Diem fails to do in judging the Catholic position (Schlier), which he judges as setting up dogma over the scriptures, is to make a distinction between the contentwise sufficiency of the scriptures and a description of their historical appearance. In the context of their historical appearance dogma -- in the form of kerygmatic formulae (prae-symbola) -- certainly did exist before scripture. In the context of the contentwise sufficiency of scripture, the bible contains all the truths

---

Dogmatiker von den Fortschritten, die die katholische Exegese in der letzten Jahrzehnten erzielt hat, nicht genugend Notiz nähmen."

necessary for salvation. This latter fact is not just a Protestant teaching but is witnessed to by a long line of Catholic theologians including Irenaeus of Lyon, Gregory of Nyssa, Augustine, Vincent of Lérin, Anselm, Thomas Aquinas, John Gerson, Capreolus, Bellarmine, Scheeben, Michael Schmaus, etc.[35]

One must, however, make a distinction between dogmas and dogmas. The dogmas which have been proclaimed since the death of the last apostle are instances of (even with the help of the Holy Spirit) purely human witnessing to the facts of revelation, that took place in the past. The dogmas, such as the resurrection or propitiatory character of Christ's death, which are witnessed to in the 'praesymbola' have more a divine character, and belong to the revelation process itself. As such the degree of their certainty and importance for the total Christian experience is more central than say, for example, the dogma which determines which books belong to the canon or the dogma of papal infallibility. These two planes of dogma -- the divine and the human -- should not be confused indiscriminately, as a controversial-polemical theology would tend to do by insisting on belief in every sentence which, if at all possible, can be denominated "dogma." It is also admittedly difficult to see exactly where the lines of separation between the two planes should be drawn.

If, however, such a distinction were made, to which we shall yet refrain from giving a name, it would be easier to see light through the haze surrounding the controversy -- scripture over dogma, or dogma over

---

35. This list of theologians teaching the contentwise sufficiency of scripture is taken from Peter Lengsfeld, *Überlieferung, Tradition und Schrift in der evangelischen und katholischen Theologie der Gegenwart*, (Paderborn, 1960), pp. 120-123. Lengsfeld lists even more theologians and gives complete references.

scripture. For on the one hand, those dogmas which derive more closely through the 'praesymbola' from the revelation process itself factually do and always will occupy a place from which the scriptures themselves will be judged (in reference to other, more peripheral dogmas, that is), and those dogmas which derive, on the other hand, from later derivation and reflexion of the post-apostolic Church (this is not the place to discuss theories of the development of dogma) upon the scriptures will always be judged themselves by the scriptures.[36]

It would seem better if those dogmas contained in the 'praesymbola' and which are more central to the total Christian mystery were called "apostolic-divine." Those dogmas then which come to explicit ecclesiastical proclamation through a process of the development of dogma could be called "Church-human."

b. Ulrich Wilkens

U. Wilkens attempts a fundamental challenge to Schlier's essay, "Kerygma und Sophia," in his own essay, "Kreuz und Weisheit."[37] Wilkens considers four points: (1) the relationship between crucifixion and resurrection according to the Pauline text of 1 Cor 1; (2) which relationship throws light on the position of the Corinthian gnostics insofar as this can be determined religious-historically from the text itself; (3) Schlier's conception of kerygma and tradition; (4) the philosophical conclusions of Schlier. Inasmuch as our present interest is limited to

36. On the critical function of scripture in relationship to dogma in Catholic theology see Leo Scheffczyk, "Die Auslegung der Heiligen Schrift als dogmatische Aufgabe," in *Was heisst Auslegung der Heiligen Schrift?*, (Regensburg, 1966), pp. 135-171, but especially pp. 168-171. This essay is also found in *Münchner Theologische Zeitschrift*, 15 (1964), pp. 190-204.
37. *Kerygma und Dogma*, 3 (1957), pp. 77-108.

Wilkens' third consideration, we go into his second point only insofar as it concerns immediately the third consideration, and into the others not at all, except for the following paragraph which intends to indicate in capsule form the jist of Wilkens first section.

Wilkens sees a great difficulty inasmuch as in the first chapter of First Corinthians Paul speaks only of the "crucified Christ" as the "wisdom of God," whereas Schlier connects considerations taken from the fifteenth chapter on both the crucifixion and on the resurrection, and applies them to his interpretation of kerygma from the first chapter.[38] But even Wilkens is ready to admit in reference to 1 Cor 1: "Das bedeutet natürlich nicht, dass die Auferweckung Christi im Zusammenhang des Gedankenganges sachlich fehlte."[39]

In the second part of his essay Wilkens attempts to clarify the actual position of the Corinthian gnostics as it can be deduced from First Corinthians. He asks Schlier how he can argue that Paul places his preaching over against a Greek, philosophical wisdom teaching, when Paul factually argues with his opponents in an anti-gnostic way. Can it be right to accuse these opponents as propounding a philosophical teaching when Paul himself addresses the "Jews" and "Hellenes" of the community at Corinth as "those who are called" in 1:24, and as "the chosen ones" in 1:26? Paul was obviously addressing himself to aberrations within the Christian community there.

It is very noteworthy that from 2:6 Paul changes his manner of presentation and begins to argue abruptly as a gnostic himself.[40]

---

38. *Ibidem*, *vd.* p. 84ff., but especially footnote 10, p. 85.
39. *Ibidem*, p. 84; *cf.* p. 89.
40. *Cf. ibidem*, p. 90, and the reference given there to Bultmann, *Glauben und Verstehen*, I, (Tübingen, 1954^2), p. 42ff.

"We do, however, speak wisdom among those who are mature..."[41] Here both
Schlier and Wilkens are agreed as to what this "wisdom" of God is, and
that it is a special charismatic gnosis that manifests itself now and
then in charismatic speech. The ability to recognize this speech and the
speech itself is given to certain "perfect ones" to whom the spirit of
God has been given. But the purely "psychic" man does not and cannot
recognize the things of God, because the Spirit of God has not been given
to him. Paul seems, according to Wilkens, to be clearly making an eschatological differentiation between those standing in different eons. Is
this not t o preach "in the wisdom of words"? What has happened to
belief in the crucified Christ?

Paul's argumentation over his kerygma in First Corinthians is
presented to an intra-Christian audience. It was not primarily addressed
to the pagan philosophical world. Nevertheless, there remains the
opposing structure of his kerygmatic speech to the charismatic, wisdom
speech which passed in Corinth as preaching according to the gospel.
Paul presented himself as the herald authoritatively approved to announce
God's message. But, Wilkens claims, gnostic speech was also accepted as
a proclamation.[42] And the speaker of this logos was himself authorized
through the redeemer sent by God. Paul's kerygma is understood as something not strictly demonstrable, but rather as a message that can be
accepted only by those who have first received the Spirit, as was the
wisdom speech of the gnostics, insofar as it allows itself to be understood from the text, not the speech of this world which imposes itself
by its rational power, but the revelation of the divine world of the

41. 1 Cor 2:6.
42. Wilkens, *op. cit.*, p. 97.

270

Spirit, which once again, cannot be reasoned to, but must be accepted in obedient faith without proof. "Ist also das religionsgeschichtliche Urteil <u>Schliers</u> über den gnostischen Charakter der Weisheitslehre in Korinth durchaus richtig, so ist dagegen historisch unrichtig, die Erörterung des Paulus als gegen eine philosophisch-erfragend-argumentier-ende Christuslehre gerichtet zu verstehen. Gegen ein <u>solche</u> Tendenz würden die korinthischen Gnostiker zweifellos genauso scharf Front gemacht haben wie Paulus selbst!"[43]

What is then the difference between Paul's understanding of the kerygma and that understanding of his Corinthian opponents? Wilkens sees it in the <u>content</u> of the speech. In Corinth Christ was preached as risen Spirit-redeemer and revealer, who at the same time was the wisdom of God. Wisdom speech is in this community the verbal expression both of the redemption happening and of the "Selbstaussprache" of the one Spirit. Between Christ and the Christians there is a relation of identity through which the transcendant world reveals itself. "Weil nach gnostischer Anschauung also der Pneuma-Offenbarer, der pneumatische Inhalt der Offenbarung und der redende bzw. hörende und beurteilende Pneumatiker identisch sind, muss sich pneumatische Weisheitsrede grund-sätzlich nicht allein durch den pneumatischen Inhalt der Lehre, sondern zugleich auch durch die pneumatische Existenz des Redenden selbst ausweisen."[44]

The last clause of the above quote is as important as its first part. The "content" so important to Wilkens for establishing the differ-ence between kerygma and wisdom speech must prove itself through the

---

43. *Ibidem*, pp. 97-98.
44. *Ibidem*, p. 98.

pneumatic existence of the proclaimer himself. This is the "proof of the spirit and of the power" of which Paul speaks.[45] Basing himself on several passages of Second Corinthians,[46] Wilkens maintains that in the process of this proof, inasmuch as the preacher announces Christ, he announces himself also.

Such a "proof of spirit and of power" Paul can give only in a paradoxical way. And that is the proof where in his own evident weakness the power of God is revealed. Wilkens believes that because Paul maintains this proof of strength in weakness so evidently, that the phrase of Schlier for the apostle, "Stimme dessen, der ihn sendet,"[47] can in no way be true. For if it were true the apostle would not have to answer at the last judgment for his words, as Paul himself affirms.[48] On the contrary, he would in his preaching only be speaking the words to which the Spirit prompts him, since both are identified in the same eschatological experience.[49]

---

45.   1 Cor 2:5.
46.   2 Cor 12:12; 13:3; 4:5.
47.   Wilkens, *op. cit.*, p. 98, quoting Schlier, *op. cit.*, p. 214.
48.   *Cf.* 1 Cor 3:12-15.
49.   Inasmuch as Wilken's argument here is difficult to follow, we append the following restatement of it for clarity's **sake**: Wilkens maintains that in proclaiming the mystery of Christ the apostle must necessarily also proclaim himself, inasmuch as through his preaching the power of the Spirit is made visible. However, the difference in Corinthian wisdom speech from Paul's preaching is that in the former it is the Spirit speaking in and through the preacher with whom he has a relationship of gnostic identity. Paul can, to the contrary, offer only a very weak "proof in spirit and power," because his own weakness is everywhere evident. The only proof that he can offer is that, despite his own personal inadequacy, the glory of God be visible "shining in the face of Christ" whom he preaches. "For we preach not ourselves, but Jesus Christ as Lord, and ourselves merely as your servants in Jesus. For God, who commanded light to shine out of darkness, has shone in our hearts, to give enlightenment concerning the knowledge of the glory of God, shining on the face of Christ Jesus. But we carry this treasure in vessels of clay, to show that the abundance of the power

If Paul then proclaims a message for which he must sometime render
an account, and he is not, through implied identification with the
Spirit, the mouthpiece of the one who has sent and commissioned him, it
can hardly be said that his role as apostle revolves around "...ihm vorgegebenes, fest und unveränderlich in fixierten Sätzen formuliertes,
traditionelles 'Kerygma' zu entfalten, dessen Legitimität als solche
nicht in Frage steht, weil es bis in seine Formulierung hinein unmittelbaren Offenbarungscharakter hat...."[50] And with this step in his reasoning Wilkens believes that Schlier's whole "neutestamentliche Grundlegung
des Dogmas" falls. The process of the formation of revelation, as
Schlier imagines it, is basicly "ungeschichtlich."

Wilkens is willing to grant to Schlier's argument that from the
form-critical research of the New Testament there were certainly very
early short kerygmatic sentences in existence, and which were the foundation for missionary preaching and teaching. "Aber zumindest im Blick auf
Paulus wird nirgendwo sichtbar, dass diese Formeln für ihn so etwas wie
'heilige Texte' seien, die von ihm nur legitim zu entfalten wären."[51]
As a matter of fact, with the exception of the Pastoral Epistles, there
is in the New Testament no method of citation by which traditional
kerygmatic sentences, as in the manner of quotes from other sources, are
are introduced. Even the places where Paul points to the paradosis, as

---

is God's and not ours." --2 Cor 4:5-7. For Paul maintains no
relationship of identity between himself and the Spirit, but considers himself only the instrument of the Spirit, who will have to
give an account of his stewardship on the last day.

So, Wilkens maintains, he can not be said (in Schlier's sense)
to be the "Stimme dessen, der ihn sendet," nor can his role as
apostle simply be the repeating of "...ihm vorgegebenes, fest und
unveränderlich in fixierten Sätzen formuliertes, traditionales
'Kerygma' zu entfalten, dessen Legitimität als solche nicht in
Frage steht."

50. Wilkens, *op. cit.*, p. 99.

1 Cor 11:23, 15:1f., and Gal 1:11, are not methods of citation.[52]

It is important that we examine yet a bit closer the way Wilkens understands the thesis of Schlier. According to Schlier the faith formulae reach back to Christ himself.[53] This depends on his revelation of his risen self and of the fact of his resurrection to the apostles. Wilkens interprets: "Diese 'Selbstbezeugung des Auferstandenen' hätten die Apostel als seine Zeugen in bestimmten Sätzen formuliert, aufgenommen und also Grundlage und Quelle aller weiteren Verkündigung weitergegeben, wo dass zu sagen sei, dass 'die Selbstbezeugung des Auferstandenen in seiner Erscheinung ein Eingehen und Offenbarwerden in die Sprache und in das Wort der Zeugen hinein' wird."[54]

In reference to 1 Cor 15ff. Wilkens allows that although by "gospel" Paul habitually means "content" of what he preaches, in this case he is certainly also quoting with attention to a particular word order -- ἐν τίνι λόγω εὐηγγελισάμην ὑμῖν. "Aber dabei ist doch zu beachten, dass dieser Wortlaut von Paulus offenbar nicht in dem Sinne als Formel einer heiligen sakrosankten Tradition gewertet worden ist, dass sie als solche abgeschlossen und irreversibel wäre."[55] This is evident from the fact that Paul fills out the formula with additional appearances of the risen one.

Wilkens finds another point of disagreement in Schlier's phrase, "Selbstoffenbarung des Auferstandenen."[56] He asserts that Paul traces the source of his vocation and mission to God, and never to Christ. He

---

51. *Ibidem*, p. 99.
52. *Ibidem*, footnote 31.
53. *Cf.* Schlier, *op. cit.*, p. 216.
54. Wilkens, *op. cit.*, p. 99; inside quote is from Schlier, *op. cit.*, p. 215.
55. **Wilkens**, *op. cit.*, p. 100.
56. *Cf. ibidem*, p. 100ff.

bases this assertion on 1 Cor 15:10, and on Gal 1:1 and Gal 1:12, which

latter passage, he insists, must be interpreted as an objective genitive

because in Gal 1:15f. the revelation -- even that of the experience on

the road to Damascus -- Paul has received is understood as an action of

God, and not as a tradition that he has in any way received.

As summary to Wilken's understanding of Schlier we can quote his

sentence: "Doch ist die Grundthese Schliers, dass die Verküngigung des

Paulus in ihrem Wortlaut den Charakter unmittelbarer, weil aus dem Munde

des Auferstandenen selbst überlieferter Offenbarung habe und darum

prinzipiell aller weiteren christlichen Verkündigung als ihr normativer,

heiliger Text zugrunde liegen müsse, im Blick auf die von ihm angeführten

neutestamentlichen Texte als verfehlt zu beurteilen."[57]   To this state-

ment Wilkens appends a long footnote, but his argument remains basicly

the same. E.g., he quotes Romans 10:17, "Also kommt der Glaube aus dem

Gehörten, das Gehörte aber διὰ ῥήματος Χριστοῦ," and adds: "...eindeutig

erscheint mir hier auf jeden Fall, dass mit dem ῥήμα Χριστοῦ nicht 'das

Wort Christi' (gen. subj.), sondern das 'Wort von Christus' (gen. obj.)

gemeint ist."[58]

Wilkens declares his **own** understanding of the traditional kerygmat-

ic formulae to be that of "summaries" of faith regarding the risen one,

inasmuch as he sees them as having more a homologus than a kerygmatic

function.

It also goes now without question that Wilkens understands Schlier

as having understood and described the basis of dogma in the New Testa-

ment in the sense that one finds there set formulae with a determined

---

57. *Ibidem*, p. 101.
58. *Ibidem*, footnote 34.

word order. "Der Nachdruck, mit dem Schlier auf die fixierte Formulierung des Evangeliums bzw. des Kerygma in bestimmten Worten und Sätzen Wert
legt, scheint dafür zu sprechen, dass er den Vorgang der Entstehung des
Kerygma in diesem Sinne als Offenbarungsvorgang versteht."[59]

Before we discuss this conclusion it will be well to take a look
at Gerhard Ebeling's statement also.

c. Gerhard Ebeling

Ebeling's critique of Schlier can be expressed precisely in a few
brief quotes from his book, *Theologie und Verkündigung*: "Der Gesichts-
punkt des wörtlichen Fixiertseins in bestimmten Sätzen ist von H. Schlier
schon in : Über das Hauptanliegen des 1. Briefes an die Korinther....und
Kerygma und Sophia."[60] "So ist also eigentlich das Dogma das Wesen des
Kerygmas und darum nach Schlier 'Glaubensprinzip'. Das heisst: Der
Glaube kommt - so muss man nun schon formulieren - nicht aus der ἀκοὴ
πιστέως, sondern aus dem Dogma. 'Die Ankunft des Dogmas' ist die grundlegende Heilstatsache."[61]

"Die These von der zeitlichen Priorität des Kerygmas als fixierter
Formel vor dem Evangelium kann nur aufrechterhalten werden unter Statu-
ierung eines nicht an Kriterien auf sein Recht prüfbaren Fixierungs-
prozesses, bei dem Anfang und Fortgang kraft dogmatischer Setzung
identisch sind."[62]

It is now clear that both Wilkens and Ebeling understand Schlier's
essay as proposing the theory that revelation insofar as it bears on the

59. *Ibidem*, p. 102.
60. *Theologie und Verkündigung*, (Tübingen, 1962), p. 116.
61. *Ibidem*, p. 118.
62. *Ibidem*, p. 119.

kerygma occured in "bestimmten Sätzen," or with a "wörtlichem Fixiertsein." It is, however, clear that they have both misunderstood the
tendency and sense of what Schlier was trying to say, for Schlier
certainly did not understand the kerygma to be a formula of set word and
phrase.

The proof that Schlier did not hold this opinion in "Kerygma und
Sophia" he gives himself on page 215 where he quotes A. Haussleiter,
Trinitarischer Glaube und Christusbekenntnis in der alten Kirche (1920),
p. 40, and comments thereto. We reproduce the quote and comment in full:

> 'Die Formel erscheint also als Norm für die den Glauben weckende
> apostolische Verkündigung. Es gab ein bestimmt geprägtes Christus-
> kerygma, auf das sich der Apostel beruft. Die Termini ὁμολογεῖν
> und ὁμολογία, die später zu geläufigen Bezeichnungen des Tauf-
> symbols überhaupt geworden sind, hafteten ursprünglich an der
> Zustimmung zum Christuskerygma, vg. die Stellen Röm. 10,9f.; 1 Tim.
> 6,12; Hebr. 4,14; 1 Joh. 4,15.' Uns ist im Zusammenhang nur der
> erste Satz von Bedeutung. Die spezielle These Haussleiters ist
> wohl kaum zu halten.

There is a great difference between simply employing a formula for
mnemonic purposes in preaching, and insisting on a sacrosanct order of
words. The latter was certainly not intended by Schlier.

Schlier had also expressed himself on the same question in an
earlier essay relative to the establishment of the teaching office in
the Church: "Das verstehende Übernehmen und Weitergeben der gewissen,
zum Teil formulierten und auch schriftlich aufbewahrten apostolischen
Überlieferung, die sich unter dem Beistand Christi und des Heiligen
Geistes vollzieht, macht diese zu einer lebendigen Lehrsubstanz, die
sich einerseits gegen Verfälschung und Auflösung straubt, andererseits
dem geschichtlichen Prozess der Erkenntnis entspricht."[63] It is here

---

63. "Die Ordnung der Kirche nach den Pastoralbriefen," in *Die Zeit der
    Kirche*, pp. 129-147.

stated that the apostolic tradition was only partially formulated. It was then hardly a "wörtliches Fixiertsein."

The final evidence that the kerygma in the Pauline epistles (the genuine and the ungenuine) does not depend on a formula of particularly set words is that different formulas are used for it, and one formula is not adhered to with a preference that excludes others.[64]

If Schlier is not speaking of a word for word statement which was handed to the apostles by the risen Christ and which they were to pass on as an unalterable formula, what does he intend? It seems that when Christ after his resurrection appeared to his apostles he thereby communicated to them that he was not dead, but alive and in the glory of God. It seems very doubtful that these facts were actually related to the disciples by Christ. It is much more likely that they were simply the overwhelming impression of his glorious and now re-experienced presence. And thereto must be coupled the commission of Christ to the apostles to give witness to him. Whether this commission was given only before the passion, as for example in Mk 9:8-9, or also in the post-resurrection appearances matters not. What matters is that the sudden and revelatory concurrence of these two facts -- the resurrection, and the commission to witness to it -- necessitated that what the apostles had to communicate be formulated in words. There was no other way. True, a person can imagine the substance of the kerygma being expressed in another form of human communication, such as art, or music, or symbol, but since the very formation of human concepts depends on words and on the dialogical disposition of the human spirit, even those methods of communication can be reductively related to the mystery of speech in

---

64. *Cf.* Rom 10:9; 1 Cor 15:1-6, 12-15, etc.; Phil 2:5-11; etc.

human understanding.

Therefore, the formulation, as also all communication of the kerygma, necessitated the use of words and of human language. In this' sense the resurrection came "zum Wort," and "zur Sprache." And in this sense the resurrection became a "Wortereignis." But this does not say that a distinctive, irreplacable, and irreformable order of words was also implied. Only that Christ is risen and sits in the glory of God. It was to this fact that the apostles had to give witness. They could do so through a variety of formulae.

The important thing is that Christ is not dead but in the glory of God. This fact can conceivably be expressed in as many ways as there were apostles. And as a matter of fact, when many people, as in a court, are called upon to give witness to a certain event, although each can tell those assembled what has happened, each does so in his own words and concepts, emphasizing those aspects that to him seem the most important or luminous in the context of the total experience. And so, when the apostles referred in their preaching and witness to the resurrection event they could all call upon ὁ καὶ παρέλαβον, as Paul did in 1 Cor 15:3, referring to the series of facts which constitute the passion and glorification of Christ. In that famous passage the emphasis is on distinctive and absolutely determinative facts, and not primarily on a distinctive and absolutely determined order of words, which is also in part there.

It is therefore completely impossible that the interpretation given to Schlier by Wilkens and Ebeling, that he holds to a determined word choice and order as necessary to the kerygma, be accepted as correct. There was in Paul's time no word-for-word set formula to the kerygma.

There is **none** today. But the content of the various forms of the kerygma in the New Testament in terms of concept is all important. And that is what the kerygma as a "Wortereignis" is all about.

CHAPTER SIX

THE CONCRETE FORMS OF THE DEVELOPING DOGMATIC FAITH

1. THE HISTORICAL STUDY OF CREEDS

Studies of the early expressions of the Christian faith have fallen
naturally into one of two categories. On the one hand there is the
collection and study of the actual and established creeds of Christendom;
on the other hand there are form critical studies which have attempted
to analyze "creedal" material within the text of the New Testament.
Studies of the first type are of an historical nature and work back
towards the New Testament; studies of the latter type work from the text
of the New Testament as a terminus a quo. These begin with a formal
analysis of the text and usually lead to the positing of a particular
and hypothetical Sitz-im-Leben as necessary to explain the text's
provenance.

It is not our purpose here to present a survey of the results of
both types of study of the early creedal material, but to select for
comment from the literature those studies which illustrate the "dogmatic"
nature of the developing faith, and which enable us to educe conclusions
relative to the concrete forms of the developing dogmatic faith as such

from several exegetical works of recent date. These works, which center on the Gattung 'hymn' in the New Testament, illustrate a direction in contemporary exegesis which is of considerable significance for the systematic theologian.

In the last century A. Hahn began the laborious work of collecting the creeds of the ancient churches. His work, first published in 1842, was revised by his son, G. L. Hahn, and became the *Bibliothek der Symbole und Glaubensregeln der alten Kirche*.[1] The largest work of pure collection was produced by P. Caspari: *Ungedruckte, unbeachtete und wenig beachtete Quellen zur Geschichte des Taufsymbols und der Glaubensregel*.[2] Caspari's work is, as the title indicates, largely the publication of material from manuscripts around the world. This was continued in his *Alte und neue Quellen zur Geschichte des Taufsymbols und der Glaubensregel*.[3] The most extensive work ever written on the Apostles' Creed alone was produced at about this time by F. Kattenbusch, *Das apostolische Symbol*.[4] Kattenbusch's great work makes no significant gain in relating the Apostles' Creed to the New Testament.[5]

Meanwhile Alfred Seeberg propounded the theory of a 'catechism' which ante-dated the composition of the New Testament and which, at least to some extent, formed the basis of the same.[6] This theory, although it deservedly found no general acceptance, did help awaken interest in forms of material which were in existence before the New Testament. This in itself was a significant step since it antedated

---

1. Breslau, 1897[3].
2. 4 vols. Christiana, 1866-69.
3. Christiana, 1879.
4. Leipzig, 1894.
5. *Cf. infra*, section 2.
6. Leipzig, 1903.

the application of the form critical method to the New Testament.

Harnack's criticism of Seeberg's 'catechism' can be taken as summary judgment on all such efforts: "Allein, dass ein solcher Katechismus nicht existiert hat, wird die Darstellung der Geschichte in den nächsten zwei Jahrhunderten lehren. Hätte er existiert, so hätte er deutlicher hervortreten müssen und hätte nicht untergehen können."[7]

Since the time of A. Hahn an immense amount of work has been done on the history of creedal forms and their use in the Christian churches. The work of surveying this long and arduous path has been excellently done by J. de Ghellinck in the first volume of his series *Patristique et Moyen Age, Études d'histoire littéraire et doctrinale, Les Recherches sur les Origines du Symbole des Apôtres.*[8] By far the greater part of this literature has been concerned with the established creeds of the Church, and has been controled by this perspective. De Ghellinck offers an appendix which lists the many publications in this area year by year from 1842 through 1949.[9] Much of this literature was occasioned by the interest which the "Apostolikumstreit" sparked in the history of creeds in 1892.[10]

In the years since the publication of de Ghellinck's work the most notable publication on the development of the creeds is, by universal

---

7. *Dogmengeschichte*, I, p. 66, footnote 1. A more balanced critique of Seeberg's total work is given by R. Deichgräber, *Gotteshymnus und Christushymnus in der frühen Christenheit*, (Göttingen, 1967), pp. 13-14.
8. Brussels, 1946; 1949[2].
9. *Ibidem*, pp. 273-299.
10. This was a recurring argument in the German Lutheran Church over the necessity of retaining the Apostles' Creed for ordination and other liturgical occasions in the light of liberal historical criticism. Harnack took a leading position in 1892 on the liberal side, maintaining that the Apostolikum should be retained but subject to criticism.

acclaim, J.N.D. Kelly's *Early Christian Creeds*.[11] Before discussing

some of its conclusions we should like to point to a work by P. Caelestis

Eichenseer, *Das Symbolum Apostolicum beim Heiligen Augustinus* which,

while principally a study of Augustine's usage and interpretation of the

Apostles' Creed, gives nevertheless a useful summary of the developmental

process toward determined word structure in creedal forms ending in the

Apostles' Creed.[12] Eichenseer's summary is useful because it lists in

full the texts of the creeds from the pages of the fathers which progres-

sively point to this development.[13] It depends heavily on Kelly.

Kelly's principal claim to fame rests on his disproving a theory

long held and propounded by Holl, Harnack, and Lietzmann, namely that

the common declaratory form of the early creeds finds its Sitz-im-Leben

in the baptismal service.[14] Kelly resolves the anomalous situation in

the early liturgical records of baptismal ceremonies which manifest both

declaratory and interrogatory creeds by showing that the declaratory

creeds belong to a very advanced stage of the catechumenate, "to the

second generation of the third century at the earliest."[15] Only in this

way can the gulf between the catechetical arrangements of a St. Justin

from those of a St. Hippolytus be explained. In the first few centuries

it was only necessary that the baptizand signify his faith by answering

to the baptizer's questioning, as in Acts 8:36-38. The traditio and

reditio of the longer declaratory creeds belongs to the logically

anterior catechumenate which, however, chronologically, belongs to the

third century.[16] Thus Kelly believes that it is obvious that a wider

---

11. London, 1960[2].
12. St. Ottilien, 1960.
13. *Cf. ibidem*, pp. 75-107.
14. *Cf.* Kelly, *op. cit.*, p. 30ff.
15. *Ibidem*, p. 49.

background must be postulated for the creeds than simply the ceremony of baptism, although in still later usage, e.g., the Roman ritual of the fourth century, the declaratory creed has its place.[17]

Simply stated then, "Declaratory creeds, conceived in the setting of their original purpose, were compendious summaries of Christian doctrine compiled for the benefit of converts undergoing instruction."[18] They were not themselves the regula fidei, but only convenient summaries of it. They subserved the purpose of instruction. Perhaps their summary character explains why even a text with the authority of the Apostles' Creed was never accorded the signal authority of later doctrinal definitions.

Evidence that the faith is larger than this summary of it is supplied in the Adoptionist controversy in the second century where the heretics are accused of falsifying "the truth of the preaching" and the "Church's belief" rather than a formulary of it.[19] For the truth of the Church's preaching is in its content rather than in its words.

Without doubt other factors such as the influence of the Trinitarian groundplan of Mt 28:19, and the developing Christology in the face of heresy, together with the exigencies of teaching have played a part in the formation of the Apostles' Creed. Nevertheless, it remains in any case only a "compendium of popular theology."[20]

Thus in the works of Justin Martyr (†165) we find only "half-formed" confessions.[21] In Irenaeus (†c. 202) there appears for the first

---

17. *Cf. ibidem*, p. 35f.
18. *Ibidem*, p. 50.
19. *Cf. ibidem*, p. 129.
20. *Ibidem*, p. 165.
21. *Cf.* Eichenseer, *op. cit.*, pp. 82-85

time "ein voll ausgebildeter christologischer Passus, das heist, das Christus-Kerygma in voll ausgeprägter Fassung," which is added to the trinitarian, sometimes binitarian, groundplan.[22]

The same development is hinted at in Hippolytus' (†235) citation of the formula for the questioning of a baptizand which contains a fuller 'Christology' in his *Traditio Apostolica*. Indeed, it is first in Hippolytus that we find a complete and fully determined confessional formula. "Diese Verschmelzung der kurzen triadischen Formel mit dem selbstständigen Christus-Kerygma muss um das dritte Viertel des zweiten Jahrhunderts erfolgt sein, da die zweite Tauffrage bei Justinus noch keinen voll entwickelten christologischen Abschnitt aufweist, während er bei Hippolyt voll ausgebildet vorliegt. Doch muss der terminus ante quem schon eine Generation vor ihm liegen, da Hippolyt in all seinen Äusserungen bekannt konservativ ist."[23]

The tendency to write formulae down which were used in the liturgy such as the creeds becomes acute in the third century. Yet even at this time absolute stability is not of prime importance, as the writings of Tertullian (c. 200) which give witness to a number of creedal formulae testify.[24]

The earliest Greek text of the Old Roman Creed (R) which has down to us is that of Marcellus of Ancyra writing to Pope Julius I about the year 340. His text runs:

πιστεύω οὖν εἰς θεὸν παντοκράτορα·
καὶ εἰς Χριστὸν 'Ιησοῦν, τὸν υἱὸν αὐτοῦ τὸν μονογενῆ,
  τὸν κύριον ἡμῶν,
τὸν γεννηθέντα ἐκ πνεύματος ἁγίου καὶ Μαρίας

---

22. *Cf. ibidem*, pp. 85-87.
23. *Ibidem*, p. 89.
24. *Cf. ibidem*, p. 93; Kelly, *op. cit.*, 98f.

τῆς παρθένου,
τὸν ἐπὶ Ποντίου Πιλάτου σταυρωθέντα καὶ ταφέντα,
καὶ τῆ τρίτη ἡμέρα ἀναστάντα ἐκ τῶν νεκρῶν,
ἀναβάντα εἰς τοὺς οὐρανοὺς καὶ καθήμενον
ἐν δεξιᾶ τοῦ πατρός, ὅθεν ἔρχεται
κρίνειν ζῶντας καὶ νεκρούς·
καὶ εἰς τὸ ἅγιον πνεῦμα, ἁγίαν ἐκκλησίαν, ἄφεσιν ἁμαρτιῶν,
σαρκὸς ἀνάστασιν, ζωὴν αἰώνιον.[25]

Marcellus' purpose in addressing himself to Pope Julius is to justify his own reputation for orthodoxy against his Arian detractors. Marcellus presents the above creed as his own faith, not necessarily as the creed of the Church of Ancyra.[26] It notably exhibits several variations from the traditional Roman creed in the earliest extant Latin version, which depends principally on the *Commentarius in Symbolum Apostolorum* of Rufinus of Aquileia from about the year 404.

Kelly reconstructs the text of R known to Rufinus with the help of two manuscripts in English libraries thus:

Credo in deum patrem omnipotentem;
et in Christum Iesum filium eius unicum,
    dominum nostrum,
qui natus est de Spiritu sancto et Maria
    virgine,
qui sub Pontio Pilato crucifixus est et
    sepultus,
    tertia die resurrexit
    a mortuis,
    ascendit in caelos,
    sedet ad dexteram patris,
    unde venturus est iudicare
    vivos et mortuos;
et in Spiritum sanctum,
    sanctam ecclesiam,
    remissionem peccatorum,
    carnis resurrectionem.[27]

Like Marcellus, Rufinus is interested in demonstrating his

---

25. Text quoted from Kelly, p. 103.
26. *Cf. ibidem*, p. 108ff.
27. *Cf. ibidem*, p. 102, and also Kelly's translation and notes in *Rufinus, A Commentary on the Apostles' Creed*, in the *Ancient Christian Writers*, (Westminster, Md., 1955).

orthodoxy with Rome, which in his case he does by explaining the points of divergence between the creed of his home Church, Aquileia, and that of Rome. Kelly reasons that, "His reason for this odd procedure was that, while he recognized that the Roman church preserved the original creed of the Apostles in its purity, he felt constrained (by natural piety, we may conjecture) to use the formula he had himself professed at baptism as his working basis."[28]

A little study reveals at least several divergences between the respective texts of Marcellus and of Rufinus. Marcellus' version omits "Father" in the first article; it adds "life everlasting" to the third article; it inserts "and" in two places in the second article. It is also noteworthy that, although Rufinus regards the creed in use at Rome as that of the apostles, he does not shirk from presenting his own orthodoxy in terms of another and variant creed, that of Aquileia. These facts underline the point that orthodoxy in the first centuries was less a question of exact words or of verbal fidelity than of content.

In attempting to assign a date to the composition of R, Kelly finds the arguments supporting the antiquity of the Greek version over the Latin not strictly conclusive since there must always have been converts who had need of the Latin version. Loof's view that the two forms are almost contemporary seems closest to the truth.

> On the whole, however, the scales are tipped slightly in favour of the priority of the Greek text, and the parallel Greek creed of St. Hippolytus brings them down heavily. The Latin text need not, of course, be much younger. ....The interesting corollary follows, however, that the original composition of R must have taken place at a time when Greek was the official language of the Roman church. We are thus able to trace it back at least a hundred years before Marcellus. It is well known that Greek was used at Rome in the

---

28. Kelly, *Early Christian Creeds*, p. 102.

liturgy and for other purposes throughout the second century. ....
But Latin was coming into official use in the first and second
generations of the third century. It therefore seems plausible
to ascribe the composition of R to the opening years of the century
at the latest. ....The fact that St. Hippolytus ...bears witness
to the existence of an almost identical formulary in the first
decades of the third century might by itself be held to be
decisive. Moreover, R exercised a powerful influence... on all
the other local creeds of the West. This can only be explained
on the assumption that its position was already firmly established
by the middle of the third century.[29]

Eichenseer is able to show that although the Apostles' Creed may

not belong to the ceremony of baptism in the strictest sense, Augustine

could recommend most strongly in his sermons "to pray it daily and

praying to contemplate it," so that "das Symbolum von neuem lebensbestim-

mend wurde und es für das Abendland blieb."[30]

2. THE NOTION OF CONFESSION

Confession means disclosure. It is the externalization of what is

within. Through the means of speech the most intimate word of a person,

his decision for or against something, is made public and brought before

the community. Hermann Zeller writes: "Das Bekenntnis kann aus freien

Stücken erfolgen, es kann unter Umständen auch zur notwendigen Pflicht

werden. Der Bekennende öffnet sein Gewissen und opfert seine Sicherheit

für das allgemeine Wohl; Gutes und Böses beim Namen nennend, bekennt er

sich zu einer objektiven Ordnung. Indem er sich vor anderen darauf

festlegt, klart und formt er seine eigenen Haltung und befähigt sie damit

auch zur gleichgerichteten Wirkung auf andere."[31]

Confession, in Latin "confessio" from "confiteri," corresponds to

29. *Ibidem*, pp. 112-113.
30. Eichenseer, *op. cit.*, p. 483.
31. "Bekenntnis" in *LThK*, II, 142-143; *cf.* the corresponding articles by
    O. Michel in *ThW* and N. Brox in *HThG*.

the Greek ὁμολογεία and ὁμολογεῖν which are derived from ὁμός, "like,"
and λεγεῖν, "to say."

In classical Greek, confession meant simply agreement with the
mind of another.[32] The word is easily translated as meaning to "admit,"
"agree," or "acknowledge." According to Plato the masses adopt opinions
in an uncritical manner, whereas philosophers come to agreement through
dialogue which proves itself as convincing. Thus agreement comes about
after the manner that a man binds himself to something freely. Prominent
in the classical era is the juristic usage of the word. One agrees to a
declaration, for example, to his guilt before a court, or to a binding
agreement, by "confessing" it.

In the protocanonical books of the Septuagint ὁμολογεῖν occurs
only three times: as translation for ידה, "to praise" (Job 40:9); for
נדר, "to vow" (Jer 44:25); for שבע, "to swear" (Ez 16:8).

Much more often ἐξομολογεῖν is found (about 120 times) and usually
as a translation of ידה, "to praise" or "confess" (e.g., 2 Sam 22:50;
Ps 106:47). ὁμολογία occurs a few times as translation for נדבה, "free-
will offering" (Dt 12:17; Am 4:5), and for "vow," נבר, and once for
"praise," תודה (1 Esd 9:8).

In the Old Testament context Martin Noth calls the phrase, "Yahweh
brought Israel out of Egypt," the "Urbekenntnis Israels."[33] It is the
"dramatische Mitte," around which the other happenings in Israel's
history are grouped. So the very frequent recitations of the deeds of
Yahweh have a confessional character, as do Exo 15:1-18, 1Chr 16:8-36,
Ps 105.

---

32. *Cf.* G. Bornkamm, "Homologia," in *Hermes* 71 (1936), pp. 377-393.
33. Quoted from Gerhard von Rad, *Theologie des Alten Testaments*, I,
     (München, 1958), pp. 177-178.

The Schema of Deut 6:4 was, however, the phrase and confession which most pithily expressed the faith of Israel. As a prayer which was recited twice daily, it has stamped the religious consciousness of Israel as no other confessional expression. Although the whole Torah was indeed the "creed" of Israel, the Schema confession of the one God unified the people in a prayable expression of agreement in monotheism.[34] Vernon Neufeld points to the fact that at the beginning of the Christian era the expression εἶς ὁ θεός sometimes took the place of the Schema.[35]

In late Judaism ὁμολογεῖν and ἐξομολογεῖν began to be used more in relation to the confessing of sins and of repentance. Examples are Dan 9:1-9 and Tob 3:1-6. This acknowledgment of guilt was also a confessing.

In the New Testament ὁμολογεῖν is found twenty-six times, of which ten occurrences are in John. ἐξομολογεῖν is found ten times. ὁμολογία occurs only six times: 2 Cor 9:13; 1 Tim 6:12, 13; Heb 3:1; 4:14; 10:23. It is remarkable that the noun always refers to the Christian confession. In Hebrews it (the confession) even seems to have a determined liturgical Sitz-im-Leben. In Second Corinthians and First Timothy the Septuagintal and classical meanings suffice.

"Am häufigsten aber wird die Begriffsgruppe in der Bedeutung gestehen, frei erklären, öffentlich bekennen verwendet."[36] So, in both Acts 24:14 and in 1 Tim 6:12 public confessions of belief in Jesus are made by Paul and Timothy respectively. In John confession has not such

---

34. *Cf.* W. D. Davies, "Torah and Dogma: a Comment," in *Harvard Theological Review*, 61 (1968), pp. 87-106.
35. *The Earliest Christian Confessions*, (Grand Rapids, Mich., 1963), p. 36ff.
36. Dieter Fürst, "Bekennen," in *Theologisches Begriffslexikon zum Neuen Testament*, (Wuppertal, 1967), p. 78.

a forensic sense as in these examples; it rather means the acknowledgment of the truth, which has come into the world in the person of Jesus.

An eschatological accent is even detectible when ὁμολογεῖν and ὁμολογεία are used in contradistinction to ἀρνέομαι, "to deny," as in: Jn 1:20; Tit 1:16; 1 Jn 2:12; Mt 10:32f.

There is a conclusion then that is unescapable, particularly since ὁμολογία is always used in some such sense as it is in Heb 3:1, "Therefore, holy brethren, partakers of a heavenly calling, consider the apostle and high priest of our confession, Jesus...." i.e., of the Christian confession. That conclusion is that the concepts ὁμολογεία and ὁμολογεῖν referred to the acceptance and acknowledgment of the Christ-kerygma, as in Rom 10:8ff.; 1 Tim 6:12; Heb 4:14; 1 Jn 4:15.[37]

Neufeld concludes his study of the nature of the homologia commenting on Rom 10:8: "The homologia, 'Jesus is Lord,' and the belief that 'God raised him from the dead' comprise the ῥῆμα τῆς πίστεως which is preached in the kerygma of the church. Thus it is clear that the essentials of the gospel which the church proclaimed were closely related to the homologia to which the Christian community adhered."[38]

3. THE FORMATIONS OF CONFESSIONS IN THE NEW TESTAMENT

To postulate fixed dogmatic formularies in the time of the composition of the New Testament has long been regarded as an anachronism. The legend popularized by Rufinus -- that each of the apostles elicited one part of the Apostles' Creed as a model for their preaching before departing on their missionary journeys -- has not been seriously accepted for

---

37. *Cf.* Neufeld, *op. cit.*, pp. 20-24.
38. *Ibidem*, p. 24.

some hundreds of years.[39] In his great work on the Apostles' Creed published in 1900, Kattenbusch sought to establish links between the Old Roman Creed and the New Testament. Elements of that creed he believed could be found there, but not the creed itself.[40] Eduard Norden made important contributions in determining formal criteria in his *Agnostos Theos, Untersuchungen zur Formengeschichte religiöser Rede* by pointing to the importance of the participial construction, relative clauses, and substantives.[41] Others such as Josef Kroll continued this work in his lectures and publications of the twenties.[42] Ernst Lohmeyer's *Kyrios Jesus* of 1928 is a landmark because it established once and for all the hymnic character of Phil 2:6-11. Taking a different tack, Paul Feine in 1925 believed he could find a rather well-formed creed behind the text of the New Testament.[43] These are the important background efforts which set the stage for more recent attempts to find creedal material in the New Testament.

a. Paul Feine

Feine's work deserves more extended consideration because it was the first work which sought in detail to link the Apostles' Creed with the New Testament. As terminus **a** quo he took the Old Roman Baptismal Creed, which was already in use in the third century, and which in an

---

39. *Cf.* Kelly, *op. cit.*, pp. 1-6.
40. *Cf.* Kattenbusch, *op. cit.*, p. 346: "Ich finde in den Schriften des Neuen Testaments, die in ihrer absoluten Mehrzahl älter sind als R, in der Gestalt von disjecta membra die 'Artikel' von R präformiert, nicht R selbst. Das Symbol ist eine originale Produktion."
41. Leipzig, 1913.
42. *Cf.* especially "Die Hymendichtung des fruhen Christentums," in *Antike* 2 (1926), pp. 258-281.
43. *Die Gestalt des apostolischen Glaubensbekenntnisses in der Zeit des Neuen Testaments*, (Leipzig, 1925.

enlarged version is the Apostles' Creed. Feine's terminus ad quem is to reestablish what he believes to be the original form of both creeds. That is to say, as the creed was soon after Pentecost. An exegete, he even maintains that there is "ein wesentlich umfangreicheres neutesta-mentliches Material" to be developed.

Feine criticizes the view according to which the oldest baptismal confession of a new Jewish convert was only the recognition of Jesus as Messiah, whereas for pagans the confession of an almighty God together with the recognition of Jesus as Lord was required. He shows that already in his first sermon Peter names Jesus "Lord and Christ" in Acts 2:36: "Assuredly let all the house of Israel know that God has made both Lord and Christ, this Jesus whom you crucified." Therefore, God's action in Christ is spoken out. And from this fact Feine reckons that the two-member baptismal creed was born.

Although the Gospel according to Matthew comes from Jewish circles, Feine assumes that the baptismal creed of Mt 28:19 is not original, but represents a liturgical usage of later date because it is so "abgeschlif-fen und kurz." In other places of the New Testament where there is mention of baptism it is only done in reference to Jesus as Messiah. So Gal 3:27 and Rom 6:3 mention baptism "into Christ." Acts 19:5 and 8:16 say, "in the name of Jesus Christ." Acts 2:38 says, ἐν τῷ ὀνόματι Ἰησοῦ Χριστοῦ, "auf Grund des Namens Jesu Christi."

Feine believes that the confession required of the Jewish convert was three-membered from the very beginning. However, the third member mentioned neither the Church nor had any reference to the Holy Spirit, because the first community "lived from the strength of the Holy Spirit," and the witnesses of the first Pentecost "saw and heard his works."

Instead the third member mentioned the goods of salvation: the forgiveness of sins, the sending of the gifts of the Spirit, eternal life.[44]

The method which Feine used was simply to point to the similarity of words between the Old Roman Creed and certain formulary-like passages in the New Testament. An example in his own words suffices:

> An den Namen Jesu Christi hat sich wahrscheinlich die Bezeichnung 'Herr' (Κύριος) angeschlossen. Die Begrundung für diese Annahme erblicke ich einerseits in der Tatsache, dass das Bekenntnis zu Jesus als dem Herrn das älteste im Neuen Testament nachweisbare Bekenntnis der Christengemeinde gewesen ist.... wenn man ein Taufbekenntnis bildete, dieses Element nicht gefehlt haben wird; andererseits darin, dass es tatsächlich im altrömischen Taufbekenntnis enthalten ist. Ob Jesus Christus von vornherein 'unser Herr genannt worden ist, lässt sich nicht mit Sicherheit sagen, ist aber nicht unwahrscheinlich, angesichts der grossen Zahl von derartigen formelhaften Stellen nicht nur in den paulinischen Briefen..... soncern auch in anderen neutestamentlichen Schriften...."[45]

Although Feine is not of the opinion that one can work out a completely determined formulation for the creed during the time of the New Testament since some things were still in flux, let us quote his own final solution. In the earliest times the apostolic baptismal creed ran so:

> Zum ersten Artikel: ich bekenne Einen Gott, den Vater, den Schöpfer des Alls, (oder: von dem das All ist, oder: von dem und durch den und auf den hin das All ist, oder: der Himmel und Erde gemacht hat, oder: Einen Gott und den Vater des Alls, der über allem und durch alles und in allem ist) (den Allmächtigen). Zum dritten Artikel: Durch welchen wir empfangen Vergebung der Sünden und die Gabe des heiligen Geistes, und die Hoffnung der Auferstehung von den Toten oder: und die Auferstehung der Toten und das ewige Leben oder: und die Hoffnung des ewigen Lebens.[46]

Feine's work is therefore so speculative as to be inconclusive. Indeed, it does not even necessarily conclude to the existence of a three-membered creed in the earliest times.

---

44. Cf. *ibidem*, pp. 30-31.
45. *Ibidem*, pp. 94-95.
46. *Ibidem*, pp. 143-144.

b. Oscar Cullmann

In his book, *The Earliest Christian Confessions*,[47] Oscar Cullmann
attempts to uncover the circumstances which are responsible for the
appearance of the first Christian confessional forms. He believes that
their Sitze-im-Leben are to be found not only on the occasion of dogmatic
disputes or of liturgical happenings, but maintains that many types of
occasions would have simultaneously contributed to their appearance.
These various circumstances are of course to be found in the period when
the New Testament had not yet assumed its authoritative position in the
Church. It will not always be possible to tell if a particular formula
owes its first formulation to one circumstance rather than another. We
name his various circumstances as he does:

1. Baptism and catechumenism;
2. Regular worship (liturgy and preaching);
3. Exorcism;
4. Persecution;
5. Polemic against heretics.[48]

Baptism

Already in the time of the Acts of the Apostles we find a type of
rudimentary baptismal liturgy which included the questioning of the
baptizand. The example in question is the baptism of the Ethiopian
eunuch. The question which is put to the baptizand reveals a stereo-
typed character: τι κωλύει: "What is to prevent me from being baptized?"
And Philip gives an answer which already seems to have a liturgical
character: "If you believe with your whole heart, you may [be baptized].[49]

---

47. The French edition of this work, *Les Premières Confessions de Foi
     Chrétiennes*, (Paris, 1943), was not available; hence the quotes are
     taken from the English edition: London, 1949.
48. *Ibidem*, p. 18.
49. This sentence (Acts 8:37) is, Cullmann admits, not found in every
     early manuscript. Yet it is a very early interpolation and cannot

Then the eunuch makes his confession: "I believe that Jesus Christ is the Son of God" (Acts 8:37-38). Cullmann believes there are remnants from early baptismal confessions in two other places, namely 1 Pet 3:18 and Eph 4:5, which will be discussed later.

Cullmann is of the opinion that there is a certain form of development among the confessional formulae in the New Testament, a development from the less complex to the more complex. He even warns against the assumption that the three-member forms may have existed from the beginning. Furthermore, he thinks that it would be wrong to assume that the single-membered confessions were only parts of the larger three-membered forms of later date.[50]

It was necessary to baptize under the name of someone, and this explains why the three names are mentioned together in Mt 28:19. Cullmann would not even allow that this formula is a baptismal creed.[51] Places such as 2 Cor 13:14, "The grace of our Lord Jesus Christ and the love of God and the fellowship of the Holy Spirit be with all of you," are also not looked upon as confessions, although they probably had a liturgical character.

By far the greatest number of confessions in the New Testament are one-membered: they name only Christ. Much more seldom are the two-membered formulae which mention Christ and God the Father. Here it seems almost as if belief in God is only a function of belief in Christ, since he is the one who has raised Jesus from the dead. Cullmann believes that the true three-membered formulae appear only later in the age of the

---

be regarded as a late addition; therefore it represents an early liturgy. *Cf. ibidem*, p. 19, note 4
50. *Cf. ibidem*, pp. 35-36.
51. *Cf. ibidem*, pp. 43-44.

apostolic fathers. "This suggests the idea of a direct development of single-membered confessions into double-membered, and then further into triple-membered."[52] He does not believe that the succeeding steps in this evolution eliminated the continuing use of the former more simple forms.

The multitude of one-membered formulae, such as "Kyrios Jesus Christus" (1 Cor 12:3), "Jesus is the Christ" (1 Jn 2:22), and "Jesus is the Son of God" (Acts 3:37) confirm that the Christ confession was in the ancient Church the heart of every confession. From time to time other elements were added, as the "according to the flesh ....according to the spirit," of Rom 1:3, or the humiliation-exaltation motif of Phil 2:6ff.

Cullmann believes that the two-membered formulae only came into being with the mission to the gentiles, for the Jewish mission could presume belief in God. He takes as proof of this the places where the two-membered formulae can be found. All such places are, he thinks, places in the text where there is question of Christianity having contact with paganism. Examples are the three places in the letters to Timothy (1 Tim 2:5; 6:13; 2 Tim 4:1f.), and the confession in 1 Cor 8:6, "One God, the Father, from whom we exist, and one Lord, Jesus Christ; through whom are all things and through whom we exist."

If the first article was added because of the gentile mission, what was the cause of the appearance of the third article? Cullmann thinks that baptism needed to be performed only under the name of one person, but the Holy Spirit was eventually added to the other two because the Spirit was manifestly the effect of baptism. Thus 1 Pet 3:20ff. is

52. *Ibidem*, p. 36.

seen as a baptismal creed. His reasoning here is extremely artful. The text mentions that Christ went after his death to the "spirits in prison." This was the occasion for preaching about baptism. But since the Spirit was one of the effects of baptism, it was eventually simply added to the two-membered creeds.

Or to express the same matter differently (as Cullmann does too), two-membered baptismal creeds were made into three-membered formulae simply because one could no longer go on with confessions such as Eph 4:4, "....one body, one Spirit....one hope....one Lord (one faith), one baptism, one God and father of all...."; for "one baptism" from Eph 4:4 could no longer stand as the third member of a creed on the same level as God-Father and God-Son. And so it was replaced with the gift of baptism, the Spirit.[53]

Regular Worship

By every meeting of the community there would have been the need to have a determined text for expressing the common faith, since agreement to a text (or confession) is that which unites a community. As examples of such formularies Cullmann suggests the Christ hymn of Phil 2:6-11, and 1 Cor 15:3-7. He admits that at the time of the New Testament there was no general and fixed text for the Christological confession. The Philipians text was an independent piece for liturgical usage. The one from Corinthians was probably used in preaching and catechetical work.

Exorcisms

Until about the year 150 _all_ the Christ confessions mention that the Lordship of Christ is over all demons, powers, authorities, as the confession in Col 1:10-20 reveals: "He is the image of the invisible God,

53. *Cf. ibidem*, p. 43.

the first-born of all creation, for in him all things were created, in heaven and on earth, visible and invisible, whether thrones or dominions or principalities or authorities..."[54] For Cullmann the simple confession, "Jesus is Lord," means that he rules over absolutely all other powers. Therefore, the very mention of his lordship in exorcisms had a great significance. So Peter attributed the miracle of healing the lame man at the gate of the temple in Acts 3 not to his own power, but to the "name of Jesus Christ the Nazorene." 'Christ' and 'Nazorene' are not to be understood as proper names but as the confession used in this healing. But the Lord, the mention of whose very name was effective in healing one held in the power of sickness, was also effective over the power of the demon, as the synoptics witness the demons themselves confessing him in Mk 2:24, 3:11, and 5:7.

Persecution

Disagreeing with other interpreters, Cullmann understands 1 Tim 6:12-16 as connected with persecutions. Verse 13, "In the presence of God who gives life to all things, and of Christ Jesus who in his testimony before Pontius Pilate made the good confession, I charge you to keep the commandment unstained and free from reproach until the appearing of our Lord Jesus Christ," together with Acts 3:13, where Pontius Pilate is also mentioned, reveal the fact that the passage in 1 Tim refers to a confessional form employed in judicial processes. The appearance of μαρτυρέω here is the first step in its eventually meaning "to suffer martyrdom." Hence the connection between "witnessing" at a judicial process and this confession.

Of particular importance was the simple confession, Κύριος Ἰησοῦς.

54. *Cf. ibidem*, pp. 23ff., and 59-60.

From its subjects Rome demanded the contrary confession, Κύριος Καῖσαρ.
Under no circumstances could a pious Christian give the title "Lord" (in
Hebrew, "Adonai") to an earthly ruler. The contradiction between Lord-
Jesus and Lord-Caesar is seen also in Acts 17:7: "These all do contrary
to the decrees of Caesar, announcing another King, Jesus."

Polemic

It is not difficult to establish that polemic against heretical
opinions also played a role in the growth of the confessions. So, the
First Johannine Epistle is a work addressed in its entirety against
Docetism; its whole content is summarized in the short confession, "Jesus
has come in the flesh" (4:2). 1 Cor 8:6, "One God, the Father,from whom
we exist, and one Lord, Jesus Christ, through whom are all things and
through whom we exist," can be understood as a polemic against pagan
polytheism. Finally, the confession of 1 Cor 15 points to the fact
that there were doubters of the resurrection, and that one of the
functions of the confession was to counter their influence.

Cullmann summarizes best his own work:

> The affirmation that several circumstances contributed to the
> formation of the confessions of faith should prevent us from postu-
> lating a _priori_ any unified and uniform formula of faith for the
> New Testament times. There were at first different formulas for
> the different requirements of the Church; each sought in the whole
> Christian tradition what appeared essential to the end in view.
> But since a formula originating, for example, in persecution,
> found employment also in worship and polemic, the road opened for
> a progressive unification and fusion, such as can be already
> affirmed of the New Testament age.[55]

We find Cullmann's elaboration of various circumstances in the
earliest period of Christianity which would have required a confession to
the faith of Christians useful; his postulation of a strict evolutionary

---

55. _Ibidem_, p. 33.

process from one-membered to two and three-membered formulas is not completely convincing.

c. Ethelbert Staufer

Ethelbert Stauffer goes much further than either his predecessors or other exegetes in proposing a primitive Christianity which already had explicit dogmatic formulae. Missionary preaching was "die ursprünglichste und beweglichste Gattung theologischer Rede in der ersten Christenheit."[56] So the preaching, even when brought to speech by different missionaries, was bound "an das Kerygma, das in festgeprägten Begriffen und Sätzen die entscheidenden Heilstatsachen ausspricht (Apg 4,10; 8,12; 9,20)."[57] In the second place after missionary preaching comes regular theological instruction in the context of which "katechismusartige Formeln als Leitfaden ....[zum] Gedächtnisstoff [waren] unentbehrlich." Texts he mentions to support this are: Acts 2:41f.; Mt 23:10; Gal 6:6; 1 Cor 12:28. Another factor contributing to the growth of dogmatic formulae was the struggle with heretical opinions, which would necessarily lead to the "Herausbildung formelhafter Schuldoktrinen."

The very greatest need for confessional formulae would undoubtedly have been the liturgy and, in the first place, baptism. So the confession fits naturally into the liturgy for, "Das Credo hat doxologischen Inhalt und ist von vielerlei Glaubensformeln durchsetzt (1 Kor 12,3; Ap 22,20). Viele Bekenntnisse haben hymnischen, viele Hymen haben bekenntnishaften Charakter (Kol 3,16; Eph 5,19...)."[58]

---

56. *Die Theologie des neuen Testaments*, (Stuttgart, 1941), p. 213.
57. *Ibidem*.
58. *Ibidem*, p. 214.

Stauffer's one contribution seems to be his listing in an appendix

of twelve formal criteria for recognizing the dogmatic formulae which

are, in his own words, embedded in the text of the New Testament as

"Kristalle in eine amorphe Gesteinsmasse."[59] We list his twelve criteria

just as he presents them:

> 1. Das sicherste Kennzeichen ist oft die Rahmenterminologie: Die
> Glaubensformeln oder ihre Elemente werden umrahmt und hervorgehoben
> durch Begriffe wie "überliefern", "glauben", "bekennen". ZB R 10,9
> 2. Oft auch macht sich das Vorhandensein einer Glaubensformel
> durch Randstörungen bemerklich. Denn durch die Einfügung der
> Glaubensformel in den Kontext hat vielfach der Kontext oder die
> Glaubensformel oder beides gelitten. ZB 1 Tm 3, 16 (ὅς!).
> 3. Oft fügt sich die Glaubensformel syntaktisch nicht in den
> Rahmentext ein. ZB Ap 1, 4.
> 4. Oft auch hat die Glaubensformel eine andere Sprache, Termin-
> ologie oder Stilgebung als der Kontext. ZB 1 Kor 16,22.
> 5. Oft beobachten wir, dass an den verschiedensten Stellen die-
> selbe Glaubensformel mit geringen Modifikationen gleichförmig
> wiederkehrt. ZB 2 K 5, 21; 8,9.
> 6. Oft fallen die Glaubensformeln auf durch ihren einfachen und
> durchsichtigen syntaktischen Aufbau. Partikel, Konjunktionen und
> komplizierte Konstruktionen werden vermieden. Der Satzbau ist
> meist parataktisch, nicht hypotaktisch, die Gedankenführung nicht
> argumentativ, sondern thetisch. ZB Ag 4,10.
> 7. Oft auch treten die Glaubensformeln durch ihren monumentalen
> stilistischen Aufbau hervor. Antithetische oder anaphorische
> Stilgebung ist beliebt. ZB 1 Tm 3,16.
> 8. Die Glaubensformeln zeigen oft rhythmische Gestaltung. Doch
> ist der Rhythmus nicht, wie in der griechischen Metrik, durch die
> Quantität der Silben, sondern durch die Anzahl der Hebungen oder
> auch der Worte bestimmt. ZB 1 K 15,3.
> 9. Die Glaubensformeln sind oft nach Stichen und Strophen geglied-
> ert. ZB Kol 1,15 ff.
> 10. Oft zeichnen sich die Glaubensformeln durch eine Vorliebe
> für Namensprädikationen und Appositionen aus. ZB Ign Eph 7,2.
> 11. Oft auch zeigen die Glaubensformeln eine Vorliebe für Partiz-
> ipien und Relativsätze. ZB R 1,3f.
> 12. Meist sprechen die Glaubensformeln in normativer Weise von
> den elementaren Wahrheiten und Tatsachen der Heilsgeschichte. ZB
> Ign Trall 9,1 f.[60]

Doubtless Stauffer has gone far beyond the measure of even the

systematic theologian (not to mention that of the exegete) in seeking the

---

59. *Ibidem*, p. 215.
60. *Ibidem*, p. 322.

foundations of the Church's dogmatic teaching in "festgeprägte Begriffe und Sätze," which express the kerygma and are to be found like gems in the text of the New Testament. Although there is assuredly a dogmatic content to the New Testament, it does not depend precisely on the exact wording of the various kerygmatic formulae to be found therein.

d. J. N. D. Kelly

Kelly criticizes both Feine and Cullmann for being too one-sided. Feine concentrates too exclusively on baptism, as if it were the only occasion which would have occasioned the use of a creed. An equally serious objection to his work is that Feine *assumes* that the apostolic Church possessed a textually determined creed. The evidence hardly supports this assumption.

In rejecting Feine's positing **of** a textually determined creed, Kelly comes to a much more finely nuanced position on the development of the apostolic doctrine. In the first place he finds Dodd's reconstruction of the apostolic kerygma excellent for revealing the pattern and content of the apostolic preaching; it suffers, however, for concentrating too exclusively on the preaching of the early Church, as if there were not also a variety of other occasions which would also call for doctrinal expression.

Certainly the apostolic Church possessed a creed in the sense of a broadly recognized body of teaching. This is usually referred to as the regula fidei. But the movement to fixity was only beginning. "Thus the reader of the New Testament is continually coming across creed-like slogans and tags, catchwords which at the time of writing were being consecrated by popular usage. In addition he lights upon longer passages which, while still fluid in their phrasing, betray by their context, rhythm and general pattern, as well as by their content, that they derive from community tradition rather than from the writer's untrammelled invention."[61]

When it comes to fixity Kelly is ready to admit that the words "creed," "confession," and "formula" are used only too loosely to describe the material. "It cannot be too often repeated that, in the proper sense of the terms, no creed, confession or formula of faith can be discovered in the New Testament, with the possible exception of such curt slogans as Kurios Iesous."[62] A true estimate of the state of fixity at the time of the New Testament requires that one posit a corpus of teaching which was the possession of the Church as a whole, and which was only beginning "to crystallize into more or less conventional patterns and forms, and sometimes set types of verbal expression."[63] To require or even to suggest a greater degree of fixity at this stage of the expression of the developing Christian doctrine is simply anachronistic.

In support of Kelly's nuanced position on fixity we can cite the consensus, or rather lack of it, on 1 Cor 15:3ff. That Paul is here passing on a catechetical summary is agreed on by all. The extent of the traditional formula within this passage, however, and the degree of the apostle's adaption of it is a problem which will probably never be solved.[64] Paul even mentions in verse 2 that he delivered the gospel in the form of a determined formula (word) to the Corinthians: τίνι λόγω

---

61. Kelly, *op. cit.*, p. 13.
62. *Ibidem*, p. 23.
63. *Ibidem*, p. 24.
64. *Cf.* Karl Lehmann, *Auferweckt am dritten Tag nach der Schrift*, (Freiburg, 1968), pp. 27-35.

εὐηγγελισάμην ὑμῖν· εἰ κατέχετε, ἐκτὸς εἰ μὴ εἰκῆ ἐπιστεύσατα.

Karl Lehmann translates this passage: "...wenn ihr es festhaltet in eben dem Wort(laut), in welchem ich es euch als Evangelium verkündigt habe..."[65] In other words, Paul insists that the Corinthians have received the gospel in the very "word" in which he has delivered it to them; yet in writing to the Corinthian community he still feels free enough to extend the formula beyond verse 5, and to mention appearances of of the risen one which were not included in the original formula. This is surely a state of fixity in the tradition which is fixed according to content, but not fixed according to the word (Wortlaut) in any absolute sense.

Kelly also criticizes the view of those (Feine, R. Seeberg, J. Hausleiter, and Cullmann) which held that the single-membered confession, "Jesus is Lord," or something like it was the first of the creedal forms, which then led progressively to the two-membered and three-membered formulae. To suppose that there has been such a progression in the development of the creed is to read back into history what a wholly modern evolutionary standpoint demands, which sees the less complex always preceeding the more complex. This evolutionary hypothesis has a certain plausibility insofar as in the apostolic age Christological confessions were certainly the most numerous. Two-membered confessions are more rare, and three-membered confessions still harder to find. So Kelly simply denies Cullmann's assertion that all the binitarian confessions are to be found in a context which suggests the gentile mission. Of 1 Cor 8:6 Cullmann's assertion may be true, but 1 Tim 6:13 "is almost certainly to be connected with baptism, and there is little to be said

---

65. *Ibidem*, p. 27.

for Cullmann's strained attempt to interpret it as referring to a judici
judicial process" before a pagan judge.[66]

Other reasons controverting the Cullmann thesis can also be brought
forward. So the phrase, "God, who has raised the Lord Jesus from the
dead," simply occurs too often to be limited to the gentile mission.
For the Church's very beliefs about Jesus are elaborated in the context
of what God the Father has accomplished in him. Moreover, the proposal
to substitute the Holy Spirit for the third article's enumeration of the
fruits of baptism, since the Holy Spirit is one of these, is simply too
ingenious. The Holy Spirit represented much more to the early Christian
than simply one, or even the greatest, of the fruits of baptism. As
we have shown earlier, the "Trinitarian groundplan" (in Kelly's phrase)
was much too embedded in the early Christians' way of thinking and the
various New Testament documents to have been occasioned by the evolutionary myth. "Our conclusion must be that one-membered, two-membered and
three-membered confessions flourished side by side in the apostolic
Church as parallel and mutually independent formulations of the one
kerygma; and this is a datum of prime importance. It is worth noting
that there is abundant confirmation of it in the documents of the second
century."[67]

e. Hans Conzelmann

In his article, "Was glaubte die frühe Christenheit?"[68] Hans
Conzelmann asks the question whether, in view of the seeming impossibil-
ity of finding a unity among the various theological conceptions of the

---

66. Kelly, *op. cit.*, p. 26.
67. *Ibidem*, p. 24.
68. *Schweizerische Theologische Umschau*, 25 (1955), pp. 61-74.

New Testament, one might look to the "fest formulierten Sätze," therein hoping to find a timeless representation of the faith, and thereby a way out of the theological impass. Is it legitimate to seek in them a "Wesen des Christentums" free of particular historical coloration?

To raise the question of the content of the confessional formulae as though they contained that certain 'minimum' of Christianity is, he believes, wrong. For to do so would be the misguided attempt to place Christian confession outside of all history, to transform it into some type of timeless principle. And Christian confession, if it is anything, is timely engagement in an historical happening. Therefore it is never divorced from the particularities of one's own history, nor from those of the history of Jesus. Within the parameters of these particularities every confession is an absolute and (at least) to this extent a timeless fides qua and fides quae. "Insofern erhebt es gerade in seiner Geschichtlichkeit den absoluten Anspruch. Dieser steht nicht auf einem fixierten, autoritativen Wortlaut -- in dieser Hinsicht bemerken wir in der Frühzeit trotz eines gewissen Grundbestandes an Begriffen, Stilformen, eine grosse Mannigfaltigkeit -- , vielmehr ergibt sich der Absolutheits-anspruch aus der Absolutheit des geglaubten Herrn."[69] A determined word choice or order is in itself then not only an unnecessary quantity; it is a quantity of questionable importance. Theology will naturally require different words (e.g., the various cultural thought forms), yes, words differing even from the simplest biblical confessions for the very purpose of expressing the same theological content. This also suggests the necessity of an authoritative teaching office in the Church.

Today the question is not precisely to seek the theology of the

---

69. *Ibidem*, p. 63.

individual New Testament writers but to seek what it was they brought to expression with their theology. πιστεύειν expressed in the first place neither trust nor a personal relationship to Christ, but the acceptation of the kerygma. To believe in Christ is to accept that which is contained in the kerygma, namely God's work of salvation in him, that God has raised him from the dead.

Next to πιστεύειν stands in the New Testament ὁμολογεῖν: both words serve "das Anführen fester Bekenntnisformeln." So 1 Jn 4:14, ὃς ἐὰν ὁμολογήσῃ ὅτι 'Ιησοῦς ἐστιν ὁ υἱὸς τοῦ θεοῦ, and 1 Jn 5:15, ὁ πιστεύων ὅτι 'Ιησοῦς ἐστιν ὁ υἱὸς τοῦ θεοῦ. On the basis of Rom 10:9, ὅτι ἐὰν ὁμολογήσῃς ἐν τῷ στόματί σου κύριον 'Ιησοῦν, καὶ πιστεύσῃς ἐν τῇ καρδίᾳ σου, ὅτι ὁ θεὸς αὐτὸν ἤγειρεν ἐκ νεκρῶν, σωθήσῃ, Conzelmann differentiates the two words seeing "homology" as indicative of that content which names Jesus as Lord, "credo" as indicative of Jesus' work of salvation.

By every expression of either homology or credo some title of Jesus must find employment. Although the titles vary, three are by far the most common: Lord, Christ, Son of God. (Christ was soon joined to Jesus and became for all practical purposes a proper name.) What is common to each of these titles is their claim to bring to expression the unconditioned: "Alle drei Begriffe drücken, jeder für sich, die Absolutheit der Stellung Jesu aus."[70] Although each of these titles has its own proper history and denotation, it is the exclusivity of claim to allegiance which they have in common.

Thus, all of these most common titles are limited in their own way -- to the particular Weltanschauung from which they stem. Their

---

70. *Ibidem*, p. 65.

universality comes not so much from what they denote, as from the universality of the claim they require in the New Testament. To this extent they do not represent the center of faith, nor the quintessential content of faith, but free modes for expressing it. Thus the question of exact words for dogmatic formulation shrinks to the level of an entirely secondary consideration.

From this basis the claim to exclusivity is something which even in the New Testament begins to be expanded to other conceptualities. This expansion becomes especially acute in the New Testament hymns. For here an expanded conceptuality prepares the way through the hymns' Sitz-im-Kult for the acclamation which is the more basic homology. So the terms μορφή and εἰκών in Phil 2 are expansive interpretations of the original homology, which lead, nevertheless back to it. "Diese Begriffe haben ihren alten, griechischen, ontologischen Sinn abgestreift; sie bezeichnen nicht mehr die Form, Gestalt, sondern die Substanz. Werden sie im Laufe der dogmatischen Entwicklung nicht mehr, wie in der kirchlichen Frühzeit, streng auf das geschichtliche Heilsgeschehen bezogen, sind die Substanzbegriffe nicht mehr primär als Interpretation, sondern als eigener Sinn der Aussage verwendet, dann ist der Weg zur spätern dogmatischen Fixierung beschritten."[71] The New Testament hymns are then an all important step toward the development and beginning of dogma.

The expansion of the three basic homologies begins already in the New Testament as within the infant Church. Gradually the distinctiveness of the faith is accentuated as it becomes necessary to set it off from polytheism with the confession of εἷς κύριος. Against the Mysterienfrömigkeit the exclussiveness of this one Lord is emphasized. And the

---

71. *Ibidem*, p. 71.

road to the future orthodoxy of the Catholic Church becomes discernable
as it is necessary to interpret the general confession, "Jesus is God's
Son," against gnosticism. For in the beginning gnosticism was not a
clearly defined party to be distinguished from the Church, but a group
within the Church which also adherred to the confession of Jesus as Son
of God. Now the confession was expanded to read that Jesus Christ "has
come in the flesh" (1 Jn 4:2).

> Und zwar wird diese Formel nicht als Neubildung verstanden,
> sondern lediglich als sachgemässe Auslegung der alten. Im nächsten
> Vers kann der Verfasser dann einfach wieder dafür sagen: "Jesus
> bekennen." Der Sinn ist: jetzt, im Akt der Auseinandersetzung über
> das Wesen des Erlösers, kann man nicht das eine -- dass er Gottes
> Sohn sei -- annehmen, das andere -- seine wahre Menschlichkeit --
> aber abweisen. Der Glaube ist unteilbar, und in dem strittigen
> Punkte wird über das Ganze des Glaubensverständnisses entschieden.
> Bis zu diesem Zeitpunkte war in der Kirche ein naiver Doketismus
> möglich; jetzt aber ist das Problem bewusst geworden; damit kann
> der Doketismus nicht mehr naiv bleiben, und die Alternative heisst
> nunmehr: Doketismus oder -- Glaube.[72]

And so Conzelmann sees the growth of the orthodox confession not
primarily as a response to a crisis such as the failure of the parousia
to take place but, simultaneous to that crisis, as the expansion of the
first confessions affirming Jesus as Messiah, as Son of God, as Lord.
This expansion was required by the prominence of variant opinions
(heresies) as much as by the succession of time and the need to
reinterpret the old confessions into a new vocabulary.

4. THE GATTUNG "HYMN" IN THE NEW TESTAMENT IN RECENT EXEGESIS

a. Gottfried Schille

G. Schille's work, *Frühchristliche Hymnen*,[73] is a form critical
work which researches what the author calls baptismal hymns in Ephesians,

---

72. *Ibidem*, p. 73.
73. Berlin, 1965. This volume is the first half of the author's 1953

Colosians, and other early Christian writings. Going considerably beyond the poineer work in this area by E. Norden,[74] as well as that of H. Gunkel,[75] Schille sets up the following philological criteria for detecting quoted material in the accepted texts:

(1) A word of introduction usually introduces the quote (γάρ, δέ, ὅτι). The same technique is employed in citing Old Testament texts, as in Rom 11:34, 2 Cor 10:17, etc.

(2) Afterwards there is a summary of the point of comparison within the quote with the point being made in the epistle. This joining is expressed through such expressions as ἄρα οὖν, μὴ οὖν τις.

(3) The quote appears then to be an excursus or, at least in part, superfluous. Thus one can ask himself why the author has not omitted the line from Ps 40:7, "In the beginning of the book it is written of me," from the quote in Heb 10:5ff.

(4) Especially noticeable are differences in style between quote and context. Thus the hymn-like style "we" abruptly contrasts with the apostle's usual manner of addressing his readers. Likewise the manuscripts are wont to change "we" to "you" or vice versa where the texts are joined.

(5) The citation exercises a certain force over the writer, inasmuch as he must marshal his thoughts to introduce it and then afterwards again mention the important point in the citation in connection with his major thought.

(6) The citation can be expanded, changed in meaning, or precised by the

thesis presented in Göttingen, *Liturgisches Gut im Epheserbrief*.
74. *Vd.* footnote 41.
75. H. Gunkel and J. Begrich, *Einleitung in die Psalmen*, 1933; and H. Gunkel, "Die Lieder in der Kindheitsgeschichte Jesu bei Lukas," in *Festgabe für A. v. Harnack*, 1921, p. 43ff.

author.

(7) The citation can also be corrected by the author, sometimes between the lines, as in Rom 10:6ff.

(8) Sometimes the burden of the citation forces the author to compromise his sentence structure.[76]

In addition to the above Schille lists other special criteria for detecting the presence of a hymn in an already found citation:

(1) When the hymn is a community hymn it will have the confessional-like "we" or the narrative-praising "he" style; more seldom the "I" style, whereas the epistle speaks to someone (2nd person).

(2) In quoting a hymn the author is citing an already given text. A narrator, on the contrary, can add to an already given example.

(3) That means that the reflexion of the author can alter his kerygma, whereas in citing a hymn one theology meets headlong another.

(4) Correction and application are seen to be separate from the hymn itself, so long as the author cites the original form of the hymn.

(5) A hymn citation will contain the general formal elements of hymns, such as the participial and relative clause style, a regular change of lines which is often clearly to be recognized through parallelismus membrorum, a characteristic structure of line and of length which, however, does not rule out irregularities at the beginning and end.

(6) An example remains clear, even when individual features must be subsequently explained, for the thoughts of a hymn follow in some order as, for example, in synonyms.

(7) Since the hymn is 'homologia of the community' it can be used as the basis for encouragement but not as an example for preaching.

---

76. Schille, *op. cit.*, pp. 16-18.

(8) For this reason hymns are often put in prominent places such as at the beginning of a writing as in Rom 1:3f., Eph 1:3ff., Col 1:12ff., and Heb 1:2ff. They serve here to point to the common faith or as the basis for more elaborations.

(9) When a hymn summarizes the kerygma it is not interested in historical representation in the stricter sense. Thus, at times there are historical inconsistencies such as Heb 5:7 which seems to think simultaneously on Gethsemane and Golgotha. He who praises the overlying meaning of an event in hymnic form is not concerned with such details.

(10) Thus the hymns speak their own language with concepts and motifs from the liturgical tradition which is in fact older than the epistles themselves. This knowledge determines their real age.

(11) The older hymnic tradition makes use of typology, especially in reference to Christ; the later sometimes relates ecclesiastical motifs to the Old Testament.[77]

Schille relates in the most explicit way all the above characteristics of hymns to the community's confession of its faith:

> Alle diese Züge erklären sich von daher, dass der Hymnus für die älteste Zeit Bekenntnis ist. "Bekennen" meint zunächst den Lobpreis Gottes als öffentliches Eintreten für den Gepriesenen. Erst allmählich hat sich der Begriffsinhalt auf die Homologie der Taufe u.ä. verengt. Wer einen Hymnus spricht, steht nach urchristlicher Anschauung in der Schar der Erlösten. Aus ihm spricht das Pneuma, das die Gemeinde zum Loben treibt und ihrer Gotteskindschaft versichert. ....Doch setzt der Hymnus stets Predigt voraus und ist also Bekenntnis der Wissenden...."[78]

Schille determines that there are three types of redeemer hymns: confessional-like redeemer hymns (bekenntnisartige Erlöserlieder), cross-triumph hymns (Kreuz-Triumph-Lieder), and remembrance type hymns

---

77. *Ibidem*, pp. 18-20.
78. *Ibidem*, p. 20.

(Anamnesen).[79] Examples of confessional-like redeemer hymns are: Phil 2:6-11; 1 Tim 3:16; Heb 5:5; 1 Pet 3:18-22; Ignatius ad Eph. 7:2; Ignatius ad Trall. 9:1f.; Ignatius ad Smyrn. 1-3; Iren, haer. I, 10:1f.; Iren. fragment; Epistula Apostolorum 3; Petr acten 20; Acta Theclae et Pauli 37; Ascensio Jesajae 3:13ff.; Oracula Sibyllina VI:1ff.; Thomas-Acten 10;39;47;141;143; Psalmen des Thomas 2-4;7;11; Heb 1:2-4. Examples of cross-triumph hymns are: Eph 2:14-18; Col 2:9-15; Heb 7:1-3; Ode Sal. 22; Ode Sal. 31:1-4; Ode Sal. 39:9-12; Ode Sal. 41:11-16: Thomas-Acten 156. Examples of remembrance type hymns are: Acts 4:24b-28; 1 Pet 2:21-24; Apo 1:5f., and 5:9f.; Thomas-Acten 158.

After researching each of the above passages, Schille comes to definite and significant conclusions about the faith contents of these hymns which precede the old Roman creed.

> Die Erlöserlieder reden vom Kommen und der Erniedrigung, vor allem aber vom überwaltigenden Sieg des Erlösers.

> (1) Der Erlöser ist schon anfangs Gott, Erbe, Arzt, Haupt oder Priester und bedarf eigentlich keiner eigenen Tat. Aber er fragt nicht darnach und gibt Wesen und Würde daran. Wird das nicht eigens erzählt, so wird es doch vorausgesetzt, indem der Tod etwa als notwendiger Triumph beschrieben wird. Der Sterbende bringt die Macht zum Sieg gleich mit.

> (2) Der Weg führt an das Kreuz und d.h. zunächst in den blutigen Tod (in die Tiefe). Der Erlöser ist gehorsam und weicht dem gewiesenen Weg nicht aus. Besonders in der Anamnese wendet man sich der Frage zu, inwiefern Christus Gottes Willen erfüllte und wofür er sterben musste.

> (3) Aber Kreuz und Tod sind nicht das Ende, sondern der Anfang seiner Rechtfertigung. Diese ist sein Machterweis. Alle Bindungen an die Mächte dieser Welt werden überwunden, an Fleisch, Schuld, Gesetz oder Tod. Der Sieg gipfelt in der Unterwerfung der Mächte.

> (4) Die Rechtfergigung bedeutet eine Verleihung von Macht und Herr-schaft. Die Wahrheit seines Namens bringt den Sieg. Von hier aus erklärt sich, dass der Liedschluss den (grösseren) Namen oder ein

---

79. *Ibidem*, p. 37.

Würdeprädikat nennt. Der Gepriesene erhält die Würde, die er
anfangs hatte beanspruchen können.

(5) So wird der Erlöser Ursache ewigen Heils für die Sänger, denen
er den Zugang zum Vater geöffnet hat. Dies Motiv kann breit ausgeführt werden, aber auch in einer winzigen Andeutung verhüllt
sein. Bisweilen enthält das Prädikat des Liedes bereits die
Bedeutung des Erlösers für die Gemeinde wie in einem Stichwort.

(6) Das Heil wird mitgeteilt, verkündet. Der Erlöser bringt die
Friedensbotschaft selbst in das Totenreich dieser Welt. Gemeint
ist kein Wort des Irdischen, sondern die gemeindegrundende Proklamation des Erhöhten. Das Wort 'verkündete' gehört direkt vor das
andere 'er fuhr auf'.[80]

Insofar as these six conclusions are the distillate of a variety of

hymns, they suggest a content to the faith regarding the redemption and

the redeemer which is doctrinally consistent despite the individual type

of hymn. Indeed, one can speak of the material in the six conclusions

as being the 'dogmatic' foundations of liturgical celebration.

      b. Reinhard Deichgräber

    R. Deichgräber maintains that there are basicly only three types

of human speech directed towards God: praise, petition, thanksgiving

(Lobpreis, Bitte und Dank).[81] Every type of prayer or hymn fits into

one of these classifications. So, for example, laments are a form of

petition. Hymns of thanks and of praise are often thought of as basicly

one type, although the thanksgiving reveals itself in the "I-Thou manner

of speaking" (Ich-Du-Redeweise), praise in the "I-He manner of speaking"

(Ich-Er-Redeweise). More often than not the I is completely omitted and

hymns of praise are simply in the third person. "So verstehen wir unter

---

80. *Ibidem*, pp. 48-50. The numbering of these six results has been
    changed to suit our purposes.
81. *Gotteshymnus und Christushymnus in der frühen Christenheit, Unter-
    suchungen zu Form, Sprache und Stil der frühchristlichen Hymnen.*
    Göttingen, 1967. *Cf.* p. 21ff.

einem Hymnus das rühmende, lobpreisende Aufzählen der Taten oder Eigen-
schaften einer Gottheit."[82]

Claus Westermann attempted to improve on H. Gunkel's classification
of many of the psalms as simply hymns by differentiating between hymns
of praise and hymns of thanks. Deichgräber finds this division artificial since the Hebrew words ברך and ידה have a wider meaning than their
corresponding translations into modern languages, or into Greek.

In the more strict sense it seems that prayer is limited to
petition and to thanks. Yet hymns are prayers too, in both their "I-He"
style as in their "I-Thou" style. The former presumes some type of
audience, the latter is pure worship. "Wir können demnach zwischen
proklamatorischen und anbetenden Hymnen unterscheiden. Der Hymnus im
Er-Stil steht an der Schwelle zwischen Gebet und Verkündigung, der Hymnus
im Du-Stil ist reines Gebet, er ist Anbetung."[83]

Although one usually thinks of hymns as being in poetic form,
Deichgräber states that they may also appear in prose form, which prose
forms are to be recognized through "Plerophorie des Ausdrucks" and
"rühmenden Grundton." He then proceeds to examine at length short
expressions of praise such as doxologies and eulogies, and finally the
longer hymns to God and to Christ. For purposes of comparison with the
other form critical studies of Schille and Sanders we shall limit our
considerations here to his Gattung of hymns to Christ.

In his chapter, "Christushymnen," Deichgräber notes that among the
Christ hymns of the New Testament only "I-He" style is found; the
"I-Thou" style belongs to a later time. "Formgeschichtlich wird darauf

---

82. *Ibidem*, p. 22.
83. *Ibidem*, p. 23.

zu achten sein, dass die Christushymnen nicht mit christologischen Verkündigungsformeln, Homologien und Bekenntnissen vermischt werden dürfen."[84] Deichgräber laments at length the fact that so often no clear distinctions have been seen between the type, "Christushymnus," and the type, "Christusbekenntnis." He points to the fact that authors such as E. Stauffer, H. Lietzmann, R. Stählin, W. Maurer, G. Bornkamm, and E. Käsemann compound the confusion by speaking even of "hymnischen Bekenntnissen."[85] E. Stauffer's phrase (*Theologie des N.Ts.*, p. 214) is typical for what Deichgräber sees as a lack of form critical acuity: "Viele Bekenntnisse haben hymnischen, viele Hymnen haben bekenntnishaften Charakter."

Deichgräber differentiates thus: "Was ist unter einer Verkündigungsformel zu verstehen? Ich verstehe darunter kurze, formelhaftgeprägte Zusammenfassungen wesentlicher Elemente urchristlicher Verkündigung, kurz gesagte Formeln, die Jesu Leiden und Sterben, Auferweckung und Wiederkunft zum Inhalt haben."[86] The prime example here is 1 Cor 15:3-5. Such "preaching formulae" show a strong relationship to παράδοσις and are rooted in the oldest Palestinian preaching. They are the τὰ στοιχεῖα τῆς αρχῆς, as Heb 5:12 puts it.

> Die Verkündigungsformeln gehören ganz und gar in das Stadium der mündlichen Tradition hinein. Sie sind keine schriftlich fixierten Bekenntnisse, wie wir sie in späteren Zeit finden, obwohl sie durchaus die Funktion eines Bekenntnisses haben. Dieser Tatbestand wird genügend bewiesen durch die Beobachtung, dass der Wortlaut der Verkündigungsformeln keineswegs absolut feststeht, sondern erweitert und variiert werden kann. Es handelt sich also auf keinen Fall um ein Bekenntnis im Sinne einer unbedingt gültigen Formulierung theologischer Lehre.[87]

---

84. *Ibidem*, p. 106.
85. *Cf. ibidem*, p. 107, foonote 1.
86. *Ibidem*, pp. 107-108.
87. *Ibidem*, p. 109, footnote 2.

The hymns, in distinction to the Verkündigung, represent a Hellenistic conceptuality and a greater degree of word fixation. The "preaching formulae" are to be distinguished from "kerygmatic summaries" such as Acts 2:22-24, 3:13-15, etc., which are sober prose historical reports. The "preaching formulae" are also to be distinguished from "acclamatory confessions" such as Rom 10:9, and from simple homologies such as Κύριος 'Ιησοῦς.

Like H. Gunkel for the psalms, Deichgräber attributes to all the Christ-hymns a liturgical Sitz-im-Leben, but just what type of liturgical background they reflect is a question that is more than hard to answer.[88]

After surveying the Christ-hymns in Ignatius of Antioch which reveal much the same problematic as the more well-known ones in the cannonical epistles, Deichgräber is able to arrive at a schema that represents in dramatic form the underlying themes of the Christ-hymns:

	Phil 2	Kol 1	1 Tm 3	Hb 1	1 Pt 2	1 Pt 3	Eph 1
Präexistenz	2,6a	1,15		1,3a			
Schöpfungsmittler		1,16		(a,2c)			
Erhaltung der							
Schöpfund		1,17b		1,3b			
Erhabenheit		1,18a					
Inkarnation	2,6.7	1,19	3,16 a				
Erniedrigung							
Leiden	2,8	1,20		1,3c	2,21ff.	3,18	
Tod							
Auferstehung		1,18b				3,18	1,20a
Erhöhung	2,9a		3,16	1,3d		3,22a	1,20b
Neuer Name	2,9b			(1,4)			(1,21)
Unterwerfung der							
Mächte	2,10f.		3,16 b	(1,6)		3,22b	1,22a
Mission			3,16 b c				
Einsetzung zum							
Haupt des Soma							1,22b

[89]

What is remarkable in this table is that it shows that there is
an underlying unity of theme in the New Testament hymns. That may in
part stem from the fact that they stem from the Hellenistic mission of
the Church, that is to say, at least one degree of removal from the
Palestinian mission. Once again, one must note that the underlying
unity of theme in the New Testament hymns betrays an underlying unity
of doctrinal belief.

c. Jack T. Sanders

Noting that the establishment of a clearly defined Gattung for the
hymns in the New Testament has not yet been considered, Jack T. Sanders
essays a working definition in his book, *The New Testament Christological
Hymns, Their Religious Background.*[90] H. Gunkel had designated one of
his four Gattungen of psalms 'hymn,' but sometimes used the expression,
'song of praise.'[91] Claus Westermann preferred the term 'psalm of
praise' to 'hymn,' and distinguished further between 'descriptive praise'
and 'narrative praise.'[92] Georg Fohrer follows Westermann separating
the thanksgiving proper from the hymn, but notes that the two are
frequently linked closely together.[93] Usually there is an introductory
call to praise, followed by a narration recounting a situation of need
and subsequent deliverance, which again is followed by the repetition
of the call to thanksgiving found at the beginning. "It seems likely
that this Gattung of thanksgiving psalm (or 'narrative praise'), so

88.   *Cf. ibidem*, pp. 132, 154, 160.
89.   *Ibidem*, p. 163.
90.   Cambridge, 1971. *Cf.* pp. 1-5.
91.   "Psalmen," in *RGG*, vol. IV (1930[2]), cols. 1612-14.
92.   *Das Loben Gottes in den Psalmen*, (Göttingen, 1961[2]).
93.   *Einleitung in das Alte Testament*, (Heidelberg, 1965[10]).

closely related to the Gattung 'hymn' (or 'descriptive praise') as to be at times almost indistinguishable, is the Gattung to which most of the New Testament passages to be discussed here belong."[94]

"Since the New Testament writers (Col. iii. 16; Eph. v. 19) apparently made no distinction among 'psalm', 'hymn', and 'thanksgiving', the term 'hymn', which is the word normally used today for religious songs, seems to be appropriate as a general designation for referring to all such passages."[95] Finally Sanders calls attention to the dramatic quality of this early Christian hymnody, which Joseph Kroll called "ardor of enthusiasm."[96] Sanders maintains that this dramatic character is "not merely a stylistic or formal observation, but refers as well to the content of the hymns, since early Christian hynody tends to deal with a divine drama, a cosmic redemption, thus with an 'exalted' subject."[97]

The first part of Sander's study is then a formal analysis of the literary structure of seven New Testament Christological hymns. We give here the arrangements of the texts he adopts.

Philippians 2:6-11

6 Who, Being in the form of God,
        Did not think it robbery to be equal with God,
7   But emptied himself,
        Taking the form of a slave.

        Becoming in the likeness of men
        And being found in fashion like a man
8   He humbled himself,

94. Sanders, *op. cit.*, p. 3.
95. *Ibidem*, p. 4.
96. *Die christliche Hymnodik bis zu Klemens von Alexandria*, (Königsberg, 1921; reprinted at Darmstadt, 1968).
97.   *op. cit.*, p. 5.

```
            Becoming obedient unto death
                [the death of the cross].

9       Wherefore God highly exalted him
        And bestowed upon him the name above every name,
10      That in the name of Jesus every knee may bow
        in the heavens and on earth and beneath the earth,
11      And every tongue confess,
        'Jesus Christ is Lord!'
                to the glory of God the father.
```

This arrangement of the hymn is essentially that of Joachim Jeremias,[98] which Sanders adopts because it shows the hymn is structured "along lines of Semitic parallelismus membrorum." The three stanzas represent "the pre-(earthly) existence, the earthly existence, and finally the post-(earthly) existence of the redeemer" respectively.[99]

Colossians 1:15-20

```
15  Who is the image of the        18b  Who is the beginning, the
    invisible God, first-               first-born of the dead,
    born of all creation,              [that he himself might
                                        be pre-eminent in
                                        everything]

16  For in him was created
    everything in the
    heavens and on earth,
    [the visible and the
    invisible,
    whether thrones or
    lordships,
    whether rulers or
    authorities]
    Everything was created     20  And through him to
    through him and                reconcile everything
    unto him.                      unto himself.

17  And he is before everything
    And everything is united in him,
18  And he is the head of the body [the church].
```

The arrangement, except for the bracketed material, is that of

---

98. "Zur Gedankenführung in den paulinischen Briefen," in *Studia Paulina in honorem Johannis de Zwaan*, edit. by J. N. Sevenster and W. C. van Unnik, (Haarlem, 1953), pp. 146-154.
99. Sanders, *op. cit.*, p. 10.

Eduard Schweizer.[100] Schweizer omitted the bracketed material. This is

only one possible reconstruction of this hymn, and very likely the

original order may never be recovered.[101] Thus, other reconstructions,

such as James M. Robinson's two strophe reconstruction is also worthy of

consideration.[102]

Ephesians 2:14-16

[For] he is our peace,

Who has made both one
And has broken down the dividing wall of the fence [the
  enmity],

In order to make the two into one new man in him [making
  peace],
And to reconcile both in one body to God [through the cross].

This reconstruction is one suggested by Sanders himself in an

earlier article.[103] It is, he says, minimal rather than definitive.[104]

In other words, just how far the wording of the hymn proceeds in the

text is uncertain. Very likely there was at one time also a first

stanza. "However the original may have looked exactly, the liturgical

elements are also prominent here. Participial predications, parallelis-

mus membrorum, and the opening αὐτός ἐστιν (cf. Col. 1:17f.) point to

the liturgical setting of this 'poem'."[105]

1 Timothy 3:16

        Who was manifested in the flesh,
            Was vindicated in the spirit,

100. "Die Kirche als Leib Christi in den paulinischen Antilegomena," in
        ThLZ, 86 (1961), col. 241.
101. Cf. Sanders, op. cit., pp. 13-14.
102. "A Formal Analysis of Colosians 1:15-20," in JBL, 76 (1957), pp.
        270-287.
103. "Hymnic Elements in Ephesians 1-3," in ZNW, 56 (1965), p. 217.
104. Sanders, The New Testament Christological Hymns, p. 14.
105. Ibidem, p. 15.

Was seen by angels,
Was proclaimed among the nations,
Was believed on in the world,
Was taken up into glory.

Eduard Schweizer has studied this passage and pointed out that it has a 'chiastic structural pattern of parallelism' which is: ab/ba/ab.[106] Although the 'formal structure' of this passage is universally admitted (it is so printed in Nestle's Greek New Testament), there is some disagreement as to whether it represents a 'hymn' or a 'confession.' Thus, the opening ὅς and the cosmic drama would link this passage with other hymns; yet it is lacking in participles, parallelismus membrorum, and is not long enough to have stanzas. "At this passage, then, the line between 'hymn' and 'confession' seems to become blurred; if a hymn would normally exhibit confessional character, and if a confession would normally be heard in a service of worship, i.e in the liturgy, then this blurring is certainly to be expected."[107]

1 Peter 3:18-22

18c Having been put to
       death in the flesh,
       Having been made alive
       in the spirit,
19   Having gone to the
       spirits in prison,
       He preached.

22   Who is at the right hand
       of God,
       Having gone into heaven,
       Angels and authorities
       and powers having been
       made subject to him.

---

106.   Schweizer, πνεῦμα, πνευματικός..." *ThWb*, vol. VI, ed. by Gerhard
       Friedrich, (Stuttgart, 1959), p. 414. *Cf.* also his *Erniedrigung
       und Erhöhung bei Jesus und seinen Nachfolgern*, (Zürich, 1962²),
       p. 105, n. 421.
107.   Sanders, *op. cit.*, p. 16.

Differing from E. G. Selwyn,[108] Sanders believes that this hymn is more closely the original basis for 1 Tim 3:16 and not the reverse. The similarities between the two 'hymns' are obvious: contrast between activities "in the flesh" and "in the spirit"; "having gone into heaven" compares with "was taken up into glory"; the shift from active to passive voice of 1 Pet 3:19's ἐκήρυξεν to 1 Tim 3:16's ἐκηρύχθη. Moreover, the Petrine version seems more likely to have been at one time composed of two stanzas. If the author of 1 Timothy quoted from 1 Peter, "then one would have to assume that the author of 1 Timothy reduced or 'refined' the hymn into a credal statement for purposes of quotation."[109]

Hebrews 1:3

3 Who, being the reflection of his glory and the stamp of his essence,
    Bearing everything by the word (ῥῆμα) of his power,
    Having made purification for sins,
    Sat down on the right hand of the majesty on high.

It was Günther Bornkamm who first recognized the hymnic character of these lines.[110] Sanders presents the above version as the more likely since it pays attention to the metric structure and 'formal parallelism' noted earlier by James Moffatt.[111] Sanders notes similarities of this passage which link it with the other hymnic forms already treated, such as "the opening ὅς, which likely tied this hymn originally to a preceding thanksgiving, the presence of participial predications employing substantive participles without the article."[112]

108. *The First Epistle of St. Peter,* (London, 1946), pp. 17f.
109. Sanders, *op. cit.*, p. 18.
110. "Das Bekenntnis im Hebräerbrief," in *Studien zu Antike und Urchristentum, Gesammelte Aufsätze*, vol. II, (München, 1959), p. 197.
111. *A Critical and Exegetical Commentary on the Epistle to the Hebrews,* (Edinburgh, 1924), p. 56.
112. Sanders, *op. cit.*, p. 19.

John 1:1-11

1   In the beginning was the Word,
    And the Word was with God,
    And the Word was God.
2   He was in the beginning with God.

3   Everything was made through him,
    And apart from him was nothing made which was made.
4   In him was life,
    And the life was the light of men.

5   And the light shines in the darkness,
    And the darkness did not overcome it.

9   He was the true light,
    Which enlightens every man,
    Coming into the world.

10 He was in the world,
    And the world was made through him.
    And the world did not know him.

11 He came to his own.
    And his own did not receive him.

This reconstruction will hardly please everyone, nor is it at all clear that this passage should be denominated a 'hymn,' since most of the general characteristics are lacking, such as participles, absence of the article, connection with thanksgiving, etc. Sanders therefore calls it "religious poetry, hence hymnic in a general sense, though perhaps not 'hymn' in the more precise sense in which the term has been used for the other passages considered."[113] In any case Ernst Käsemann agrees that verse 11 is the end of the second stanza of this 'hymn.'[114] Sanders agrees with Bultmann in omitting verses 6 and 8, since they disturb the chain of "accented words."[115] The result is a poetic structure of which verses 1-5 and 9-11 make up, with "a reasonable degree

113. *Ibidem*, p. 21.
114. "Aufbau und Anliegen des johanneischen Prologs," in *Libertas Chris-
      tiana, Festschrift für Friedrich Delekat*, ed. by W. Matthias,
      (München, 1957), p. 87.

of certainty," the original passage quoted by the author of the Fourth
Gospel.[116] Moreover, one notes a certain analogy between verses 5 and
11, the concluding verses of the two stanzas. Sanders reasons therefore:

> Both describe the movement of the redeemer into a realm ('dark-
> ness', 'his own') in the first line, and in the second line relate
> what that realm did not do to him--in both cases an aorist form of
> a compound of λαμβάνω. Assuming, then, as a working hypothesis,
> that these two lines form in either case the conclusion of a
> stanza, one sees that the lines prior to the concluding two lines
> fall in either case rather readily into two strophes--of four
> lines each in the second stanza. The first strophe thus describes
> the pre-existent position of the Word, the second strophe states
> his role as creator and as himself existing in creation as the
> light and life of men(whereby his role as redeemer may be implied),
> and the concluding two lines narrate his cosmic movement, the
> beginning of redemption, from the realm of light into the realm of
> darkness. In the next stanza, the Word successfully enters the
> cosmos (strophe 1), yet the cosmos does not know him (strophe 2),
> and when he goes to 'his own' (concluding two lines), even they do
> not receive him. His rejection is complete.[117]

The general conclusion from Sanders' investigation of the literary
and hymnic structure of all the above passages is most interesting, for
it illustrates, as he says, that all these pericopes are more closely
related one to another than simply being in a broad sense 'Christological.' For, although there are many points of detail where they do not
agree and, very likely, the reconstructions will never be perfectly
recovered or agreed upon, the same redeemer myth, involving his partici-
pation in creation, his descent and ascent to and from the world, and
finally his work of redemption recurs in each. Sanders represents this
emerging pattern as follows:

1. The redeemer possesses unity or equality with God; Phil.
2:6; Col. 1:15 ('image of the invisible God'); Col. 1:17 ('before
everything'); Heb. 1:3 ('reflection of his glory and stamp of his
essence'); John 1:1f.

---

115. *Cf.* Bultmann, *Das Evangelium des Johannes*, (Göttingen, 1959[16]),
     p. 2f.; p. 5, n. 5.
116. *Cf.* Sanders, *op. cit.*, pp. 21-24.
117. *Ibidem*, pp. 23-24.

2. The redeemer is mediator or agent of creation: Col. 1:16; John 1:3.

3. The redeemer is himself a part of (or is the sustainer of) creation: Col. 1:15 ('first-born of all creation'); Col. 1:17f. ('everything is united in him, and he is the head of the body'); Heb. 1:3 ('bearing everything'); John 1:4.

4. The redeemer descends from the heavenly to the earthly realm: Phil. 2:7; John 1:5,9.

5. He dies: Phil. 2:8; Col. 1:18 ('first-born of the dead')' 1 Tim. 3:16 and 1 Pet. 3:18 ('manifested in the flesch', 'put to death in the flesh').

6. He is made alive again: Col. 1:18 ('first-born of the dead'); 1 Tim. 3:16 and 1 Pet. 3:18 ('vindicated in the spirit', 'made alive in the spirit').

7. He effects a reconciliation: Col. 1:18 ('the beginning'); Col. 1:19f.; Eph. 2:14-16; 1 Tim 3:16 ('proclaimed among the nations, believed on in the world') and 1 Pet. 3:19; Heb. 1:3 ('having made purification').

8. He is exalted and enthroned, and the cosmic powers become subject to him: Phil. 2:9-11; 1 Tim. 3:16 ('seen by angels, taken up into glory') and 1 Pet. 3:22; Heb. 1:3 ('sat down on the right hand').[118]

In other words, there was at the time of the composition of these New Testament books an "emerging mythical configuration which could be attached, in the literature and in the religious consciousness of the Jew of the day, to various and different redeemer or revealer figures."[119] In the subsequent course of his investigation Sanders locates the provenance of this 'emerging configuration' in the psalmography of the Wisdom school, from which also come the Odes of Solomon.[120]

Like the other investigations of the New Testament hymns by Schille and Deichgräber, Sanders work leads also the the conclusion that the unity of faith expressed in the various New Testament hymns was an underlying datum of belief which manifests a doctrinal consistency even on the level of the earliest oral tradition.

---

118. *Ibidem*, pp. 24-25.
119. *Ibidem*, p. 96.
120. *Cf. ibidem*, pp. 133-139.

5. CONFESSION -- HYMN -- DOGMA

In this chapter we have seen that the words ὁμολογεῖν and
ὁμολογεία are used quite frequently in the New Testament for the
'confession' that takes place when one accepts the Christ-kerygma.
Yet if the verbal form refers to the act of 'confessing' the faith, the
noun form refers to the content of that confession, the word of faith
that has been revealed.

A fruitful line of research has been followed by Eduard Norden,
Ethelbert Stauffer, Ernst Lohmeyer, Oscar Cullmann, Gottfried Schille,
Reinhold Deichgräber, and Jack Sanders in determining form critical
criteria for discerning quotes from hymns and preaching formulas quoted
in the New Testament.

F. Kattenbusch was not able to establish a version of the Old
Roman Creed behind the text of the New Testament, despite the presence
there of many of its elements. Paul Feine's work along the same lines
must be judged harshly. A. Seeberg's efforts to find a catechism behind
the New Testament text were equally unsuccessful. The recent work of
Eichenseer and Kelly show that fully formed creeds of a declaratory
nature date from towards the time of Hippolytus (✝235) at the earliest.

Before the later part of the second century there are indications
of various types of creedal and catechetical material, all of which show
that there was no formula universally agreed upon yet. Indeed, the 'rule
of faith' at this time was not a formula but the content of the Church's
preaching.

What research on the early history of the creeds has revealed is
that in the time before the fixation of either the text of the Old Roman
Creed or of the canon of scripture, the form the homologies of the Church

assumed was rather fluid. Indeed, Kelly's research leads to the conclusion that the time of fluidity stretches from before the time of the composition of the New Testament until the beginning of the third century. Yet during these several centuries the Church was not without its dogmas or "decisions" of faith. Towards the end of that period we find the early forms of the Old Roman Creed. At the period's beginning we find "creedal" formulae embedded in the text of the New Testament.

Since Kelly disavows the word, "creed," for this material in the New Testament, we find Schlier's expression, the "praesymbola," the more appropriate. As we have repeatedly seen, the state of fixity at this level is at most one of content, hardly of words.

Conzelmann even comes to the conclusion that at the earliest level of Christological confession the expressions, "Lord" and "Christ" and "Son of God" are secondary as regards fixity to what he calls the "Absolutheitsanspruch" demanded by the confessing of Jesus.

Indeed, the conceptuality of the Christological titles only prepares the way for the Christological hymns of the New Testament. They are expansive interpretations of the original Christological homologies. The New Testament hymns are the important middle step between the titles and the later creeds. As homologies taught, prayed, and confessed by the Church they are the dogma of the Church in the time of their flourishing.

In the final part of this chapter we find in three of the most recent exegetical works on the New Testament hymns that each of the exegetes concludes to a type of "dogmatic" substratum of Christian belief which the various hymns seek to express.

G. Schille finds that the hymns teach that: the redeemer is from the beginning God; his way is that of suffering on the cross; cross and death are not the end, but the beginning of justification; justification brings power and victory in his name; he is therefore the cause of our salvation; he establishes peace even in the realm of the dead.

R. Deichgräber lists the themes of the Christ-hymns as: preexistence, mediator in creation, conserver of the creation, sublimity, incarnation, abasement, suffering, death, resurrection, elevation, a new name, conquest of the powers, mission, installation as head of the body.

J. T. Sanders finds behind all the hymns evidence of a redeemer myth in connection with which certain truths are taught: the redeemer's unity or equality with God; the redeemer is the mediator or agent of creation; the redeemer is sustainer of the creation; the redeemer descends to the earthly from the heavenly realm; he dies; he is made to live again; he brings about reconciliation; he is exalted and the cosmic powers become subject to him.

These are then the dogmas of the Church in its earliest stages, for they represent the consensus of faith, the homologies or 'praesymbola' which united the Christian community and to which it testified.

CONCLUSION

THE BEGINNING OF DOGMA AND THE LIFE OF THE CHURCH

1. CAN THE CHURCH DETERMINE ITS FAITH IN SET WORDS?

The subject of this work is the beginning of dogma. We have seen that the solution proposed by Harnack (a creation of the Greek spirit in the fourth century on the foundation of an enthusiastically received gospel), as well as the solution proposed by Werner (the historically necessitated reinterpretation of eschatological faith) are insufficient. Dogma is not a reality several steps or several centuries removed from scripture or the source of revelation.

H. Schlier's essay, "Kerygma und Sophia" has fulfilled its intention as expressed in its subtitle: "Zur neutestamentlichen Grund-legung des Dogmas." In his newly coined expression, the 'praesymbola,' Schlier has pointed to those creedal formulae which served the function of dogma in the Church at the time of the redaction of various books in the New Testament, and which ante-date the later and more determinedly expressed creeds. Harnack may be excused for not having begun his history of dogma with the New Testament since at the time of his literary activity form criticism had not yet revealed the presence of the various creedal formulae within the New Testament. Yet no one can begin the history of dogma today at a degree of removal from the New Testament, as the more recent attempts by Alfred Adam and Peter Meinhold demonstrate.

One can, however, hardly excuse Harnack for his misconstruing the nature of dogma. Etymologically dogma means "decree" or "decision." It also means "opinion" and "teaching." Only since the time of the Council of Trent and Melchior Cano has the word assumed in ecclesiastical circles the controversial sharpness that accompanies it today. We were able to prove that Melchior Cano was the first to use the word in the sense adopted by the First Council of the Vatican.

If we concentrate on dogma's meaning as decision or statement of teaching, it is easy to see how it was already realized in the various creedal fragments in the New Testament. Despite their varying literary genres, they represent the homologies of the Church at that time, therefore its dogmas.

It is wrong to look upon these creedal and kerygmatic formulae as simply confessions of the believing Church. For in Schlier's words, "Die sogenannten Glaubensformeln, in denen das Kerygma fixiert ist, sind also der Sache nach im wörtlichen Sinn hervorgerufen durch die Selbstbezeugung des Auferstandenen vor den Zeugen." They are positively caused by revelation in the active sense. Schlier even emphasizes that these homologies or 'praesymbola' fulfill the requirements of Vatican I for dogma: "veritates a Deo revelatae et ab ecclesia propositae."

We have found it important to emphasize that a determined order of words is not necessary to a dogma. That was the opinion of Harnack and the error of Gerhard Ebeling and Ulrich Wilckens in interpreting Schlier's essay.

The point is not that dogmas are to be found in a very precise word order, but simply that they are found in one or other type of formulary -- catechetical summary, hymn, acclamation, etc. -- and that therefore they represent a certain consensus on the faith which was in turn found worthy of incorporation into the New Testament literature at the time of its redaction. That is to say, a certain word selection and order are not necessary for a dogma, but they may reveal the presence of a formulary which, once revealed, will probably contain one or other aspects of dogmatic reflection, simply because the acceptance into the canon of a formulary manifests a degree of consensus regarding its usage and universality.

In the course of our long journey through history we have traced a certain evolution in the concept of dogma and have also been able to discern a residue of meaning which retains a significant usefulness. For dogma is the Church's 'decision' or 'teaching' on what the faith that is in the Church and which constitutes it says. It therefore partakes in both the nature of revelation -- insofar as it expresses it, and of confession -- insofar as it acknowledges God's act of revealing himself. Using human words because they are the only tools at hand, dogma nevertheless somehow makes the divine present, for it summons the response of faith and, as Thomas Aquinas wrote, "actus autem credentis non terminatur ad enuntiabile, sed ad rem."

2. CHRISTIANITY WITHOUT DOGMA?

The suggestion that there ever has been, or could be, a Christianity without dogma has proved ridiculous. For working from the most basic meaning of dogma as "decision," we have been able to show a certain continuity from the time of Plato and his statement that the state is a place for the life of a group of men having common "dogmas" through the New Testament and Fathers of the Church, even to the somewhat controversially oriented expression of Vatican I. For dogma is a decision of the Church that a revealed truth is normative for its life of faith at a particular time in history.

We do have to agree with M. Elze and W. Elert that the notion of dogma cannot simply be defined according to its biblical usage. However, the meanings of "opinion," or "teaching," and "determination" which are found in the scriptural usage are certainly relevant for the further employment of the term in the Church today. One reason these meanings are still applicable is that every authoritative representation of Church doctrine is a particular "opinion" or "teaching," even when this is brought about through the massive machinery of an ecumenical council. For dogma is still today basically a "teaching" as much as it was among the schools of Greek philosophy in antiquity. A second reason which also underlines the applicability of the ancient meaning of dogma as "determination" is that what the Church teaches is determined by what the Church is -- the authoritative spokesman of the revealing and redeeming God in the world -- and which has therefore the authority to make doctrinal "determinations."

There is then always and necessarily a certain absolute quality to dogmatic expression -- for although formulated in imperfect human words and language, it brings to focus the divine imperative in human life. Dogmas serve the gospel by witnessing to it.

While the First Vatican Council must be credited with fixing the final evolution of this relationship between dogma and faith, the Second Vatican Council in its *Decree on Ecumenism* reminds us that not every official teaching or dogma has a like importance. For there "exists an order or 'hierarchy' of truths, since they vary in their relationship to the foundation of the Christian faith."[1] Moreover, if we can admit the basic function of faith witnessing to Christian truth as the purpose of dogma, then the concept loses something of its controversial sharpness.

The problem of the beginning of dogma has not been an embarrassment for Catholic theologians. This explains why it has hardly received

---

1. II, 11. Quoted from Walter M. Abbott, *The Documents of Vatican II*, (New York, 1966), p. 354.

mention in their works. Indeed, Catholic theology has always assumed a certain continuity between exegesis and the science of dogmatics. Yet this continuity need no longer remain an assumption. We have been able to demonstrate, following the hints of Schlier's suggestive essay, that dogma is already present in the New Testament.